Essentials of Financial Accounting in

Michael Bendrey is a Chartered Management Accountant, a Chartered Certified Accountant and holds an MSc in Business Administration. He has held a variety of financial appointments in the Chemical, Electrical, Printing, Packaging and Newspaper Industries, and since 1976 has been engaged in education and training at all levels.

He has taught on professional, undergraduate and postgraduate programmes at the Universities of the West of England (where he was Faculty Chairman at Bristol Business School), Bristol, Bath, Exeter and Ballarat (Australia). Michael has combined this academic career with consultancy activities, and advised on the appraisal and financing of large infrastructure projects in the Middle East (Syria, Jordan and Oman), Africa (Ethiopia, Zambia, Tanzania and Mozambique), and old Eastern Bloc countries (Latvia, Poland and Russia). He has also worked in Cyprus and Turkey on similar projects, and acted as a consultant to UK companies.

Roger Hussey is Dean of the Odette Business School at the University of Windsor, Canada, and Visiting Professor at Bristol Business School, University of the West of England. His first career was as an accountant in industry, and he is still a Fellow of the Association of Chartered Certified Accountants. He went on to study for an M.Sc in Industrial Relations at Bath University, and followed this with a Ph.D. in Management at the same university.

On leaving Bath, Roger went to St Edmund Hall, Oxford University, as Director of Research into Employee Communications for 6 years. This was followed by 15 years at Bristol Business School before moving to Canada in 2000.

Companion title

Essentials of Management Accounting in Business: Mike Bendrey, Roger Hussey and
  Colston West

Essentials of Financial Accounting in Business

Mike Bendrey, Roger Hussey and Colston West

THOMSON

Australia • Canada • Mexico • Singapore • Spain • United Kingdom • United States

Essentials of financial accounting in business

Copyright © Mike Bendrey, Roger Hussey and Colston West 2004

The Thomson logo is a registered trademark used herein under licence.

For more information, contact Thomson Learning, High Holborn House, 50-51 Bedford Row, London WC1R 4LR or visit us on the World Wide Web at:
http://www.thomsonlearning.co.uk

British Library Cataloguing-in-Publication Data
A catalogue record for this book is available from the British Library

ISBN 1-84480-089-X

Published by Thomson Learning 2004
Reprinted 2005 by Thomson Learning

Typeset by RefineCatch Limited, Bungay, Suffolk
Printed in the UK by TJ International, Padstow, Cornwall

CONTENTS

PREFACE

In recent years developments in financial accounting have moved at a bewildering pace. Fortunately, the basic techniques and concepts are fundamentally the same, and regulatory changes have often clarified particular aspects of accounting. In this volume we have concentrated primarily on explaining the fundamentals of the discipline and providing ample opportunity for students to practice before moving on to more advanced topics, such as the accounts of limited companies and financial reporting standards.

Many lecturers and students find the comprehensive nature of the book, and its easily accessible style, allow it to be used successfully on a variety of courses where accounting and finance are studied. This includes certificate and diploma courses in a range of disciplines as well as introductory courses at the degree level. Although mainly intended as a class text, previous editions have been used with success by students for individual study.

We have kept the chapters short and focused on a particular topic. This allows the material in a chapter to be covered thoroughly in a lecture and, when students already have some understanding of accounting, the pace can be accelerated. The chapters are presented in a logical order and the principles established in one chapter serve as the platform for subsequent chapters.

At the end of each chapter we provide an array of tasks, questions and tests. Where time permits and the students have little or no work experience, the tasks are an excellent opportunity for individual and group learning. The questions and tests can often be answered by reference to the relevant section of the chapter. Where a new point is being introduced answers are given at the back of the book. Answers are also given for all of the objective tests.

Students frequently find accounting difficult in the early stages. We hope that this book will help to alleviate these difficulties. However, accounting is a substantial discipline and as a key part of business is subject to dynamic change. Even with over 100 years of lecturing experience between them, the authors still find that there are many new developments. This book should give students a firm foundation of knowledge and the ability to progress their career in any business of their choice.

Mike Bendrey
Roger Hussey
Colston West

PART I

THE BUSINESS WORLD

CHAPTER 1

The providers of information

1   OBJECTIVES

At the end of this chapter you should be able to:

- define the different organisational forms;
- describe the main features of different organisational forms;
- explain the significant differences between the organisational forms;
- list the advantages and disadvantages of different organisational forms;
- indicate the main reporting requirements of the different organisational forms;

2   INTRODUCTION

Business organisations in the UK take a number of different forms and these are defined by legislation. The way in which a business is managed, conducts its affairs, borrows money, the type of financial information it generates and the people who receive such information are to a great extent matters related to the legal structure of the organisation. We will examine the different *organisational structures* and their features in detail later in this chapter. For our purposes, the most important are:

- The sole trader: one individual running the business for his or her own exclusive benefit.
- The partnership: two or more people own the business.
- Companies limited by shares, also known as limited liability companies: these may be owned by many people who have no part in the day-to-day management of the company.

Choosing the most suitable organisational structure for a business depends on a number of factors. The main ones are:

- The nature of the activity. To take an extreme example, it is evident that running a nuclear power station will require greater resources and administration than having a window cleaning business.
- The number of people involved. Two or more people could not launch a business as a sole trader.
- The amount of money needed to start the business. Few people are rich enough to launch a large business venture with their own money alone.

- The amount of financial risk involved. If a venture is very risky there is a good argument for spreading the possibility of financial failure.

In deciding which is the most appropriate organisational form for a particular business, it is important to consider both the nature of the proposed business and the wishes of the owners. The different organisational forms have their own particular advantages and disadvantages and these are considered in the sections which follow.

> *You should now be able to attempt Question 1.1 at the end of this chapter.*

3 | INDIVIDUALS IN BUSINESS

One person in business alone with a view to making a profit is known as a *sole trader*. The business may simply be in the name of the person or may have a business name such as 'Quickclean Windows'. The business trading name does not have to be registered, but if one is used the owner's name should appear on all letterheads and so forth.

If you start a business as a sole trader you are the owner of that business, taking all the profits but also suffering any losses. You are totally responsible for the business, although you may decide to employ people to do some of the work or to manage the business for you. But they will be employees; you are the person with the final responsibility.

When starting the business you will have to provide all the finance. If you are unable to do this from your own savings, you will have to borrow the money from other people. You will be responsible for paying them back, even if the business is unsuccessful. Banks and other financial institutions, if asked to lend money, usually want to see detailed plans of the proposed business.

If the business runs into financial problems, you will be called upon to resolve them. This means that if the business ends up owing money, then you will be personally responsible for paying the debts, even if this means selling your house, car and any other possessions of value you may have. In the worse possible circumstances, if you cannot pay all the debts you may be declared legally bankrupt.

The *advantages* of being a sole trader are:

- It is very simple to start the business; there are no legal formalities.
- You make all the decisions without having to consult any other person.
- You enjoy all the profits.
- You have total control over the business.

The *disadvantages* of being a sole trader are:

- You may not have sufficient money to start the business and you may not be able to borrow what you need.

- If the business makes a loss, you will suffer all of it.
- You will have to provide all the management expertise, unless you can afford to employ other people.
- You are personally responsible for the debts of the business, which means you can be made legally bankrupt if you are unable to pay.
- You are liable to pay tax on the profits of the business.

4 | PARTNERS IN BUSINESS

A *partnership* can be defined as two or more people carrying on a business with a view to profit. The maximum number of partners allowed is 20, apart from professional firms such as accountants and solicitors who can exceed this number. Partnerships are very common, although you may not appreciate that many of the businesses with which you come into contact have this organisational form. It is quite usual for professional people such as dentists, doctors, solicitors and accountants to offer services not by themselves but with two or more colleagues. In other words, they are trading their services as a partnership. In addition, estate agents, barbers, shops and other small businesses offering a range of services from painting and decorating to catering for a wedding, may be owned by two or more people; they have formed a partnership.

The partners are all owners of the business; they jointly share in the decisions and the running of the business. As in the case of a sole trader, they may operate under a business name which does not have to be registered and need not include any wording to show it is a partnership. For example, The Daw and Jakes Partnership is clearly a partnership, but 'Quickclean Windows', the name we used as an illustration for a sole trader could also be a partnership; you cannot tell from the name. However under the *Business Names Act 1985* the names of the partners must appear on the firm's stationery.

It may be easier to raise the finance to start a business as a partnership because each of the partners may be able to contribute a sum of money. All the partners will expect a share of any profit the business earns, but they must also take a share of any losses. Partners normally ask a solicitor to draw up a legal agreement showing the proportions in which they will share any profit or loss and other matters.

It may be that because one partner spends more time in the business than the others, he or she is entitled to a larger share of the profit, or even a salary. This should be stated in the Partnership Agreement. If the partners fail to draw up an agreement, the rules of the *Partnership Act 1890* apply. This can be very important in the event of a dispute between partners and in Chapter 17 we look at these rules more closely.

As in the case of a sole trader, the owners of the business, i.e. the partners, are personally responsible for the debts of the business. This may cause great hardship because should one partner disappear to South America, the remaining partner(s) is/are personally liable for all the debts of the business.

The *advantages* of a partnership are:

- More capital can be raised to start the business.
- The pressures of running and controlling the business are shared.
- Legal requirements are few (but remember the Partnership Act 1890 applies if the partners fail to draw up an agreement).
- If the business makes a loss it is shared amongst the partners.

The *disadvantages* of a partnership are:

- You do not have sole control and the other partners may overrule your decisions.
- You do not enjoy all the profits but have to share them.
- If the business runs into financial problems, you will be personally responsible for the debts of the partnership.

> You should now be able to attempt Question 1.2 at the end of this chapter.

5   LIMITED LIABILITY COMPANIES

A *limited liability company* (often just referred to as a limited company) can be defined as a 'legal person' and is separate from the owners. This feature is so distinctive and important that we will discuss it now before we consider any other feature of limited companies.

In the case of a sole trader or a partnership, the people are the business even though, for example, John Smith may trade under the name of Futuristic Events; he and the business are one and the same. If you want to take legal action you will be suing John Smith and he will be responsible. It is the same with a partnership. But matters are very different with a limited company. If you and two of your friends decide to form a small limited company called 'Threesome Limited', from a legal point of view there will be four of you: the three shareholders, i.e. you and your two friends, and a fourth legal person, the limited company.

Because a limited company is regarded as being separate from its owners, it is often referred to as a *legal entity*. The most important consequence of this is that the company is responsible for the debts incurred in trading. If the business is unable to pay its debts, then the company can be sued in its own name. The owners of the company (the *shareholders*) are responsible for the amount of money they have invested and/or agreed to invest in the company, but their liability is limited to that amount. In some countries the term stockholder is used instead of shareholder.

If the company is unable to pay its debts, it may go into liquidation and have to stop trading. This will not affect the shareholders. Although they may lose the amount they have agreed to invest in the company they will not be expected to sell their personal possessions. If you look back at the personal responsibilities of small traders and partnerships, you will appreciate the crucial difference.

All shareholders in limited companies have a great advantage over sole traders and partnerships. By forming a limited company they have reduced the risk of losing money, as they are only liable for the amount they have invested or agreed to invest. Because of this great benefit there are a number of legal burdens placed on limited companies.

On the formation of the company certain documents must be registered with the *Registrar of Companies*, which is a part of the Department of Trade and Industry. In addition, every year a limited company must send certain financial information to all its shareholders and register certain information with the Registrar. As any person may consult the files of the Registrar, the data submitted by the companies become public documents.

As well as having a legal personality and existence separate from its owners, the identity of the company is not affected by changes of ownership and the company can enter into contracts without necessarily having to refer to its owners. The owners of a limited company, particularly the larger ones, do not run it on a day-to-day basis themselves but appoint directors to do it for them.

Companies limited by shares are the most important form of business organisation, not because of their number, but because of their size. All the major organisations in the private sector are companies limited by shares. Companies whose shares can be offered to the public are known as *public limited companies (plc)* and these words must appear after the name. You will find that most major organisations such as the high street banks, Boots, Sainsburys and Marks & Spencers, are public limited companies, although in conversations and in press reports the words 'public limited company' may not be added to the name. In some countries the words Corporation or Inc. (Incorporated) are often used.

As well as public limited companies, there are *private limited companies* whose shares may not be offered to the public. Private companies must put the word 'limited' in their name. A public company can choose to offer its shares to the public through the *Stock Exchange*; a private company cannot do this.

The *advantages* of limited companies are:

- The liability of the owners (also known as members) of a company for the debts it incurs is limited to the amount they have agreed to subscribe for shares.

- It can be easier to raise large sums of money.

- The company can be professionally managed by directors.

- Owners can sell their shares in a public limited company if they wish to relinquish their ownership because the Stock Exchange is a market place for dealing in shares.

The *disadvantages* of limited companies are:

- It is more expensive to start business as a limited company than as a partnership or sole trader (although it is possible to form a limited company for approximately £100).

- Any decisions you make about the company may be vetoed by other shareholders.

- There are considerable legal requirements to be fulfilled.
- Some of the financial affairs of a limited company become public property.

> *You should now be able to attempt Task 1.1 and Question 1.3 at the end of this chapter.*

6   TRENDS IN BUSINESS OWNERSHIP

Employee-owned companies and management buy outs

Companies are sometimes owned by the employees who do the work for them. Many smaller companies are owned by the individuals who founded them, but there is a growing trend today for employees to buy significant stakes of larger companies. The current pattern is for this ownership to take the form of *employee stock ownership plans*, or *ESOPs*.

An ESOP is essentially a trust established on behalf of the employees. A corporation might decide, for example, to set up an ESOP to stimulate employee motivation or to fight a hostile takeover attempt. The company first secures a loan, which it then uses to buy shares on the open market. A portion of the future profits made by the company is used to pay off the loan. The shares, meanwhile, are controlled by a bank or other trustees. Employees gradually gain ownership of the shares usually on the basis of seniority, but even though they might not have physical possession of the shares for a while, they control their voting rights immediately. With some companies, the managers, with other employees, may buy out the original owners. This management buy out (MBO) usually takes place when managers believe that they can run the company better than the owners.

Strategic alliances

A strategic alliance, or joint venture, involves two or more enterprises co-operating in the research, development, manufacture, or marketing of the product. Companies might choose to engage in a joint venture for several reasons. One major reason is that it helps spread the risk.

Another reason for joint ventures is that each firm thinks it can get something from the other. It may be able to offer finance or management skills in exchange for production know-how or access to new markets.

Demutualisation

This occurs when an organisation, owned by its members, such as a building society or an insurance company, decides to become a publicly traded company. The reasons for doing this are the desire of the organisation to gain access to stock markets. It is agreed that they can more easily acquire money at a cheaper rate and that the organisation becomes more commercial and efficient. The existing members of the organisation are awarded by receiving cash or shares in the new organisation in proportion to the value of their membership. In the UK there was a spate of 'demutualisations' in the 1990s and they have also been common in north America with life insurance companies.

<table>
<tr><td>7</td><td>REPORTING REQUIREMENTS</td></tr>
</table>

7 REPORTING REQUIREMENTS

In this chapter we have looked at the essential features of different organisational structures. At this stage it is useful to examine the difference in the types of information which they must disclose. In subsequent chapters we will deal with this more thoroughly and in the following sections only the main legal requirements will be considered.

Sole traders

A *sole trader* has very few legal requirements to fulfil. The most important ones are:

- If the value of the taxable supplies of the sole trader is over a certain sum per annum, the business must be registered with HM Customs and Excise for Value Added Tax purposes. The Chancellor of the Exchequer sets this figure each year in his annual budget. It is a legal requirement that businesses registered for VAT maintain accurate records.

- The Inland Revenue collects tax from a profitable business. It is not necessary for a sole trader to ask an accountant to attend to the tax affairs, but many consider it wise to do so. To ensure that the correct amount of tax is paid, proper accounting records should be maintained.

- A sole trader may well be interested in the amount of profit the business has made in the year, but there is no legal requirement to produce a statement showing this. (The Inland Revenue will expect to see one or it may not believe the amount of tax the sole trader thinks should be paid.) Where the sole trader does produce a financial statement showing the profit of the business for the year, this remains confidential information and need not be shown to any other person without the sole trader's permission.

- The *Business Names Act 1985* applies to sole traders (and partnerships) carrying on a business under a name that does not consist solely of their name (with or without their initials or forenames). This is designed to prevent a person carrying on a business using a name that gives the impression that the business is connected to the government or any local authority, or uses certain words or expressions which are prohibited under the Act. If the Act applies the name and address of the owner must be displayed on all business premises and stationery.

Partnerships

The comments relating to VAT, the Business Names Act and the Inland Revenue for sole traders are also pertinent to *partnerships*. In addition, the *Partnership Act 1890* requires the following:

- Proper books of accounts must be kept.

- Capital must be distinguished from profits and losses.

- A record must be kept of profit shares and drawings.

- Partners are bound to render true accounts and full information of all things affecting the partnership to any partner or his legal representative.

The requirements placed on partnerships are therefore more onerous and in a subsequent chapter we will study these in detail. It is important to stress that the partnership is not legally required to make any financial information about itself available to the general public. This is very different from limited companies, as we will see in the following section.

> *You should now be able to attempt Question 1.4 at the end of this chapter.*

Limited liability companies

The legal reporting requirements surrounding *limited liability companies* are complex and are contained in the *Companies Act 1985*. This was not the first companies Act. A number of different Acts have been passed from the middle of the last century, but all limited companies are now regulated by the provisions of the 1985 Act. This Act has now been amended and added to by the *Companies Act 1989*. You will find, however, that people still refer to the Companies Act 1985 and it is implied that they mean 'as amended by the Companies Act 1989'.

There are variations depending on the type of company and its size but the main general provisions are:

- Every limited company must keep accounting records to show and explain the company's transactions.

- At the end of each financial year every limited company must prepare final accounts that comprise:

  the profit-and-loss account;

  the balance sheet;

  the auditor's report;

  the directors' report.

- These final accounts are given to each shareholder, debenture holder and any persons entitled to attend the *Annual General Meeting* of the company, prior to the date of such a meeting. The accounts should also be lodged with the Registrar of Companies. In this way they become public documents and for a small fee anyone can obtain a copy of them. Many large companies now have their own Web sites and often provide a considerable amount of financial information

In addition to the requirements of the Companies Act 1985 and the amendments in the Companies Act 1989, financial statements intended to give a *true and fair view* (see Chapter 4), are subject to *accounting standards*, with some exceptions. This is particularly important in respect of limited liability companies. The accounting profession has been very involved in establishing accounting standards.

Knowledge of accounting standards is crucial when considering the accounts of limited companies and we will discuss the operation of accounting standard setters in a later chapter when we consider the accounts of limited companies. Accounting standards are also relevant to particular aspects of sole traders and partnerships and we will discuss those issues as they arise.

If a public limited company wishes to be listed (wishes its shares to be traded) on the Stock Exchange then it must also comply with the specific rules that the Stock Exchange has concerning disclosure of information.

There are a number of terms and phrases above that you may be encountering for the first time. We will explain them fully in later chapters. At this stage it is only important to appreciate that limited liability companies have to comply with strict legislation concerning their financial activities and certain information will be publicly available.

> *You should now be able to attempt Tasks 1.2 and 1.3 and Question 1.5 at the end of this chapter.*

8 | SUMMARY

In this chapter we have considered the various forms of organisational structures and their reporting requirements.

A *sole trader* is a person trading alone with a view to making a profit. This is a very easy way to start a business and gives the owner complete control. The sole trader is personally responsible for all the debts of the business. The sole trader does not have to make any financial information about the business publicly available.

A *partnership* is two or more people carrying on a business with a view to profit. The Partnership Act 1890 applies to partnerships in the absence of any other agreement. Partnerships do not have to make any financial information publicly available, but partners are individually liable for the debts of the partnership.

A *limited liability company* is a legal person as distinct from the owners. The financial responsibility of the owners is limited to the amount they have invested or agreed to invest in the company. There are very strict disclosure of information regulations applied to all limited liability companies through the Companies Act 1985.

> *You should now be able to attempt the objective test at the end of this chapter.*

Student activities

Task 1.1
Make a list of different limited companies whose products or services you use in one day. Some of the companies you may know already as plc's. With other companies you will find the words (usually in very small print) on the label of their products or stationery.

Task 1.2
Surf the Internet and see how many companies you can find which provide financial information.

Task 1.3
You have decided to start a business with two friends delivering sandwiches to office workers. One of your friends argues that you should form a limited company and the other believes that you should form a partnership. Bearing in mind the type of business you are envisaging, write a letter to your friends giving your opinion and explaining the reasons.

Question 1.1
Select the correct response to the following statements:

	True	False
i) It only needs one person to start a partnership.	☐	☐
ii) A limited company is the simplest way for an individual to start a small business.	☐	☐
iii) The amount of money required to start a business is important in determining the most appropriate organisational form.	☐	☐
iv) A sole trader is a business owned by one person.	☐	☐

Question 1.2
Select the correct response to the following statements:

	True	False
i) All sole traders must call their business by a different name from their own.	☐	☐
ii) A sole trader is personally responsible for all debts incurred by the business.	☐	☐
iii) A sole trader does not have to pay tax on the profits of the business.	☐	☐
iv) If two or more persons own a business they must include the word 'partnership' in its name.	☐	☐
v) If partners do not make an agreement on the share of profit the rules of the Partnership Act 1890 apply.	☐	☐
vi) Only partners who receive a salary from the partnership must contribute to any debts incurred by the business.	☐	☐

Question 1.3

Select the correct response to the following statements:

		True	False
i)	All shareholders are personally responsible for all debts incurred by the limited company in which they have invested.	☐	☐
ii)	A private limited company is exactly the same as a partnership.	☐	☐
iii)	In the event of one of the shareholders dying, a limited company would have to cease business.	☐	☐
iv)	Only a public limited company can offer its shares to the public.	☐	☐
v)	By forming a private limited company, all its financial affairs can be kept secret.	☐	☐

Question 1.4

Which of the following statements refer to sole traders, which to partnerships, and which to both?

i) If the turnover of the business is above a certain figure it must be registered for VAT.

ii) No financial information about the business has to be made publicly available.

iii) Apart from tax responsibilities, there are no legal requirements stating what financial records the business must maintain.

iv) It is important to distinguish between capital and profit shares and drawings.

Question 1.5

Complete the missing items in the following statement:
All limited companies are regulated by the Companies Act ————. This requires companies to prepare ———— at the end of each financial year. Both private limited companies and ———— must deposit certain information with the ———— and it thus becomes public.

Objective test

i) To form a business as a sole trader you must:

    a) have a bank loan   ☐

    b) register your name with the Department of Trade and Industry   ☐

    c) be willing to take all the financial risks by yourself   ☐

    d) make public your financial results   ☐

ii) To form a partnership you must:

    a) have at least four partners   ☐

    b) register the business name with the Department of Trade and Industry   ☐

    c)   have at least two partners □

    d)   make public your financial results □

iii) A limited company offers the advantage of:

    a)   being very easy to establish □

    b)   complete financial secrecy □

    c)   no legal formalities to meet □

    d)   limited financial risk to its owners □

iv) The Companies Act 1985 applies only to:

    a)   all limited companies □

    b)   all partnerships □

    c)   all public limited companies □

    d)   all private limited companies □

v) Demutualisation is when:

    a)   One company takes over a partnership □

    b)   A management buy out takes place □

    c)   An organisation owned by its members becomes a public company □

    d)   Two companies form a joint venture □

CHAPTER 2

Potential users of financial information

1 | OBJECTIVES

At the end of this chapter you should be able to:

- identify the potential users of financial information;
- explain the types of decisions they make;
- identify the types of information they require.

2 | INTRODUCTION

In this chapter we are concerned with the *potential users of financial information* about a business. The owners of shares will be interested in the financial performance and stability of the business, but so may other groups such as trade unions, creditors, employees and financial analysts. There are a number of *sources of financial information* and we will discuss the main ones and the type of information they contain.

3 | SOURCES OF FINANCIAL INFORMATION

Certain people and organisations have no difficulty in obtaining any financial information they require about a particular company. Managers inside the company often receive very detailed information to allow them to do their job properly. The Inland Revenue and HM Customs & Excise have extensive powers to demand information from a company, but there are various other groups of people, such as prospective shareholders, creditors and trade unions, who are not in such a favourable position. These groups depend on the information that the company makes publicly available.

Sole traders and partnerships do not have to make any of their financial information publicly available, but limited companies are required to make certain financial information available to each of their shareholders and the public. This chapter is concerned with that information and its potential users.

The most useful and important financial document for those outside the company is the *annual report and accounts*. This is sent to each shareholder of the company and to the Registrar of Companies. In a later chapter we will take a closer look at this document. There are many other sources of information, many of them freely available from your local library. Some contain scant financial information, but give details of the company's products, markets, structure and even the proper address, which will help you to investigate further. It would be impossible to list all potential sources of information, but the following is a selection of the better known sources and the type of information provided. You should be able to find most of these publications in your library.

The Financial Times

This is the most important daily source of financial information. As well as giving extensive and excellent news of general business and commercial topics, it provides comprehensive coverage of UK and international companies' activities and their finances.

Investors Chronicle

This is a weekly guide to the activities of the City and financial news. It also provides valuable reviews of selected companies and industries.

Kompass

This guide is published annually in two volumes. Volume 1 is a classified catalogue of products and services, giving the names of manufacturers, wholesalers and distributors. Volume 2 contains information on over 30,000 companies, including the names of directors, details of share capital, turnover, number of employees, nature of business and product group.

Kelly's Manufacturers and Merchants Directory

This is an annual directory covering some 90,000 UK manufacturers, merchants and wholesalers. The firms are listed with addresses, telephone and telex numbers and telegraphic addresses.

The Stock Exchange Official Year Book

This is the only reference book giving authorative information about what is bought and sold on the Stock Exchange. It is the prime source of information about the operation of the London Stock Exchange and gives information on the companies' directors, capital, accounts and dividends.

Who Owns Whom

This is an annual directory in two volumes. The parent companies and their subsidiaries are listed in Volume 1 and the second volume is an index of subsidiaries and associate companies showing their parent companies.

Extel Cards

These are sometimes available in the business section of libraries. There are a number of different Extel Card Services, each providing comprehensive financial information on certain types of companies. For example, the UK Listed Companies Service covers every company listed on the London and Irish Stock Exchanges.

CD ROM databases

Many libraries have databases of corporate and stock exchange information stored on CD ROM. These disks are regularly updated with information and their advantage over printed information sources is that they are easily accessed and you can set up your own search strategy. Examples are Datastream and Fame (Financial Analysis Made Easy).

Summary financial statements

The full annual report and accounts is a very lengthy and complex document. Legislation has been passed that allows public limited companies to send shareholders Summary Financial Statements (SFSs) instead of the full document. Summary Financial Statements must include certain financial information, but this is a very reduced amount of non-financial information about products, markets and events within the company.

The Internet

Another increasingly important source of information is the Internet. Many public companies have their own Web sites and disclose significant amounts of financial information. However, care should be taken when using information from the Internet. Although some companies will put the complete information in the published annual report and account of the Internet, there may be many omissions.

> You should now be able to attempt Task 2.1 at the end of this chapter.

4 POTENTIAL USERS OF FINANCIAL INFORMATION

There are a number of *potential users of financial information*. We say potential users because the extent to which they use company financial information and the value it is to them is not fully known. It is possible to suggest why and how they might use such information, but insufficient research has been conducted to know if the potential users do this. The main groups of potential users are:

- shareholders
- lenders
- trade unions and employees
- business contacts
- analysts and advisers

We will examine each of these user groups separately in the following sections.

5 | SHAREHOLDERS

The rights of *shareholders* to information about a company arise from the direct financial relationship between them. The amount of information required by a shareholder depends to some extent on the size of the shareholding and whether the investor is a private shareholder or a financial institution employing professional investors.

The number of individual shareholders has risen in this country in recent years. However, many of these new investors have very modest shareholdings, often in one company. They do not actively trade on the stock market by regularly buying and selling shares, but keep their original holding until they decide to sell. Possibly, one of the main reasons they choose to sell their shares is that they require the money for other purposes, such as a holiday or to buy a new car. There are some individual shareholders who take a great interest in the stock market and have sizable holdings. These investors often rely on the services of a professional adviser such as a broker. Because of the size of their investment, their need for information may be greater than the individual who has acquired only a few hundred shares in a single company.

Approximately 75 per cent of all UK equities is held by institutional investors such as pension funds, unit trusts and insurance companies. They employ people to invest funds on the stock market. These professional investors are dealing with huge sums of money that do not belong to them but to their employer. Although professional investors have no personal stake in the share transactions, the decisions made by them affect the success of the financial institutions that employ them. The professional investor, therefore, has the motivation and the time to conduct detailed research on a company.

Whatever type of shareholder we are considering, there are three basic decisions to be taken by investors:

- to buy more shares;
- to hold on to the shares already owned;
- to sell all or part of the shares owned.

The way these decisions are made depends on the investor's view of the prospects of the stock market as a whole, the particular company in which the investment is made, and the industry in which the company operates. The important thing to stress is that the investor is interested in the future. What has happened in the past will be of value only in so far as it helps to predict what is likely to happen in the future. By attempting to predict the future, investors hold one or both of two main objectives: to secure a regular and attractive income from the investment in the form of a dividend paid by the company and/or to achieve capital growth. The latter will be achieved if the market value of the shareholding increases. In other words, if the shares can be sold for a higher price than that paid, the investor will make a capital gain.

The shareholder may place far greater emphasis on one of these objectives and than the other. A retired person, for example, may want a regular and secure income and have no interest in capital growth, apart from keeping pace with inflation. A professional investor may buy shares in the belief that they will

18

rapidly increase in price and a profit can be made by selling them and not be concerned much with dividends. Whatever the objectives of the shareholder and the decisions to be made, financial information is required. Although the financial information will not forecast the future, it will enable conclusions to be drawn about the past and present financial performance of a company. This assists in judging what is likely to happen in the future.

> *You should now be able to attempt Question 2.1 at the end of this chapter.*

6 LENDERS

A business may have a number of sources from which it has borrowed money. One of the main sources is likely to be a bank. The loan from the bank may be long term, for a period of, say, over five years, or short term, such as an overdraft that is repayable on demand. In addition, most businesses transact their trade on credit; goods are supplied but payment is not made until some weeks later.

If a *lender* has made a long-term loan to a company or has been asked to do so, a number of financial judgements must be made. The lender will wish to assess the long-term economic stability of the company. There is no sense in making a long-term loan to a company that is likely to go out of business in a few months. The lender will also want to ensure that there is every prospect of the loan being repaid and the degree of risk involved. If the worst should happen and the organisation goes out of business, the lender will want to know the possibility of the loan being repaid out of the proceeds of the sale.

Short-term lenders and *trade creditors* are interested in the company's cash and near cash position and how they are likely to change in the future. They will want to estimate the risk and consequences of the organisation not being able to pay any outstanding debt.

7 EMPLOYEES

Individual *employees* and *trade unions* are also interested in the finances of a company. The future livelihood and prospects of employees depend on the financial stability and success of the company that employs them. An employee may wish to assess the security of employment and will be interested in any indications of the position, progress and prospects of the company. Employees may not only wish to avoid the risks of redundancy, but may be seeking to ascertain career prospects. It is also natural that an employee, who spends a large part of the day working for an organisation, has a general interest in its financial performance. A large number of organisations realise this and produce simplified financial accounts for employees and sometimes show employees videos giving financial information.

8 TRADE UNIONS

Trade unions representing employees in a particular organisation require financial information for the same reasons as employees. The trade unions are interested in security of employment and the prospects of the business. Financial information is also required for the purposes of collective bargaining when the trade union attempts to negotiate improvements in the pay and conditions of its members. However, trade unions are more likely to take a broader view of the organisation than an individual employee. They are also more likely to have the resources and knowledge to enable them to conduct a more detailed financial analysis. A number of trade unions employ research officers, who are qualified accountants and skilled at analysing financial information. In addition to requiring the same type of information needed by investors and lenders, trade unions need information for the following reasons:

- to estimate the future prospects of the organisation, particularly its ability to make wage increases;

- to predict future levels of employment and changes in skill demands in the company;

- to evaluate managerial performance, efficiency and objectives;

- to assess the prospects of individual factories and other parts of a large organisation or group of companies.

 You should now be able to attempt Task 2.2 at the end of this chapter.

9 BUSINESS CONTACTS

An organisation has a large number of *business contacts*. Suppliers of goods and services to the organisation rely on it for the success of their own businesses. The customers may be dependent on it if there are few or no other organisations offering the same goods or services. Its competitors may be interested in take-overs or mergers and may also wish to make comparisons of efficiencies, market share and new products. All these business contacts require *financial information*.

Suppliers of goods and services require information on the business's ability to pay. Suppliers are also interested in its long-term prospects. If it appears that the business is highly successful and likely to expand, suppliers may wish to improve their own production capacity or make other significant changes in order to benefit from the opportunities offered.

Customers also want information about the products and services offered. In particular, customers are interested in details of prices, product specifications, delivery dates and likely product improvements. If the customer is relying on the organisation for continuing supplies or its ability to complete a long term contract, a longer term view will be taken. Information on the financial position of the organisation and its profitability may help customers to make decisions.

Competitors may seek financial information because they wish to invest in the business or launch a takeover bid. In this case the competitor will require the same information as the professional investor. In addition, competitors often require information so that they can make comparisons and therefore judge their own efficiencies. If a similar business in the same industry is much more profitable, there is a need to examine where improvements can be made. Competitors are interested in all aspects of an organisation's affairs, including information about pricing and marketing policies, production methods, research and development initiatives, investment plans and overall profitability. Some of this information will be confidential, but some will be publicly available.

10 FINANCIAL ANALYSTS AND ADVISERS

There are a large number of *financial analysts and advisers* in the industry. The financial press carries many articles that analyse in depth the financial affairs of particular companies and industries. Stockbrokers use their own analysts so that they can advise their clients. Companies, trade unions, the government and other institutions all employ analysts and advisers.

The information needs of the analysts and advisers are similar to the needs of the client for whom they are working. For example, stockbrokers need information to advise their clients on the investments they should make and therefore seek the same financial information as the investor. A researcher working for a trade union will require financial information relating to pay, prospects and job security. Analysts and advisers are likely to need more complex information and, in turn, will produce sophisticated and highly informed observations on the activities of companies. A considerable amount of the information used will come from the annual report and accounts published by companies. We will discuss this in detail in a later chapter. To interpret this information, accounting ratios will be used, which we examine in a subsequent chapter.

You should now be able to attempt Task 2.3 and Questions 2.2 and 2.3 at the end of this chapter.

11 B2B

A recent trend that may have a significant impact on the provision and use of financial information is B2B, which stands for business-to-business electronic commerce. You will be familiar with B2C (business-to-commerce) transactions such as buying books, clothes and CDs over the Internet for personal use. Although these transactions are important, B2B is far more significant in value.

If you are a manufacturer, you will wish to purchase from suppliers and will want certain product specifications, delivery times, quantities and prices. The Internet provides an excellent opportunity for a number of suppliers to make this information available. It also has the result that a number of companies are trading electronically and sharing considerable financial information.

12   DISCLOSURE AND CONFIDENTIALITY

Limited companies are legally obliged to make available certain information to their shareholders and register this with the Registrar of Companies thus making it public. Public limited companies that are quoted on the Stock Exchange will provide more information than legally required and the annual report and accounts is, to some extent, a public relations document designed to promote the name and image of the company.

However, there are certain types of information a company would be unwilling to give. The reason for this is known as commercial confidentiality. Put quite simply, this means that it might cause harm to the company if this information was disclosed. For example, if a company had invented a new product, it would not want its competitors to know all the details. Similarly, a company would not want its customers to know all its costs and the profit made on each product.

This commercially confidential information is often the very information that the potential users would like to receive. If we knew that a major drugs company had just discovered a wonder drug that would cure every disease, it would be very useful information. It would be even more useful if we knew this before others, because we could buy the company's shares. When the news of the drug became common knowledge, there would be a demand for the company's shares, because investors would consider the company had a successful future. This demand for shares would push up the price and we could sell our holding and make a profit.

If we had bought the shares because we had carefully examined information that was public, and through our general knowledge had predicted there was the possibility of a new drug being discovered, there is no problem. However, if the chief chemist of the company had told us in private, we would be in receipt of privileged information. If we had bought shares on this basis, we would be guilty of insider dealing, which is an offence.

13   SUMMARY

In this chapter we have considered the main sources of readily available information on *limited companies*. *Sole traders* and *partnerships* do not have to make financial information publicly available.

We have identified the main potential users of such information. *Shareholders* have a legal right to receive certain financial information and will require such information to make decisions on their investments. *Trade unions* and *employees* rely on the financial stability and success of the company for their future livelihood and future prospects. They require information to assess these matters, but employees may also have a general interest in the financial welfare of their employer. *Business contacts*, whether lenders, suppliers, customers or competitors, are interested in the financial information of a company. *Financial analysts and advisers* interpret the financial information and comment on its significance.

Although limited liability companies must disclose certain information, there may be concerns over *confidentiality*. A company may believe that the disclosure of some types of information might cause it harm.

> *You should now be able to attempt the objective test at the end of this chapter.*

Student activities

Task 2.1
Choose one very well known company with a household name and a small local company. Go to your library and by using the various reference books and papers see how much information you can obtain on each of them. Conduct a similar search on the Internet and compare the information you have obtained.

Task 2.2
See if you can obtain any copies of financial reports that have been produced by companies specifically for employees. You may find working relatives may receive them. Business libraries sometimes have copies and well known companies will often send a copy if you write to them. Compare the information in the report for employees with the annual report for shareholders which companies are legally obliged to publish. What are the similarities and differences in the contents and the way the information is presented?

Task 2.3
Using a well-known company name as an example, draw up a list of the information you would like if you were a supplier to the company. Ask a friend draw up a list as a customer of that company. Compare your lists and attempt to explain any differences in the type of information you require.

Question 2.1
Select the correct response to the following statements:

	True	False
i) Partnerships have to disclose financial information to the public if requested to do so.	☐	☐
ii) Only limited companies quoted on the Stock Exchange have to produce an annual report and accounts.	☐	☐
iii) If you know the correct name of a subsidiary company it is possible to find out the name of the holding company.	☐	☐
iv) Shareholders are only interested in buying shares in companies which pay large dividends.	☐	☐
v) If an investor sells shares for a higher price than was originally paid a capital gain has been made.	☐	☐

23

Question 2.2

Why would a private shareholder want financial information about a company and how useful do you consider the annual report and accounts is in meeting these needs?

Question 2.3

Match the potential users of information with the purpose for which they may require it in the following list:

a)	Customers	i)	To ensure that a loan will be repaid
b)	Trade unions	ii)	For dealing in shares
c)	Lenders	iii)	To evaluate products and services
d)	Employees	iv)	For producing highly informed observations
e)	Investors	v)	To negotiate improvements in pay
f)	Analysts	vi)	To assess security of employment

Objective test (tick the appropriate box)

i)   The best source of financial information about a company is:

   a)   the *Financial Times*   ☐

   b)   the *Stock Exchange Official Year Book*   ☐

   c)   the annual report and accounts   ☐

   d)   the *Investor's Chronicle*   ☐

ii) If a bank makes a short-term loan to a company, the most important information for the bank is:

   a)   the balance sheet for the last five years   ☐

   b)   the predicted cash position   ☐

   c)   the share price of the company   ☐

   d)   the profit for the last five years   ☐

iii) A creditor of a company is someone who:

   a)   is owed money by the company   ☐

   b)   owes money to the company   ☐

   c)   wants to buy shares in the company   ☐

   d)   wants to sell shares in the company   ☐

iv) By law a company's annual report and accounts must be sent to:

   a)   the bank   ☐

   b)   institutional investors only   ☐

   c)   shareholders with over 500 shares only   ☐

   d)   all shareholders   ☐

v) Insider dealing is when you buy shares because:

    a) the share price is going down   ☐

    b) you are in possession of privileged information   ☐

    c) you have loaned money to the company   ☐

    d) you are an employee of the company   ☐

CHAPTER 3

The role of the accountant

1 │ OBJECTIVES

At the end of this chapter you should be able to:

- explain what is meant by the term 'accounting';
- describe the structure of the accounting profession;
- explain the role of the accountant;
- compare the main forms of accounting;
- describe the various areas of accounting work.

2 │ INTRODUCTION

The words *accounting* and *accountant* are frequently used by people without any understanding of what the terms convey. Accounting in its broadest sense is concerned with the measuring, recording and communicating of the financial aspects of business activities and accountants are the people who carry out these tasks. This description gives some impression of the subject, but in this chapter we will examine the various subdivisions of accounting and the different types of accountants and the tasks they carry out.

There are two main forms of accounting and accountants will often refer to their own work in this way. There are a number of subdivisions and variations, but the two main forms are *financial accounting* and *management accounting*.

3 │ FINANCIAL ACCOUNTING

Financial accounting is concerned with classifying and measuring the transactions of a business and recording them. At the end of a period of time, usually a year but possibly more frequently, a *profit-and-loss statement* is prepared to show financial performance over that period of time and a *balance sheet* to show the financial position of the business at the end of the period. The preparation of these two financial statements at the end of the period is for the benefit of the owners of the business, although other people may also be interested in them.

Financial accounting is concerned with giving a *true and fair view* of the business. To ensure this, considerable attention is paid to any *accounting conventions and concepts* that influence the preparation of financial accounts. In the case of limited companies, attention will be paid to the legal requirements of the *Companies Act 1985* as amended by the *Companies Act 1989* and the requirements of Accounting Standards. If a company is listed on the Stock Exchange, the reporting *regulations of the Stock Exchange* must also be complied with.

Financial accounting can be divided into a number of specific activities, such as auditing, taxation advice, insolvency and bookkeeping. We will look at some of these more closely later in the chapter but we will concentrate on bookkeeping at this stage.

Bookkeeping is concerned with the recording of business transactions. It is an essential business activity and modern bookkeeping was developed in Italy in the fourteenth and fifteenth centuries. The records kept by bookkeepers were originally in handwritten ledgers, although many businesses now use computers. Although bookkeeping is a crucial aspect of accounting in a business, the skills and knowledge of a highly qualified accountant are not required for the work. It is normal therefore for a business to employ someone who is not able to carry out all accounting functions, but has sufficient knowledge and experience to be able to carry out bookkeeping competently.

If you look in the local Press under 'situations vacant' you will find jobs advertised for bookkeepers. These will often state that the applicant should be experienced to trial balance. This is the stage of accounting before the preparation of a profit-and-loss account, but where all the records have been summarised at the end of a period.

4   MANAGEMENT ACCOUNTING

The main function of *management accounting* is to provide financial information to managers. Such information will be needed by the managers so that they can plan the progress of the business, control the activities and see the financial implications of any decisions they may have to take.

Originally management accounting was concerned mainly with working out the actual cost of the products and services. An organisation needs to know how much it costs to make one of its own products and will want a breakdown of these costs into various categories, such as materials, labour and overheads. At this early stage the term *cost accounting* was used. If you start to study management accounting, you will find that the introductory lessons are still concerned with costing.

As management accounting developed various methods and techniques, it became possible to provide management with information on alternative courses of action, the financial implication of decisions and to answer 'what if' questions. Increasingly management accounting has become more concerned with the strategy of the organisation.

A financial accountant needs to ensure that the information complies with established conventions, concepts and legal requirements. A management accountant, however, needs to ensure that the information is of value to managers. Management accounting uses a range of techniques and methods to provide the information. The main point to remember is that management accounting is concerned with identifying why the information is required so that the most appropriate technique can be used to supply information to managers which will be of value to them.

 You should now be able to attempt Question 3.1 at the end of this chapter.

5 | AUDITING

Most members of the public tend to associate accounting with auditing. Although auditing is a critical part of the accounting profession, it is not a main area of work for accountants. In a later section we will discuss the structure of the accounting profession and the nature of the accounting qualifications. Only those accountants who have received the appropriate training are permitted to conduct external audits. An external audit is performed by a trained accountant in public practice and is a legal requirement for most companies. It should be remembered that it is the responsibility of the directors to prepare the financial statements and the auditor expresses an opinion on them.

In addition to external auditors, who are responsible to shareholders, many major companies employ internal auditors. These will be responsible to managers and they ensure that the accounting system and procedures in an organisation are properly maintained.

6 | FORENSIC ACCOUNTING

The integration of accounting, auditing and investigative skills yields the specific discipline known as forensic accounting. This is a fairly recent addition to the tasks of accountants and forensic accounting provides an accounting analysis that is suitable in a legal case and will form the basis for discussion, debate and ultimately resolution.

Forensic accounting encompasses both litigation support and investigative accounting. Litigation support provides assistance of an accounting analysis that is suitable in involving existing or pending litigation. It deals primarily with issues related to the quantification of economic loss resulting from a breach of contract. Investigative accounting is often associated with investigations of criminal matters. A typical investigative accounting assignment might be an investigation of employee theft. Other examples include securities fraud, insurance fraud, bribes and proceeds of crime investigations.

Forensic accountants can be retained to analyse, interpret, summarise and present complex financial and business related issues in a manner which is both understandable and properly supported. They may be working in public or employed by insurance companies, banks, police forces, government agencies and other organisations.

The types of work that a forensic accountant may be called upon to perform are:

- Investigation and analysis of financial evidence;
- Development of computerised applications to assist in the analysis and presentation of financial evidence;
- Assistance in legal proceedings, including testifying in court as an expert witness and preparing visual aids to support trial evidence.

In order to perform these services a forensic accountant must be familiar with legal concepts and procedures. In addition, the forensic accountant must be able to identify substance over form when dealing with an issue.

7 THE STRUCTURE OF THE ACCOUNTING PROFESSION

What do we mean when we speak about a person being a qualified accountant? A number of people know something about accounting and may have a Certificate or Diploma in business and finance or a degree in accounting, but are not regarded as being qualified. To become a qualified accountant you must pass the examinations and become a member of a *recognised professional body*. When you have done this you can put designatory letters after your name.

There are a number of accounting bodies, but the major professional bodies of accountants are shown in Table 3.1, together with recent figures of members and

Table 3.1 Membership of professional accounting bodies

Accounting body	Designation	2001 Membership	
		Members	Students
Institute of Chartered Accountants in England & Wales (ICAEW)	FCA or ACA	120,000	10,000
Institute of Chartered Accountants in Ireland (ICAI)	FCA or ACA	12,500	1,000†
Institute of Chartered Accountants in Scotland (ICAS)	CA	15,000	1,500*
Association of Chartered Certified Accountants (ACCA)	FCCA or ACCA	87,000	175,000
Chartered Institute of Management Accountants (CIMA)	FCMA or ACMA	57,000	74,000
Chartered Institute of Public Finance and Accountancy (CIPFA)	IPFA	13,400	2,200

* Approximation   † New trainees

students. The numbers are given as an indication of size only and all of the professional bodies are experiencing significant growth.

None of these professional bodies is better than another. The members of all of them are considered as qualified accountants. If you wish to become an accountant, the professional body you choose will depend on the way you wish to train and the type of work you wish to do when you are qualified.

The first three professional bodies used to require their students to train with professional firms in practice although these rules are now being relaxed. This means that you will be working for a firm of accountants. The firm can be just one accountant – a sole practitioner – or a large partnership employing a few thousand people. Once you are qualified you may choose to remain working in the profession, as a sole practitioner or for a firm of accountants. Approximately half of the members of the first three bodies work in professional practices.

Members of the *Association of Chartered Certified Accountants* can choose to train in the profession or in industry or commerce, working for a company. Some of the largest organisations such as British Rail, Rolls Royce, CEGB. run special training schemes. On qualifying, approximately 25 per cent of *certified accountants* choose to work in practice, 15 per cent in financial and public administration, and the remainder in industry.

Members of the *Chartered Institute of Management Accountants* do their training in industry and commerce and usually continue to work there when they are qualified. Members of the *Chartered Institute of Public Finance and Accountancy* work in local authorities, the National Health Service, and other similar public bodies.

You should now be able to attempt Task 3.1 at the end of this chapter.

8 THE NATURE OF ACCOUNTANCY WORK

The accountant, whether in practice or working in industry, commerce or the public sector, has an important role in collating, recording and communicating financial information. As well as communicating the implications of financial information, accountants are expected to give advice on a wide range of matters which will include the following:

- How financial affairs can be best arranged so that the lowest amount of tax may be paid. This could be for an individual with a small income or a very large company.
- The best way to borrow money for a specific project. This could range from individuals building extensions to their homes or a company building a complete factory.
- The costs of offering a new product or service.
- The financial benefits of introducing new technology.

- The total costs of a pay offer to be put to the trade unions.
- The profit to be made from organising a huge pop concert.

The above list gives only a few examples. Wherever there is a need for financial information and advice, the accountant has a key role. Because of the very different types of work there are, accountants tend to specialise in particular areas.

It is impossible to list the many areas of activity in which a management accountant in industry is involved as they are so varied and different. The primary task is to assist the other managers in their work. This involves examining alternative courses of action and determining the future activities of the company; measuring the activities of the company and comparing with the plans so that control can be maintained; analysing the financial consequences of taking certain decisions.

With financial accounting there are some activities that can be identified, although these only give an indication of the types of work undertaken. The main areas of work concerning the financial accountant are:

Accounts preparation

This is a large area of activity, both for financial accountants working in industry or commerce and for accountants working in practice. Limited companies are obliged under the *Companies Act 1985* to keep proper books of account and produce certain financial statements. Most limited companies will employ an accountant to carry out this task. In large companies there will be many qualified accountants.

Even sole traders and partnerships will have to declare their profits to the Inland Revenue. If the business is so small that there is insufficient work to employ an accountant, then the proprietor will go to an accountant working in the profession to get the work done.

Auditing

The law provides that the accounts of a limited company must be subject to audit by a registered accountant. An audit is a thorough examination of the financial records of the company to confirm that the profit-and-loss account and balance sheet that are prepared from these records give a true and fair view.

An audit can be conducted on any financial statement, not only the annual accounts of a limited company. However, the audit of the limited companies accounts is required by legislation and the law states clearly who is qualified to conduct the audit. Only those who are properly supervised and appropriately qualified can be appointed as company auditors. The audits must be carried out properly, with integrity and with a proper degree of independence.

Taxation

If you are an employee of a company and that is your only source of income, you have little opportunity to adjust the amount of tax you pay. However, people who are self-employed and enjoy a significant income will need an accountant to handle their tax affairs. The accountant will attempt to arrange the individual's financial affairs in such a way that the lowest amount of tax possible is paid, although, of course, what is legally due to the Inland Revenue must be paid.

Limited companies are subject to corporation tax and this is a complex area needing the knowledge of an accountant to ensure that the correct amount of tax is paid.

> *You should now be able to attempt Task 3.2 at the end of this chapter.*

9 | BECOMING AN ACCOUNTANT

Becoming a member of any of the professional bodies of accountants mentioned in this chapter takes a considerable amount of time and lots of effort. As well as doing accountancy work, you will have to take a number of rigorous examinations. The failure rate in the examinations is very high and even a student with an accounting degree, who passes all the examinations the first time, can expect to take three years to qualify. For many students the period will be five to six years.

The rewards, both financially and in terms of job satisfaction, are very high for qualified accountants. The work can be as varied as resolving someone's taxation problems in the Bahamas, calculating the cost of building a road in Africa or auditing the books of a small company in an English country town. It is these opportunities that makes accounting an exciting career and the general requirements for two of the professional bodies are shown below.

To become a *chartered accountant* you must train with a firm of chartered accountants for three or four years by entering into a training contract. This will allow you to gain practical experience as well as preparing to take the professional examinations. The Institute of Chartered Accountants has introduced a scheme allowing students to qualify in industry.

Certified accountants can train and work in industry, commerce, local and central government, nationalised industries and practice. Although students must be doing recognised accounting work, the Association allows moves between different sectors of employment during the training period. The prospective student must be highly motivated. There is a wide choice of ways to study for the examinations. Students may have day or block release at college, go to evening classes or take a correspondence course.

> *You should now be able to attempt Questions 3.2 and 3.3 and Task 3.3 at the end of this chapter.*

10 THE INFLUENCE OF ACCOUNTANTS

Because of their specialised knowledge and training, accountants can be very influential in a number of ways. As individuals, they are likely to command respect in the organisation in which they work and their advice is likely to be listened to. They may also be influential in the local community by being members of bodies such as the Chamber of Commerce. At a national level, accountants often sit on committees that provide guidance to government and other national bodies; they sometimes make the front pages of the newspaper when a financial scandal is announced. Usually this is because the accountant has been called in to investigate the scandal, rather than because he or she is the cause of the scandal.

Accountants are also influential through their professional bodies. In Chapter 1 we commented on the importance of the professional bodies of accountants in setting up a system for setting accounting standards in the UK. Although the role of the professional bodies is not so dominant since the establishment of the *Accounting Standards Board (ASB)*, they remain highly influential. *The Department of Trade and Industry (DTI)*, which is the part of the government responsible for company legislation, the ASB, which is responsible for accounting standards, and the Stock Exchange, which is responsible for regulating limited companies whose shares are publicly available, all seek the advice and views of the professional bodies on any proposals or changes they wish to introduce. The professional bodies are also important because they regulate the work of their members. They, therefore, seek to ensure the highest standards of competence and ethics from the members.

However, not everyone is willing to accept that this influential role played by the accounting bodies is entirely beneficial. Some argue that accountants not only set the rules of the financial game, but also act as the referees and the investigators when there are problems. They would prefer to see a number of different aspects of accountancy regulated by bodies who are independent of the accounting profession. Some argue that the success of the ASB compared with the *Accounting Standards Committee (ASC)*, which it replaced, is partly due to the ASB's independence. Of course, whichever body carries out these responsibilities, whether it is part of the accounting profession or a government department, it must be paid for and the individuals involved are likely to be qualified accountants.

11 SUMMARY

In this chapter we have looked at the two main forms of accounting. Financial accounting is concerned with classifying, measuring and recording the transactions of a business. Management accounting is concerned with providing financial information that is useful to managers.

Accountancy work is very broad in its nature and accountants have an important role in industry, commerce and the public sector, as well as in practice.

You should now be able to attempt Task 3.3 and the objective test at the end of this chapter.

Student activities

Task 3.1
Read through the situations vacant columns of national newspapers and collect all the advertisements for accountants. Analyse these to see if there is a pattern between the type of work and the accountancy qualification required.

Task 3.2
Look at the advertisements for accountants in the financial press. Make a list of the various types of work specified and attempt to classify them into either financial or management accounting.

Task 3.3
Conduct a survey in your college to ascertain how many students intend to pursue a career as an accountant and if so which professional body they are going to choose. Ask them for their reasons for choosing a career in accounting.

Question 3.1
Classify the following activities into those that are financial accounting and those that are management accounting:

i)   Keeping the financial records of a company.

ii) Providing financial information to be used by managers.

iii) Ensuring compliance with the Companies Act 1985.

iv) Preparing the profit-and-loss account and balance sheet at the year end.

v)   Analysing the financial implications of management decisions.

vi) Managing the tax affairs of a company.

vii) Auditing the books of a company.

Question 3.2
Select the correct response for the following statements:

		True	False
i)	Bookkeeping is the most technical activity a qualified accountant undertakes.	☐	☐
ii)	Under the Companies Act 1985 limited companies are obliged to maintain proper books of account.	☐	☐
iii)	To become a qualified accountant you must train with a firm of accountants working in practice.	☐	☐
iv)	Management accounting is primarily concerned with producing financial information that is valuable to managers.	☐	☐

	True	False
v) To pass all the examinations of any of the main professional bodies of accountants normally takes at least two years.	☐	☐

Question 3.3

Nick Adams has just finished his first year's training as a painter and decorator. He has been operating as a sole trader and his wife, June, who has a BTEC qualification, has been keeping his accounts. Nick's brother asks him if he can join the business, but Nick refuses saying that as a partnership they would have to have a properly qualified accountant to audit the books and that would be very expensive.

Required

Write a letter to Nick explaining the legal position on auditing. Identify any advantages there may be for Nick in employing a qualified accountant instead of June and explain the different types of accounting qualifications.

Objective test (tick the appropriate box)

i) Management accounting is mainly concerned with:

   a) providing financial information to managers ☐

   b) recording information for tax purposes ☐

   c) communicating financial information to shareholders ☐

   d) auditing the accounts of a company ☐

ii) An audit is a:

   a) method of recording financial information ☐

   b) examination of the financial records of an organisation ☐

   c) process of constructing a profit statement ☐

   d) statement issued by the professional bodies of accountants ☐

iii) The two main forms of accounting are:

   a) bookkeeping and auditing ☐

   b) taxation and investment appraisal ☐

   c) financial and management accounting ☐

   d) profit statement and balance sheet ☐

iv) If you want to pursue a career in local government, the most appropriate accounting qualification is to become a member of the:

   a) Institute of Chartered Accountants ☐

   b) Association of Chartered Certified Accountants ☐

   c) Chartered Institute of Management Accountants ☐

   d) Chartered Institute of Public Finance and Accountancy ☐

v) It is a legal requirement that an audit is carried out on the financial records of:

a) a sole trader ☐

b) a partnership ☐

c) a limited liability company ☐

d) none of these ☐

CHAPTER 4

Accounting concepts and conventions

1 OBJECTIVES

At the end of this chapter you should be able to:

- explain the importance of accounting concepts and conventions;
- describe the main concepts and conventions;
- explain the limitations of financial statements;
- calculate the impact on profit if a company is inconsistent in its accounting policies.

2 INTRODUCTION

So far in this book we have told you how you should carry out certain accounting activities. Some of you will have wondered why these activities are dealt with in one particular way when another method would seem to be just as good. You may have also found yourself wondering what you should do when you come up against a problem for which we have not given you specific guidance.

Even with accounting in the workplace, there is no huge book that states precisely the correct accounting treatment for every transaction and eventuality. Accountants in business, however, and students require some framework and guidance and this is found in the Generally Accepted Accounting Principles (GAAP), which describes the basis on which financial statements are prepared. The GAAP are not a rigid, highly defined set of statements but covers specific rules, practices and procedures for particular circumstances and also broad principles and conventions of general application.

This does mean that GAAP has flexibility. Alternative methods of accounting are sometimes available and accountants must use their professional judgement to choose the most appropriate alternative accounting approach to resolve financial reporting issues. Professional judgement must be exercised cautiously because GAAP has become increasingly complex and specific in certain accounting treatments. The main framework of GAAP in the UK is derived from:

- Company legislation, although this is less important at the level we are studying and is only briefly covered in a later chapter.
- Accounting Standards are set by the Financial Accounting Standards Board in the UK. To understand the financial statements of limited companies it is

essential to have an understanding of Accounting Standards. In later chapters, we will deal with this topic at the introductory level but it is still essential that you appreciate the great importance of Accounting Standards on financial accounting.

- Accounting concepts and conventions may already be contained in legislation or Accounting Standards. However, some are so fundamental to doing accounting that they can be regarded as the basic 'rules of the road'. In this chapter, we will look at these concepts and conventions and this will help in understanding future chapters.

3   OBJECTIVES OF FINANCIAL REPORTING

In an earlier chapter we gave, as part of a definition of accounting, the communication of financial information. The entire process of financial accounting is carried out so that somebody receives information about the organisation. Much of this information will be in the form of financial statements. With limited companies the financial statements will be accompanied by narrative reports and a considerable amount of text that expands on and explains the financial statements.

There are a number of potential users of financial statements, as explained in Chapter 2. They will have different information needs and preferences and, for a large company, it is impossible to meet all these needs. The financial statements should therefore be a general purpose document intended to meet as many of the needs as possible.

In meeting these needs, however, certain basic assumptions are made as to general reasons why users require information. Two assumptions have been made that, to a large extent, are in conflict and raise a number of issues. The two assumptions are that accounts are needed either for stewardship purposes or for decision making.

Where it is assumed that accounts are needed for stewardship purposes great emphasis will be placed on accounting for past transactions. Investors and owners are interested in how the funds they have already put into the business have been used. It is the responsibility of a steward to account for any assets held and any liabilities accrued. Accounting with a stewardship objective will, therefore, be historical.

If it is assumed that accounts are for decision-making purposes, information must be up to date and, preferably, have some predictive value. For someone interested in decision making it is less important to know what a factory building or any other asset cost when it was first purchased, which may have been years ago. It is far more important to know what the value of the building is now, or what it may be worth in the future.

Unfortunately such information is often less reliable and less certain. In a later chapter we will consider the problems there are with deciding the present value of an asset. Whatever the drawbacks of stewardship and 'historical' accounting, there is no denying that the information it provides is highly reliable.

4 | MONEY MEASUREMENT CONVENTION

Financial statements are prepared by measuring items in *monetary values*. For example if a business sells 500 tins of baked beans in a year and 250 bags of sugar, we can record the information in this way. But if we wish to prepare financial statements, these transactions must be recorded in terms of money so that we have a sales figure for the profit statement.

A business may look at its fixed assets at the end of the year in terms of being 5,000 square metres of office space, 5 cars and 15 personal computers. If we are summarise these items on a balance sheet a common unit of measurement must be used. This unit is monetary value and can be expressed in any currency, such as pounds sterling, euros or dollars, as long as we do not mix the different currencies in the same financial statements.

Unfortunately, there are a number of serious disadvantages with the money measurement concept. Items that cannot be measured in money terms are ignored. A company may have very loyal and creative employees, but this will not be shown in any of the financial statements. Another company may have a large number of highly dissatisfied customers, but this will not be shown in the financial statements.

It is true that in the long term one would expect that the company with loyal employees would prosper and the company with dissatisfied customers would go out of business. These are some of the reasons for the success or failure of the business, but these reasons are not shown anywhere on the financial statements. Only the consequences are measured in monetary terms.

Another difficulty with using money as a measure is that it is not stable due to inflation. If you measure your desk and it is one metre long, you would expect it to be one metre long next year, and the year after. If you replaced your desk with another that is one metre long, you would be very surprised if you put the two side by side and one was longer than the other. However, if your desk originally cost £150 two years ago and you wished to replace it, you would expect, possibly, to pay more because of inflation. The same desk may now cost £165. The type of desk has not changed, but the money measure is different.

If you consider the balance sheet, the fixed assets will all be shown at cost less their cumulative depreciation to give their written value. If the fixed assets have been bought at different times, then the money measure of cost will be different. A company may have identical computers, but if they were bought in different years the cost will not be the same and this fact will not be evident from the balance sheet. The written values that are shown on the balance sheet may not be a good guide as to what the items are now worth and there will be no information given as to how much it would cost if they were to be replaced.

Despite the severe drawbacks to the money measurement concept, it is in universal use. A number of proposals have been made for adjusting financial statements to show the effects of inflation. These have not been successful so far but the issue is constantly being considered by accountants and alternatives sought.

You should now be able to attempt Task 4.1 and Question 4.1 at the end of this chapter.

5 BUSINESS ENTITY CONVENTION

Financial statements describe the business as if it were entirely separate from its owner. If Josie Stamen owns a flower shop and we prepare the financial statements for the shop, we regard the shop as being a *separate entity*, a thing with a real existence. When we produce a profit-and-loss account, the profit will have been 'earned' by the business and it will be shown on the balance sheet as a liability that the business owes to Josie.

This view is a very artificial one because Josie runs the flower shop, but it is very helpful. When we are preparing financial statements, we have to draw some boundaries on what we are going to describe. Josie, as well as owning the flower shop, may also run a keep fit class two nights a week for which she is paid, be restoring a yacht, and may inherit £5,000 from her grandmother which she is using for speculating on the Stock Exchange. These are important activities for Josie and the people who know her, but if we set out to prepare financial statements for her flower shop, we need to concentrate on the activities that are related to that business. This task is made easier if we regard the business as a separate entity.

You will remember from Chapter 1 that an important feature of a limited company is that it is regarded as a distinct legal entity. This is of crucial importance in determining the financial liabilities of the owners of the business.

6 GOING CONCERN CONCEPT

A profit-and-loss statement and balance sheet are prepared for a business on the assumption that it will continue trading in the foreseeable future: in other words that it is a *going concern*. In the vast majority of cases this is true and there is no intention to close the business or reduce any of its activities significantly.

If the business is not a going concern, the financial statements can be very misleading. Some of the assets owned by the business may have a very different value placed on them from that shown in the balance sheet. For example, an aeroplane manufacturer will have very specialised factories and equipment shown in the balance sheet at written down values. If the business were to close, it is very doubtful if there would be many buyers, apart from other aeroplane manufacturers, of the fixed assets and they may not sell for the figures shown on the balance sheet.

Because of the going concern basis, financial statements can mislead and the possible consequences of closure are not shown. Apart from fixed asset valuation, there are other items that are not revealed. For example, when a business is wound up, it will have to pay redundancy compensation to its employees, and this information is not shown.

You should now be able to attempt Task 4.2 and Question 4.2 at the end of this chapter.

7   MATCHING CONCEPT

In later chapters we will examine the preparation of two major financial statements, the *profit-and-loss account* and the *balance sheet*. A major concept that is used in the preparation of these statements is known as the *matching concept*. The matching concept means that there must be a matching exercise so that expenses and revenues both refer to the same goods and the same financial period. Thus, the receipt and payment of cash are not the only information required for the preparation of financial statements: *accruals* and *prepayments* must also be taken into account. These terms will be discussed in later chapters.

Some writers divide the matching convention into a number of topics or show some of the implications under different headings. These are:

- *The period concept*, which means that a profit-and-loss account and balance sheet must be prepared at regular time intervals, for example each year. Unfortunately, business activities do not divide neatly into these periods and there are difficulties in dealing with this. For example, fixed assets last for a number of financial periods and business activity may not always correspond with the financial period selected.

- *The realisation concept*, which is concerned with ensuring that when a transaction occurs it is recorded in the correct financial period. This is particularly relevant to sales. With cash sales there are no problems, but imagine that a shipbuilder has received an order for a luxury yacht which will take two years to build and will require further finishing after the owner has used it for six months. It is important to determine when the sale takes place and when the costs are incurred so that the correct figure of profit can be shown for a particular financial period.

8   CONSISTENCY CONCEPT

This means simply that once a particular method of accounting treatment has been selected it should be used to account for similar transactions and in subsequent financial periods. Failure to do this would mean that the financial results would be distorted and comparisons over a period of time would be impossible.

The importance of the *consistency concept* can be illustrated by a simple example. Imagine that a business has reported that it made a profit of £3,000 each year in the first two years of trading. Upon investigation you find that the business bought fixed assets of £50,000 in the first year. In year one the business decided to depreciate on a straight line basis with a life of five years and a nil scrap value. In year two it changed to the reducing balance method over a different estimated life to give a depreciation charge of £8,000 for the year.

In year one the depreciation charge would have been £10,000, but by changing its method and the life, the depreciation charge in year two is reduced by £2,000.

If we are consistent and use the straight line method, the profit in year two is only £1,000.

> You should now be able to attempt Task 4.3 at the end of this chapter.

9 | PRUDENCE CONCEPT

This concept means that when you are preparing financial statements you should be a pessimist and not an optimist. Do not include revenues or profits unless you are certain that they will be realised.

On the other hand, all known liabilities should be included, even when the amount is not known with certainty and a best estimate has to be made. Thus on the profit-and-loss account accruals should be made for all expenses incurred, even if the invoice has not been received and the actual amount is not known. Similarly, a provision for bad debts will be made and deducted from the debtors on the balance sheet if we are not confident that all the money will be received.

Another example of accountants using the concept of prudence is in the valuation of stock held by a business. Stock at the year end will be valued at the lower of cost or net realisable value. Net realisable value can be taken as the estimated proceeds of selling the stock less all the costs required to put it into a marketable condition less all the costs to be incurred in marketing, selling and distributing the stock.

In recent years, the importance of the prudence concept has tended to reduce. Accountants wish the information they produce to be as objective as possible and the prudence concept gives information a 'negative' aspect. There is some tension, however, as we do not want to move from being too pessimistic to being too optimistic.

This debate is particularly relevant when the issue of stewardship and decision-making objectives are being discussed. There is a danger that in trying to ensure that financial information is appropriate for decision making, an overoptimistic approach may be taken and the information will be low on reliability.

> You should now be able to attempt Question 4.3 at the end of this chapter.

10 | THE TRUE AND FAIR CONCEPT

You may have heard accountants saying that financial statements must give a *true and fair view* of the financial affairs of an organisation. Although most people intuitively sense what the concept means, the concept of true and fair is not defined in any of the legislation or other regulations. The Accounting Standards

Committee (ASC) sought legal advice on the issue in 1983. The opinion given was that the matter must be decided by a judge. However, the advice went on to say that in reaching the decision the court would regard accounts complying with Generally Accepted Accounting Principles as, on the face of it, giving a true and fair view. Generally Accepted Accounting Principles are a reflection of the day-to-day practices of accountants and in many areas these practices are guided by accounting standards.

There are still attempts to try to arrive at a more precise definition of true and fair, but it seems unlikely that this will ever be achieved. As a result, it remains a somewhat vague concept, albeit a crucial one. Undoubtedly the truth and fairness of financial statements rests on the fact that Generally Accepted Accounting Principles have been followed and, in many instances, these principles will be guided by accounting standards.

11 SUMMARY

Accounting has a number of *concepts* and *conventions* that are used in maintaining accounting records and preparing financial statements. The concepts and conventions provide a *framework* and are essential in accounting. As well as providing a common basis for understanding accounts, the concepts and conventions also set some limitations on the usefulness of financial information.

You should now be able to attempt the objective test at the end of this chapter.

Student activities

Task 4.1
Consider a business such as an advertising agency or a hairdressing salon. Which aspects of the business do you think are important, but do not show on the financial statements?

Task 4.2
Make a list of local businesses and decide where there may be differences in the valuation of fixed assets as shown on the balance sheet under a going-concern basis and the actual amounts that may be received if the businesses close. Do not worry about trying to get the figures, merely identify the major items.

Task 4.3
Make a list of the various transactions of a business that, if not dealt with in a consistent manner, would affect the financial statements.

Question 4.1
State the main disadvantages of using money as a unit of measurement to record business transactions.

Question 4.2

Select the correct response to the following statements:

		True	False
i)	The value of items shown in the balance sheet is a good guide to what it would cost to replace them.	☐	☐
ii)	Items that cannot be measured in monetary terms are omitted from financial statements.	☐	☐
iii)	A sole trader's business is a separate legal entity.	☐	☐
iv)	Businesses with very specialised assets do not have to produce financial statements on a going concern basis.	☐	☐
v)	Inflation has no effect on the values of assets shown in the balance sheet.	☐	☐

Question 4.3

Keith Wilson trades in furniture. During the year he bought 80 coffee tables for £25 each and sold 60 of them for £27. At the year end he sees that a competitor is selling the tables for £24 each. Keith decides that his remaining tables require polishing, which will cost £1.50 each, and that he will have to advertise in the papers, which will cost £60, if he wishes to sell the remaining stock. What would be the stock valuation of the tables in the balance sheet at the year end?

Objective test (tick the appropriate box)

i) A profit-and-loss account and balance sheet are usually prepared for a business on the assumption that:

    a) it will close the next day   ☐

    b) it is a going concern   ☐

    c) it will continue for only one year   ☐

    d) it will continue for only one month   ☐

ii) If fixed assets are shown on the balance sheet at cost it means that:

    a) this is the cost of replacing them now   ☐

    b) this is the cost if you wished to buy them   ☐

    c) this is the original cost at which the business bought them   ☐

    d) this is the cost of keeping them maintained   ☐

iii) A major advantage of using money as a unit of measurement is that:

    a) it is not stable due to inflation   ☐

    b) it allows a value to be put on employees' loyalty   ☐

    c) fixed assets are shown on the balance sheet at current values   ☐

    d) it allows different activities to be summarised in the accounts   ☐

iv) When valuing the stock held by a business, an accountant will use:

    a)   the selling price ☐

    b)   the lower of cost or net realisable value ☐

    c)   the lower of cost or the selling price ☐

    d)   the replacement price ☐

v) If the owner of a business changed the method of depreciating fixed assets, it would be contrary to the:

    a)   matching concept ☐

    b)   prudence concept ☐

    c)   going concern concept ☐

    d)   consistency concept ☐

PART II

ACCOUNTING FOR ECONOMIC TRANSACTIONS

CHAPTER 5

Identifying transactions

OBJECTIVES

At the end of this chapter you should be able to:

- identify the source of information on transactions
- explain the purpose and features of source documents;
- prepare a document for a specific purpose;
- construct a flow diagram for source documents.

INTRODUCTION

In this chapter we are going to look more closely at the transactions and the documents needed by organisations in the course of their business activities. Organisations carry out many of the transactions between themselves on credit. If a manufacturing company sells goods to a retailer, payment is not always made in cash or by cheque immediately, but a period of credit is taken. The manufacturer must therefore issue an *invoice* to obtain the payment. This is a *source document*. When purchasing goods a business usually sends an *order* specifying the exact goods required, when they are required, and the address to which they should be sent. The sending and receipt of the goods needs both of the organisations concerned to issue a number of documents.

As well as requiring documents to record external transactions, a system of documentation is set up by most businesses for internal planning and control. For example, it may be necessary to record the amount of time that a worker has spent on a particular job or the amount of raw materials used in a manufacturing process. The documents used to measure these activities form the source from which the financial records of the organisation are drawn up. All the documents used by a business are designed for its own needs and purposes. However, there will be a great similarity between the documents used by different businesses. There is certain information that must be included on an invoice, such as the date and the amount due, although the business name, invoice design and colour of paper and print may vary. Even with internal documents there are likely to be many similarities between one organisation and another because the need to record certain types of information is common.

In this chapter we will look at the main source documents used, explain their purposes and the procedures adopted for issuing and controlling the documents. We will use standard formats for the documents and you should take the opportunity, wherever possible, to examine documents issued by various organisations to see the individual differences in practice. But first it will be useful to look at the accounting cycle.

You should now be able to attempt Task 5.1 at the end of this chapter.

3   THE ACCOUNTING CYCLE

The accounting cycle is the process and procedures to be completed to prepare financial statements such as the profit-and-loss account. Each time financial statements are prepared, and this will be at least annually and could be more frequent, the accounting cycle must be completed. The typical stages in the accounting cycle are described in Table 5.1.

Table 5.1 Stages in the accounting cycle

Stage	Process
Identifying transactions	Obtaining or generating a source document so that the transactions can be entered in the organisation's records.
Journalising and posting	Journalising is recording the information from the source documents into a journal. These entries in the journal are then aggregated and posted into the appropriate account. In this book we will commence with entering information into accounts before looking at the journal as this gives a better understanding of the process.
Preparing a trial balance	A trial balance is a list of the account balances as at a specific date. If there have been a number of errors and omissions in the accounting records it may also be necessary to prepare an adjusted trial balance.
The financial statement	From the trial balance, a profit-and-loss account and balance sheet is prepared for the financial period and the accounting cycle starts again at the beginning of the new financial period.

As part of the accounting cycle, an organisation will also have an internal control system. This is a set of procedures and policies designed to ensure that all transactions are correctly identified and entered in the accounting records. The internal control system should safeguard the organisation's assets and help prevent fraud and innocent errors. The organisation may appoint internal auditors to assure themselves of the efficiency of the internal control system and the external auditors will be very interested in the operation of the system.

4 PURCHASING GOODS

When an organisation purchases goods on credit a number of documents are raised by both the business buying the goods and the business selling the goods. The following flow diagram shows the documents which may be issued by a large organisation and the internal records maintained.

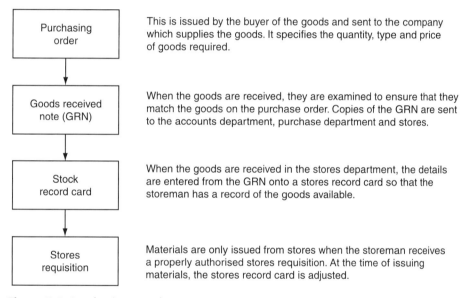

Figure 5.1 *Purchasing goods*

The document that starts off this chain is the *purchase order*. The essential information that must appear on the purchase order is:

- The name of the business buying the goods and the address to which the goods are to be delivered.
- The name and address of the supplier of the goods.
- Description of the goods, the quantity required and the price.
- Date of the purchase order, a reference number and the signature of the person in the company responsible for ordering the goods.

Below is an example of a purchase order for *Seth's Martial Arts Stores*. Having sent this order the next stage in the transaction for Seth's Martial Arts Stores is the receipt of the goods. If Seth's Stores is large with goods being delivered from a number of suppliers, a record of the receipt of the goods is made. The layout and information used for the internal documents such as the goods received note and

51

SETH'S MARTIAL ARTS STORES

The Judokai, Pleasant Street, Newcastle NW5 3SR
Tel: (0782) 315234

PURCHASE ORDER NO: 9011   Date: 10th May 2003

Please supply to the above address:

```
    250    Size 4    Colour White Belts @ £2.60 each
    160    Size 6    Colour Blue Belts @ £2.90 each
    120    Size 6    Colour Black Belts @ £3.05 each
```

Delivery required by 1st June 2003

Authorised by: ....

Chief Buyer

To:
Eastern Clothing Company
135, Blissford Avenue
LONDON EC2 4ER

Figure 5.2 *Purchase order*

stores requisition depends on the system maintained by the company. However, the essential details to be given on all such documents are:

• Date and reference number.

• Description and quantity of goods.

• Signature of person authorising the document.

> *You should now be able to attempt Task 5.2 at the end of this chapter.*

5 | SELLING GOODS

On receipt of an order the seller sends the goods to the buyer and ensures that payment will be received by issuing an invoice. The main documents that may be issued by a large organisation are shown in Figure 5.3.

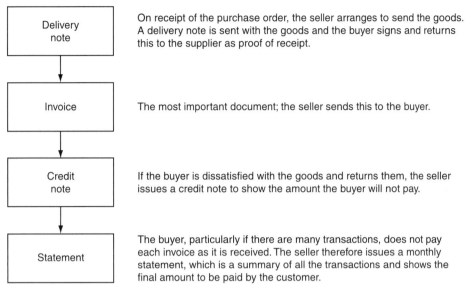

Figure 5.3 *Main sales documents issued by a large organisation*

The *invoice* issued by the seller is a most important document and contains a considerable amount of information as follows:

- Name and address of seller.
- Name and address of buyer.
- Reference number and date.
- Details of goods supplied and purchase order number.
- Date by which payment is required and if a cash discount is given for prompt payment.
- The total net price of the goods.
- The amount of Value Added Tax (VAT), if any.
- Total amount due from customer including Value Added Tax.

Figure 5.4 shows a typical design for an invoice.

Should the buyer decide the goods are faulty, not of a suitable standard, incorrectly despatched or otherwise unacceptable they will be returned and a credit note will be issued by the supplier as in Figure 5.5.

 You should now be able to attempt Question 5.1 at the end of this chapter.

INVOICE

From:

Eastern Clothing Company	Tax point/Date	10th June 2003
135, Blissford Avenue	Invoice No	2876A
LONDON EC2 4ER	Purchase Order No	9011

Quantity	Description	Unit Price	Amount
250	Size 4 Colour White belts	£2.60 each	£650
160	Size 6 Colour Blue belts	£2.90 each	£464
120	Size 6 Colour Black belts	£3.05 each	£366
		Sub Total	£1,480
		VAT (17.5%)	£259
		Invoice Total	£1,739

To:

Seth's Martial Arts Stores
The Judokai
Pleasant Street
Newcastle NW5 3SR

Payment due within thirty days of invoice date

VAT Reg No: 860 1856 40

Figure 5.4 *Tyical design for an invoice*

6 STATEMENTS

The buyer does not pay on each invoice as it is received, but waits until a *statement* has been received from the supplier. The statement sent by the seller is a summary of the transactions with a particular purchaser over a period of time (usually a month). The main information shown is:

- Names and addresses of seller and purchaser.
- Invoices and credit notes sent and any payments received.
- Date and reference number.
- Balance due from purchaser.

As with invoices, the design of a statement may vary, but Figure 5.6 is an example showing the information that should be given as a minimum.

> *You should now be able to attempt Question 5.2 at the end of this chapter.*

CREDIT NOTE

From:

Eastern Clothing Company
135, Blissford Avenue
LONDON EC2 4ER

Credit Note No   331C
Tax point/Date   22nd June 2003
Invoice No   2876A
Purchase Order No   9011

Quantity	Description	Unit Price	Amount
6	Size 4 Colour White belts	£2.60 each	£15.60
2	Size 6 Colour Blue belts	£2.90 each	£5.80
		Sub Total	£21.40
		VAT (17.5%)	£3.75
		Invoice Total	£25.15

Goods returned due to colour staining,

To: Seth's Martial Arts Stores
The Judokai, Pleasant Street
Newcastle NW5 3SR

VAT Reg No: 860 1856 40

Figure 5.5 *Credit note*

STATEMENT

From:

Eastern Clothing Company
135, Blissford Avenue
LONDON EC2 4ER

Number   565S
Date   30th June 2003

Date	Reference	Amount
10 June	Invoice No 2876A	£1,739.00
22 June	Credit Note 331C	£25.15
		£1,713.85

To:

Seth's Martial Arts Stores
The Judokai, Pleasant Street
Newcastle NW5 3SR

VAT Reg No: 860 1856 40

Figure 5.6 *Statement*

7   RECORDING LABOUR

Wages paid to the workforce are an important item of expenditure, particularly in a manufacturing organisation. For many companies this represents a very large proportion of their annual expenditure and it is important that the business controls every aspect of this activity and properly records it. In a large organisation with well established systems, the procedures that are established will show:

- The actual number of hours spent by workers on the factory premises. This may mean the recording of hours by each worker having an individual clock number and using a clock card in a machine at the factory entrance to print starting and leaving times.

- The actual hours spent by the workers on specific production activities. It should be possible to reconcile this figure with the actual hours spent on the factory premises.

In addition to the above information, details will be maintained in the wages office of each individual worker. These show the remuneration of each employee, including rates, allowances, tax codes and statutory deductions.

> *You should now be able to attempt Task 5.3 at the end of this chapter.*

8   TIME SHEETS AND JOB CARDS

To record the actual time spent on specific production activities a system of either *time sheets* or *job cards* is used. Time sheets are completed on a weekly or daily basis by the employees themselves and countersigned by their supervisor. The time sheet shows how much time has been spent on a particular job for a client. Accountants working in professional offices complete time sheets so that they may charge their clients correctly for the time spent on their affairs. Job cards are for a specific job and each employee completes the time spent on that particular job so that a record is built up of the total hours it has taken to complete all the work.

9   THE WAGES OFFICE

A *payroll* is prepared that shows the details of each employee's pay. The clock cards, which show the attendance time of the employees, are reconciled to the job cards, which show the amount of time recorded on each job. The total labour cost is calculated and the wages paid and the labour costs analysed for entry into the cost records. Figure 5.7 illustrates the procedure.

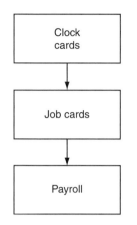

These show the amount of time spent on factory premises.

These record the amount of time spent on each job and will be reconciled to the clock cards.

This permits the calculation of wages from the clock cards for workers paid on a time basis and from the job cards if there is an incentive scheme.

Figure 5.7 *Labour costs*

You should now be able to attempt Question 5.3 at the end of this chapter.

10 | ROLE OF THE ACCOUNTANT

In a very large organisation the system and procedures for source documents are very complex. It is essential that the system is efficient. If there are deficiencies in the system, the business may fail to collect the money due to it; pay for goods which were not received or were faulty; fail to pay the correct wages; or run out of its stock of goods. These are only some of the problems. In addition there is always the danger of fraud. If the system for controlling and recording the transactions is weak, there is a possibility that unscrupulous employees will exploit it to their own advantage.

The responsibility for establishing good systems and procedures and ensuring that they are operated efficiently is that of the *accountant*. In a small company the external auditors ensure, as part of their regular examination, that there are no deficiencies. If there are, they bring this to the notice of the directors of the company. In a large company there is frequently an internal audit department. This employs accountants whose task is to conduct investigations into the systems and procedures of the company, to ensure that, if there are any weaknesses, corrective action is taken to remedy them.

As well as providing a primary record of business transactions and permitting controls to be maintained, the source documents are the first stage in the preparation of two key financial statements produced by businesses: *the profit-and-loss account* and the *balance sheet*. These two financial statements show the financial performance of a business for a period of time and the financial position of the business at the end of that period respectively. They are the product of system of record keeping known as double-entry bookkeeping which we examine in Chapter 6.

You should now be able to attempt Questions 5.4 and 5.5 at the end of this chapter.

11   SUMMARY

Organisations carry out many business transactions on credit. It is essential that there are the proper documents to support these transactions. When a company buys goods it normally sends an *order* to the supplier. When the supplier sends the goods to the buyer a *delivery note* is sent with them. To obtain payment the supplier sends an *invoice* to the buyer and may also send a *statement* at the end of the month.

As well as completing the correct documents for external transactions, a business must maintain procedures for recording and controlling internal activities. One important item of expenditure in many organisations, particularly if they are manufacturers, is *wages*. It may be necessary to record the time spent by workers on certain jobs through the use of *time sheets* and *job cards*.

Source documents are the basis of a system of record keeping known as *double-entry bookkeeping* (see Chapter 6). This system allows us to produce the two main financial statements of an organisation, the *profit-and-loss account* and *balance sheet* (see Chapters 10 and 11 respectively).

You should now be able to attempt the objective test at the end of this chapter.

Student activities

Task 5.1
Collect a selection of invoices from companies. Draw up a table to illustrate the differences and similarities. Analyse the design of the invoice separately from the contents.

Task 5.2
Design an appropriate goods received note for Seth's Martial Arts Stores. As it as a document that is only used inside the company, it should be plain and simple, but contain the essential information.

Task 5.3
Design a purchase order and an invoice for a television company that wishes to promote a glossy, dynamic image on all its business documents.

Question 5.1

Select the correct response to the following statements:

		True	False
i)	A company will always issue an invoice when a cash payment has been made.	☐	☐
ii)	When a company orders goods it normally sends a delivery note to the supplier.	☐	☐
iii)	A company selling goods on credit will always send an invoice to the purchaser.	☐	☐
iv)	If goods are returned by a buyer because they are unacceptable, the seller will usually issue a credit note.	☐	☐
v)	A credit note must be paid in full by the buyer.	☐	☐
vi)	A goods received note will show the quantity and description of the goods which the buyer has received.	☐	☐
vii)	Buyers will not compare the goods received note with a copy of their original purchase order.	☐	☐

Question 5.2

Tick the items from the following that you might normally expect to see on an invoice:

i)   the name and address of buyer

ii)   the profit made by the seller

iii) the amount of Value Added Tax, if any

iv)   the total net price of the goods

v)   details of the goods supplied

vi)   details of credit notes issued in the previous month

vii) goods received note reference

viii) purchase order number

Question 5.3

Match the appropriate documents with their descriptions in the lists below:

Document

a) Time sheet

b) Invoice

c) Purchase order

d) Goods received note

e) Statement

f) Credit note

Description

i)   A summary of sales transactions for a period of time

ii)   A request for goods of a particular type and quantity

iii) A record of how much time an employee has spent on a particular job

iv)   A request for payment showing the amount due

v)   A notification to the purchaser of amounts not due for payment

vi)   A record of the goods actually received by the purchaser

Question 5.4

List some of the difficulties that can arise if an organisation does not have a proper system of source documents.

Question 5.5

Natalie Hodges has a thriving business that employs ten people to sell high quality silk clothing by mail order. After six months' trading, she is concerned that the profit is not as high as expected and she suspects that theft is taking place. At the end of the six months she has 425 garments in stock.

Required

Write a brief report to Natalie Hodges explaining which documents she can use and how they can help her calculate how many garments should be in stock.

Objective test (tick the appropriate box)

i)   A company wishing to buy goods from another company on credit would send:

  a)   a delivery note   ☐

  b)   a purchase order   ☐

  c)   a goods received note   ☐

  d)   a credit note   ☐

ii)   Which of the following information would not be shown on a purchase order:

  a)   the quantity of items required   ☐

  b)   the price of each item   ☐

  c)   the Value Added Tax to be paid   ☐

  d)   the delivery address   ☐

iii) What information is shown on a clock card:

  a)   the income tax to be paid by an employee   ☐

  b)   the number of hours the employee has spent on the premises ☐

   c)   the number of hours the employee has spent on a particular job   ☐

   d)   the National Insurance to be paid by an employee   ☐

iv) Which of the following will not be shown on a statement issued by a company:

   a)   any payments received from the customer   ☐

   b)   credit notes issued to the customer   ☐

   c)   goods received notes issued by the customer   ☐

   d)   invoices issued to the customer   ☐

v) A stock record card will be used by a company so that it knows:

   a)   the price of goods it sells   ☐

   b)   the amount of goods it has available   ☐

   c)   the amount of VAT it has to pay   ☐

   d)   the number of orders it has received   ☐

CHAPTER 6

Recording transactions

1 OBJECTIVES

At the end of this chapter you should be able to:

- explain the principles of double-entry bookkeeping;
- record entries for assets and liabilities;
- record entries for expenses and sales;
- make entries in a journal.

2 INTRODUCTION

Bookkeeping is that part of accounting that is concerned with making records of financial transactions. In this chapter we describe a system for keeping accounting records known as *double-entry bookkeeping*. It is thus called because every financial transaction is recorded twice. This not only reflects the dual nature of economic transactions in the business world, but has the advantage of providing a mathematical check on the accuracy of the record keeping. It also enables two key financial statements to be conveniently constructed. These are the profit-and-loss account and the balance sheet and we will introduce these statements in later chapters.

Double-entry bookkeeping is the foundation of accounting. Even in large, complex businesses that use computers for record keeping, the same principles are used. In this chapter we will concentrate on explaining these principles and illustrate them as if manual records were being kept in a ledger. It will help you to remember that the business is always regarded as a separate entity from its owners when it carries out its activities. Because it is separate from its owners it can enter into transactions with them. This applies even if there is only one owner and the business is very small.

The reason why double-entry bookkeeping is important is because it is essential that accurate records are kept of all transactions entered into by a business. This information is used to run the business and may also be required by outside parties, such as the Inland Revenue, shareholders, investment analysts, etc. Double-entry bookkeeping has been found to be the best method for maintaining accounting records.

In practice, most businesses will use journals, a specific type of accounting record, to first enter transactions from the source documents. For accounting students it is essential to fully understand journal entries, but the topic is less important for general business students. At the end of this chapter we explain how journal entries are made and how this fits in with the double-entry book-keeping system.

3 | BASIC PRINCIPLES

In order to operate, all businesses need *resources*. These resources are known as the business's *assets*. Examples of assets include:

- premises;
- plant and machinery;
- office furniture and equipment;
- vehicles;
- stocks of materials and goods;
- cash.

In order to acquire assets, a business must obtain *funds*. In a new business, the owner is usually the main source of funding. The investment is referred to as *capital*. Capital is a *liability* of the business because the business is liable to, or owes the money to the owner. If no one else has funded the business, the assets of the business are equal to the capital. This can be written as an equation:

$$\text{Assets} = \text{Capital}$$

However, in addition to any capital supplied by the owner, the business may have to acquire funding from the bank in the form of a loan. In this case, the equation becomes:

$$\text{Assets} = \text{Capital} + \text{Liabilities}$$

In a later chapter you will see that the above *accounting equation* is fundamental to the financial statement known as the *balance sheet*. At this stage, however, you need only to remember that the equation must always balance.

Example
A business buys a new machine for £5,000.

Required

Show how this affects the accounting equation if the business finances the purchase by borrowing money from the bank.

Solution

The business will increase its assets by £5,000 (the new machine), but it will also increase its liabilities by £5,000 (the loan from the bank). Using the accounting equation to show these changes:

$$(\text{Assets} + £5,000) = \text{Capital} + (\text{Liabilities} + £5,000)$$

In a manual record-keeping system, all transactions are recorded in an *account*.

The word 'account' means 'a history of'. In double-entry bookkeeping, each account is kept on a separate page with printed columns and rows where details of the individual transactions can be recorded. Although the pages may be loose-leaf or bound, they are kept in a book. These books of accounts are referred to as *ledgers*. In the above example the business purchased a machine with a loan from the bank. The accounts where this transaction will be recorded are the *machine account* and the *loan account*. The following illustration shows the machine account.

Machine account

Date		£	Date		£

As you can see, the page is divided into six columns. The left-hand side is referred to as the *debit* side and the right-hand side is called the *credit* side. The date that the transaction takes place is inserted in either the first or the fourth column, the nature of the transaction in the second and fifth columns, and the amount involved in the third and sixth columns.

Before we look at how transactions are recorded in practice, a word of warning about debits and credits. These terms are often a source of anxiety for students, some of whom are inclined to believe that they hold mystical powers that, if they were only able to understand them, would guarantee success in every examination. This is not the case. As far as double-entry bookkeeping is concerned, debit always means the left-hand side of the account and credit always means the right-hand side. In other words, if you are going to debit an account, you should enter the item on the left-hand side; a debit entry means one that is on the left-hand side of the account. If you are going to credit an account, you should enter the item on the right-hand side of the account; a credit entry means one that is on the right-hand side of the account.

In order to keep the accounting equation balanced, every transaction conducted by a business must be entered twice: once on the debit side of one account and once on the credit side of another account. To know whether you should enter a transaction on the debit (left) or the credit (right) side on an account, you need to learn the rules, which we will examine next.

> *You should now be able to attempt Task 6.1 at the end of this chapter.*

4   RECORDING ASSETS AND LIABILITIES

The rules for recording transactions which involve *assets* and *liabilities* are as follows:

- To show an increase in an asset, debit the asset account.
- To show a decrease in an asset, credit the asset account.
- To show an increase in a capital or liability account, credit the account.
- To show a decrease in a capital or liability account, debit the account.

Example

To illustrate these rules we will take a business that commenced on 1 January 2003. The owner of the business is Gavin Salcombe and he has invested £5,000 in the business. His girlfriend, Suzanne, has given the business a loan of £2,000. All the money is kept in the bank. Therefore, there are two transactions to record: the capital invested by Gavin and the loan given by Suzanne. Each transaction will require a debit entry to be made to one account and a corresponding credit entry of the same amount made to another account.

Three accounts need to be opened:

- a capital account for the money invested by the owner, Gavin;
- a loan account for the loan from Suzanne;
- a bank account to show the money held at the bank.

Required

Make the necessary entries in the appropriate accounts.

Solution

Capital account

2003		£	2003		£
			1 January	Bank	5,000

Loan account

2003		£	2003		£
			1 January	Bank	2,000

Bank account

2003		£	2003		£
1 January	Capital	5,000			
1 January	Loan	2,000			

If you study these accounts, you can see that the rules for recording transactions have been stringently applied. The transaction of the owner introducing £5,000 capital has been shown as a credit in the capital account and because the assets of the business have increased by this same amount, the bank account has been debited with £5,000. Thus, there is a corresponding debit entry for the credit entry.

With regard to the loan, when Suzanne gave the £2,000 loan to the business, its liabilities increased by that amount, so the loan account has been credited. Having made a credit entry in that account, a debit entry must be made in another account. In this case it is the bank account, because the loan means an increase in the assets of the business. As you can see, for each transaction you need to record the date, the name of the account where the corresponding entry is made and the amount. This allows you to trace it at a later date if you have any problems with the records.

Example

We will now extend our example by showing the transactions entered into by the business on 2 January 2003. Gavin Salcombe pays £3,000 from the bank account for premises; £1,000 for machinery and £500 for equipment. The bank account is already open, so you can continue to use it. However, you need to open three new asset accounts to record these latest transactions.

Required

Make the necessary entries in the appropriate accounts.

Solution

Bank account

2003		£	2003		£
1 January	Capital	5,000	2 January	Premises	3,000
1 January	Loan	2,000	2 January	Machinery	1,000
			2 January	Equipment	500

Premises account

2003		£	2003		£
2 January	Bank	3,000			

Machinery account

2003		£	2003		£
2 January	Bank	1,000			

Equipment account

2003		£	2003		£
2 January	Bank	500			

These records reflect the results of the transactions. For example, the bank account is an asset account. When the business received the capital of £5,000 from Gavin and the loan from Suzanne, these amounts were debited to the bank account to show the increase in assets represented by the amount of money held at the bank. When the business paid for items such as the machinery, the bank account was credited. If you take the total of all the debit entries in the bank account and deduct the total of all the credit entries, the resulting figure is £2,500. This is the amount of money the business now has left at the bank.

   We will finish this section by looking at a further example of recording assets and liabilities.

Example

On 3 January Gavin Salcombe repays £1,500 to Suzanne. On the same day, the business returns £250 worth of equipment to the supplier because it is faulty and receives a refund, which is paid into the bank.

Required

Make the necessary entries in the appropriate accounts.

Solution

Bank account

2003		£	2003		£
1 January	Capital	5,000	2 January	Premises	3,000
1 January	Loan	2,000	2 January	Machinery	1,000
3 January	Equipment	250	2 January	Equipment	500
			3 January	Loan	1,500

Loan account

2003		£	2003		£
3 January	Bank	1,500	1 January	Bank	2,000

Equipment account

2003		£	2003		£
2 January	Bank	500	3 January	Bank	250

You should now be able to attempt Task 6.2 at the end of this chapter.

5 RECORDING REVENUES AND EXPENSES

A business aims to make a profit. For example, if it is a manufacturing business, it will hope to sell its goods for more than it costs to make them. If it is a retailing business, it will try to sell its goods for more than it cost to purchase them from the wholesalers or manufacturers. If it is providing a service, it will try to sell its services for more than it costs to supply them. Therefore, as well as needing accounts for its assets and liabilities, a business must have accounts for its *revenues* and *expenses*. Revenue is the monetary value of the sale of goods or services to customers. Expenses are the monetary value of assets used to obtain those revenues.

The rules for making debit and credit entries in these accounts are as follows:

- To show an increase in an expense account, debit the account.
- To show a decrease in an expense account, credit the account.
- To show an increase in a revenue account, credit the account.
- To show a decrease in a revenue account, debit the account.

As you will see, every transaction involves making a credit entry to one account and a debit entry to another account. First we will explain what is meant by an increase in an expense account and an increase in a revenue account.

Example

Let us suppose that Gavin Salcombe spends £200 on printing advertisements in the form of promotional leaflets, and £20 on posting them to potential customers. Prior to this date the business has not incurred any expenses, so the monetary value was nil. Now it has incurred some and you need to show the increase in the appropriate expense accounts.

Required

Make the necessary entries in the appropriate accounts.

Solution

Bank account

2003		£	2003		£
1 January	Capital	5,000	2 January	Premises	3,000
1 January	Loan	2,000	2 January	Machinery	1,000
3 January	Equipment	250	2 January	Equipment	500
			3 January	Loan	1,500
			4 January	Advertising	200
			4 January	Postage	20

Advertising account

2003		£	2003		£
4 January	Bank	200			

Postage account

2003		£	2003		£
4 January	Bank	20			

As the business has paid for the advertising leaflets and postage, its cash assets at the bank must have decreased by the amount of these expenses. Therefore, these two transactions resulted in debit entries to the expense accounts and both were credited to the bank account.

We will now take this example a step further.

Example

On 5 January Gavin Salcombe pays £50 for the cleaning of the premises. On 6 January the business lets two of its rooms for a one-day conference and receives £350 in rent.

Required

Make the necessary entries in the appropriate accounts.

Solution

Bank account

2003		£	2003		£
1 January	Capital	5,000	2 January	Premises	3,000
1 January	Loan	2,000	2 January	Machinery	1,000
3 January	Equipment	250	2 January	Equipment	500
6 January	Rent received	350	3 January	Loan	1,500
			4 January	Advertising	200
			4 January	Postage	20
			5 January	Cleaning	50

Cleaning account

2003		£	2003		£
5 January	Bank	50			

Rent received account

2003		£	2003		£
			6 January	Bank	350

You should not have had too much difficulty with this example. The cleaning expenses were a pair of straightforward entries. The receipt of rent may have caused you to think because we have not illustrated any similar transactions. However, as long as you remembered the rule that you show an increase in revenues by crediting the revenue account (in this case, rent received), the corresponding entry had to be to debit the bank account to show an increase in cash assets of £350.

> *You should now be able to attempt Task 6.3 at the end of this chapter.*

6 | RECORDING PURCHASES AND SALES

Of course, it is not much use a business advertising its goods unless it has *purchased* some it can *sell*. Buying goods is an expense and therefore it is necessary to open a *purchases account* to record such transactions. As the purchase account is an expense account, when the business buys goods, the transaction is recorded as a debit. However, when the business sells the goods, they are *not* shown as a credit in the purchases account for two reasons. Firstly, they will not be sold at the same price as they were purchased for, because the business wants to make a profit. Because we want to show the profit on a financial statement known as the *profit-and-loss account*, we do not want to lose it in the detail of the purchases account. The second reason is that at the end of a financial period it is likely that there will be some unsold goods left, which are known as *stock*. Stock required special treatment and we will be discussing this in Chapter 8.

Instead of crediting sales to the purchases account, a *sales account*, which is a revenue account, is opened. If the goods are sold to customers for cash, the sale is shown as a credit in the sales account and the corresponding entry is a debit in the bank account. The latter entry reflects the increase in cash assets held at the bank. We look at a new example to shown how this is done.

Example

Hannah Johnson starts off a retail business on 1 July by investing £10,000 in the business. On that day she purchases equipment costing £4,000, stock costing £4,000 and pays £500 for advertising. On 2 July she sells stock for £2,800 and buys a small, second-hand car for £1,000. On 3 July she sells stock for £3,500 and purchases further stock for £2,000.

Required

Make the necessary entries in the appropriate accounts.

Solution

Capital account

2003		£	2003		£
			1 July	Bank	10,000

Bank account

2003		£	2003		£
1 July	Capital	10,000	1 July	Equipment	4,000
2 July	Sales	2,800	1 July	Purchases	4,000

Bank account—continued

2003		£	2003		£
3 July	Sales	3,500	1 July	Advertising	500
			2 July	Car	1,000
			3 July	Purchases	2,000

Equipment account

2003		£	2003		£
1 July	Bank	4,000			

Advertising account

2003		£	2003		£
1 July	Bank	500			

Purchases account

2003		£	2003		£
1 July	Bank	4,000			
3 July	Bank	2,000			

Sales account

2003		£	2003		£
			2 July	Bank	2,800
			3 July	Bank	3,500

Motor vehicle account

2003		£	2003		£
2 July	Bank	1,000			

In the above example we have referred to the goods that the business is buying and selling as *stock*. However, we will not use a *stock account* until the end of the financial period. Instead, the purchases and sales of goods have been recorded in separate accounts, named *purchases account* and *sales account* respectively. Accountants use the term *purchases* by itself to mean purchases of goods for resale. Do not confuse this with purchases of other assets, such as equipment or machinery.

There is one final aspect of purchases and sales of goods that we must consider. Perhaps the business has purchased goods and had to return them to the supplier because they were faulty, or for other reasons. Alternatively, perhaps a customer returns goods to the business. The first transaction requires a *returns outward account* (or *purchases returns account*) to be opened. The second transaction requires a *returns inward* (or *sales returns account*) to be opened. We will start by illustrating the returns outward account.

Example

On 1 July Hannah Johnson purchases goods from her usual supplier. However, she subsequently finds that £200 worth are faulty and returns them to the supplier on 12 July and receives a refund of £200 that day.

Required

Make the necessary entries in the appropriate accounts.

Solution

Bank account

2003		£	2003		£
1 July	Capital	10,000	1 July	Equipment	4,000
2 July	Sales	2,800	1 July	Purchases	4,000
3 July	Sales	3,500	1 July	Advertising	500
14 July	Returns outward	200	2 July	Car	1,000
			3 July	Purchases	2,000

Returns outward account

2003		£	2003		£
			12 July	Bank	200

As you can see, the bank account has been debited to show the increase in cash assets due to the cash refund by the supplier, but rather than crediting the purchases account to record the goods which were returned, a returns outward account has been opened and this provides an accurate record of what has happened. This information will be used when the profit-and-loss account is drawn up.

The same principles are applied if one of the business's customers returns goods.

Example

One of Hannah Johnson's customers returns £500 worth of goods to the business on 14 July and the business gives the customer a refund that day.

Required

Make the necessary entries in the appropriate accounts.

Solution

Bank account

2003		£	2003		£
1 July	Capital	10,000	1 July	Equipment	4,000
2 July	Sales	2,800	1 July	Purchases	4,000
3 July	Sales	3,500	1 July	Advertising	500
12 July	Returns outward	200	2 July	Car	1,000
			3 July	Purchases	2,000
			14 July	Returns inward	500

Returns inward account

2003		£	2003		£
14 July	Bank	500			

You should now be able to attempt Question 6.1 at the end of this chapter.

7 | CREDIT TRANSACTIONS

In the examples we have shown so far, all the receipts and payments have been for cash. For example, the business has received cash from customers and has paid cash to suppliers and all these cash transactions have been either into or out of the bank account. However, in practice the majority of transactions in a business are made on credit, where the actual cash receipt or payment does not take place until a later date. This requires accounts to be opened for *creditors* (those individuals and entities to whom the business owes money) and *debtors* (those individuals and entities who owe the business money). A debtor is an *asset* and a creditor is a *liability* to the business. The rules of double-entry bookkeeping for making entries into asset and liability account therefore apply to debtors and creditors.

First we will consider an example where a customer of the business has not paid cash but has obtained goods or services on credit.

Example

Continuing to use the example of Hannah Johnson's business, let us assume that the goods that were sold for £2,800 on 2 July were bought on credit by John Juniper. This means that he did not pay cash for them on that date, but will pay for them at a later date. The entry in the sales account will still be a credit, but instead of debiting the bank account as an increase in cash assets, you will need to debit John Juniper's account. This is because, by obtaining the goods on credit, John is a debtor because he has not yet paid for the goods.

Required

Make the necessary entries in the appropriate accounts.

Solution

Sales account

2003		£	2003		£
			2 July	John Juniper	2,800

John Juniper account

2003		£	2003		£
2 July	Sales	2,800			

As you can see, because John Juniper is an asset account, we have followed the rules for asset accounts. Before 2 July he owed the business nothing, but after the sales transaction on that date, he owed Hannah Johnson's business £2,800. This increase in debtor assets is shown by debiting the John Juniper account. The debtor's account has been opened in John Juniper's name so that a record can be kept of who owes Hannah Johnson's business money.

We can extend this example as follows.

Example

On 20 July John Juniper pays £750 of the money he owes to Hannah Johnson.

Required

Make the necessary entries in the appropriate accounts.

Solution

Bank account

2003		£	2003		£
1 July	Capital	10,000	1 July	Equipment	4,000
3 July	Sales	3,500	1 July	Purchases	4,000
12 July	Returns outward	200	1 July	Advertising	500
20 July	John Juniper	750	2 July	Car	1,000
			3 July	Purchases	2,000
			14 July	Returns inward	500

John Juniper

2003		£	2003		£
2 July	Sales	2,800	20 July	Bank	750

As long as you remembered the rules for asset and liability accounts, you should have had no difficulty with recording this transaction. You can see that cash assets have increased by £750 and debtor assets have decreased by the same amount.

Note that in the bank account we have deleted the entry on 2 July for sales of £2,800 because we have now decided that John Juniper did not pay cash but had his goods on credit. The debit entry is therefore to the John Juniper account and the sales account remains untouched.

Now we will consider a case where the business itself has not paid cash but has obtained goods or services on credit. In such a case the business has acquired a liability and you will need to use the double-entry rules for increasing and decreasing liability accounts.

Example

On 26 July Hannah Johnson purchases goods on credit from Bob Lytham for £1,500. On 28 July she pays the debt in full.

Required

Make the necessary entries in the appropriate accounts.

Solution

Purchases account

2003		£	2003		£
1 July	Bank	4,000			
3 July	Bank	2,000			
26 July	Bob Lytham	1,500			

Bob Lytham

2003		£	2003		£
28 July	Bank	1,500	26 July	Purchases	1,500

Bank account

2003		£	2003		£
1 July	Capital	10,000	1 July	Equipment	4,000
3 July	Sales	3,500	1 July	Purchases	4,000
12 July	Returns outward	200	1 July	Advertising	500
20 July	John Juniper	750	2 July	Car	1,000
			3 July	Purchases	2,000
			14 July	Returns inward	500
			28 July	Bob Lytham	1,500

You should now be able to attempt Question 6.2 at the end of this chapter.

8 AN OVERVIEW OF RULES

Double-entry bookkeeping is in, principle, simple although you may find that some transactions can be confusing. This is particularly the case in the examination room. The main rule is to always go back to first principles and remember that for every debit value there must be a credit of an equal amount.

Many accountants, when they are working out problems, use 'T' accounts, which represent 'proper' accounts with all the details, with the left side being the debit and the right side of the 'T' being a credit. We can use 'T' accounts to demonstrate the rules in this chapter.

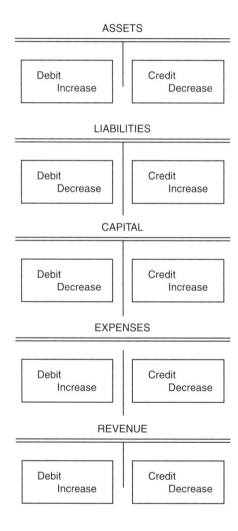

Figure 6.1

If you reflect on the expenses and revenues accounts, there are certain common-sense assumptions you can make. Normally, most entries to revenues accounts will be credit entries as you expect the revenues account to increase every time you sell something. Also, when you purchase something you would normally expect the expenses account to increase and thus it will have a debit entry.

9   THE JOURNAL

Most organisations use a journal to document their activities before entering them into the accounts themselves. We will take for example from the section 6.4 of Gavin Salcombe to demonstrate the principles underlying journal entries.

Gavin commences a business on 1 January 2003 with £5,000 of his own money and a loan from his girlfriend of £2,000. The journal entries are:

1 January 2003
Dedit Cash	£5,000	
Credit Capital		£5,000

This being the investment of the owner at the commencement of the business.

1 January 2003
Debit Cash	£2,000	
Credit Loan Account		£2,000

This being a loan by Suzanne at the commencement of the business.

In the above example we are journalising assets and liabilities. We can look at revenues and expenses by going back to the example under Section 6.5 where Gavin, amongst other transactions, spends £200 on printing leaflets and lets two rooms for a conference for £350. First looking at the expenses, the entries in the journal will be:

4 January 2003
Debit Advertising Account	£350	
Credit Rent Received Account		£350

This being the rent for two rooms.

10   SUMMARY

Double-entry bookkeeping is a crucial procedure for recording accounting transactions. The system ensures that the records are mathematically correct and permits the profit-and-loss account and balance sheet to be prepared. It captures the dual nature of transactions by making a debit and a corresponding credit entry for every financial transaction. A debit entry is recorded on the left-hand side of the account and a credit entry on the right-hand side.

There are separate rules for recording assets and liabilities, revenues and expenses. At the end of a financial period, which may be for any convenient length of time, the accounts are balanced.

Student activities

Task 6.1

Look for examples of the terms *debit* and *credit* in documents such as invoices and receipts.

Task 6.2

Give examples of three transactions that involve the use of asset and liability accounts and show the entries in the appropriate accounts.

Task 6.3

Open a set of accounts to show the financial transactions you have entered into in the last week. For example, you may have paid your rent, borrowed money, made purchases, etc. You could include an entertainment account to record buying a meal or a drink, hiring a video, or going to a club, cinema, theatre, and so forth.

Question 6.1

Ben Clark starts a delivery business on 1 March with £10,000 capital and a loan of £3,000 from the bank. He purchases a delivery van for £7,500 on the same date and pays £50 for offices services for the week. On 2 March he pays £35 to advertise in the newspaper and £20 for petrol. On 3 March he carries out a number of deliveries and his total sales for the day amount to £180.

Required

Open accounts for these transactions and enter the appropriate figures.

Question 6.2

On 1 April Tony O'Hara has the following accounts.

Capital account

2003		£	2003		£
			1 April	Bank	20,000

Bank account

2003		£	2003		£
1 April	Capital	20,000	2 April	Purchases	4,000
3 April	Sales	2,500	4 April	Purchases	3,000

Purchases account

2003		£	2003		£
2 April	Bank	4,000			
4 April	Bank	3,000			
5 April	A. Stewart	6,000			

Sales account

2003		£	2003		£
			3 April	Bank	2,500

A. Stewart

2003		£	2003		£
			5 April	Purchases	6,000

On 6 April, the following transactions take place: sales of £7,500 are made to L. Lombard on credit; A. Stewart is paid £3,500; equipment is purchased for £1,200. On 7 April £2,500 is received from L. Lombard; sales of £1,300 are made to S. Gray on credit; purchases of £1,000 are made from K. Davison on credit. On 8 April creditors are paid all amounts owing to them.

Required

Make the entries in the appropriate accounts.

Question 6.3

Taking the example of Ben Clark from Question 6.1 make the journal entries for all the transactions.

Objective test

i) The accounting entries to record a loan taken out by a business are:

   a) debit the bank account and debit the loan account ☐

   b) credit the loan account and debit the bank account ☐

   c) credit the loan account and credit the bank account ☐

   d) credit the bank account and debit the loan account ☐

ii) If a business purchases goods for cash for later resale, the accounting entries are:

a) debit the stock account and credit the bank account ☐

b) credit the stock account and debit the bank account ☐

c) debit the purchases account and credit the stock account ☐

d) debit the purchases account and credit the bank account ☐

iii) If a customer who has received goods on credit subsequently pays the business, the accounting entries are:

a) debit the creditor's account and credit the bank account ☐

b) debit the debtor's account and credit the creditor's account ☐

c) credit the debtor's account and debit the bank account ☐

d) credit the creditor's account and debit the bank account ☐

iv) At the end of a financial period, a credit balance outstanding on a stock account suggests that:

a) assets have increased over the period ☐

b) there has been no change in assets during the period ☐

c) assets have decreased over the period ☐

d) a bookkeeping error has been made ☐

v) If you wished to show an increase in an asset account, you would expect to see

a) a debit to the sales account ☐

b) a credit to the asset account ☐

c) a debit to the purchases account ☐

d) a debit to the asset account ☐

CHAPTER 7

Controlling cash

1 | OBJECTIVES

At the end of this chapter you should be able to:

- explain the importance of cash control;
- describe the procedures for cash control;
- compare a cash book and a petty cash book;
- record cash receipts and payments in the correct manner.

2 | INTRODUCTION

Whatever the size of a business, the *control of cash* is critical. In this context the word *cash* means cash itself as well as cheques, postal orders and other means of transferring money from one person or organisation to another. Both a large multinational company and the newspaper seller on the street corner are deeply interested in cash. Without adequate amounts of cash they would not be able to pay their bills and would therefore go out of business.

Businesses often obtain bank loans and overdrafts to help them pay their bills, but these loans have to be paid back at some stage. Although a loan may be useful as a temporary measure, over a long period of time a business must ensure that it has more cash coming in than it pays out. If it is unable to do this it will go out of business.

Because of the critical importance of cash, businesses pay particular attention to recording the amounts of cash coming into and going out of the business. Regular checks are made to ensure that the actual amount of cash held at any one time agrees with the records. It is obvious that cash must be kept in a safe place as carelessness in doing so could lead to theft.

3 | PROCEDURE FOR RECORDING CASH

In most organisations it is normal to give one person the responsibility for maintaining the *cash records*. This person is known as the *cashier*. In a very large organisation the task may require more than one person. If there are payments made of small amounts, a petty cashier will be appointed to record them.

The main responsibilities of the cashier are:

- to record receipts of cash and cheques;
- to pay cash and cheques received into the bank;
- to make cash payments and record them;
- to prepare cheques for signature and record them;
- to keep safely any amounts of actual cash (known as cash floats);
- to ensure the petty cashier has sufficient cash;
- to reconcile the cash records maintained with bank statements.

4   CASH BOOK

The recording of cash is carried out in a *cash book*. This may be maintained on a computer, or be a standard book that can be obtained from any stationers, or be designed for the company's own particular needs. A page of a typical cash book is shown below with notes explaining its features.

Example

Cash book

Receipts					Payments				
Date	Details	Ref	Cash	Bank	Date	Details	Ref	Cash	Bank
			£	£				£	£

All receipts are shown on the left-hand side and payments on the right-hand side. Actual cash received and paid is recorded in the cash column whereas receipts and payments by cheques are shown in the bank column. The details column shows the type of transaction and often includes a reference, for example the cheque number or receipt number. Where cash is drawn out of the bank for cash payments to be made or where actual cash received is paid into the bank, this is known as a *contra entry*. This means that both parts of the transaction are shown in the same book. We have omitted VAT for the purposes of simplicity.

Example
Andrew Sodbury has just started in business and the transactions for the first week are:

June 1 Paid £2,000 into bank account

June 1 Paid office rent of £250 by cheque

June 2 Took £250 cash from bank for business use

June 2 Bought stationery for £50 cash

June 2 Bought design materials for £175 cash

June 3 Received £300 cheque from client

June 3 Paid cheque of £125 for promotional material

June 4 Received £200 cash from client

June 5 Paid £150 cash into bank

You are the cashier of the company and must enter up the cash book.

Solution

Cash book

Receipts				Payments			
Date	*Details*	*Cash*	*Bank*	*Date*	*Details*	*Cash*	*Bank*
		£	£			£	£
June 1	Capital		2,000	June 1	Rent		250
June 2	Bank (contra)	250		June 2	Cash (contra)		250
June 3	Sales		300	June 2	Stationery	50	
June 4	Sales	200		June 2	Design material	175	
June 5	Cash (contra)		150	June 3	Promotional material		125
				June 5	Bank (contra)	150	

You should now be able to attempt Task 7.1 at the end of this chapter.

5   BALANCING THE CASH BOOK

At the end of the week Andrew may wish to know how much actual cash he has available and how much money he has in the bank. To find this out we will *balance the cash book*. This is done at least monthly.

Example

1. Add up all the columns putting the totals in pencil. For Andrew Sodbury these pencil totals are:

Cash book

Receipts				Payments			
Date	Details	Cash	Bank	Date	Details	Cash	Bank
		£	£			£	£
		450	2,450			375	625

2. Enter the difference between the two cash column figures and the difference between the two bank columns on the lowest side so that both cash columns and both bank columns now total the same. In this case the figures will be £75 for cash and £1,825 for bank. These will both be entered on the right-hand side of the page with the words 'balances carried down' put in the details column.

Cash book

Receipts				Payments			
Date	Details	Cash	Bank	Date	Details	Cash	Bank
		£	£			£	£
				June 5	Balance c/d	75	1,825

3. The final stage is to add both sides and rule them off. The balances you have entered are then shown as the opening balances on the opposite side. In the description column you write the words 'Balances brought down'. The cash book now looks like this:

Cash book

Receipts				Payments			
Date	Details	Cash	Bank	Date	Details	Cash	Bank
		£	£			£	£
June 1	Capital		2,000	June 1	Rent		250
June 2	Bank (contra)	250		June 2	Cash (contra)		250

Cash book—continued

Receipts				Payments			
Date	Details	Cash	Bank	Date	Details	Cash	Bank
		£	£			£	£
June 3	Sales		300	June 2	Stationery	50	
June 4	Sales	200		June 2	Design material	175	
June 5	Cash (contra)		150	June 3	Promotional material		125
				June 5	Bank (contra)	150	
				June 5	Balances c/d	75	1,825
		450	2,450			450	2,450
June 6	Balances b/d	75	1,825				

Just a final word on the balances before you attempt a question. By transferring the closing balances on 5 June to the opposite side of the cash book as the opening balances on 6 June, we are showing Andrew Sodbury's position. On 6 June, he has £75 cash and this can be checked by counting it. He also has £1,825 in the bank and this can be checked by telephoning the bank or requesting a bank statement. Later in this chapter we will discuss what happens if the figures on the bank statement and the cash book do not agree and have to be reconciled.

In this example the closing balances were on the right-hand side and were transferred to the left-hand side to show how much money Andrew Sodbury has. It is possible at the end of the period that the closing bank figure will be on the left-hand side and will be brought down as an opening balance on the right-hand side. This shows that the business has no money in the bank of its own and must have an overdraft.

> You should now be able to attempt Question 7.1 at the end of this chapter.

6   CASH DISCOUNTS

In business a *cash discount* is given sometimes to encourage customers to pay early. For example, goods may have been sold to the value of £100 and the customer is told that a cash discount of 5 per cent will be given if payment is made within 30 days. If the customer pays on time, an amount of £95 only will be paid. To record this, a third column may be added to the cash book to show all the cash discounts received and allowed by the company. The amount of cash paid or received is entered in the appropriate cash or bank column.

Recording transactions would continue in the same fashion until it is decided to balance the cash book. The bank and cash columns are balanced in the way we explained earlier in the chapter. The discount columns would be individually totalled – they are not balanced. The total of each of the discount columns is then transferred to another ledger and appears in the trading and profit-and-loss accounts.

It is important to remember that only *cash* discounts are recorded and not *trade* discounts.

Example

David Corsham has the following transactions:

Jan 1   Received £195 cheque from a customer, a discount of £5 having been allowed.
Jan 2   Customer sent cheque for £390 having deducted £10 discount.
Jan 4   Paid cheque for £192 having taken a £8 discount.

Required

Prepare the cash book showing the cash discount received and allowed by the company.

Solution

Cash book

Receipts					Payments				
Date	Details	Dis-count	Cash	Bank	Date	Details	Dis-count	Cash	Bank
		£	£	£			£	£	£
Jan 1	Sales	5		195	Jan 4	Goods	8		192
Jan 2	Sales	10		390					

You should now be able to attempt Question 7.2 at the end of this chapter.

7 THE PETTY CASH BOOK

All businesses are called on to make numerous small payments. These may be for such things as postage, purchasing a small amount of stationery, bus or taxi fares and so forth. It is not appropriate to write cheques for such amounts and cash payments are made. However, such transactions may be quite numerous and the main cash book is a record of great importance and should not include the details of insignificant amounts. As a record must be kept of all cash payments, it is normal to use a *petty cash book* to enter items of small expenditure.

The method of making entries in the petty cash book is the same as the cash book and a typical layout is as follows. You will see that we have added a column for the separate recording of Value Added Tax.

Petty cash book

Receipts					Payments				
Date	Details		Total		Date	Details	Total	VAT	Net
			£				£	£	£

In some businesses the payments made by petty cash are analysed into separate columns in the petty cash book so that they can be easily incorporated into the accounting system. If at the end of the period the totals for each column of analysed expenditure are added, the amount should agree with the main total column. This is known as cross casting and ensures the arithmetical accuracy of your workings and that the same amount is entered in the total column as well as the analysed column.

> *You should now be able to attempt Question 7.3 at the end of this chapter.*

8 THE IMPREST SYSTEM

In some businesses the petty cashier will ask the main cashier for more cash when it is needed. The system most commonly used, however, is known as the *imprest system,* This allows better control of cash and the procedure is as follows:

1. The cashier gives the petty cashier a starting sum of cash known as the float or the imprest.

2. The petty cashier makes payments when a properly authorised petty cash voucher is submitted.

3. Periodically, say every month, the cashier checks the accuracy of the petty cash book. If everything is correct the cashier reimburses the petty cashier for all payments made. This returns the imprest to the original amount.

4. At intervals a senior member of staff checks the petty cash book. The total of the current petty cash vouchers held by the petty cashier and the amount of cash held should agree with the original imprest amount.

Example

A petty cashier is given an imprest of £50.00 on 1 January. On 15 January the petty cashier holds vouchers for £18.60. On 31 January the amount of cash held by the petty cashier is £4.60.

i)   What was the balance of cash held by the cashier on 15 January?

ii) What sum needs to be reimbursed by the cashier to restore the imprest to its original sum?

Solution

		£
i)	Original imprest amount	50.00
	Cash paid against vouchers	18.60
	Cash held on 15 January	31.40
ii)	Original imprest amount	50.00
	Cash held on 31 January	4.60
	Amount required to restore imprest	45.40

You should now be able to attempt Question 7.4 at the end of this chapter.

9   BANK RECONCILIATION

When you reach the end of a financial period and have calculated your closing balances, the figures in the cash book should be checked. The actual cash held should be counted and should agree with the cash column. Differences can be due to the following:

- Incorrect recording in the cash book.

- Theft or loss of cash.

- Incorrect additions.

- Omission of entries in the cash book.

Any differences should be investigated and action taken to rectify them. However, the position is not so straightforward with the bank column in the cash book. A number of differences may arise and the reasons may be:

- The bank has made a mistake.
- A mistake has been made in the cash book.
- Items are shown in the cash book but not on the bank statement.
- Items are shown on the bank statement, but not in the cash book.
- There are timing differences.

The first two reasons for the differences, if they arise, should be investigated and put right. The third point can occur for a number of reasons. One frequent cause is that a cheque has been received and entered into the cash book, but has been subsequently dishonoured (bounced) and is not on the bank statement. The fourth reason may be due to a variety of causes. Although the business is informed of transactions it may have forgotten to put them in the cash book. Examples are standing orders, direct debits, cashpoint withdrawals and bank interest and charges. The fifth reason is the most common cause and it is normal to prepare a bank reconciliation to show that the difference in the cash and bank figures arise from timing differences. These differences are due to two main reasons:

- The business has sent out a cheque that has been entered in the cash book, but the recipient has not paid it into his account by the end of the period.
- The business has received money that it has shown in the cash book as being paid into the bank, but it has not yet been entered on the bank statement. There is usually only a day or two delay.

The procedure for carrying out a *bank reconciliation* is as follows:

1. Tick all the entries in the cash book against those made on the bank statement.

2. If no mistake has been made by the bank then correct the cash book for those entries which should be shown.

3. Total the cash book to give the new correct balance.

4. Identify the differences between the bank statement and cash book which are due to timing differences only.

5. Draw up a bank reconciliation statement proving that the cash book and bank statement agree apart from the transactions involving timing differences.

Example

John Westbury finds that his cash book and bank statement do not agree. He adjusts his cash book for errors and obtains a new balance of £227. The balance shown on the bank statement is £271 and John notices that £52 he had paid into the bank on the last day of the period has not yet been shown in his account. Further investigation reveals that the last two cheques drawn for £96 in total have not yet been presented to their bankers by the recipients. Draw up a bank reconciliation.

Solution

Bank reconciliation statement

	£
Balance on the bank statement	271
Add Deposits not yet cleared	52
	323
Less Cheques not yet presented	96
Balance as per cash back	227

Note that details of the deposits not yet cleared and the cheques unpresented would be shown. The cash figure shown at the bottom of the reconciliation statement of £227 is the figure that would appear in the balance sheet and not the bank statement figure.

> *You should now be able to attempt Task 7.2 and Question 7.5 at the end of this chapter.*

10 | SUMMARY

The control of cash is critical in all organisations. The person responsible for recording transactions is known as the *cashier*. All cash and cheque receipts and payments are recorded in a *cash book*. The cash book is balanced at regular intervals and checks made to ensure that the correct amounts are held either in immediate cash or at the bank. Where small cash payments are made, they are recorded in a *petty cash book*. This is normally controlled on the *imprest system*.

If the balance in the bank column of the cash book does not agree with the bank statement, a *bank reconciliation* is drawn up. This shows the reasons for the differences and adjustments are made to the cash book if errors need correcting.

> *You should now be able to attempt Task 7.3 and the objective test at the end of this chapter.*

Student activities

Task 7.1
Visit a good stationery shop and examine the cash books on display. Note the differences in format and compare them with the examples we have used in this chapter.

Task 7.2
Draw up a cash book for your own receipts and expenditures as they occur during the next month. At the end of the month obtain a bank statement and prepare a bank reconciliation.

Task 7.3

Design a standard form that might be used in a small business for carrying out monthly bank reconciliations.

Question 7.1

You have been appointed as cashier to Warminster & Sons. The cash book on 1 January has the following balances.

Cash book

Receipts				Payments			
Date	Details	Cash	Bank	Date	Details	Cash	Bank
		£	£			£	£
Jan 1	Balances b/d	450	2,185				

During the month of January the following transactions take place:

January 2   Paid cheque of £1,250 for materials
January 3   Paid cheque of £500 for rent
January 6   Received £200 cash for sales
January 8   Paid delivery charges of £150 cash
January 9   Bought packaging materials for £185 cash
January 12 Received £1,000 cheque from customer
January 16 Paid cash of £115 for advertising
January 19 Customer paid £650 cheque
January 20 Drew £200 from bank for business use
January 24 Paid cheque of £3,000 for machinery
January 27 Paid electricity bill of £135 in cash
January 29 Cheque of £500 from customer

Required

Draw up the cash book for January showing the opening balances for 1st February.

Question 7.2

i) A company buys goods for £250 cash. What would the entry in the cash book be?

ii) At the end of a month the cash book shows cash receipts of £425 and cash payments of £297. What entries would be needed to balance the cash book?

iii) Cash of £350 is drawn from the bank for business purposes. What entries should be made in the cash book?

iv) An amount of £3,250 has to be inserted in the left hand bank column so that the two totals agree at the end of the month. Does this represent money that the business has in the bank or an overdraft?

v) A supplier offers you a trade discount of 5 per cent if you purchase goods to the value of £1,000. What figures should be entered in the cash book if you pay by cheque?

vi) If a cash book showed an opening balance in the cash column on the right hand side, what would you conclude?

vii) What is a contra entry?

Question 7.3

The following transactions need to be analysed in the petty cash book. The first two transactions have been entered. Complete the entries and total the columns. Cross cast your analysed columns at the end to ensure that there are no errors. Note that only the payments side of the petty cash book is given and VAT has been ignored.

> July 1 Bought envelopes for £12.00
> July 1 Rail fare to Nottingham £16.20
> July 1 Meal purchased at station £3.60
> July 2 Writing paper and envelopes £5.20
> July 2 Taxi fare to attend meeting £2.45
> July 3 Coffee and milk for office £1.35
> July 3 Postage of parcel £4.45
> July 4 Paper clips, drawing pins and pens £6.55
> July 4 Rail fare to Leicester £6.20
> July 5 Postage stamps £3.80
> July 5 Window cleaner £2.40
> July 6 Biscuits for office £1.10

Petty cash book

Payments					
Date	Details	Total	Postage & Stationery	Travelling expenses	Misc
		£	£	£	£
July 1	Envelopes	12.00	12.00		
July 1	Rail fare	16.20		16.20	

Question 7.4

David Stroud is responsible for the petty cash book. On the first of September an imprest of £50 is given to David. During that month the following amounts are paid by David.

September 1   Rail fare £4.25
September 2   Tea and coffee for the office £1.80
September 3   Taxi fare for client's meeting £2.25
September 6   Envelopes and paper £3.45
September 7   Recorded delivery parcel £1.65
September 7   Cleaning cloths and disinfectant for office £2.65
September 10   Postage stamps £1.90
September 12   Special inking pen £1.05
September 14   Bus fares £0.40
September 16   Milk for office £2.20
September 17   Taxi fare £2.20
September 17   Recorded delivery parcel £3.00
September 18   Printer ribbon £1.80
September 21   Postage stamps £1.90
September 22   Manilla envelopes £3.00
September 24   Receipt book £1.00
September 24   Tea and coffee for office £1.80
September 24   Polish and cleaners £2.80
September 26   Bus fares £0.75
September 28   Rail fare £3.20
September 28   Meal £3.60

Required

Draw up the petty cash for the month analysing the expenditure into

- Postage and stationery
- Travelling expenses
- Miscellaneous

Give the entry on 1 October restoring the imprest.

Question 7.5

Bob Chipping has a pet shop. At 30 June his cash book balance was £332, but when the bank statement was received it showed a balance in his favour of £607. On investigation Bob finds that cheques have been entered in to the cash book for £539 and sent to suppliers, but had still not been presented to the bank. On 30 June Bob had paid £264 into his bank account. This had been recorded in his cash book, but did not appear on his bank statement until 2 July. Prepare a bank reconciliation statement as at 30 June.

Objective test (tick the appropriate box)

i)   David Bowood has received an invoice for £280 and pays this promptly in order to obtain the cash discount of 2.5 per cent. What is the actual amount David pays:

a)   £7.00   ☐

b)   £287.00   ☐

c) £273.00 ☐

d) £277.50 ☐

ii) If at the end of a financial period you have £5.60 in the petty cash, you would expect to see this figure in the petty cash book as:

a) the closing balance on the right-hand side ☐

b) the opening balance on the right-hand side ☐

c) a total figure on the left-hand side ☐

d) a total figure on the right-hand side ☐

iii) If a company receives a trade discount, the cash book would:

a) show it on the left-hand side ☐

b) show it on the right-hand side ☐

c) not show it ☐

d) show it on both sides ☐

iv) The imprest system is a method whereby at the end of a period the petty cash is:

a) restored to its original amount ☐

b) put in the company bank account ☐

c) used to buy stationery ☐

d) counted three times ☐

v) Cheques that have been drawn but not yet presented are cheques that have been:

a) paid into the bank, but are not yet cleared ☐

b) paid to suppliers, but are not yet on the bank statement ☐

c) received from debtors, but not yet paid into the bank ☐

d) none of these ☐

CHAPTER 8

Balancing the books

At the end of this chapter you should be able to:

- balance accounts;
- discuss the treatment of stock;
- construct a trial balance;
- record adjusting entries;
- discuss possible problems of a trial balance.

2   INTRODUCTION

At the of a financial period, a business will 'close' all its accounts; that is calculate the balance on each account. Those balances will be listed on a special statement which is drawn up on a specific date. The first purpose of a trial balance is to see whether the sum of all the accounts' endings debit balances equals the sum of the accounts' ending credit balances.

If you review the last chapter you will see that for every debit entry you also made a credit entry of the same amount on another account and vice versa. If this is done consistently then the sum of all the debit balances will equal the sum of the credit balances. In real life, and in the examination room, this is rarely the case. In all probability there will have been omissions and errors. These are corrected with adjusting entries and, if there are a sufficient number, an adjusted trial balance may need to be prepared.

Once you are satisfied that the trial balance is correct, the financial statements in the form of the profit-and-loss account and balance sheet may be drawn up.

In this chapter we will show you how to close accounts and construct a trial balance. This will complete this section of the book on 'accounting for economic transactions' and will lead to the next section, which will look at the financial statements of individuals in business.

3   CLOSING THE ACCOUNTS

Having worked through the examples in the preceding chapter, you may have noticed how easy it is to make a mistake and enter a transaction as a credit or a debit in both accounts, rather than as a credit on one account and a debit on the other. At the same time, it is quite likely that you found the whole process some-what tedious. We commiserate with you, but it is essential that you understand these important principles. Not only will you find this a prerequisite for under-standing later chapters in this book, but if your employment involves accounting you will need to have acquired these basic skills.

Having recapped why double-entry bookkeeping is worth learning, we are now ready to look at the problem of how to ensure that the records are mathematically correct. We will also demonstrate how the information can be conveniently summarised so that it can be communicated to others, by periodically *closing the accounts* and constructing a *trial balance*.

The rules for closing the accounts are very straightforward. At the end of a financial period, which may be the end of the month, the end of the quarter, the end of the year, or any other period decided by the business, all the individual bookkeeping accounts are closed using the following rules.

1. If the account contains entries on each side which are equal to one another, they can be double underlined to close the account for that financial period. The Bob Lytham account is an example of this.

Bob Lytham

2003		£	2003		£
28 July	Bank	1,500	26 July	Purchases	1,500

2. If the account contains only one entry, insert the balancing figure on the opposite side and carry this down to the same side as the original entry to start the next period. The term *carried down* is often abbreviated to c/d; *brought down* is abbreviated to b/d. Hannah Johnson's motor vehicle account provides an example of this. You can see that we have complied with the rules of double-entry bookkeeping: for every debit entry there is a corresponding credit entry and vice versa. We have credited the closing balance of £1,000 and debited an opening balance of the same amount.

Motor vehicle account

2003		£	2003		£
2 July	Bank	1,000	31 July	Balance c/d	1,000
1 Aug	Balance b/d	1,000			

3. If the account contains a number of entries, add up both sides.

   • If both sides are the same, insert the totals and double underline them. An extension of Hannah Johnson's debtor account for John Juniper provides an example of this.

John Juniper

2003		£	2003		£
2 July	Sales	2,800	20 July	Bank	750
5 July	Sales	200	28 July	Bank	2,550
8 July	Sales	100			
12 July	Sales	200			
		3,300			3,300

- If both sides do not agree, first insert the balancing figure on the side with the lower amount, insert the totals which should now be equal and double underline them. Complete the entry by carrying down the balancing figure on the opposite side as the opening balance for the new financial period. Hannah Johnson's bank account provides an example of this.

Bank account

2003		£	2003		£
1 July	Capital	10,000	1 July	Equipment	4,000
2 July	Sales	3,500	1 July	Purchases	4,000
12 July	Returns outward	200	1 July	Advertising	500
20 July	John Juniper	750	2 July	Car	1,000
28 July	John Juniper	2,550	3 July	Purchases	2,000
			14 July	Returns inward	500
			28 July	Bob Lytham	1,500
			31 July	Balance c/d	3,500
		17,000			17,000
1 August	Balance b/d	3,500			

You should now be able to attempt Task 8.1 and Question 8.1 at the end of this chapter.

4 | TRIAL BALANCE

When all the accounts have been balanced off, some of them will have been closed completely and will show no balance brought down to commence the next financial period, whereas others will show either a *debit* or a *credit* balance. The debit balances normally represent the assets and expenses of the business and the credit balances normally represent the capital, revenue and liabilities of the business. The list of balances is drawn up in a financial statement at a particular point in time known as a *trial balance*.

If you have made a debit entry for every credit entry and vice versa, the total of the debit balances should be equal to the total of the credit balances. If errors are present, it may require a number of trials to get the two columns to balance. When you have achieved this, the mathematical accuracy of the double-entry bookkeeping system is proven and the trial balance can be used to prepare the important financial statements known as the *profit-and-loss account* and the *balance sheet*, which we will examine in a later chapter.

Example

Continuing to use the example of Hannah Johnson in Chapter 6, calculate the closing balances for the accounts and construct a trial balance.

Solution

See the trial balance laid out below.

Looking at the two columns, you will see that the debit column is a list of all the expenses (for example, purchases), which will appear on the *profit-and-loss account*, and assets (for example, premises) that will appear on the *balance sheet*. The credit column is a list of the capital and the liabilities that will appear on the *balance sheet* and the sales or revenues which will appear on the *profit-and-loss account*. We will be looking at the profit-and-loss account and balance sheet in Chapters 10 and 11.

Hannah Johnson
Trial balance as at 31 July 2003

	Debit £	Credit £
Capital at beginning of year		10,000
Sales		6,800
Purchases	7,500	
Cash at bank	3,500	
Equipment	4,000	
Motor vehicles	1,000	
Returns inward	500	
Returns outward		200
Advertising	500	
	17,000	17,000

Note: at 31 July the business had stock of £4,000.

You will see that at the end of the trial balance there is a note that states that the business has stock of £4,000 at 31 July. As discussed earlier, when goods are purchased, a debit is made to the purchases account and when goods are sold, a credit is made to the sales account. However, it is likely that at the end of a financial period the business will still have stock remaining that it will hope to sell in the next financial period and make a profit. To account for this properly, the business must carry out a stock take at the end of the financial period. Some businesses close to allow a manual counting of stock and its valuation to take place; others operate an automated stock control system that allows up-to-date stock figures to be read off at any time. In this example the stock is valued at £4,000 at the end of the period. In later chapters we will show you how this figure is incorporated into the profit-and-loss account and balance sheet. We also discuss how to cope with transactions that have not yet been entered into the records and those that have been entered but refer to a future financial period.

Finally, we need to consider what a trial balance does not do, because there are some accounting errors that it does not reveal. These are known as:

- *errors of omission*, where the transaction has not been recorded in the books of accounts at all;

- *errors of commission*, where the transaction has been recorded in the wrong accounts; for example, in the premises account instead of the equipment account;

- *errors of principle*, where the transaction has been recorded in the wrong class of account; for example, in an asset account instead of a liability account;

- *errors of original entry*, where the transaction has been correctly recorded, but the wrong amount was entered;

- *errors of reversed entries*, where the transaction has been recorded in the correct accounts, but on the wrong side of both accounts.

You should now be able to attempt Tasks 8.2 and 8.3 and Questions 8.2 and 8.3 at the end of this chapter.

5   ACCRUALS AND PREPAYMENTS

So far we have assumed that all of the transactions that the organisation has undertaken have been recorded on the books of account. Unfortunately, that is not normally the case. In some instances the organisation may have bought goods and received them or incurred operating expenses that it has not paid. Similarly there may be revenues that it has received but for some reason the source documents have not passed through the system.

You must remember that business will continue as normal even though it is the end of the financial period. The accountant would most likely prefer to close the business for a week or a month until the books are balanced and the financial statements are drawn up. This does not happen. The business will continue to run, goods will be sold and purchased, expenses will be incurred and the other normal transactions will take place.

This mismatch of timing in real life is also a favourite area for examiners. They will want to test how well students deal with these issues when preparing financial statements from a trial balance. We will deal with these topics fully in Chapter 16 when we deal with incomplete records. At this stage we will introduce two important terms.

Accruals

An accrued expense is an expense that has been incurred at the trial balance date but it has not been paid for and it has not been recorded. For example, telephone bills are rarely received by the trial balance and the organisation has had the benefit of using the telephone, but no record will appear in the organisation's books until the invoice is received.

An accrued revenue is revenue that has been earned but no payment has been received and no entry has been recorded to recognise the revenue. For example, an organisation may have a deposit with a bank on which it receives interest. At the trial balance date it may not have received notification of the interest that it has earned.

Prepayments

Frequently, economic activities overlap more than one accounting period. This means that the appropriate amount of revenue or expense must be allocated to a future period. One regular example that appears on examination papers is that of insurance. An organisation may be paid for an insurance premium for a period ending on the 31 December in the year prior to that 31 March, part of the premium will need to be adjusted.

6 | SUMMARY

At the end of a financial period, usually 12 months but sometimes more frequent, the organisation will close the accounts. There are specific rules on how this is done. The closing balances are listed on a trial balance and the sum of the debit balances should equal the sum of the credit balances. The trial balance, therefore acts as a mathematical check on the correctness of the record keeping. However, there can be errors that are not detected by the trial balance.

When the necessary adjustments are made and the trial balance is mathematically correct, the financial statements can be constructed. However, there are usually a number of transactions that will not have been recorded in the accounts at the date of the trial balance. These are known as accruals and prepayments.

Student activities

Task 8.1
Construct a diagram to explain the rules for closing accounts.

Task 8.2
Explain the errors which may occur on a trial balance date

Task 8.3
Give 3 examples of accrual which may occur at the trial balance date

Question 8.1
Design examples to illustrate the rules for closing accounts

Question 8.2
Using the example of Gavin Salecombe in Section 6.5 of Chapter 6, close all the accounts and draw up trial balance as at 6 January. Remember to use the most recent bank accounts in your answer.

Question 8.3
Using the example of Tony O'Hara in Question 6.2 in Chapter 6 close the accounts and construct a trial balance.

Objective test (tick the appropriate box)

i) A trial balance sheet is designed to:

    a) show the amount of profit made ☐

    b) catch those committing fraud ☐

    c) demonstrate the mathematical correctness of the accounts ☐

    d) show how much the organisation is worth ☐

ii) To close an account with only one entry you should:

    a) enter a zero on the opposite page and double underline ☐

    b) insert a balancing figure on the opposite page and double underline ☐

    c) insert a balancing figure on the opposite side and carry down to the same side as the original entry ☐

    d) do nothing as it will not appear on the trial balance ☐

iii) One would expect that at the trial balance date a sales account would normally have:

    a) no entries in it ☐

    b) only debit entries in it ☐

    c) debit and credit entries which agree ☐

    d) only credit entries in it ☐

iv) An error of commission on a trial basis is where:

   a) the transaction has never been recorded in the account ☐

   b) the transaction has been recorded in the wrong accounts ☐

   c) only the debit entry has been recorded ☐

   d) the entry has been recorded on the wrong side ☐

v) An accrued expense is where:

   a) the organisation has failed to pay an invoice ☐

   b) an expense has been incurred but not paid for or recorded ☐

   c) the organisation has paid in advance for insurance ☐

   d) good have been returned to a supplier ☐

Brother trouble

Context

Your brother, who is at art college, has come home for the weekend. He confesses to you that he has some money problems that have arisen because of a business he has started. He has been buying jewellery made by some of his fellow students and selling it to shops. Everyone has been happy with the arrangement, but one of the students, Terry Spinks, wishes to buy a motorbike and has asked your brother to pay all the money that is owed to him. Unfortunately, your brother has not maintained a proper bookkeeping system and does not know how much he owes Terry.

After a lengthy discussion you establish that the jewellery was purchased from the students on credit and when your brother had some cash he paid them odd amounts 'to keep them happy'. The sales to the shops were on credit, but your brother arranged that they would settle in cash within 10 days. Your brother believes he has put £550 of his own money into the business and has £6 left. From the few receipts and various notes kept by your brother, and relying on his memory, you have been able to draw up the following lists of transactions.

Purchases of jewellery from students on credit

Date		Student	£
January	2	Terry Spinks	282
	2	Jan Davis	202
	15	Tariq Elefonte	64
	18	Terry Spinks	86
	19	Jan Davis	220
	23	Terry Spinks	86
	23	Tariq Elefonte	220

Jewellery sold on credit

Date		Shop	£
January	6	Kellers Boutique	210
	8	Silver Stores	352
	24	Kellers Boutique	335
	25	Silver Stores	482

Cash paid to students

Date		Student	£
January	18	Terry Spinks	50
	18	Jan Davis	100
	28	Tariq Elefonte	250
	28	Jan Davis	200
	28	Terry Spinks	400

In addition, your brother informs you that Kellers Boutique paid him £210 on 10 January and Silver Stores £352 on 16 January, but he has received no money from them since. He also remembers that he bought display boxes, business cards and some advertising brochures for £106 on 5 January.

Student activities

i) Use a double-entry bookkeeping system to record all the transactions of your brother's business.

ii) Close the accounts at the end of January and prepare a trial balance.

iii) Inform your brother of the amount owing to Terry Spinks at the end of January.

iv) Advise your brother on how he can keep better financial control of his business activities.

Format

A note is required for your brother that shows:

● the double-entry bookkeeping system;

● the trial balance as at 31 January;

● the amount owing to Terry Spinks;

● advice on how your brother can keep better control of his business.

Objectives

In this assignment the student will apply the principles of double entry-bookkeeping in a situation which is fairly unstructured and extract detailed information as well as explaining the basis and advantages of maintaining proper financial control of business activity.

References

Chapter 8 will be of particular use in this assignment.

PART III

INDIVIDUALS IN BUSINESS

CHAPTER 9

Cash-flow statements

1 OBJECTIVES

At the end of this chapter, you should be able to:

- explain the purposes and importance of a cash-flow statement;
- define the terms positive cash flow, negative cash flow and net cash flow;
- construct a personal or business cash-flow forecast manually or using a spreadsheet.

2 INTRODUCTION

For both individuals and organisations, the control of *cash* is a most important activity. In a later chapter we shall look at the difference between cash and profit; in this section we concentrate on cash. By cash we mean coins, notes or cheques; that is, money that is held either as cash in a safe (or elsewhere) or as a balance at the bank.

Cash flows in and out of an organisation. Cash flowing in, known as *positive cash flow*, is cash received; for example, from debtors or from customers paying cash. Cash flowing out, known as *negative cash flow*, is cash paid out; for example, cash paid to suppliers or as wages to employees. The difference between cash flowing in and cash flowing out is known as the *net cash flow*. This may be a *surplus* (more cash flowing in than out), or a *deficit* (more cash flowing out than in). Never refer to these as a profit or loss.

3 CASH-FLOW FORECASTS

A *cash-flow forecast* is a simple statement which shows the predicted movement of cash (the cash flow) for an individual or an organisation. It allows cash flows to be *planned* and gives financial information which can be used in the following ways:

- to establish whether there is enough cash to carry out planned activities;
- to check that the amount of cash coming in is sufficient to cover the cash going out;

- to ensure that they do not run out of cash and that they receive early warning that a bank overdraft or other loan is required;
- to enable decisions to be made about the investment of any cash surplus.

> *You should now be able to attempt Question 9.1 at the end of this chapter.*

An easy way to construct a *cash-flow forecast* is to adopt the following procedure:

- The heading should state the name of the person or organisation and the period to which the forecast refers.
- The columns should be labelled with the months to which they relate.
- The cash coming in is itemised separately in the first rows and subtotalled.
- The cash going out is itemised separately in the next rows and subtotalled.
- The subtotal of cash out is deducted from the subtotal of cash in, to give the cash surplus or deficit for the month.
- The final rows calculate the cumulative cash position.
- The final column shows the total of all cash movements for that particular item.

Example

At the end of December Peggy Lin decides that she wants to go on holiday at the beginning of July. She has savings of £250, but will need £500 by the end of June to be able to afford this holiday. Her net salary is £700 each month and she predicts that her monthly cash expenditure will be as follows:

- Rates are £320 per annum, payable in two instalments in April and October.
- Rent is £200 per month, payable monthly at the start of each month.
- Electricity is £180 per quarter, payable at the end of each quarter.
- Travel is estimated at £50 per month, payable each month.
- Insurance is £10 per month, payable each month, with extra premiums due for payment: £30 in February and £120 in April.
- Sundries are expected to total £120 per month, payable monthly.
- Food is estimated at £150 per month, payable monthly.
- The holiday will cost £500 and falls due for payment in June.

Solution

Peggy Lin's cash-flow forecast is shown opposite. The layout shows the difference between cash coming in and going out for each month (the net cash flow). It also shows the cumulative cash position (the *total amount* of cash that Peggy has at the end of each month). The June and Total columns both show that Peggy

Peggy Lin: Cash-flow forecast January to June

	Jan £	Feb £	Mar £	Apr £	May £	Jun £	Total £
Cash inflows:							
Salary	700	700	700	700	700	700	4,200
Total inflows (A)	700	700	700	700	700	700	4,200
Cash outflows:							
Rates	–	–	–	160	–	–	160
Rent	200	200	200	200	200	200	1,200
Electricity	–	–	180	–	–	180	360
Travel	50	50	50	50	50	50	300
Insurance	10	40	10	130	10	10	210
Sundries	120	120	120	120	120	120	720
Food	150	150	150	150	150	150	900
Holiday	–	–	–	–	–	500	500
Total outflows (B)	530	560	710	810	530	1,210	4,350
Net cash flow (A–B)	170	140	(10)	(110)	170	(510)	(150)
Balances:							
Start of month	*250	420	560	550	440	610	*250
End of month	420	560	550	440	610	100	100

  * Savings at 1 January

should have £100 in hand at the end of June; the other monthly columns show that there is adequate cash in hand.

Note how the cumulative cash flow is calculated. If the difference for the net cash flow is negative, you should show the figure in brackets. In calculating the cumulative figure, follow the usual rules of arithmetic: add a positive net cash flow to a positive net cash flow, deduct a negative cash flow from a positive cash flow or add a negative cash flow to a negative cash flow.

If Peggy has drawn up her cash-flow forecast and finds that she should have adequate cash in hand at the end of June after paying for her holiday, she has carried out a valuable planning exercise. However, as she has only predicted the cash flows, it is unlikely that the actual cash flows will be exactly as forecast. To ensure control, Peggy should record the actual cash flows each month and compare them with her plan. If at the end of any month there are significant differences between the plan and what actually happened, she can decide what action is necessary to improve the situation.

4   USING SPREADSHEETS

Although you can prepare a cash-flow forecast, or indeed any other financial statement, using mental arithmetic or a calculator, there is an ever increasing array of individual spreadsheet programs and integrated software packages now on the market that make the task even easier. Most of these are mouse operated in the user-friendly Windows environment with icons (picture symbols), menus and on-screen help. Facilities available include mathematical functions such as addition, subtraction, multiplication and division, as well as a wide range of statistical functions and integrated graphical packages.

Spreadsheet programs perform calculations on numerical data which is entered into a worksheet. A worksheet is a large matrix of rectangles called *cells*. A cell can contain numbers (the numerical data), words (labels and headings) or a formula (such as sum this column or row of cells). When you open a spreadsheet program, the screen usually shows an empty worksheet ready for you to insert data. The columns are already labelled A, B, C, and so forth and the rows numbered 1, 2, 3, and so on. This allows you to identify particular cells in the worksheet when inserting formulae. For example, the *address* of the cell in the top left-hand corner is A1.

You can construct a cash-flow forecast (and other financial statements) quickly and easily using a spreadsheet program. Providing you enter the formulae and data accurately, using a spreadsheet ensures that you get it right every time! We have used Excel to construct ours, but if you do not have access to this program, you will find the principles are the same for most other programs.

Example

In the example in Figure 9.1, we show the labels and formulae you should enter on the spreadsheet in order to construct the cash-flow forecast for Peggy Lin. You can format the labels and the numerical data using bold, italics, underline, left justify, centre and right justify in the same way as you can when using a word-processing program However, do not format the formulae. These should be typed into the cells exactly as illustrated, with no spaces between characters and paying careful attention to the punctuation and signs used.

Once you have set up your *pro forma*, name the file and save it on a floppy disk so that you can adapt it for use on other occasions. The sort of changes you may want to make to your pro forma in the future are likely to include amending the labels for the different types of cash inflows and outflows and this may require inserting or deleting rows of cells.

For example, you may want to insert a row above 'Total inflows' (row 6 in our example) so that you can record a second source of cash inflow. You can do this by moving your cursor to cell A6, clicking on Insert in the toolbar at the top of the screen and selecting Rows from the pull-down menu. A new row 6 will appear, moving the 'Total inflows' row down to row 7 and so on down the spreadsheet. However, you must remember that the data you enter into this new row 6 will need to be included in the 'Total inflows'. This means that cell B5 should now contain the formula SUM(B5:B6); the formula in cell C5 should read SUM(C5:C6), etc., across the whole row. If you insert a row by mistake, and realise straightaway before clicking or typing anything else, simply click on *Edit* and select. *Undo Insert Rows*. This is a very useful command; in fact, the spreadsheet editor almost always allows you to undo your last action.

You may find that you have too many rows in the cash outflows part of the pro forma and want to cut a row. To do this, highlight the row you want to delete (say, row 15 in our example) by clicking on the number 15. Next, click on *Edit* in the toolbar at the top of the screen and select *Delete*. The row will disappear and all the other rows move up to take its place, adjusting their numbers accordingly.

	A	B	C	D	E	F	G	H
1	Peggy Lin: **Cash flow forecast - January to June**							
2		Jan £	Feb £	Mar £	Apr £	May £	Jun £	Total £
3								
4	*Cash inflows:*							
5	Salary							=SUM(B5:G5)
6	**Total inflows**	=SUM(B5:B5)	=SUM(C5:C5)	=SUM(D5:D5)	=SUM(E5:E5)	=SUM(F5:F5)	=SUM(G5:G5)	=SUM(H5:H5)
7	*Cash outflows:*							
8	Rates							=SUM(B8:G8)
9	Rent							=SUM(B9:G9)
10	Electricity							=SUM(B10:G10)
11	Travel							=SUM(B11:G11)
12	Insurance							=SUM(B12:G12)
13	Sundries							=SUM(B13:G13)
14	Food							=SUM(B14:G14)
15	Holiday							=SUM(B15:G15)
16	**Total outflows**	=SUM(B8:B15)	=SUM(C8:C15)	=SUM(D8:D15)	=SUM(E8:E15)	=SUM(F8:F15)	=SUM(G8:G15)	=SUM(H8:H15)
17	**Net cash flow**	=B6-B16	=C6-C16	=D6-D16	=E6-E16	=F6-F16	=G6-G16	=H6-H16
18	*Balances:*							
19	Start of month		=B20	=C20	=D20	=E20	=F20	=B19
20	End of month	=B17+B19	=C17+C19	=D17+D19	=E17+E19	=F17+F19	=G17+G19	=G20
21	(B19 and H19 = Savings at 1st January)							
22								

◄ ◄ ► ►I Sheet1 ╱ Sheet2 ╱ Sheet3 ╱ Sheet4 ╱ Sheet5 ╱ Sheet6 ╱ Sheet7 ╱ Sheet ╱

Figure 9.1 *Spreadsheet example*

When you delete a row like this, you will find that you do not need to edit the simple formulae we have used as they will automatically adjust themselves to take account of the deletion of the row. If you realise straightaway that you have deleted a row by mistake, simply click on *Edit* and select *Undo Delete* and the row will reappear; any formulae affected by the change will automatically adjust themselves.

Once you are happy that you have entered the labels and formulae correctly, the next stage is to enter the data into the cells where you have not entered a formula. If you enter something into a cell with a formula by mistake, you will overwrite the formula instructions and will need to re-enter it. Once you have checked that it is correct, save it and print it in the usual way. On the screen your finished forecast should look like this:

	A	B	C	D	E	F	G	H
1	Peggy Lin: Cash flow forecast January to June							
2		Jan	Feb	Mar	Apr	May	Jun	Total
3		£	£	£	£	£	£	£
4	*Cash inflows:*							
5	Salary	700	700	700	700	700	700	4,200
6	**Total inflows**	**700**	**700**	**700**	**700**	**700**	**700**	**4,200**
7	*Cash outflows:*							
8	Rates	–	–	–	160	–	–	160
9	Rent	200	200	200	200	200	200	1,200
10	Electricity	–	–	180	–	–	180	360
11	Travel	50	50	50	50	50	50	300
12	Insurance	10	40	10	130	10	10	210
13	Sundries	120	120	120	120	120	120	720
14	Food	150	150	150	150	150	150	900
15	Holiday	–	–	–	–	–	500	500
16	**Total outflows**	**530**	**560**	**710**	**810**	**530**	**1,210**	**4,350**
17	**Net cash flow**	**170**	**140**	**(10)**	**(110)**	**170**	**(510)**	**(150)**
18	*Balances:*							
19	Start of month	*250	420	560	550	440	610	*250
20	End of month	420	560	550	440	610	100	100
21	* Savings at 1st January							
22								

Sheet1 / Sheet2 / Sheet3 / Sheet4 / Sheet5 / Sheet

Figure 9.2

As events often do not turn out to be exactly as predicted, it is important to establish *control* of the cash movements on a regular basis by comparing the actual movements cash against the original plans. A simple *cash-flow statement* can be *drawn up to do this* and is useful for making decisions about whether to revise planned activities so that plans become more realistic and therefore more likely to be achieved.

5 | SIMPLE CASH-FLOW STATEMENTS

Example

The following cash-flow statement for Peggy Lin reflects shows the actual cash flows for the first three months. The title reflects the fact that it is no longer a forecast, but a statement of the actual cash flows. You will see that at the end of March she only had £430 cash, instead of the planned figure of £550.

Peggy Lin: Cash-flow statement January to March

	Actual			Revised forecast			
	Jan £	Feb £	Mar £	Apr £	May £	Jun £	Total £
Cash inflows:							
Salary	700	700	700				
Total inflows (A)	700	700	700				
Cash outflows:							
Rates	–	–	–				
Rent	200	200	200				
Electricity	–	–	220				
Travel	50	60	60				
Insurance	10	60	10				
Sundries	120	150	130				
Food	150	150	150				
Holiday	–	–	–				
Total outflows (B)	530	620	770				
Net cash flow (A−B)	170	80	(70)				
Balances:							
Start of month	*250	420	500				
End of month	420	500	430				

* Savings at 1 January

Peggy's original forecast was to have £100 cash at the end of June after paying for her holiday, but the actual cash outflows have exceeded the forecast figures by £120 (£60 in February and £60 in March) This means that even if the forecast is strictly adhered to during April, May and June, she will be £40 overdrawn at the end of June.

Being somewhat overweight, Peggy decides to cut her food bill by £40 per month, thus reducing it to £120 for the next three months, and to try to keep to the original budget for the other items of expenditure. This means that she should still have £100 cash at the end of June after paying for her holiday. Fill in the revised forecast figures in the above table, and then compare your figures with the solution given opposite.

Solution

Peggy Lin: Cash-flow statement January to June

	Actual			Revised forecast			
	Jan £	Feb £	Mar £	Apr £	May £	Jun £	Total £
Cash inflows:							
Salary	700	700	700	700	700	700	4,200
Total inflows (A)	700	700	700	700	700	700	4,200
Cash outflows:							
Rates	–	–	–	160	–	–	160
Rent	200	200	200	200	200	200	1,200
Electricity	–	–	220	–	–	180	400
Travel	50	60	60	50	50	50	320
Insurance	10	60	10	130	10	10	230
Sundries	120	150	130	120	120	120	760
Food	150	150	150	110	110	110	780
Holiday	–	–	–	–	–	500	500
Total outflows (B)	530	620	770	770	490	1,170	4,350
Net cash flow (A−B)	170	80	(70)	(70)	210	(470)	(150)
Balances:							
Start of month	*250	420	500	430	360	570	*250
End of month	420	500	430	360	570	100	100

* Savings at 1 January

> You should now be able to attempt Task 9.1 at the end of this chapter.

6   CASH PLANNING FOR A NEW BUSINESS

It is essential for individuals thinking of starting a *new business* to prepare a cash-flow forecast. This allows them:

- to see if the business will generate sufficient cash – as we will see in a later chapter, a business can make a profit, but still not have sufficient cash to meet its needs;

- to decide on the timing of cash inflows and outflows – as a general rule in a business, you want the cash to come in as quickly as possible, but go out as slowly as possible. A business with a shortage of cash may attempt to achieve this by collecting the money it is owed as soon as it can, but delay any payments it has to make.

- to calculate the amount of capital (cash) they should invest in the business;

116

- to ascertain what additional funds they require – the owners of a new business may be able to provide some cash of their own, but a cash-flow forecast will show if they will need to obtain a loan from outside sources such as a bank.

> *You should now be able to attempt Task 9.2 at the end of this chapter.*

Example

Carol Dumant sets up as a manufacturer of sports equipment. She has £25,000, which she pays into a business bank account on 1 July and budgets as follows:

- Machinery to be purchased on 1 July for £30,000, and this will have to be paid for by the end of the month.
- Wages: £3,000 per month.
- Rent of factory will be £48,000 per annum, payable in monthly instalments at the start of each month.
- Other costs incurred in the running of the business (excluding material purchases): will be £15,000 per month, payable (on average) in the month following the month in which the costs are incurred.
- Materials will be supplied on one month's credit (i.e. materials purchased in July will have to be paid for by the end of August).
- Half of the sales are expected to be for cash; the remaining half on credit. Although her quoted terms are to be 'net monthly account', Carol is realistic enough to budget for two months' credit being taken, an average, by her credit customers (i.e. credit sales in July will not be settled until September).
- After careful market research, Carol expects a steady but rapid expansion in her business. Her forecast for sales and purchases of materials is as follows.

	Sales £	Purchases £
July	40,000	16,000
August	60,000	24,000
September	80,000	32,000
October	100,000	40,000
November	120,000	48,000
December	140,000	56,000

Required

Prepare a monthly cash-flow forecast for Carol Dumant for the six months from July to December.

Solution

Carol Dumant: Cash-flow forecast for six months ending 31 December (£'000)

	Jul £	Aug £	Sep £	Oct £	Nov £	Dec £	Total £
Cash inflows:							
Capital	25	–	–	–	–	–	25
Cash Sales	20	30	40	50	60	70	270
Credit Sales	–	–	20	30	40	50	140
Total inflows (A)	45	30	60	80	100	120	435
Cash outflows:							
Machinery	30	–	–	–	–	–	30
Wages	3	3	3	3	3	3	18
Rent	4	4	4	4	4	4	24
Other Costs	–	15	15	15	15	15	75
Materials	–	16	24	32	40	48	160
Total outflows (B)	37	38	46	54	62	70	307
Net cash flow (A−B)	8	(8)	14	26	38	50	128
Balances:							
Start of month	0	88	0	14	40	78	0
End of month	8	0	14	40	78	128	128

7 PLANNING CAPITAL REQUIREMENTS

Sometimes you know the amount of cash coming in and the amount going out, but you need to calculate the amount of cash required at the start of the financial period to ensure that the individual or business does not require an overdraft. This is particularly important if for some reason this is not obtainable.

The way to tackle this kind of problem is to draw up a cash-flow forecast using the figures supplied, but leaving the opening cash balance (or the amount to be inserted for capital introduced) blank. Proceed with all the calculations as usual. The highest cumulative figure of *negative* cash in the period (the bottom line of the layouts used so far) will be the sum required at the start to ensure that there is not a cash deficit (i.e. an overdraft) at any time.

Example

David McLeod plans to start a business on 1 January manufacturing and selling haggis. His plans include the following:

• Equipment will cost £20,000 and will be purchased and paid for on 1 January.

- Factory rent will be £500 per month, payable monthly at the start of each month.

- Overheads are estimated at £1,000 per month, payable monthly during the month in which they are incurred.

- Sales are estimated at £6,000 per month for the first three months, then increasing to £7,500 per month from April onwards. Realistically, David budgets to give all his customers two months' credit (receipts from January sales will materialise in March.

- Materials are estimated at one-third of sales value and friendly suppliers have reluctantly agreed to give David one month's credit.

- The bank has agree to grant David a loan of £10,000 from 1 January. Interest will be charged at 20 per cent per annum and charged to his bank account at the end of each quarter (i.e. at the end of March, June, September and December).

Required

a) Prepare a monthly cash-flow forecast for the six months to June, ignoring any capital which David may have to introduce.

b) How much capital will this have to be in order to ensure that David does not incur a cash deficit during the first six months' trading?

Solution

David McLeod: Cash-flow forecast for the six months ending 30 June

	Jan £	Feb £	Mar £	Apr £	May £	Jun £	Total £
Cash inflows:							
Capital	[ ]						[ ]
Loans	10,000						10,000
Sales	–	–	6,000	6,000	6,000	7,500	25,000
Total inflows (A)	10,000	–	6,000	6,000	6,000	7,500	35,500
Cash outflows:							
Equipment	20,000	–	–	–	–	–	20,000
Rent	500	500	500	500	500	500	3,000
Overheads	1,000	1,000	1,000	1,000	1,000	1,000	6,000
Materials	–	2,000	2,000	2,000	2,500	2,500	11,000
Interest on loan	–	–	500	–	–	500	1,000
Total outflows (B)	21,500	3,500	4,000	3,500	4,000	4,500	41,000
Net cash flow (A−B)	(11,500)	(3,500)	2,000	2,500	2,000	3,000	(5,500)
Balances:							
Start of month	0	(11,500)	(15,000)	(13,000)	(10,500)	(8,500)	0
End of month	(11,500)	(15,000)	(13,000)	(10,500)	(8,500)	(5,500)	(5,500)

£15,000 is the amount of capital which would have to be introduced by David McLeod in order to eliminate the highest cash deficit which is at the end of February.

> *You should now be able to attempt Questions 9.2 to 9.6 at the end of this chapter.*

8 | SUMMARY

A *cash-flow forecast* is a financial statement showing the movements of cash in and out and is essential for cash planning and decision making. Whereas a cash-flow forecast shows predicted figures, a *cash-flow statement* shows the actual figures (or a combination of actual and forecast figures). Control can achieved by regularly comparing the predicted cash flow with the actual cash flow.

To draw up a cash-flow forecast or statement, you must know the *amount* and the *timing* of each movement of cash. This can be done manually or using a spreadsheet. Providing you have entered the formulae and data accurately, the latter offers a fast and accurate method. The most common mistakes made by students are entering the correct cash flow in the incorrect month and calculating the cumulative cash figures incorrectly.

> *You should now be able to attempt Task 9.3 and the objective test at the end of this chapter.*

Student activities

Task 9.1
Draw up a personal cash-flow forecast for the next six months, using a spreadsheet and the figures from your bank or building society statement.

Task 9.2
Visit your local bank and ask if they can give you a pro-forma cash-flow forecast. Most banks have a supply of these for customers wishing to apply for a business loan. Compare the bank's layout with the examples we have given in this chapter.

Task 9.3
In groups, select a business you would like to start; for example, a restaurant, a second-hand book shop, a hairdressing salon or a fitness centre. Make a list of the information you would require in order to construct a cash-flow forecast and the sources from which you would obtain it.

Question 9.1
Why do individuals and organisations need to plan and control their cash flows?

Question 9.2

Using a spreadsheet, recalculate the cash-flow forecast for David McLeod in Section 9.7, entering the figure for capital in the square brackets under cash inflow as £15,000.

Question 9.3

If David McLeod in Section 9.7 did not have sufficient capital to introduce to prevent the cash deficits, what do you suggest he does, apart from obtaining a further loan?

Question 9.4

Robert Morgan is a shoe manufacturer who has been in business for several years. He is thinking of expanding his business in three months' time, and wishes to know how this will affect his cash flow for the next six months, April to September. His budgeted figures for this period are as follows:

- Cash sales are expected to be £10,000 per month, for the first three months, and £20,000 per month from 1 July onwards.

- Credit sales of £55,000 per month have been achieved during the period January to March this year and this is likely to continue until the end of June, after which it is hoped that they will double. Customers are allowed two months' credit.

- Material purchases have been £10,000 per month for the last few months and this is likely to be the pattern until 30 June, after which they will double. Suppliers allow one month's credit.

- Wages are £15,000 per month until 30 June, after which they will double.

- Overheads are £20,000 per month until 30 June, after which they are expected to increase to £35,000 per month.

- In order to achieve the increased production, new machinery will have to be purchased in June at a cost of £100,000, with payment due in July.

- An extension to the factory will be necessary and this will be *built during April and May*, and payment of £150,000 will be due in July.

- On 31 March, he had a credit balance on his business bank account of £140,000.

Robert can foresee a cash flow problem in July, and has an appointment to see his friendly bank manager, who wants to see a cash-flow forecast for the next six months.

Required

Using a spreadsheet, prepare a cash-flow forecast for Robert Morgon and append a few brief but relevant comments.

Question 9.5

In December 2003 Joan Norton plans to take a trip abroad the following August. Although she has savings of £150, the holiday costs £500 and she will have to pay for it on 1 July 2004. Her net salary is £800 per month and she predicts that her expenditure for 2004 will be as follows:

- Rent is £300 per month, payable at the beginning of each month.
- Electricity is estimated at £230 per quarter, payable at the end of each quarter.
- Food is estimated at £200 per month.
- Travel expenses are expected to be £50 per month.
- Insurance premiums are £10 per month, with an additional premium of £30 in February and £50 in April.
- Her endowment policy is £30 per month.
- Clothes and entertainment are estimated at £70 per month.

Required

Using a spreadsheet, construct a cash-flow forecast for Joan Norton for the period January to June 2004. If she does not have sufficient cash to go on holiday, what actions would you advise her to take so that she has the necessary sum by 1 July?

Question 9.6

Tom Cherry is planning to start a business manufacturing wet suits for water sports. He has carried out a market survey and has found that at a retail price of £125 each, he can expect to sell the following number of wet suits:

Month	Forecast sales
January	10
February	20
March	30
April	60
May	80
June	80
July	60
August	50
September	50
October	40
November	40
December	30

He expects that half his customers will pay cash and the other half will take one month's credit. He has found suitable premises in a seaside town with a work-room and a showroom. The rent is £10,000 per annum, payable at the beginning of each quarter. Overheads, such as heating and lighting, are expected to be £400 per month, payable in the month following the month in which they are incurred. He estimates that his other costs will be as follows:

- Telephone is expected to be £250 per quarter, payable in the first month of the following quarter.
- Printing and stationery costs are estimated at £50 per month, payable in the month following the month in which they are incurred.

- Insurance will be £300 per quarter, payable at the beginning of each quarter.

- Regular advertising costs will be £60 per month, but extra advertising will be needed in April, May and June. This will cost an additional £500 which will be paid in two instalments in March and July.

- The cost of materials for making each wet suit is £65 and the suppliers will allow two months' credit.

- Packaging will cost £3 per wet suit sold and the supplier is prepared to allow one month's credit.

A friend has agreed to cut out the wet suits for £5 per suit and she will be paid monthly. Tom plans to make 50 wet suits per month The cost of equipment for making the wet suits is £16,000 and will be due for payment in January. The equipment will be depreciated over five years. The cost of fitting the showroom is estimated at £3,500 and must be paid for by 31 March.

Required

i) Using a spreadsheet, draw up a cash-flow forecast for Tom Cherry for the twelve months January to December.

ii) How much capital does he require to make his business financially viable?

Objective test (tick the appropriate box)

i) Positive cash flow is:

    a) cash inflow into an organisation ☐

    b) cash flowing out of an organisation ☐

    c) payments made to suppliers ☐

    d) money taken out of the business by the owner ☐

ii) If more cash has come in than has gone out, this is known as:

    a) a profit ☐

    b) a cash deficit ☐

    c) a negative cash flow ☐

    d) a cash surplus ☐

iii) Constructing a cash-flow forecast is:

    a) a method for ensuring control ☐

    b) a valuable planning exercise ☐

    c) a way of recording a business's debts ☐

    d) a check on statements issued by the bank ☐

iv) If a business anticipates a cash deficit, it can improve the position by:

    a) not collecting any money from its customers ☐

    b) making all payments as soon as possible ☐

   c)   withdrawing any money it has in the bank ☐

   d)   delaying any payments it has to make ☐

v)   If you are trading on credit, you should enter the money owed by your customers on the cash-flow forecast:

   a)   as soon as the sale is made ☐

   b)   when the customer first places the order ☐

   c)   when you expect the customers to pay ☐

   d)   two weeks after each sale is made ☐

Starting a business

Context

A local school has recently introduced a scheme designed to improve sixth-form pupils' understanding of business. The pupils are divided into groups of four and they have to examine the problems and advantages of setting up their own business. To make the project realistic, each group has to decide on the type of business it would like to run and construct a business plan.

To assist the pupils, the school arranges for a series of outside speakers to come and talk on relevant topics. You have been asked if you would give a talk on different forms of business organisations and the various sources of finance available, with particular reference to the local situation. The school has asked you to make the talk as relevant as possible to the types of business proposed by the pupils and these are:

- hairdressing salon;
- car valeting service;
- fish-and-chip van;
- job agency for Saturday staff;
- wedding photography.

Student activities

i) Conduct research into local sources of finance and advice for small businesses.

ii) Draw up a list of recommendations for appropriate organisational structures for the proposed businesses.

iii) Prepare an outline of the presentation you will give to the pupils.

iv) Prepare overhead transparencies or flip charts to be used during your presentation.

v) Prepare a handout for the pupils covering the main points in your presentation and provide a list of addresses from which they can obtain further advice and information.

Format

You should assemble the material for the presentation, which should include:

- notes for your speech;
- handout for the pupils;
- visual material you intend to use.

Objectives

In this assignment the student will experience the process of conducting research and will gain knowledge of the local position in respect of sources of finance and advice for small businesses. The student will also understand the value of organising and structuring material for a presentation.

References
Chapters 1 and 9 are of particular value to this assignment.

CHAPTER 10

Profit-and-loss account

1 OBJECTIVES

At the end of this chapter you should be able to:

- explain what is meant by a trading account;
- explain what is meant by a profit-and-loss account;
- define such terms as *realisation convention* and *matching convention*;
- construct a simple trading account and profit-and-loss account for a sole trader.

2 INTRODUCTION

In this chapter we shall be looking at a financial statement known as a *profit-and-loss account*. A profit-and-loss account measures *performance over a period*. At the end of the period it shows what *profit* has been achieved. *Profit* is not an easy concept to describe. It normally has very little to do with *cash*, except in very simple circumstances. If you bought an article yesterday for £2, paying cash for it, and then sell it today for £3, also for cash, then you will have £1 cash more today than you had yesterday. Also, you will have made a profit of £1.

However, if you did not pay cash yesterday, but bought the article on credit, and today you sell the article, not for cash, but to someone who says he will pay you next month, also on credit, then no cash has changed hands. But, in accounting terms, you will still have made a profit of £1. The position, whether or not any cash has changed hands, is that:

the *sale* is	£3
the *cost of sale* is	£2
and the *profit* is	£1

Profit can therefore be described as *sales* less the *cost of sales*.

We shall now look at the *profit-and-loss account* for a sole trader (see Chapter 1) in more detail, and describe at the various accounting conventions which are employed in the calculation of *profit*.

3   THE PROFIT-AND-LOSS ACCOUNT – OVERVIEW

Strictly speaking, the full name for this account is the *trading and profit-and-loss account*. A simple account would look something like this:

Example

	£
Trading account	
Sales	10,000
Less Cost of goods sold	4,000
= Gross profit	6,000
Profit-and-loss account	
Less Expenses	5,000
= Net profit	1,000

4   TRADING ACCOUNT

The following example and solution illustrates various principles and accounting conventions.

Example

Thomas Tenby trades as Tenby & Company. The business sells standard computers to educational establishments. He buys them at £700 each and sells them for £1,000 each.

1. At the start of January 2003, Thomas had 25 computers in stock.

2. During January he bought 60 computers from his supplier.

3. On 25 January he paid his supplier for the 70 computers that he had bought in the previous month of December.

4. During January he sold 75 computers to various educational establishments.

5. During January he received payment for 45 computers that he had sold in December.

6. On 25 February he paid his suppliers for the 60 computers that he bought during January.

7. During February he received payment for 55 of the 75 computers that he sold in January.

Required

Calculate how much gross profit Tenby & Company has made, during the month of January.

Solution

To the uninitiated, this must seem an awful mess. Accountants, however, have developed a set of rules or conventions that make it easier to sort the wheat from the chaff.

Anything to do with cash payments or cash receipts is *irrelevant* in calculating profit (or loss). Therefore items 3, 5, 6 and 7 are irrelevant (though this information would be essential for producing cash-flow statements, balance sheets, and managing the business). This leaves items 1, 2 and 4 that are relevant. We can express the computer position as follows:

Item 1 Stock at 1 January	25
Item 2 *Add* Purchases during January	60
	85
Item 4 *Less* Sales during January	75
= Stock at 31 January	10

We can produce a trading account as follows:

Tenby & Company

Trading account for the month ending 31 January 2003

	£
Sales of computers 75 @ £1,000	75,000
Less Cost of computers sold 75 @ £700	52,500
= Gross profit	22,500

The account is now shown in greater detail.

Tenby & Company

Trading account for the month ending 31 January 2003

				£	£
a)					
b)					
c)	Sales of computers	75	@ £1,000 =		75,000
d)	*Less* Cost of sales:				
e)	Opening stock	25	@ £700 =	17,500	
f)	*Add* Purchases	60	@ £700 =	42,000	
g)	available for sale	85	@ £700 =	59,500	
h)	*Less* Closing stock	10	@ £700 =	7,000	
i)	(Therefore cost of sales is)	75	@ £700 =		52,500
j)	= Gross profit				22,500

Notes

There are a number of important points to notice, and reference will be made to the letter at the start of each line of the detailed trading account above.

a) Always give an account a title that includes the name of the business. In this case it is Tenby & Company, a business entity that is accounted for separately from T. Tenby himself.

b) Always give the period to which the account relates. In this case we show that we are not interested in December or February.

c) Sales of computers. This recognises the *realisation convention*. Accountants only recognise a profit *when goods are sold*, i.e. when the goods pass to a customer who is 'invoiced' for them, irrespective of when that customer is likely to pay for them.

d) Cost of sales. This is a heading that precedes the calculation in lines (e), (f), (g) and (h). Line (i) is the result of the calculation. In the answer, we have tried to make this clear by repeating the heading: (Therefore cost of sales is), though this is usually omitted.

i) The cost of sales means the cost of the number of computers sold. This recognises the *matching convention*, which requires that the costs of sales should be *matched* with the sales (or revenue) for the period covered by the statement. This *matching convention* applies not only to the *trading account* (cost of goods sold), but also to the *profit-and-loss account* (expenses for the period), and we shall look at this in more detail later on.

In the above example we have shown the detailed calculations required to obtain the total amount for example 75 computers at £1,000 = £75,000. This is for illustrative purposes only and normally you would only show the full amounts.

> *You should now be able to attempt Question 10.1 at the end of this chapter.*

5   PROFIT-AND-LOSS ACCOUNT

In the previous example we saw that Tenby & Company made a *gross* or *trading profit* of £22,500. Unfortunately for Thomas, that is not the end of the story. In operating his computer business, he will have costs or expenses other than buying computers from his suppliers.

These expenses might include:

- Rent of premises
- Business rates (if not included in rent)
- Electricity for lighting and power
- Gas for heating
- Telephone
- Stationery
- Cleaning costs
- Insurances

- Accountancy and legal fees
- Delivery van expenses
- Depreciation of delivery van
- Depreciation of equipment
- Bad debts and provision for doubtful debts
- Interest on loans and/or bank overdraft
- Salaries of sales and technical staff

All these expenses effectively reduce his *gross profit* to a *net profit*, out of which he will have to pay tax and draw his living expenses. These terms may be new to you and some of them are explained more fully in later chapters (for example depreciation and bad debts), but it is necessary now to go through this list, item by item, to show you how an appropriate amount is calculated for inclusion under the heading 'Expenses' for *one month only*, so that we can arrive at Thomas Tenby's *net profit*.

Rent of premises

Thomas rents premises where he can demonstrate computers to prospective customers and keep his stock of computers. The rent is £12,000 per annum, payable quarterly in advance. On January 2nd he paid £3,000 for the January–March quarter. Would he therefore include £3,000 in his expenses for January? Answer: *no!* Remember that in the example we ignored cash payments and applied the *matching convention*. Here we ignore the cash payment of £3,000, and match the cost of rent against the period of the account: January. Assuming for practical purposes that each month is one-twelfth of a year, the cost of rent for January is £1,000. (The fact that Thomas paid £3,000 in January means that he has pre-paid £2,000 in respect of February and March. This will be important when we look at balance sheets.)

Business rates (not included in rent)

These are charges by local authorities and usually cover the 12-month period April to March. Many authorities require payment in two instalments, April to September (payable in advance in April) and October to March (payable in advance in October). Some authorities allow payment of one-tenth, payable from, say, March to January. Thomas paid £3,000 last year (1998), for the period October to March. The matching convention requires that we include one-sixth of this in the expenses for January, i.e. £500.

Electricity

Thomas receives a quarterly account from the electricity board, who sent him a bill for £450 on 5 January relating to electricity used for the quarter October to December. Thomas paid this on 30 January. What can we include for electricity for January? Unless Thomas has read his own meter on 31 January, he will not know the actual cost. However, we can estimate the cost at £150, using the last quarter's bill as a basis for the estimate.

Gas for heating

The situation is similar to that for electricity, and we estimate £50, based on previous bills.

Telephone

Thomas finds it easier to pay British Telecom £300 per month by direct debit. Last year, this, in fact, resulted in only a slight overpayment, so we shall include £300 in January's expenses. In this case the cash payment (by direct debit) does correspond with the amount to be included in expenses.

Stationery and postage etc.

This is quite difficult to estimate. In the calendar year 2002, the total amount spent on stationery etc. was £8,476, but costs are likely to increase this year because Thomas is hoping to embark on a mail-shot campaign, costing about £3,500. It would seem reasonable to estimate £1,000 for January.

Cleaning costs

This heading includes for two cleaners costing currently £9,770 per annum, and materials which last year cost £1,848. Allowing for inflation this year, it would seem reasonable to include £1,100 for January.

Insurances

Payment for these can be complicated. Most policies require payment annually in advance, but where, for example, the premium is expressed as a percentage of wages paid, a balancing premium is often payable after the year end, when the amount of wages paid is known. In the case of Thomas, the insurance brokers estimate that the premiums for 2003 are £7,200, i.e £600 per month.

Accountancy and legal fees

These again are irregular payments. However, an estimate for 2003 can be made on the basis of costs in 2002, and, allowing for likely increases in 2003 we estimate £500 per month in 2002, and include this amount for January.

Delivery van expenses

These can be divided under two headings:

a) Those which are paid at long or irregular intervals, for example road tax, insurance, servicing and repairs. These are best totalled for a year; a monthly estimate can then be included in the monthly expenses, for example

	£
Road tax, paid August 2002	100
Insurance, paid August 2002	450
Servicing and repairs, 2002	370
	920

Therefore include for January 2003 (£920 ÷ 12) say £80.

b) Petrol and oil, continuous costs. Thomas pays for these by cash as needed. Therefore there is no reason why the actual payments for January 1999 should not be regarded as the actual costs: £70

Depreciation of van

Depreciation will be discussed in detail in Chapter 12, and we shall include for January £90.

Depreciation of equipment

Again we shall discuss this aspect in Chapter 12, and include for January: £120.

Bad debts and provision for doubtful debts

We shall discuss this in detail in Chapter 13, and we shall include for January: £125 as a provision for a doubtful debt.

Interest on loans and/or overdraft

Thomas has an overdraft. The bank charges interest, which appears quarterly on his bank statement. On his bank statement for December 2002 appeared:

18 Dec   Charges to 4 Dec £470.28

This does not help much with what the charges will be during January, but an estimate can be made by multiplying the average overdraft figures for January by the interest rate, say, £170.

Salaries of sales and technical staff

Thomas employs two staff, and their gross pay plus employer's National Insurance for January was £1,250.

Example

We will now look again at Tenby & Company, and, using the above data concerning Thomas's expenses, prepare a trading and profit-and-loss account for January.

Solution

Tenby & Company
Trading and profit-and-loss account for the month ending 31 January 2003

	£	£
Trading account		
Sales		75,000
Less Cost of sales:		
Opening stock	17,500	
Add Purchases	42,000	
	59,500	
Less Closing stock	7,000	52,500
Gross profit		22,500
Profit-and-loss account		
Less Expenses:		
Rent of premises	1,000	
Rates	500	
Electricity	150	
Gas	50	
Telephone	300	
Stationery	1,000	
Cleaning	1,100	
Insurances	600	
Accountancy and legal fees	500	
Delivery van expenses	150	
Depreciation of van	90	
Depreciation of equipment	120	
Doubtful debt provision	125	
Interest on overdraft	170	
Staff salaries	1,250	7,105
Net profit		15,395

Some students are surprised at all this estimating. They say that they have always assumed that accountants are very precise, and that the accounts prepared by them are correct to the penny. Bookkeeping is precise. Cash paid or received is recorded meticulously. An invoice for £99.99 is for £99.99, no more, no less. Bookkeeping records all the monetary transactions of a business entity. Accounting inevitably requires some estimating.

For example, in the profit-and-loss account for the year to 31 December 2003, electricity charges to 31 November 2003 may be known and recorded. But if the accounts are prepared on 17 January 2004, and the electricity meters have not been read on 31 December 2003, then the quarterly charge for the period 1 December 2003 to 28 February 2004 will not be known, and an estimate of the charges for December 2003 will have to be made and added to the known expenses for the year to 31 December 2003, in order to conform with the matching convention, i.e. the matching of expenses to the period covered by the accounts.

What usually happens, very roughly, in the preparation of accounts such as the profit-and-loss account and the balance sheet, is as follows. The accurate figures resulting from bookkeeping are extracted from the accurately kept records, and are listed down the left-hand side of a large piece of paper. This is known as the *trial balance*. In the middle section of the paper, all kinds of adjustments are made in order to conform with the *matching convention*, and it is here that some estimates have to be made. On the right-hand side of the paper, the accountant, taking the adjustments in the middle section into account, produces the profit-and-loss account for the period under consideration, and the balance sheet as at the date at the end of that period. This working paper is called an *extended trial balance*.

It is the *matching convention* that necessitates the estimating. However, in the long run, any overestimates or underestimates cancel out, and ultimately (for example when the business is wound up) complete accuracy is (or should be) restored.

You should now be able to attempt Questions 10.2 and 10.3 at the end of this chapter.

6 | SUMMARY

Sales (or sales revenue) are recognised when the goods are transferred to the customers, irrespective of when payment is made for them. This is known as the *realisation convention*. Trading profit is calculated as sales less cost of sales. Cost of sales is opening stock plus purchases less closing stock. This conforms to the *matching convention* – the matching of sales with the cost of sales.

Net profit is trading (or gross) profit less expenses. Expenses are those costs that are incurred during the period covered by the profit-and-loss account, irrespective of when payment is made for them. This also conforms to the *matching convention* – the matching of expenses with the period covered by the account.

Bookkeeping is a precise process but accounting inevitably requires some estimating.

You should now be able to attempt Tasks 10.1, 10.2, 10.3 and the objective test at the end of this chapter.

Student activities

Task 10.1

Make a list of the various types of expenses that you think a small business would incur. Tick those that you consider you would know with certainty by the year end. Explain why you would have to do some estimating with the others, and how you would do this.

Task 10.2

The Confederation of British Industry wishes to find out the extent to which sole traders understand the profit-and-loss account. A self-completion questionnaire will be used for the survey. Construct three questions to be included in the questionnaire that you consider would test the understanding of the sole traders.

Task 10.3

You have been asked by a local school to give a speech to sixth formers on the importance of calculating the profit for a business. Write notes for your speech.

Question 10.1

This question follows on from the example of Tenby & Company given in this chapter. During February, Thomas purchases 100 computers, but the price has decreased to £650 per computer. Thomas had been aware that the price decrease was imminent, and had accordingly kept his stocks low. He has informed his customers that his selling price would drop to £950 per computer in February. During February he sold 90 computers. He values his closing stock at the revised purchase price.

Required

Calculate how much gross profit Thomas has made and set out the trading account in a proper format.

Question 10.2

Stephen Milward, trading as Pembroke Croquet Company, has for several years sold medium-priced croquet sets by mail order. For the second quarter (April to June) of 2003, the following details of his business are available:

Opening stock (1 April 2003): 50 sets valued at cost £4,900

Purchases: 200 sets @ £102 each £20,400

Sales, inclusive of postage and packing: 190 sets @ £149 each £28,310

Closing stock is valued at £102 per set

Postage £950

Packing materials £660

Rent of premises (which includes rates) is £3,200 per annum, payable quarterly at the start of each quarter.

Advertising: advertisements are placed regularly in monthly magazines and occasionally in Sunday newspapers. The cost of advertising for the quarter was £1,000

Insurance: this is payable annually early in January, and £840 was paid to insurance brokers on 17 January.

Electricity: Milford pays £50 monthly by direct debit to the electricity company. Last year this system resulted in a slight overpayment for the whole year.

Depreciation of office equipment: this is £480 per annum.

Part-time wages (clerical and packing): amounted to £500

Stationery: costs last year were £500 and are expected to be £60 more this year.

Telephone: a telephone bill received on 4 July recorded:

   quarterly charge 1 July to 30 September: £39.20p

   metered units 28 March to 24 June: 3200 units @ 4.40 pence: £140.80p

Required

Prepare a trading and profit-and-loss account for Stephan Milward business for the three months ending 30 June 2003. All items in this account should be rounded to the nearest £1.

Question 10.3

Alun Owen owns a small concern trading as Llanelli Language Courses that has developed a popular language course in the Welsh language for English-speaking people. The course consists of a set of cassette tapes, tutorial book and dictionary, and a small personal stereo cassette player, all attractively packaged. He buys the package from a manufacturer and sells it by mail order in response to advertisements in selected journals.

Last year (ending 31 December 2002) Mike sold 2,900 packs at £89 each. He started the year with 350 packs, valued at £19,250 and ended the year with a stock of 600 packs. During the year he received 3,150 packs from his manufacturer, who charged him £59 per pack; this price is the figure that Alun uses to value his closing stock.

Alun employs part-time staff, and their salaries and wages totalled £14,500. Postages worked out at £2 per pack sold, and packing at 50 pence per pack sold. Alun rented a small warehouse at £1,000 per month.

Advertising bills totalled £15,000 and an invoice for a further £500 is still awaited.

Insurance premiums paid were £3,500, but of this amount £650 refers to the current year, 2003.

Bills for power, light and heat have been received for £2,900, with a further bill for the last quarter of 2002 expected to be approximately £500.

Alun uses a computer for administrative and customer records, and this, together with word-processing equipment, cost £4,000 in 2000. Alun reckons this equipment will last about five years, so he allows £800 per annum in his accounts for depreciation. In addition to this, his stationery bill totalled £1,350.

During 2002, he received four telephone bills, totalling £3,500, of which £200 relates to rental in advance for 2003. In the previous year (2001) rental in advance of £150 (relating to the first quarter of 2002) had been deducted from the bills for 2001 in arriving at the expenses for 2001.

Alun also spent £5,100 on research and development of his product, which resulted in minor improvements to his language pack, with work well advanced on a new edition of the pack, planned for 1994. Alun's policy on research and development is to write off all expenditure in the year in which it is incurred; he feels this is prudent, since research work may not prove to be productive.

Mike's accountants are very busy, and are not expected to produce figures for 2002 until next month. Mike asks you to give him an idea of his profit for 2002.

Required

Prepare a trading and profit-and-loss account for Llanelli Language Courses for the year ending 31 December 2002.

Objective test (tick the appropriate box)

i)   The trading account of a business shows:

    a)   the cash left after sales less cost of sales ☐

    b)   the gross profit of a business ☐

    c)   the net profit of a business ☐

    d)   none of these ☐

ii)   Cost of goods sold requires, for its correct calculation, inclusion of:

    a)   all expenses, suitably matched for the period ☐

    b)   all expenses, suitably matched for the period, but excluding depreciation ☐

    c)   all expenses, suitably matched for the period, but excluding depreciation, plus the cost of goods purchased ☐

    d)   closing stock of goods ☐

iii)   The realisation convention in the trading account means that profit is only realised when:

    a)   cash is received and paid ☐

    b)   goods are paid for ☐

    c)   goods are sold ☐

    d)   expenses are correctly matched ☐

iv)   The matching convention requires that for any specified period:

    a)   revenues should be matched with associated costs ☐

    b)   cash receipts and payments should refer only to that period ☐

    c)   expenses paid should relate to the appropriate revenues ☐

    d)   all costs for that period should relate only to the purchases for that period ☐

v)   For company X, electricity charges for the period April 2002 to March 2003 were £2,743. At the end of April 2003, no account has been received. The meter has not been read, and the electricity company has stated that charges are to be increased by 5 per cent as from 1 April 2003. Consumption of electricity does not fluctuate significantly from month to month. The amount to be included as an expense in the profit-and-loss account for the month of April 2003 is:

a) £ 228 ☐

b) £ 342 ☐

c) £ 240 ☐

d) £ 230 ☐

CHAPTER 11

Balance sheet

1 | OBJECTIVES

At the end of this chapter, you should be able to:

- explain what is meant by the accounting equation;
- define such terms as assets and liabilities;
- describe the purpose of a balance sheet;
- construct a simple balance sheet for a sole trader.

2 | INTRODUCTION

For any business to operate, it needs *resources* which may include the following:

- the *premises* that the business owns and from which it operates;
- *equipment*, *plant* and *machinery*, so that production and/or trading can take place;
- *desks*, *telephones* and other *furniture* and *equipment*, so that administration, selling and distribution departments can operate;
- *stocks* of *raw materials* will be required by a manufacturer, so that these can be turned into finished goods for resale;
- *stocks* of *goods* for sale will be required by a trader, whether wholesaler or retailer;
- *cash* will be needed to buy any of the above items.

3 | THE ACCOUNTING EQUATION

All the above *resources* are known as *assets*. For a new business to acquire *assets*, it will have to obtain some money. Usually, it is the *owner* of the business who is the main source of such money.

The money supplied by the owner is known as the business *capital*, and the *business* will owe this *capital* to the *owner*. Capital is therefore a *liability* of the business, something for which the business is liable to the owner who supplied it. If no person, other than the owner, has supplied funds to the business, then:

$$Assets = Capital$$

In addition to the owner, other people may lend money to the business. For example:

- a bank may approve a loan or agree to an overdraft;

- suppliers of *raw materials* or *goods for resale* may supply goods but grant credit arrangements whereby the business does not have to pay until some agreed date. Until payment is made, these suppliers are known as *creditors*.

These sources of funds are known generally as *liabilities*.

At any one point in time, all the *assets* owned by the business will exactly equal the amount of the *capital* supplied by the owner plus all these other outstanding *liabilities*. This relationship is known as the *accounting equation* and can be expressed thus:

$$Assets = Capital + Liabilities$$

This *accounting equation* always holds true. If we know any two of the three items in the accounting equation, we can calculate the third.

A business cannot increase its total *assets* without increasing its total of *capital* and *liabilities*. An *individual* asset can increase (for example, stocks can increase), but only if capital or a liability also increases, or if another asset decreases by a similar amount. This principle is known as the *dual nature of transactions* and can be illustrated by the following example.

Example

Complete the columns below to show the effect of the following transactions for the business known as Pier Supplies, owned by F. Shastri.

You should enter the names of the assets or liabilities that you think are affected by the transaction in the appropriate column, showing whether they have increased or decreased. We have done the first one for you.

	Transaction	Assets	Capital	Liabilities
a)	Pier Supplies buys a delivery van on credit	+ Van		+ Creditors
b)	Pier Supplies repays a loan paying cash			
c)	Pier Supplies buys stock, paying by cheque			
d)	F. Shastri takes some cash out of the business for a holiday			

Solution

	Assets	Capital	Liabilities
a)	+ Van		+ Creditors
b)	– Cash	– Loan	
c)	+ Stock		
	– Bank		
d)	– Cash	– Capital	

You should now be able to attempt Questions 11.1, 11.2 and 11.3 at the end of this chapter.

4 | THE BALANCE SHEET

A *balance sheet* is a statement of the financial position of a business at *one point in time*. It shows in greater detail the financial relationship expressed by the *accounting equation* and details the *assets* owned by the business and its *capital* and *liabilities*. In this chapter we shall use the *horizontal format* of presentation: *assets* on the left-hand side, and *capital* and *liabilities* on the right-hand side. There are other formats for presenting the balance sheet, but we shall leave these until a later chapter. The *horizontal format* is easy to understand at this stage, because it reflects the *accounting equation*.

The following worked example will consolidate what you have learned so far, and illustrate how balance sheets can be presented to show the day-to-day progress of the business.

Example

1. B. Sinha starts a business known as Rambal & Company on 1 January 2002 with £10,000.

   If we describe the business by using the accounting equation, we can see that the business will have an asset (cash) of £10,000, which will equal the capital supplied by the owner. On the balance sheet this will be shown as follows:

Rambal & Company
Balance sheet as at 1 January 2002

	£		£
Cash	10,000	*Capital*	10,000

2. On 2 January the business purchases fixtures for £5,500 and stock of goods for £3,500.

Rambal & Company
Balance sheet as at 2 January 2002

	£	£		£
Fixed assets			*Capital*	10,000
Fixtures		5,500		
Current assets				
Stock	3,500			
Cash	1,000	4,500		
		10,000		10,000

Note that the assets have been classified into *fixed assets*, those resources that the business means to keep in the long term, and *current assets*, such as stock and cash, which are items that are part of the trading cycle, and that will be used up in the day-to-day activities.

3. On 3 January, the business buys a further £1,000 of stock, but does not pay the supplier, and therefore incurs the liability of having a trade creditor

Rambal & Company
Balance sheet as at 3 January 2002

Fixed assets	£	£	Capital	£ 10,000
Fixtures		5,500		
Current assets			Current liabilities	
Stock	4,500		Trade creditors	1,000
Cash	1,000	5,500		
		11,000		11,000

4. On 4 January the business sells for £3,000 in cash stock which it purchased for £2,500.

Rambal & Company
Balance sheet as at 4 January 2002

Fixed assets	£	£	Capital	£ 10,000
Fixtures		5,500	Profit	500
Current assets			Current liabilities	
Stock	2,000		Trade creditors	1,000
Cash	4,000	6,000		11,500
		11,500		11,500

Note that the profit of £500 earned on the stock (sales £3,000 less cost of sales £2,500) belongs to the owner of the business and, as we are dealing with the accounts of a sole trader, the amount of profit is shown as an addition to his capital. In other words, the business (Rambal & Company) now has a new liability of profit, which it, owes to the owner, B. Sinha.

5. On 5 January the business purchases equipment of £1,000 for cash, and a further £4,500 of stock on credit.

Rambal & Company
Balance sheet as at 5 January 2002

Fixed assets	£	£	Capital	£ 10,000
Fixtures	5,500		Profit	500
Equipment	1,000	6,500		
Current assets			Current liabilities	
Stock	6,500		Trade creditors	5,500
Cash	3,000	9,500		
		16,000		16,000

6. On 6 January:

a) the owner of the business, B. Sinha, withdraws £200 cash for his own use, and

143

b) the business sells £3,000 worth of stock for £4,000 to customers on credit: these customers are expected to pay the amount they owe in one month's time. Until they pay, they are known as debtors to the business.

Rambal & Company
Balance sheet as at 6 January 2002

	£	£		£	£
Fixed assets			Capital		10,000
Fixtures	5,500		Previous profit	500	
Equipment	1,000	6,500	New profit	1,000	1,500
Current assets					11,500
Stock	3,500				
Debtors	4,000		*Less:* Drawings		200
Cash	2,800	10,300			11,300
			Current liabilities		
			Trade creditors		5,500
		16,800			16,800

You should now be able to attempt Tasks 11.1 and 11.2 at the end of this chapter.

5 CONSTRUCTING A BALANCE SHEET

The following is a useful procedure for constructing a balance sheet for a sole trader.

1. Identify and list all the assets of the business.

2. Identify and list all the capital and liabilities of the business.

3. Ensure that the total of assets = capital + liabilities.

4. Head up paper with name of the business *and* 'Balance sheet as at ...', ensuring that you put in the correct date.

5. On the *left-hand side* of the balance sheet:

   • Divide the assets into *fixed* and *current*.

   • List the assets within each group in the order of permanence, i.e. start with the most permanent asset (for example, land) and finish with the least permanent asset, usually cash.

   • It is usual to show a sub-total for each group.

6. On the *right-hand side* of the balance sheet:

   • Show the amount of *capital*. Add any profit and deduct any drawings.

144

- Next, show any long-term liabilities, for example bank loans for over one year.

- Finally, list current liabilities under the appropriate headings, and subtotal them.

7. Total both sides of the balance sheet on the same line, even if this means leaving a space on one side.

8. Ensure that the totals agree.

Example

Draw up a balance sheet for Audrey Wong as at 31 March 1998, from the following information:

	£
Capital	16,000
Machinery	10,500
Creditors	1,150
Stock	2,150
Debtors	620
Bank balance	6,840
Loan from S. Seaford	2,960

Solution

Audrey Wong
Balance sheet as at 31 March 1998

	£	£		£
Fixed assets			*Capital*	16,000
Machinery		10,500		
Current assets			Loan	2,960
Stock	2,150			
Debtors	620		*Current liabilities*	
Bank	6,840	9,610	Creditors	1,150
		20,110		20,110

6 DEDUCING THE AMOUNT OF CAPITAL

If the figure of capital is not given in the question, the procedure is as follows:

1. List all the assets of the business, and total.

2. List all the liabilities of the business, and total.

3. Remembering the accounting equation, deduct the liabilities from the assets, and the balance will represent the capital.

Example

L. Assaf sets himself up in a new business. Before starting trading, he buys:

Motor lorries:	£30,000
Premises:	£60,000
Stock:	£8,000

He still owes £3,000 in respect of the above stock purchase.

He has borrowed £25,000 from P. Pevensey.

After these events, and before starting trading, he has £1,000 cash in hand, and £9,000 cash at his bank.

Required

Calculate the amount of Assaf's capital at the start of trading.

Solution

L. Assaf

Balance sheet as at start of trading

	£	£		£
Fixed assets			*Capital*	X
Premises	60,000			
Motor lorries	30,000	90,000	Loan	25,000
Current assets			*Current liabilities*	
Stock	8,000		Creditors	3,000
Bank	9,000			
Cash	1,000	18,000		
		108,000		X + 28,000

As capital + liabilities = assets, X + £28,000 = £108,000

Therefore X (capital) = £80,000.

> *You should now be able to attempt Question 11.4 at the end of this chapter.*

---

7   THE IMPACT OF TRANSACTIONS

A balance sheet reflects the financial position of a business *at one point in time*. The next transaction undertaken by the business will alter the previous balance sheet.

Example

In this question, you are given the balance sheet for L. Haque at 30 June 2002. There follows a list of transactions. You are required to draw up a new balance sheet after each transaction, five balance sheets in all.

L. Haque
Balance sheet as at 30 June 1998

	£	£		£
Fixed assets			Capital	146,000
Buildings	65,000			
Vehicles	35,000	100,000	Loan	24,000
Current assets			*Current liabilities*	
Stock	22,000		Creditors	10,000
Debtors	38,000			
Bank	20,000	80,000		
		180,000		180,000

The following transactions take place:

a) 2 July   Haque pays £4,000 to a creditor.

b) 4 July   Haque buys some more stock on credit for £9,000.

c) 6 July   Haque buys office equipment for £8,000 by cheque.

d) 8 July   A debtor pays Haque £3,000 by cheque.

e) 10 July   Haque pays off £10,000 of the loan by cheque.

Solution

L. Haque
Balance sheet as at 2 July 2002

	£	£		£
Fixed assets			Capital	146,000
Buildings	65,000			
Vehicles	35,000	100,000	Loan	24,000
Current assets			*Current liabilities*	
Stock	22,000		Creditors	6,000
Debtors	38,000			
Bank	16,000	76,000		
		176,000		176,000

L. Haque
Balance sheet as at 4 July 2002

	£	£		£
Fixed assets			Capital	146,000
Buildings	65,000			
Vehicles	35,000	100,000	Loan	24,000
Current assets			*Current liabilities*	
Stock	31,000		Creditors	15,000
Debtors	38,000			
Bank	16,000	85,000		
		185,000		185,000

L. Haque
Balance sheet as at 6 July 2002

	£	£		£
Fixed assets			Capital	146,000
Buildings	65,000			
Vehicles	35,000		Loan	24,000
Office equipment	8,000	108,000		
Current assets			*Current liabilities*	
Stock	31,000		Creditors	15,000
Debtors	38,000			
Bank	8,000	77,000		
		185,000		185,000

L. Haque
Balance sheet as at 8 July 2002

	£	£		£
Fixed assets			Capital	146,000
Buildings	65,000			
Vehicles	35,000		Loan	24,000
Office equipment	8,000	108,000		
Current assets			*Current liabilities*	
Stock	31,000		Creditors	15,000
Debtors	35,000			
Bank	11,000	77,000		
		185,000		185,000

L. Haque
Balance sheet as at 10 July 2002

	£	£		£
Fixed assets			Capital	146,000
Buildings	65,000			
Vehicles	35,000		Loan	14,000
Office equipment	8,000	108,000		
Current assets			*Current liabilities*	
Stock	31,000		Creditors	15,000
Debtors	35,000			
Bank	1,000	67,000		
		175,000		175,000

Instead of drawing up a balance sheet after each transaction, you could make pencil adjustments to the original balance sheet for each of the items affected. Note that *two* adjustments are required for each transaction. This method would show the *cumulative* effect of all the transactions on every item upon the balance sheet. For instance, in the above example, the bank figure changes like this:

			£
	Bank at 30 June		20,000
2 July	Cheque paid to creditor	*(deduct)*	4,000
			16,000
4 July	No change		–
			16,000
6 July	Cheque paid for office equipment	*(deduct)*	8,000
			8,000
8 July	Payment received from debtor	*(add)*	3,000
			11,000
10 July	Cheque paid to reduce loan	*(deduct)*	10,000
			1,000

The final figure of £1,000 is the same as your figure on the final balance sheet. You could have pencilled in these changes against the item of Bank on the original balance sheet, like this:

$$£20,000 - £4,000 - £8,000 + £3,000 - £10,000 = £1,000.$$

> *You should now be able to attempt Task 11.3 and Questions 11.5 and 11.6 at the end of this chapter.*

8   SUMMARY

Assets are resources which the business owns or has use of. *Capital* is money invested in the business by the owner. *Liabilities* are monies owed by the business. The *accounting equation* demonstrates the relationship between assets, capital and liabilities:

Assets – Capital ı Liabilities

A balance sheet is a statement of the financial position of the business at any *one point in time*. The most common mistakes made by students when drawing up a balance sheet are:

- not heading up the balance sheet with owner's name or the name of the business, and the date of the balance sheet;
- not correctly identifying assets and liabilities;
- forgetting how to calculate the capital figure, if this is not given;
- not listing the assets and liabilities correctly within their respective groups.

> *You should now be able to attempt the objective test at the end of this chapter.*

Student activities

Task 11.1
The following advertisement has appeared in an accounting magazine.

Required
Submit your entry to the competition.

Grand Christmas Competition
Write a humorous poem or piece of prose

The writer of the best entry concerned with balance sheets will receive a prize of a leather-bound cash book. All entries should be received by 5 April. The judges' assessment will be final. Length limit: 200 words

---

Task 11.2
At a recent meeting, the chief accountant of the company you work for referred to the balance sheet as 'a financial snapshot of the business'. One of the marketing managers asked you after the meeting what this phrase meant. Send him a memorandum giving a clear explanation.

Task 11.3
You work for a training company that is developing an open learning course for students. One unit is an introduction to balance sheets. Construct a glossary of the main terms found on the balance sheet for inclusion in the unit.

Question 11.1
Complete the gaps in the following table. The answers to (a) and (b) have been placed in square brackets to show you the idea.

	Assets £	Capital £	Liabilities £
a)	13,000	[8,000]	5,000
b)	15,500	7,500	[8,000]
c)	8,000		2,700
d)	9,700	2,800	
e)		11,900	6,400
f)	42,000		19,700
g)	119,400	43,900	
h)		15,632	14,739

Question 11.2
Classify the following business items into assets, capital and liabilities by ticking the appropriate column:

	Assets	Capital	Liabilities
Motor vehicles			
Loan from bank			
Cash at bank			
Fixtures and fittings			
Cash in hand			
Overdraft			
Creditors			
Machinery			
Stock of raw materials			
Owner's stake in the business			
Loan from owner's brother			

Question 11.3

Complete the columns below to show the effect of the following transactions for a business owned by Gino Brusso, who runs an ice-cream van business known as Ideal Ice-cream. Follow the same instructions as for F. Shastri in Section 11.3.

	Assets	Capital	Liabilities
a) Gino Brusso increases the capital of his business by paying £1,000 of his own money into Ideal Ice-cream's bank account.			
b) Ideal Ice-cream sells an old van for cash.			
c) Ideal Ice-cream buys a supply of cornets on credit.			
d) Gino Brusso takes home some ice-cream for his daughter's birthday party.			
e) Ideal Ice-cream pays by cheque the supplier who provided the cornets in (c) above.			

Question 11.4

Draw up the balance sheet of Cathy Chen at 31 December 2002, from the following items:

	£		£
Lorries	47,000	Buildings	50,000
Loan (long-term)	32,000	Balance at bank	6,000
Stocks	17,000	Creditors	15,000
Cash in hand	2,000	Debtors	21,000

You will have to deduce the amount of capital.

Question 11.5

Ann Josic has the following items in her balance sheet as at 31 March 2003:

	£
Capital	85,000
Creditors	5,000
Loan from A. Lauzon	15,000
Fixtures and fittings	45,000
Stocks	24,000
Debtors	17,000
Bank balance	19,000

During the first week of April, A. Josic did the following:

- Bought more stock on credit for £7,000.
- Repaid A. Lauzon all she owed him.
- Collected a cheque for £7,000 from a debtor.
- Bought more fixtures and fittings, paying £5,000 for them by cheque.
- Paid one of her creditors £3,000 by cheque.

Required

Draw up the balance sheet for Ann Josic as at 7 April, after all the above transactions have been taken into account.

Question 11.6

Brennan Nantais is a wholesaler trader in railway memorabilia. At 30 June 2002; he had a balance sheet which showed the following items:

	£
Capital	100,000
Long-term loan from S. Shaban	20,000
Overdraft at bank	2,000
Trade and other creditors	18,000
Debtors	17,000
Stocks	9,000
Delivery van (at book value)	12,000
Fixtures and fittings	8,000
Warehouse and offices	94,000

During the three months ending 30 September, the following transactions were recorded:

- Purchased £63,000 worth of stock on credit.
- Sold £55,000 worth of stock to his credit customers for £86,000.
- Received £83,000 from his credit customers, all of which he paid into the bank.
- Paid off £5,000 of his long-term loan from S. Shaban.
- Paid his trade creditors £59,000.
- Bought (and paid for) some new fixtures and fittings for £4,000.

- Traded in his old van for its book value and bought a new van for £15,000, paying the balance by cheque.
- Paid out £11,000 in expenses, all of which were chargeable against profits.

Required

Draw up the balance sheet for Brennan Nantais's business as at 30 September 2002, after all the above transactions have been taken into account.

Objective test (tick the appropriate box)

i)   On a horizontal-style balance sheet, the figure of capital will appear:

   a)   at the top on the left-hand side ☐

   b)   under fixed assets ☐

   c)   under current liabilities ☐

   d)   at the top on the right-hand side ☐

ii) The horizontal-style balance sheet shows:

   a)   assets on the right-hand side ☐

   b)   capital and liabilities on the right-hand side ☐

   c)   capital and liabilities on the left-hand side ☐

   d)   assets and capital on the left-hand side ☐

iii) Those items which a business owns or has use of in the long term are known as:

   a)   current assets ☐

   b)   capital ☐

   c)   current liabilities ☐

   d)   fixed assets ☐

iv) If a business purchases a motor van (which it intends to use in the business) on credit, the van will be classified as a:

   a)   current liability ☐

   b)   current asset ☐

   c)   fixed asset ☐

   d)   long-term liability ☐

v)   A business buys equipment for £5,000 on credit. The effect of this transaction will be to:

   a)   increase assets and decrease liabilities ☐

   b)   increase assets and increase liabilities ☐

c) decrease assets and decrease liabilities ☐

d) decrease assets and increase liabilities ☐

vi) A business sells part of its factory premises, and is paid £5,000. The effect of this transaction will be to:

a) decrease fixed assets and decrease capital ☐

b) decrease fixed assets and increase cash ☐

c) decrease fixed assets and decrease cash ☐

d) increase fixed assets and increase capital ☐

vii) If the figure of capital is missing in a question, it may be found by:

a) adding fixed assets and current assets ☐

b) deducting liabilities from total assets ☐

c) adding liabilities to total assets ☐

d) deducting liabilities from current assets ☐

viii) A business has assets of £15,000 and liabilities of £8,000. The capital is therefore:

a) £23,000 ☐

b) £7,000 ☐

c) £8,000 ☐

d) £15,000 ☐

ix) A business has fixed assets valued at £5,000, current liabilities of £4,000 and current assets of £3,000. Its capital is therefore:

a) £12,000 ☐

b) £4,000 ☐

c) £6,000 ☐

d) £7,000 ☐

x) A business has capital of £12,200, fixed assets of £8,050 and current liabilities of £2,250. The value of its current assets is therefore:

a) £4,150 ☐

b) £14,450 ☐

c) £6,400 ☐

d) £5,800 ☐

CHAPTER 12

Presentation and principles

1 OBJECTIVES

At the end of this chapter you should be able to:

- understand and prepare a balance sheet in vertical format for a sole trader;
- differentiate between accruals and prepayments, and incorporate them correctly in the accounts of a sole trader;
- prepare trading and profit-and-loss accounts and balance sheets, including the correct treatment of:

  bank balances;

  carriage inwards and carriage outwards;

  drawings;

  discounts allowed and discounts received;

  returns inwards and returns outwards;

  rents receivable.

2 INTRODUCTION

In Chapter 11, we presented the balance sheet of a sole trader in what is known as the *horizontal format*, with assets in a column on the left and liabilities on the right. In this chapter we shall look at the *vertical format* where all items, both *assets* and *liabilities*, are set out according to accepted conventions in columnar form *down* the page. We shall also consider other principles that are important to an understanding of profit-and-loss accounts and balance sheets.

3 VERTICAL FORMAT OF THE BALANCE SHEET

We said in the previous chapter that the horizontal format of the balance sheet had the advantage of reflecting the *accounting equation*. However, sometimes we may wish to communicate clearly other important facts on the balance sheet. We may wish to show how much money has, in total, been invested in the fixed assets combined with the working capital (current assets less current liabilities). This cannot be found immediately on a horizontal type of balance sheet without calculation, deducting the current liabilities on the right-hand side from the total assets on the left-hand side. Many businesses now use the vertical format of balance sheet because it is possible to provide this information more easily than in the horizontal format.

In Chapter 11, we considered the balance sheets of Rambal & Company. Here is the balance sheet as at 6 January 2002, in *horizontal format*.

Example

Rambal & Company
Balance sheet as at 6 January 2002

	£	£		£	£
Fixed assets			*Capital*		10,000
Fixtures	5,500		Previous profit	500	
Equipment	1,000	6,500	New profit	1,000	1,500
Current assets					
Stock	3,500				11,500
Debtors	4,000		*Less* Drawings		200
Cash	2,800	10,300			11,300
			Current liabilities		
			Trade creditors		5,500
		16,800			16,800

Now we shall re-present it in *vertical format*:

Rambal & Company
Balance sheet as at 6 January 2002

	£	£	£
Fixed assets			
Fixtures		5,500	
Equipment		1,000	6,500
Current assets			
Stock	3,500		
Debtors	4,000		
Cash	2,800	10,300	
Less Current liabilities			
Trade creditors		5,500	
Working capital (or *Net current assets*)			4,800
Capital employed			11,300
Represented by (or financed by):			
Capital			10,000
Add Previous profit		500	
New profit		1,000	
		1,500	
Less Drawings		200	1,300
			11,300

Compare Figure 12.1 with the figures for Rambal & Company above.

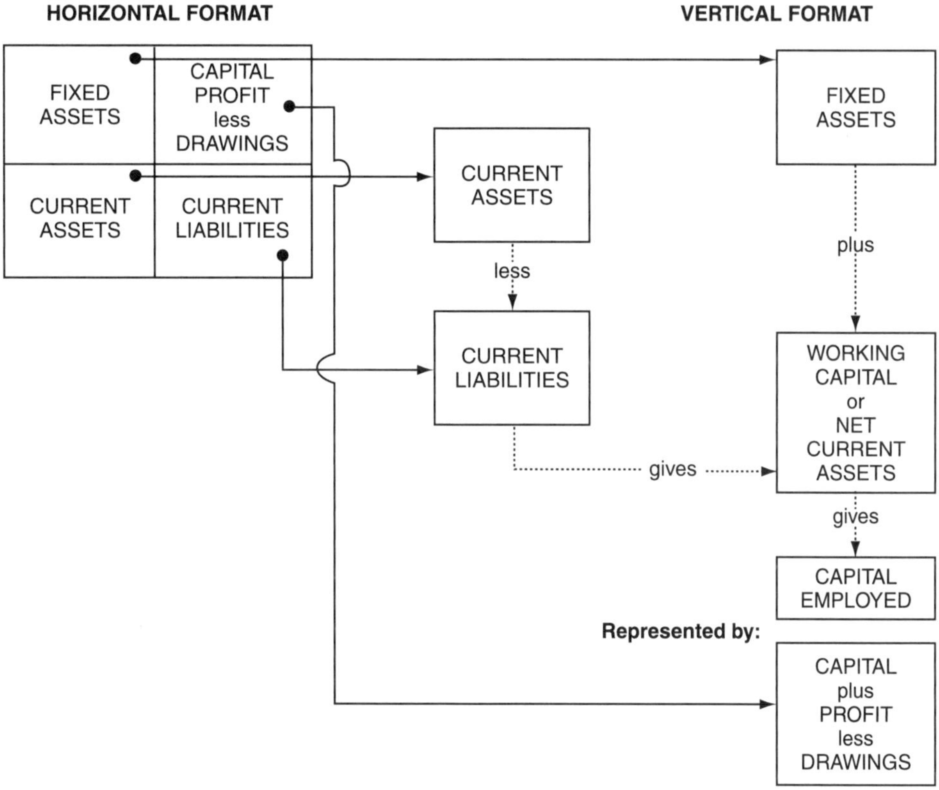

Figure 12.1 *Horizontal and vertical formats compared*

You should notice the following differences between the two formats:

Horizontal	Vertical
i) The total of the left-hand side shows the *total assets* (*fixed* plus *current*). The total of the right-hand side shows *total liabilities* (*long-term* plus *current*).	i) The total of the top half shows the *capital employed* (*total assets* less *current liabilities*). The total of the bottom half shows the *owner's worth* (which is the same figure as *capital employed*).
ii) *Working capital* (also known as *net current assets*) is *not* shown. (You would have to work it out by deducting *current liabilities* from *current assets*.)	ii) *Working capital* is shown as a deduction of *current liabilities* from *current assets*.

continued overleaf

157

Horizontal	Vertical
iii) Offset figures (to show sub-totals clearly) are not as pronounced as in the vertical format.	iii) Offset figures are employed to the extent of using three (or even four) columns. For example: *Current assets* are listed in the third column from the right, with a sub-total in the second column from the right. This enables the sub-total for *current liabilities* to be deducted from that for current assets and the result shown in the last column. This result (the *working capital*) can then be added to the total for *fixed assets*, to give the *capital employed*.

Example

In Chapter 11 the balance sheet for L. Haque on 10 July 2002 was as follows:

Balance sheet as at 10 July 2002

	£	£		£
Fixed assets			*Capital*	146,000
Buildings	65,000			
Vehicles	35,000		*Loan*	14,000
Office equipment	8,000	108,000		
Current assets			*Current liabilities*	
Stock	31,000		Creditors	15,000
Debtors	35,000			
Bank	1,000	67,000		
		175,000		175,000

Required

Represent this balance sheet in vertical format.

Solution

L. Haque
Balance sheet as at 10 July 2002

	£	£	£
Fixed assets			
Buildings		65,000	
Vehicles		35,000	
Office equipment		8,000	108,000
Current assets			
Stock	31,000		
Debtors	35,000		
Bank	1,000	67,000	

continued

Current liabilities		
Creditors	15,000	
Net current assets (or Working capital)		52,000
Capital employed		160,000
Less Loan		14,000
		146,000
Represented by:		
Capital		146,000

4 LOANS

When you attempted this question, you may have wondered where to put the *loan* of £14,000. You may have shown it like this:

	£	£
Capital employed		160,000
Represented by:		
Capital	146,000	
Loan	14,000	160,000

It may seem that this is is a satisfactory presentation because it shows the calculation of capital employed (fixed assets plus working capital), and how it has been financed (capital plus loans). However, the presentation in the answer is the one that conforms with commonly accepted practice. You will see that the first figure of £146,000 is the capital employed *less* the loan, and the second figure of £146,000 is the capital. The idea of this is to show the *inside* financing of the business, which the owner of the business has provided (*capital*) and the retained profit which has accrued to that capital. The *loan* is *outside* financing, which has been provided by a party other than the owner, for example by a bank or finance house. Thus the second total of £146,000 shows what the owner is worth, and the first figure of £146,000 shows all the assets less all the liabilities, both short-term (current liabilities) and long-term (loans).

You will note that *creditors* are classified as a current liability, whereas the *loan* is a long-term liability. The distinction between the two is that:

• *current liabilities* represent *creditors*: amounts due within one year;
• *long-term liabilities* represent *creditors*: amounts due after more than one year.

In fact, in the reports and accounts issued annually by public limited companies to their shareholders, these definitions are very often printed, rather than the shorter titles of current liabilities and long-term liabilities. When we consider the balance sheets of public limited companies later, we shall use the longer titles to conform with accepted practice.

In this chapter we are dealing with the accounts of sole traders. But there is no reason why we should not conform with what is now considered to be customary formats of presentation.

> *You should now be able to attempt Task 12.1 and Question 12.1 at the end of this chapter.*

5   CAPITAL AND REVENUE EXPENDITURE

It is important to distinguish between *capital expenditure* and *revenue expenditure*. *Capital expenditure* relates mainly to *fixed assets*, assets that are not completely used within a financial year. For example, machinery: the cost of buying it, transporting it in, installing it and subsequently modifying or improving it. This type of expenditure appears on the *balance sheet*, under the heading of *fixed assets*.

    Revenue expenditure relates to day-to-day running costs, such as wages and salaries, rent and rates, insurances, heating and lighting, and so forth. For example, machinery: running costs, maintenance and repairs. This type of expenditure appears in the *trading* and *profit-and-loss account*. We examine this in greater detail in a subsequent chapter.

6   DRAWINGS

Drawings are an appropriation of the owner's profit. They represent what the owner has drawn out of the business *for his or her own personal use*, both cash and other assets such as stock. They therefore represent a reduction of capital, just as profit represents an addition to capital. They are shown on the balance sheet as a deduction from the opening capital, to which may have been added any net profit for the period covered by the profit-and-loss account.

    For an example of presentation, look back at the balance sheet of Rambal & Company as at 6 January 2002 earlier in this chapter.

7   ACCRUALS

Accruals arise as a result of the *matching convention* discussed in Chapter 4.

Example

Accounts are prepared to 31 December 2003. The last invoice received for electricity was for the period to 30 November 2003. Estimated electricity cost for December is £500.

Profit and loss account: Add £500 to the expense of electricity.

Balance sheet: Show £500 as an accrual under current liabilities.

Sometimes accruals are grouped together with creditors as creditors and accruals.

8 PREPAYMENTS

Prepayments also arise as a result of the *matching convention* discussed in Chapter 4.

Example

Accounts are prepared to 31 December 2003. Rates for the period 1 October 2003 to 31 March 2004 were paid on 6 October 2003, in the sum of £2,000. Since £1,000 of this sum refers to the period 1 January 2004 to 31 March 2004:

Profit-and-loss account: Deduct £1,000 from the expense of rates.

Balance sheet: Show £1,000 as a prepayment under current assets.

Sometimes prepayments are grouped together with debtors as 'debtors and prepayments'.

9 BANK BALANCE

If there is money in the bank, show this as *bank* under current assets on the balance sheet. If there is an overdraft, show this as a current liability. An overdraft, which can be recalled at any time, is usually shown as a current liability, even if in practice the facility is available for more than one year. Loans are usually secured on the assets of the business, and are usually for periods in excess of one year, in which case they are treated as long-term, and deducted from the capital employed as described earlier in this chapter.

10 STOCK VALUATION

The general rule given in Accounting Standards is that closing stock values should be shown on the profit-and-loss account and in the balance sheet at the lower of cost or net realisable value. Cost is the amount incurred in bringing the stock to the state and condition existing at the date of the stock valuation. Net realisable value is the income the stocks will generate if sold less any costs in getting the stock to the customers.

Usually the net realisable value will be higher than the cost because the business hopes to sell its goods at a profit, but sometimes the net realisable value may be lower. For example, a trader may have bought some toys at £15 each, hoping to sell them for £20 each. The demand for toys drops dramatically by the time the trader is preparing the profit-and-loss account and balance sheet and he considers that he could sell the toys for £12 each. This is their net realisable value and, as it is lower than the cost of £15 each, it will form the basis for the closing stock values to be shown on the profit-and-loss account and balance sheet.

Determining the cost of stock can prove a problem if prices are fluctuating. Assume that a trader buys ten items at £5 each from his wholesaler in May. In June a further eight items are purchased, but the price has now increased to £6 for each item. If the trader then sells 15 of the items the question arises as to what is the cost of the three items unsold for calculating the stock values. Is the correct figure for the stock values three items at £5 each or three items at £6 each? There are a number of approaches accountants use to resolve this dilemma, including the calculation of an 'average' cost. In the UK we tend to use a method known as First In, First Out (FIFO). We assume that the items purchased first will be the ones sold first. Any unsold items will therefore be the last ones we bought and in our example the stock value would be three items at £6 each = £18.

In the examples we have used we have concentrated on the business of a trader; the buying and selling of goods. The problems of stock valuation at the end of a financial period become more difficult if we look at a manufacturing organisation. At the year end there will be not only finished goods waiting to be sold, but raw materials waiting manufacture into the finished product, and also work-in-progress where the manufacturing process is only part complete. For example, a car manufacturer will have a stock of partly finished cars that require engines, wheels or electrics to complete them. Although stock valuation in these circumstances is complex, the general rule of of valuing stock at the lower of cost or net realisable value must be applied.

11   PROFIT-AND-LOSS ACCOUNT ITEMS

There are a number of items that need to be shown on the *profit-and-loss account* in a particular way. It is not possible to give a list of everything you might meet, but listed below are the most common ones.

- *Carriage outwards*
  This represents the cost of delivery of finished goods to customers. Show as an expense in the profit-and-loss account.

- *Carriage inwards*
  This represents the cost of bringing in goods, raw materials, etc. Add to the cost of purchases in the trading account.

- *Discounts allowed*
  These are discounts allowed to debtors. They are deducted by customers from the balances due for sales when paying their accounts. Show as an expense in the profit-and-loss account.

- *Discounts received*
  These are discounts which a business has deducted from balances payable for purchases, effectively reducing the cost of those purchases. Add to the gross profit in the trading account.

- *Returns inwards*
  These are goods which have been returned by customers for various reasons. For example, they may be faulty or unsuitable. They can therefore be regarded as a reduction of sales. Deduct from sales in the trading account.

- *Returns outwards*
  These are goods which a business returns to suppliers for various reasons. For example, they may be faulty or unsuitable. They can therefore be regarded as a reduction of purchases. Deduct from purchases in the trading account.

- *Rents receivable*
  A business may let some of its premises to a third party. Such rent is not part of normal manufacturing or trading income. It should not therefore be shown as sales income. Add to gross profit in the trading account.

- *Depreciation*
  This deserves separate consideration and is discussed in Chapter 12.

- *Bad debts and provision for doubtful debts*
  These also deserve separate consideration and are discussed in Chapter 13.

12 | TRIAL BALANCE AND FINAL ACCOUNTS

In Chapter 8 we explained how to construct a *trial balance* at the end of a *financial* period. This is a preliminary to drawing up the *final accounts* of a business.

Example

The following trial balance has been drawn up from the accounts of *End Pages Bookshop*

End Pages Bookshop
Trial balance as at 31 December 2003

	£	£
Sales		151,500
Purchases	103,500	
Salaries and wages	18,700	
Office expenses	2,500	
Insurance	1,100	
Electricity	600	
Stationery	2,400	
Advertising	3,500	
Telephone	800	
Rates	3,000	

continued

	£	£
Discounts allowed	100	
Discounts received		200
Rent received		2,000
Returns inwards	1,500	
Returns outward		3,500
Opening stock as at 1 January 2003	46,000	
Premises	80,000	
Fixtures and fittings	5,000	
Debtors and creditors	4,800	7,500
Cash in hand	200	
Overdraft		12,000
Capital as at 1 January 2003		111,000
Drawings	14,000	
	287,700	287,700

Notes:

Value of stock at 31 December 2003	£41,000
Insurance paid in advance	£400
Electricity accrued	£300
Advertising expenses accrued	£200
Rates prepaid	£600

The trial balance has been drawn up using the principles we explained in Chapter 8. The expenses and assets are shown in the left-hand column, and the revenues, liabilities and capital in the right-hand column. The main difference is that the above trial balance is followed by some notes. These have arisen because some of the transactions have not yet been properly recorded at the year end.

Some of the notes refer to items known as *accruals*. These are amounts that the business knows it must pay at a future date, such as electricity and advertising in our example. These items will be added to the expenses shown in the trial balance before entering them on the profit-and-loss account. Other notes refer to amounts known as *prepayments*, which the business has paid but that refer to the next financial period, such as insurance and rates in our example. These items will be deducted from the expenses shown in the trial balance before entering them on the profit-and-loss account. Prepayments also appear on the balance sheet as assets.

Before you start drawing up a profit-and-loss account and a balance sheet, you may find the following advice useful. If you tick each figure every time you use it, when you have finished you will find that all the items in the trial balance will be ticked once (and only once), but all the notes will be ticked twice.

Example

Using the trial balance and notes for *End Pages Bookshop*, prepare a trading and profit-and-loss account for the year ending 31 December 2003 and a balance sheet in vertical format as at that date.

Solution

End Pages Bookshop

Trading and profit-and-loss account for the year ending 31 December 2003

	£	£	£
Sales		151,500	
Less Returns inward		1,500	150,000
Less Cost of sales:			
Opening stock		46,000	
Add Purchases	103,500		
Less Returns inwards	3,500	100,000	
		146,000	
Less Closing stock		41,000	105,000
Gross profit			45,000
Add Rents received		2,000	
Discounts received		200	2,200
			47,200
Less Expenses:			
Salaries and wages		18,700	
Office expenses		2,500	
Insurance (£1,100 – £400)		700	
Electricity (£600 + £300)		900	
Stationery		2,400	
Advertising (£3,500 + £200)		3,700	
Telephone		800	
Rates (£3,000 – £600)		2,400	
Discounts allowed		100	32,200
Net profit			15,000

End Pages Bookshop

Balance sheet as at 31 December 2003

	£	£	£	£
Fixed assets				
Premises			80,000	
Fixtures and fittings			5,000	85,000
Current assets				
Stock		41,000		
Debtors	4,800			
Add Prepayments (£400 + £600)	1,000	5,800		
		200	47,000	
Current liabilities				
Creditors	7,500			
Add Accruals (£300 + £200)	500	8,000		
Overdraft		12,000	20,000	
Net current assets (*Working capital*)				27,000
Capital employed				112,000

continued

	£	£	£	£
Represented by:				
Capital at start of year		111,000		
Add Profit for year		15,000		
		126,000		
Less Drawings		14,000		112,000

> *You should now be able to attempt Questions 12.2 and 12.3 at the end of this chapter.*

13 SUMMARY

A *balance sheet* may be shown in *vertical or horizontal format*. In either case it will balance, although the totals differ from one format to another because of the way in which the figures are presented and calculated.

There are a number of items, such as *capital* and *revenue expenditure*, *drawings* and *stock values*, which must be treated correctly on the *profit-and-loss account*. Other items, such as discounts and returns, must be shown in a particular way when arriving at the figures of gross and net profit.

Balance sheets

a) Horizontal format: Assets on the left; liabilities on the right.
b) Vertical format:

	£	£
Fixed assets		X
Current assets	X	
Less Current liabilities	X	
Net current assets		X
Total net assets		X
Less Long-term loans		X
Owner's worth		X
Opening capital	X	
Add Net profit for year	X	
	X	
Less Drawings	X	
Owner's worth		X

> *You should now be able to attempt Tasks 12.2 and 12.3 and the objective test at the end of this chapter.*

Student activities

Task 12.1

Obtain a vertical balance sheet of a business from the published accounts of a public limited company and convert it into a horizontal format.

Task 12.2

Your aunt has a small business and has given you the following example of a balance sheet she has drawn up for her business.

	£		£
Stock	1,000	What I owe suppliers	5,000
Car	5,000	*Less* What I am owed (debtors)	3,000
Land	5,000		
Buildings	6,000		
	17,000		2,000
Less Profit	3,000	Capital I invested in the business	12,000
	14,000		14,000

Required

Redraft the balance sheet in a more conventional form and write a letter to your aunt explaining what you have done and why.

Task 12.3

Conduct a survey amongst members of your class to find out which balance sheet format is preferred by most students and why.

Question 12.1

Joe Zhou has been in business for several years as a manufacturer of fishing nets. At 31 December 2003 you find that his assets and liabilities are as follows:

	£'000
Stocks	29
Creditors	12
Premises	90
Overdraft	14
Capital at 1 January 2002	150
Profit for year to 31 December 2003	21
Debtors	24
Vehicles	27
Drawings for year to 31 December 2003	16
Plant	30
Long-term loan	20
Cash in hand	1

Required

Prepare a balance sheet for J. Zhou as at 31 December 2003, setting it out in vertical format, with good style and presentation.

Question 12.2

Lilian Fung is a sole trader, and one of her businesses trades as Oriental Imports. At 30 June 2004 you have extracted the following balances from her books:

	£
Sales	47,600
Purchases	22,850
Office expenses	1,900
Insurances	700
Wages	7,900
Rates	2,800
Heating, lighting	1,200
Telephone	650
Discounts allowed	1,150
Opening stock at 1 July 2003	500
Returns inwards	200
Returns outwards	150
Premises	40,000
Plant and machinery	5,000
Motor vehicles	12,000
Debtors	12,500
Bank balance (in credit)	7,800
Creditors	3,400
Long-term loan	10,000
Capital	60,000
Drawings for the year	4,000

In addition, the following information is available, as at 30 June 2004:

		£
i)	Stock is valued at	550
ii)	Heating, lighting costs accrued	300
iii)	Insurances prepaid	150
iv)	Rates prepaid	700

Required

Construct a trial balance and prepare a trading and profit-and-loss account for the year ending 30 June 2004, and a balance sheet as at that date for Oriental Imports in vertical format.

Question 12.3

David Dolgellau owns the *Dolgellau Camping Equipment Company*, which has been operating successfully for a number of years. The following figures are available from the bookkeeping records as at 31 March 2004.

	£
Sales	378,500
Discounts received	2,400
Rent received for sub-let of warehouse	7,500
Returns outwards	7,700
Creditors	18,700
Overdraft at bank	30,000
Capital at 1 April 2003	287,500
Purchases	261,700
Salaries and wages	45,700
Office expenses	8,400
Insurance premiums	3,100
Electricity	1,600
Stationery	6,200
Advertising	8,400
Telephone	2,100
Business rates	7,500
Discounts allowed	600
Returns inwards	4,100
Opening stock at 1 April 2003	120,600
Warehouse, shop and office	210,000
Fixtures and fittings	12,800
Debtors	13,000
Cash in till and petty cash	500
Drawings during the year	26,000

In addition, the following information is available:

Stock at 31 March 2004 is valued at	£102,500
Electricity charges accrued at 31 March 2004	£700
Advertising expenses accrued at 31 March 2004	£500
Insurance premiums paid in advance at 31 March 2004	£900
Business rates prepaid at 31 March 2004	£1,500

Required

Construct a trial balance and prepare a trading and profit-and-loss account for the year ending 31 March 2004, and a balance sheet as at that date in vertical format for the Dolgellau Camping Equipment Company.

Objective test (tick the appropriate box)

i)   On a vertical style of balance sheet, capital employed represents:

  a)   net current assets plus long-term liabilities ☐

  b)   fixed assets plus working capital ☐

c) current assets plus fixed assets ☐

d) the total of all assets and liabilities ☐

ii) On a vertical format style of balance sheet, without further calculation, it is not possible to find the figure for:

a) net current assets ☐

b) capital employed ☐

c) working capital ☐

d) total assets ☐

iii) Drawings, for a sole trader, are shown:

a) as an expense in the profit-and-loss account ☐

b) as a current asset on the balance sheet ☐

c) as a deduction from capital and profit on the balance sheet ☐

d) as an accrual under current liabilities on the balance sheet ☐

iv) Carriage outwards is shown:

a) as an expense in the profit-and-loss account ☐

b) as an addition to purchases in the trading account ☐

c) as an addition to gross profit in the trading account ☐

d) as a deduction from purchases in the trading account ☐

v) Discounts allowed are shown:

a) as an addition to purchases in the trading account ☐

b) as a deduction from debtors on the balance sheet ☐

c) as an addition to gross profit in the trading account ☐

d) as an expense in the profit-and-loss account ☐

vi) Rents receivable are best treated in the accounts:

a) as an addition to sales in the trading account ☐

b) as an expense in the profit-and-loss account ☐

c) as an addition to gross profit in the trading account ☐

d) as a current asset on the balance sheet ☐

vii) Returns inwards are shown:

a) as a deduction from sales in the trading account ☐

b) as a deduction from purchases in the trading account ☐

c) as a deduction from debtors on the balance sheet ☐

d) as an expense in the profit-and-loss account ☐

viii) An accrual is dealt with in the accounts by:

    a)   adding the amount to the appropriate expense in the profit-and-loss account ☐

    b)   including the amount under current liabilities in the balance sheet ☐

    c)   both (a) and (b) ☐

    d)   none of these ☐

ix) A prepayment is dealt with in the accounts by:

    a)   including the amount under current liabilities in the balance sheet ☐

    b)   adding the amount to the appropriate expense in the profit-and-loss account ☐

    c)   both (a) and (b) ☐

    d)   none of these ☐

x) Amounts that fall due after more than one year include:

    a)   overdrafts ☐

    b)   bank balances ☐

    c)   long-term loans ☐

CHAPTER 13

Dealing with fixed assets

1 OBJECTIVES

At the end of this chapter, you should be able to:

- understand the concept of depreciation;
- calculate depreciation using the straight-line method, and the reducing balance method;
- prepare accounts incorporating depreciation into the profit-and-loss account, and the balance sheet.

2 INTRODUCTION

Depreciation is a concept that is frequently misunderstood. We saw in Chapter 10 that when a business incurs costs such as electricity, telephone or wages, these costs are matched to the period to which the profit-and-loss account relates, matched to the period in which the benefits arise from these costs. A problem arises, however, with the cost of purchasing an asset such as a van. If a business buys a van in year 1 for £10,000, it would not be observing the matching convention if it set the whole cost of the van as an expense against the profits for year 1. Suppose the van is likely to have fairly heavy use, and estimate that it will be sold in four years time for about £2,000. This means that the van will have cost £8,000 over the next four years. If we apportion the cost evenly over those four years, we could say that the cost of the van is £8,000 ÷ 4 years = £2,000 per annum. There are various ways of looking at this:

- We could say that the benefits are spread over the four years.
- We could say that the business uses up the fixed asset over the period of four years, and that this using up is therefore a *cost* or *expense*.
- We could also say that the £2,000 per annum we propose to charge to expenses is a charge for the use of the van.
- We could say that the £2,000 per annum is an attempt to spread the expenditure incurred in acquiring the asset over its useful life.
- We could say that the van is wearing out and therefore dropping in value over the four years. This is rather more difficult to justify, because at the end of year 1, we are saying that the van has dropped in value by £2,000 (from £10,000 to £8,000), whereas it is common for new vehicles to drop in value much more in their first year than in second and subsequent years. However, the future is

always uncertain, and the principle still holds good even if the figures prove to be somewhat unrealistic.

The term used generally for all these five descriptions is *depreciation*. Accountants prefer to consider depreciation as a method of allocating the total cost of an asset over the years of a business that will benefit from its use. They do not consider it as a method of valuation. There are two main methods of calculating depreciation: the *straight-line method* and the *reducing balance method*.

3 STRAIGHT-LINE METHOD

The *straight-line method* of depreciation is the method used above concerning the van. The calculation is as follows:

$$\frac{Original\ cost\ less\ estimated\ scrap\ value}{Number\ of\ years\ of\ expected\ use} = Annual\ depreciation\ charge$$

For the van described above, this gives:

$$\frac{£10,000 - £2,000}{4\ years} = £2,000\ per\ annum$$

Entries in the profit-and-loss accounts and balance sheets for the four years would be:

	Profit-and-loss accounts charged to *Expenses* under *Depreciation of vans*		less	Balance sheets at year ends shown under *Fixed assets: Vans*	
Year	£	Fixed assets at cost £		Accumulated depreciation £	= Net book value (NBV) £
1	2,000	10,000		2,000	8,000
2	2,000	10,000		4,000	6,000
3	2,000	10,000		6,000	4,000
4	2,000	10,000		8,000	2,000

On the balance sheet, fixed assets are required to be shown at cost less *accumulated* depreciation to the date of the balance sheet. It is the *net book value*, sometimes known as the net book amount (NBA) or *written-down value (WDV)* which is the figure used to balance the balance sheet. The other figures (cost and accumulated depreciation) are, in a sense, only notes to show how the net book value has been calculated.

Example

A. Cautaro bought a generator on 1 January 2003 for £6,000. He expects this to last 5 years at the end of which time he hopes to sell it for £1,000. He uses the straight-line method of depreciation.

Required

Show the entries relevant to depreciation for his profit-and-loss account for the year ending 31 December 2004, and his balance sheet as at that date.

Solution

Profit-and-loss account for the year ending 31 December 2004 (Extract)

Expenses:
Depreciation of generator   £1,000

Balance sheet as at 31 December 2004 (Extract)

Fixed assets	*Cost*	*Accumulated depreciation*	*Net book value*
Generator	£6,000	£2,000	£4,000

You should now be able to attempt Question 13.1 at the end of this chapter.

4 | DISPOSALS

It is not proposed in this book to describe the bookkeeping entries for the *disposal* of fixed assets, but you should understand what happens. Suppose that the van described earlier in this chapter is sold at the start of year 5 for £1,500, before additional depreciation for year 5 has been incurred. Then it could be said that there has been an apparent loss of £500, because, at the date of the sale, the net book value is still £2,000. This £500 would be shown as 'Loss on sale of van: £500' under expenses in the profit-and-loss account for year 5.

Similarly, if the van is sold for £2,500 instead of £1,500, then the profit of £500 could be shown as a negative expense under expenses. Alternatively, the profit on the sale of the van could be shown at the end of the trading account, as an addition to gross profit, before the listing of expenses.

There would, of course, be no entry on the balance sheet at the end of year 5, because the asset would no longer be owned by the business.

5 | REDUCING BALANCE METHOD

The *reducing-balance method* of depreciation is an alternative method of calculation. A fixed percentage rate is applied to the *net book value* (not the cost) at the end of each period. As a very rough rule of thumb, the percentage required is nearly double that required for the straight-line method. The following example is based on the van.

Example

Cost £10,000

Depreciation rate: 40 per cent per annum on the reducing balance.

Year		*Profit-and-loss account* Depreciation	Cost	*Balance sheet* Accumulated depreciation	Net book value
		£	£	£	£
1	40% of £10,000	4,000	10,000	4,000	6,000
2	40% of £6,000	2,400	10,000	6,400	3,600
3	40% of £3,600	1,440	10,000	7,840	2,160
4	40% of £2,160	864	10,000	8,704	1,296

Another way of presenting this is as follows:

	£
Original cost	10,000
Year 1 depreciation	4,000
Reduced balance	6,000
Year 2 depreciation	2,400
Reduced balance	3,600
Year 3 depreciation	1,400
Reduced balance	2,160
Year 4 depreciation	864
Reduced balance	1,296

The reduced balance at the end of year 4 is £1,296 compared with £2,000 using the straight-line method. This shows that our rough rule of thumb of doubling the rate results in rather more depreciation being applied to the asset over the 4 years (£8,704 compared with £8,000).

In order to obtain the exact rate, which under the reducing balance method would result in a scrap value of £2,000, we could use the following formula:

$$r = 1 - t\sqrt{\frac{s}{c}}$$

where

r = rate of depreciation required

t = time (number of years)

s = scrap value

c = cost of the asset

e.g. $r = 1 - \sqrt[4]{\dfrac{2,000}{10,000}} = 1 - \sqrt[4]{0.2} = 1 - 0.687403 = 0.3312597 = 33.12597\%$

Therefore:

	£
Original cost	10,000.00
Year 1 depreciation	3,312.60
Reduced balance	6,687.40
Year 2 depreciation	2,215.27
Reduced balance	4,472.13
Year 3 depreciation	1,481.44
Reduced balance	2,990.69
Year 4 depreciation	990.69
Reduced balance	2,000.00

This degree of accuracy is not normally required and the above has been demonstrated purely for illustrative purposes. In practice, if a scrap value of £2,000 is required after 4 years, a depreciation rate of 33 per cent would result in a reduced balance of £2,015, which is near enough.

6 CHOOSING A METHOD

The straight-line method is popular because it is simple to understand and calculate. Those who favour the reducing balance method argue that it produces high depreciation in the early years and lower depreciation in the later years and that:

- it relates more accurately to normal experience; for example, new cars usually drop in value heavily in the first year;

- it offsets low maintenance costs in the early years and higher maintenance costs in the later years.

Those who favour the straight-line method would reply that:

- apportioning depreciation unequally over a period of time fails to conform with the matching convention, which requires that the charge for the use of the asset should be spread evenly over the period during which the asset is being used;

- offsetting high maintenance costs in the later years with low depreciation tends to obscure the true factual high level of maintenance costs.

Example

Using the data from the A. Cautaro example we used earlier, what would the answer be if A. Cautaro employed the reducing balance method of depreciation, with a depreciation rate of 30 per cent on the reduced balance?

Solution

Calculation:	£
Original cost	6,000
Depreciation 2003	1,800
Reduced balance 31 December 2003	4,200
Depreciation 2004	1,260
Reduced balance 31 December 2004	2,940

Profit-and-loss account
for the year ending 31 December 2004 (Extract)

Expenses:
Depreciation of generator   £1,260

Balance sheet
as at 31 December 2004 (Extract)

Fixed assets	Cost £	Accumulated depreciation £	Net book value £
Generator	6,000	3,060	2,940

You should now be able to attempt Question 13.2 at the end of this chapter.

The following example includes the calculation of depreciation and its incorporation into the accounting documents. This example also calls upon skills learnt in previous chapters of this book.

Example

On 31 December 2002, the accountant of Bolton Bakeries produced a balance sheet which included the following information.

	£
Stocks	4,400
Bank balance	2,800
Creditors	4,000
Debtors	2,200
Fixed assets at net book value	
Motor vehicles	40,000 (original cost £50,000)
Plant and equipment	22,500 (original cost £30,000)

During 2003, Bolton Bakeries purchased another vehicle for £15,000 and new plant and equipment for £16,000. At the end of 2003 the books and other records showed the following:

- Customers owed £2,600
- Suppliers were owed £4,500

- Stocks were valued at £3,700
- The cash book showed a bank balance of £9,400

Bolton Bakeries adopt the following principles in calculating depreciation:

- Depreciation is charged on the straight-line basis at a rate of 20 per cent of original cost for vehicles and 25 per cent of original cost for plant and equipment.
- Depreciation for a full year is charged on all assets purchased during a year, irrespective of the date of purchase.

Required

Calculate the capital of Bolton Bakeries as at 31 December 2002.
   Prepare a balance sheet for Bolton Bakeries as at 31 December 2003.

Solution

	£	£	£
Fixed assets			NBV
Motor vehicles			40,000
Plant and equipment			22,500
			62,500
Current assets			
Stocks	4,400		
Debtors	2,200		
Bank	2,800	9,400	
Less Current liabilities			
Creditors		4,000	
Net current assets (Working capital)			5,400
Therefore *Capital* at 31 December 2002 was			67,900

Bolton Bakeries
Balance sheet as at 31 December 2003

	£	£	£
Fixed assets	Cost	Acc.Dep'n	NBV
Motor vehicles	50,000	20,000	30,000
Add New vehicles	15,000	3,000	12,000
	65,000	23,000	42,000
Plant and equipment	30,000	15,000	15,000
Add			
New plant and equipment	16,000	4,000	12,000
	46,000	19,000	27,000
Total fixed assets	111,000	42,000	69,000
Current assets			
Stocks	3,700		
Debtors	2,600		
Bank	9,400		
		15,700	

Less Current liabilities
Creditors   4,500
Working capital (Net current assets)   11,200
Capital employed   80,200

Represented by:
Capital as at 31 December 2002   67,900
Add Profit for year ending 31 December 2003   12,300*
Capital as at 31 December 2003   80,200

* This is the balancing figure.

> *You should now be able to attempt Question 13.3 at the end of this chapter.*

7 | THE PROBLEMS OF DEPRECIATION

Fixed assets and depreciation can cause more difficulties than it would first appear. There are two types of fixed assets: tangible and intangible. For individuals and partnerships the main concern will be with tangible fixed assets; those that you can see and touch such as buildings and machinery. For large organisations, particularly limited liability companies, there may be also intangible assets on the balance sheet such as goodwill, licences, brands and trademarks. When we look at limited companies in later chapters, we will discuss intangible assets. At this stage we will concentrate on tangible assets.

Any tangible fixed asset that has a limited useful economic life should be depreciated over that life, on a systematic basis down to its residual value if any.

To calculate the depreciation charge, the following factors should be considered:

- the carrying amount of the asset (whether cost or valuation);
- the length of the asset's expected *useful economic life* to the business, bearing in mind the possibility of obsolescence; and,
- the estimated *residual value* of the asset at the end of its useful economic life.

The residual value of the asset is what could be obtained from disposing of it less any costs incurred. The price you expect must be based on prices prevailing at the date you acquired the asset.

8 | SUMMARY

Depreciation is a charge for the use of an asset over the period of its useful life. There are two methods of calculation. The *straight-line method* uses the following formula to calculate the annual depreciation charge

$$\text{Annual depreciation charge} \frac{\text{Original cost} - \text{Estimated scrap value}}{\text{Number of years of expected life}}$$

The *reducing balance method* calculates the annual depreciation charge by applying a fixed percentage to the previous net book value.

The *annual depreciation charge* is shown as an expense in the profit-and-loss account and is added to the accumulated depreciation charge at the beginning of the year in the balance sheet. The total accumulated depreciation at the year end is deducted from the original cost of the asset in the balance sheet to give the *net book value.*

> *You should now be able to attempt Tasks 13.1, 13.2 and 13.3 and the objective test at the end of this chapter.*

Student activities

Task 13.1

As a group, make a list of the fixed assets that a business may own. Individually, decide what you think would be a reasonable life for each asset. Compare your answers and where there are any significant differences discuss why these have arisen.

Task 13.2

Obtain the published reports and accounts of a number of companies. Look for the section on their accounting policies and write down their depreciation policies for each class of asset. Do any of the companies you have chosen have a very different policy from the others? If so, have they explained why in the report and accounts?

Task 13.3

Construct line graphs to illustrate the differences between the straight-line method and the reducing balance method of depreciation. You can use your own figures or those given in this chapter.

Question 13.1

Harry Heysham bought a ferry on 1 January 2003, and the cost was £500,000. Anticipated life of the boat is 10 years, at the end of which time it is hoped that the boat can be sold for £100,000. The straight-line method of depreciation is employed for calculations.

Required

Show the entries relevant to depreciation for Harry's business profit-and-loss account for the year ending 31 December 2007, and the balance sheet as at that date.

Question 13.2

Using the data from the previous question, what would the answer be if Harry Heysham employed the reducing balance method of depreciation, with a depreciation rate of 20 per cent on the reduced balance?

Question 13.3

Ken Grosas started a business on 1 January 2002, trading as the Preston Packaging Company. He started with a capital of £120,000 and made a profit during the first year of trading of £23,300.

Buildings cost £100,000 on 1 January 2002, and the policy is not to allow for depreciation in the accounts. Fixtures and fittings cost £40,000 on 1 January 2002, and Ken decided to depreciate them on a reducing balance basis, using a 20 per cent rate on the written-down value at the end of each year. The net book value at the end of 2002 was therefore £32,000.

Motor vehicles cost £30,000 on 1 January 2002, and Ken decided to write them off over four years on a straight-line basis. The net book value on 31 December 2002 was therefore £22,500. On 2 February 2003, a new vehicle was purchased for £12,000, and Ken decided to apply a whole year's depreciation to this vehicle for the year ending 31 December 2003.

Figures for the year to 31 December 2003 were as follows:

	£	£
Salaries and wages		19,600
Office expenses		3,500
Heating and lighting		1,800
Telephone		1,400
Rates		3,600
Premises		100,000
Fixtures and fittings (NBV)		32,000
Motor vehicles – original (NBV)		22,500
Motor vehicles – new		12,000
Stock at 1 January 2003		20,000
Sales		307,000
Purchases		247,400
Debtors		40,000
Bank balance (in credit)		8,000
Creditors		21,000
Loan (long-term)		50,000
Capital at 1 January 2002	120,000	
Add profit for year to 31 December 2002	23,300	143,300
Drawings for year ended 31 December 2003		9,500

Additional information relative to 31 December 2003

Stocks:	£30,000
Heating and lighting accrued:	£300
Rates prepaid:	£900

Required

Prepare a trading and profit-and-loss account for Ken Grosas for the year ending 31 December 2003, and a balance sheet as at that date, relating to the business of the Preston Packaging Company.

Question 13.4

Cindy Zhang owns a fashion shop that she bought in 2004. She started trading in April 2004 and has built up what she considers to be a successful business. The following figures are available from the bookeeping records as at 31 March 2007:

	£
Sales	147,900
Creditors	14,300
Capital at 1 April 1996	201,790
Purchases	89,600
Salaries and wages	18,500
Administrative and general expenses	3,400
Insurance premiums	1,400
Light and heat	720
Stationery and postages	840
Advertising	1,530
Telephone	900
Business rates	6,500
Opening stock at 1 April 2006	19,400
Shop premises	150,000
Fixtures and fittings	32,000
Estate car	10,800
Debtors	1,400
Cash at bank	13,560
Cash in till and petty cash	240
Drawings during the year	13,200

In addition, the following information is available:

Stock at 31 March 2007 is valued at: £21,500

Electricity charges accrued at 31 March 2007: £270

Insurance premiums paid in advance at 31 March 2007: £200

Business rates prepaid at 31 March 2007: £1,300

The value of the shop premises (£150,000) is the original cost when purchased in 2004, and Cindy's policy is not to allow for depreciation in the accounts.

The fixtures and fittings of the shop cost £40,000 in April 2004, and Cindy decided to depreciate them on a straight-line basis over ten years. The written-down value at 1 April 2006 was therefore £32,000, after allowing for two years of depreciation.

Cindy bought an estate car in April 2006 which cost £18,000 and has used it for collecting and delivering goods. She decided to depreciate it over five years on a straight-line basis, ignoring any scrap or resale value it might have at the end of the five years. The written-down value at 1 April 2004 was therefore £10,800, after allowing for two years' depreciation.

Required

Prepare a trading and profit-and-loss account for the year ending 31 March 2007 and a balance sheet as at that date in vertical format, for Cindy Zhang's fashion shop.

Question 13.5

Cindy Zhang, whom we met in the previous question, is not happy with her depreciation policy for fixtures and fittings and her estate car. She feels that the fixtures and fittings will not last the ten years originally planned, because a new look to her shop may become essential within a shorter period of time; however, she considers that the original items will still have a good resale value when she decides to replace them. Also, concerning the estate car, she feels that five years is the time after which she will need to replace the car, but that it will have some resale value.

As a result she has asked you to make theoretical calculations that will show the figures that would have resulted if the following depreciation policies had been followed from the beginning, in April, 2004:

Fixtures and fittings: 20 per cent per annum on a reducing balance basis (instead of 10 per cent straight-line)

Estate car: 20 per cent per annum on a reducing balance basis (instead of 20 per cent on a straight-line basis)

Required

i)   Prepare a table that compares the original (straight-line) and suggested (reducing balance) calculations for depreciation of Cindy's fixtures and fittings, and (separately) her estate car, for the three separate years ending 31 March 2001. The table should show the depreciation charge against profits for each year and also the reduced balance or written down value at the end of each year.

ii) Calculate how much more (or less) depreciation the suggested revised policy would have been charged against profit in the first two years, the years ending 31 March 2005 and 2006.

iii) Calculate the revised figure for Cindy's opening capital at 1 April 2006 (which at present is £201,790), assuming the revised policy had been applied from April 2004.

iv) Calculate the revised figure for net profit for the year ending 31 March 2007, again assuming the revised policy had been applied from April 2004.

v)   Calculate the revised figure for 'Owner's worth' at 31 March 2007, again assuming the revised policy had been applied from April 2004.

vi) Which depreciation policy would you have recommended to Cindy in April 2004?

vii) What would you advise now, concerning the accounts for the third year ending 31 March 2007, assuming that the accounts for the first two years cannot now be altered?

Objective test *(tick the appropriate box)*

i)   A machine is purchased at the start of year 1 for £12,000 and is depreciated over five years on a straight-line basis. At the end of year 3, the net book value (or written-down value) is:

   a)   £6,000 ☐

   b)   £7,200 ☐

   c)   £4,800 ☐

   d)   £3,600 ☐

ii) Another machine is purchased at the start of year 1 for £30,000, and is depreciated on the reducing balance method, applying each year a depreciation rate of 12 per cent on the written-down value. At the end of year 3 the written-down value is (to the nearest £):

   a)   £23,232 ☐

   b)   £20,444 ☐

   c)   £17,991 ☐

   d)   £19,200 ☐

iii) Office furniture is purchased at the start of year 1 for £15,000, and is depreciated on a straight-line basis over six years. The accumulated depreciation at the end of year 4 is:

   a)   £10,000 ☐

   b)   £12,000 ☐

   c)   £ 7,500 ☐

   d)   £ 5,000 ☐

iv) The net book value of a motor vehicle at the end of three years (from date of purchase) is £10,000. If the depreciation each year is £2,500, calculated on a straight-line basis, the original cost was:

   a)   £12,500 ☐

   b)   £20,000 ☐

   c)   £15,000 ☐

   d)   £17,500 ☐

v)   A baker's oven, during the second year of its life, has been depreciated by £855, and its written-down value at the end of this second year is £7,695. Depreciation has been calculated on the reducing balance method by applying each year a percentage of 10 per cent to the reduced balance: The oven originally cost:

a) £9,618 ☐

b) £9,405 ☐

c) £9,500 ☐

d) £9,310 ☐

CHAPTER 14

Accounting for non-payment

1 OBJECTIVES

At the end of this chapter you should be able to:

- understand what is meant by bad debts;
- understand what is meant by a provision for doubtful debts;
- distinguish between them;
- apply the principles to a set of accounts for a sole trader.

2 INTRODUCTION

Whenever a sale is made *on credit*, the effect is that *sales* increase in the profit-and-loss account and *debtors* increase on the balance sheet. What happens if:

a) a debtor fails to pay up, or

b) at the time of the preparation of the balance sheet, it appears that a debtor or debtors are unlikely to pay up?

The answer to a) is that a *bad debt* is created. The answer to b) is that a *provision for doubtful debts* is created.

The difference between a) and b) is sometimes the cause of confusion and it is best if they are regarded as separate items. Some text books sometimes refer to *provisions for bad debts* but we prefer to use the term provision for *doubtful debts* to emphasise the difference between the two items.

3 BAD DEBTS AND PROVISION FOR DOUBTFUL DEBTS

Bad debts represent monies that are irrecoverable. It may be that a debtor has become bankrupt, or a business has gone into liquidation with an indication that amounts owing to their creditors are unlikely to be paid. In this case, the amount of the irrecoverable debt is charged to the profit-and-loss account as a business expense, and deducted from the previous total of debtors on the balance sheet.

In Chapter 4, we discussed the matching convention. The treatment of bad debts above, charging the bad debts to the profit-and-loss account an an expense for the period in which the sale took place, conforms with the matching convention. However, quite often it is not possible to ascertain whether a debt is irrecoverable until after the accounting period in which the sale took place. It is therefore prudent to make what is known as a *provision*, in an accounting period, for the estimated expense for debts that may ultimately prove to be irrecoverable or bad. Obviously, this provision can never be more than a prudent estimate. Such estimates can be made in various ways:

- A list can be made of debtors who can be regarded as doubtful. In fact, sometimes the provision is called *provision for doubtful debts* or *provision for bad and doubtful debts*.

- Where this is difficult, some accountants simply apply a percentage to the amount for debtors outstanding at balance sheet date, this percentage being based on past experience, adjusted up or down depending on the state of the economy at the time.

- A more realistic method, an extension of the above, is to prepare an *ageing schedule* where the debtors are analysed according to the length of time that the debt has been outstanding, and to apply percentages increasing with the age of the debt.

Example

Period debts outstanding	Amounts totalling £	Estimated bad debts %	Provision for doubtful debts £
Less than one month	100,000	0	NIL
1–3 months	50,000	2	1,000
4–6 months	30,000	3	900
6–12 months	20,000	5	1,000
over 12 months	10,000	50	5,000
	210,000		7,900

Using these figures as an illustration, they would appear in the accounts as follows:

In the *profit-and-loss account* (under expenses)

	£
Provision for doubtful debts	£7,900

In the *balance sheet* (under current assets)

	£	£
Debtors	210,000	
Less Provision for doubtful debts	7,900	202,100

4	CHANGES IN PROVISION FOR DOUBTFUL DEBTS

Provision for doubtful debts is similar in concept to provision for depreciation, in that it is *cumulative*. The following table illustrates this.

Example

Year	Provision for doubtful debts charged to profit-and-loss account £		Cumulative amount of provision to be deducted from debtors on the balance sheet £
1	1,000		1,000
2	500	(increase)	1,500
3	500	(increase)	2,000
4	(200)	(decrease)	1,800
5	700	(increase)	2,500

In the case of year 4, it was obviously felt that the £2,000 cumulative provision brought forward from year 3 was too much for the position at the end of year 4. Hence a reduction of £200 to £1,800 was applied. This reduction of £200 would be shown under expenses in the profit-and-loss account as a negative (bracketed) amount, or possibly as an addition to gross profit at the end of the trading account, before deducting expenses.

Example

Tony Ferrone manufactures and sells mint cake. During the year ending 31 December 2005 his sales totalled £96,000, and his debtors at the end of the year amounted to one month's sales. This was after allowing for two of his debtors who had gone 'bad'. One of these had become bankrupt, owing Tony £300, and other, who had owed him £550, had given a fictitious address and was untraceable.

Last year (ending 31 December 2004), Tony had made a provision for doubtful debts in his accounts of £400, and now feels, in view of experience, that this provision should be increased to £1,000 for this year.

Required

Show the relevant entries in Tony Ferrone's accounts for the year ending 31 December 2005.

Solution

Tony Ferrone

Profit-and-loss account for year ending 31 December 2005 (extract)

	£	£
Sales		96,000
Expenses:		
Bad debts	850	
Increase in provision for doubtful debts	600	

Balance Sheet as at 31 December 2005 (extract)

	£	£
Current assets		
Debtors	8,000	
Less Provision for doubtful debts (£400 + £600)	1,000	7,000

You should now be able to attempt Question 14.1 at the end of this chapter.

The following example illustrates the accounts of a sole trader, and covers aspects of this and previous chapters.

Example

Lou Petro, a local commercial photographer, is thinking of joining forces with a friend who is also a photographer. This friend has asked to see Lou's balance sheet, and Lou has asked you to prepare one for him. Lou has provided you with the following information as at 30 April 2003:

	£
Photography equipment, original cost	20,000
Estate car, original cost	12,000
Stocks of materials	2,000
Balance at bank (in credit)	4,300
Debtors	5,000
Creditors	2,400
Drawings during the past year	12,000
Long-term loan	5,000

Additional information provided is:

- Both the photographic equipment and the car were purchased on 1 May 2002, and are depreciated on a straight-line basis. The photography equipment has an expected life of five years, and the car four years, with insignificant scrap or resale value.

- Lou owes rent of £400 in respect of the past year.

- Included in debtors is a client who has owed £500 for over 11 months, and seems very unlikely to pay.

You have prepared a profit-and-loss account for Lou, allowing for the above adjustments, and the net profit for the past year amounted to £15,000.

Required

Prepare a balance sheet, in vertical format, as at 30 April 2003, for Lou's photographic business.

Solution

Lou Petro – Photographic Business
Balance sheet as at 30 April 2003

	£	£ Cost	£ Acc.Dep'n	£ NBV
Fixed assets				
Photography equipment		20,000	4,000	16,000
Estate car		12,000	3,000	9,000
		32,000	7,000	25,000
Current assets				
Stocks		2,000		
Debtors	5,000			
Less Provision for doubtful debt	500	4,500		
Bank		4,300	10,800	
Current liabilities				
Creditors		2,400		
Rent accrued		400	2,800	
				8,000
				33,000
Less Long-term loan				5,000
				28,000
Financed by:				
Opening capital (1 May 2002)*			25,000	
Add Net profit for year			15,000	
			40,000	
Less Drawings			12,000	28,000

* Lou's opening capital has to be deducted from the other figures – it is the balancing figure.

> *You should now be able to attempt Task 14.1 and Questions 14.2 and 14.3 at the end of this chapter.*

5 | SUMMARY

Sales are shown in the profit-and-loss account in total, regardless of the amount of cash received. This raises the problem of customers who may not pay. *Bad debts* are shown as an expense in the profit-and-loss account and represent money that is known to be irrecoverable. *Provision for doubtful debts* is an estimate of the amount of money owed by debtors which may not be recovered. Only the increase or decrease in the cumulative provision for doubtful debts is shown in the *profit-and-loss account*. The cumulative figure is shown as a deduction from debtors in the *balance sheet*.

You should now be able to attempt Tasks 14.2, 14.3 and the objective test at the end of this chapter.

Student activities

Task 14.1

Your friend works in an American company. The accountant there has a sign on his desk saying *Sales are a gift until the cash comes in*. Explain to your friend what principles are involved in this statement.

Task 14.2

You work for a company where your representatives make sales without worrying about the creditworthiness of the customers. Write a circular that explains how the company is affected by bad debts.

Task 14.3

You have just started to work for a small company where the practice has been to make a provision for doubtful debts at the year end as a percentage of outstanding debtors. Write a memorandum to the managing director stating the other methods that can be used, and the one you recommend.

Question 14.1

B. Rauti manufactures and sells furnaces, trading as Barrow & Company. During the year ending 31 March 2004, he incurred bad debts totalling £8,500. His sales for the year totalled £2,500,000.

At the end of the previous year (ended 31 March 2003), his cumulative provision for doubtful debts was £12,000. At 31 March 2004, the position of his debtors was as shown in the following ageing schedule:

Period debt outstanding	Debtors £	Estimated bad debts %
Less than one month	250,000	0
1–3 months	120,000	3
4–6 months	50,000	4
6–12 months	10,000	5
over 12 months	6,000	75
	436,000	

Required

Show the relevant entries in the accounts for Barrow & Company for the year ended 31 March 2004.

Question 14.2

Foreign Products is a trading business owned by R. Kucharski. Her books show the following figures at 30 June 2004:

	£	£
Buildings at cost	55,000	
Fixtures at cost	14,000	
Provision for depreciation of fixtures		5,600
Debtors	17,000	
Creditors		12,650
Cash at bank	1,850	
Stock at 1 July 2003	42,250	
Purchases	84,750	
Sales		130,500
Delivery expenses	1,350	
Discounts allowed	270	
Interest on loan	3,800	
Salaries and wages	16,500	
Office expenses	2,470	
Insurances	5,300	
Bad debts	1,610	
Provision for doubtful debts		3,000
Long-term loan		42,000
R. Kucharski: Capital at 1 July 2003		52,400
	246,150	246,150

At 30 June 2004, the following information is also available:

- Stock is valued at £55,300.

- Wages unpaid amount to £350.

- Office expenses accrued are £130.

- Insurances prepaid are £400.

- The provision for doubtful debts is to be reduced to 10 per cent of debtors.

- Depreciation of fixtures is to continue on a straight-line basis at the rate of 10 per cent on cost. Buildings are not depreciated.

Required

Prepare for Foreign Products, in vertical format:

i)   a profit statement (profit-and-loss account) for the year to 30 June 2004;

ii) a balance sheet as at 30 June 2004.

Question 14.3

David Moore, who trades as Golf Links, started business on 1 January 2005 buying and selling sports equipment. He has asked you to prepare some accounts for him for the year to 31 December 2005. He has left the following message on your answering machine:

'Aunt Gertie left me £5,000 in her will, and this formed my initial capital in my Golf Links account at my bank. A friend also loaned me £2,000 at 10 per cent per annum interest. He gave me a cheque, which I also banked. I bought an estate car to help with my collection and delivery of stock, and I made £500 profit on this car deal. The salesman wanted £1,700 for the car but I beat him down to £1,200, and I paid him by cheque. I reckon the car is good for four years before it goes to the scrapyard.

'I rent a garage to keep my stock in, and this costs me £400 per annum. I've paid £500 so far (by cheque) as the owner insists on quarterly payments in advance.

'My first bit of trading was to buy 3,000 pairs of trainers for £9,000. I've paid a cheque to the supplier for £6,000, and shall have to pay the balance soon. I've sold 2,500 pairs so far for £9,500 cash, and am owed £500. Twenty per cent of this is dodgy, but the rest should be collectable. I've banked all the cash received so far.

'Then I bought some golf clubs – a job lot of 200 for £4,000 (by cheque). I've sold 180 of these for £5,400 cash, but the remainder are faulty, and I've found someone who says he can repair them, and will take them off my hands for £100.

'I also do a good line in wind cheaters. All 300 of them cost me only £1,500. I haven't paid for them yet, since a number of them appear to have faulty stitching. I've complained to the supplier who says he will reduce the price to £900. I think I'll agree, since I know someone who will look them all over and repair as necessary for £2 a garment. I can sell them for £10 each, and make a profit of £1,500, if my maths is right.

'The cash I got for the golf clubs I've used to pay some bills: petrol for the estate car came to £500, and electricity for the garage £200. I've also spent £4,500 on myself; after all, a man has to eat!

'I also had a holiday in August, which cost £700, but I paid for that by cheque from the Golf Links account. I must also pay the first year's interest on the loan soon, I suppose.'

Required

Prepare a trading and profit-and-loss account for Golf Links for the year ending 31 December 2005, and a balance sheet as at that date. Show the cash and bank balances separately on the balance sheet, and present the figures in vertical format.

Objective test (tick the appropriate box)

i) Bad debts are dealt with in the accounts of a trader by:
   a) showing them as a deduction from debtors on the balance sheet ☐
   b) increasing the provision for bad debts ☐
   c) charging them as an expense in the profit-and-loss account ☐
   d) both (a) and (c) above ☐

ii) A provision for doubtful debts is dealt with in the accounts of a trader by:
   a) charging the current year's adjustment of the provision as an expense in the profit-and-loss account ☐
   b) deducting the provision from debtors on the balance sheet ☐
   c) adjusting the gross profit in the profit-and-loss account ☐
   d) both (a) and (b) above ☐

iii) In the accounts of a sole trader, last year's provision for doubtful debts amounted to £800. This year, debtors are £7,000 and the provision is to be 10 per cent of debtors. The following is true:

  a) £1,500 is shown as a provision for doubtful debts in the profit-and-loss account ☐

  b) £100 is deducted from debtors on the balance sheet with the heading 'less provision for doubtful debts' ☐

  c) The profit-and-loss account shows 'reduction in provision for doubtful debts: £100' ☐

  d) £700 is charged to the profit-and-loss account as 'provision for bad debts' ☐

iv) The ageing schedule of XYZ Company is as follows:

Period debt outstanding	Debtors £	Estimated bad debts %
less than one month	9,000	0
1–3 months	4,000	5
4–6 months	2,000	10
over 6 months	1,000	15

Select the correct response to the following statements:

  a) The profit-and-loss account is charged with £550 bad debts. ☐

  b) £550 is added to last year's doubtful debts provision. ☐

  c) Debtors are reduced by 10 per cent on the balance sheet. ☐

  d) None of these. ☐

v) Using the ageing schedule in Question (iv), if the provision for doubtful debts last year was £600, the provision this year should be:

  a) increased by £550 ☐

  b) increased by £50 ☐

  c) decreased by £50 ☐

  d) none of these ☐

CHAPTER 15

Relationship between financial statements

At the end of this chapter you should be able to:

- appreciate the relationship between budgeted cash-flow forecasts, profit-and-loss accounts and balance sheets;
- construct these inter-related documents using budgeted data;
- appreciate the difference between budgeted profits and budgeted cash flows.

2	INTRODUCTION

In this section we have been looking at the accounts of a sole trader, particularly the *profit-and-loss account* and the *balance sheet*. We have been looking at these documents as records of what has actually happened in the past. In this chapter we shall be looking at the future – *forecast* or *budgeted profit-and-loss accounts* and *balance sheets*, and seeing how they relate to a document we considered in Chapter 9: the *cash-flow forecast*. If you have forgotten how to prepare a cash-flow forecast, you would be well advised to revise Chapter 9 at this stage.

3	RELATIONSHIP BETWEEN CASH-FLOW FORECASTS, BUDGETED PROFIT-AND-LOSS ACCOUNTS AND BALANCE SHEETS

Example

Ramosh Rajendra has inherited £30,000, and plans to commence a confectionery business trading as Sweet Meats on 1 April 2003.

His plans include the following:

- Equipment costing £16,000 will be bought and paid for on 1 April. Further equipment will be bought and paid for on 1 July, costing £8,000. He estimates that this equipment will last ten years with no scrap value, and he will charge depreciation in his accounts from the date of purchase on a straight-line basis.

- Wages will be £2,000 per month for the first three months, and £3,000 per month thereafter.

- Selling and administration costs are expected to be £1,200 per month for the first three months, rising to £1,400 per month thereafter, payable in the month when the costs are incurred.

- Premises will be rented at £7,200 per annum, payable quarterly in advance starting on 1 April 2003.

- Selling price of goods is calculated at purchase price plus 50 per cent.

- Terms of trade are for customers to pay in the month following receipt of goods, and Ramosh has arranged with his suppliers for payment to be made two months after the month of purchase.

- Ramosh's planned sales and purchases are:

	Sales (£'000)	Purchases (£'000)
April	12	30
May	16	24
June	20	20
July	24	20
August	24	20
September	24	20
	120	134

Required

Prepare the following *budgeted* documents for Sweet Meats:

i) Cash-flow forecast for the first six months' of trading, showing the expected bank balances at the end of each month.

ii) Trading and profit-and-loss account for the six months to 30 September 2003.

iii) Balance sheet as at 30 September 2003.

iv) A brief report on the viability of the project.

Solution

Workings:

	Sales (£'000)		Purchases (£'000)	
i)	Invoiced	Cash received	Invoiced	Paid
April	12		30	
May	16	12	24	
June	20	16	20	30
July	24	20	20	24
August	24	24	20	20
September	24	24	20	20
Totals	120	96	134	94
	Debtors	24	Creditors	40
		120		134

ii) Depreciation of equipment: £
   £16,000 × 10% p.a. = £1,600 p.a. ∴ 6 months = 800
   £8,000 × 10% p.a. = £800 p.a.   ∴ 3 months = 200
                                                  1,000

iii) Stock: See trading account. This is calculated as follows:

Sales are £120,000 (data) which is 50 per cent on cost of sales. Cost of sales is therefore two-thirds of sales value, i.e. £80,000. Stock is therefore the difference between purchases of £134,000 (data) and cost of sales of £80,000.

i)

Sweet Meats
Cash-flow forecast for the first six months of trading

	April £	May £	June £	July £	Aug £	Sept £	Total £
Receipts							
Capital	30,000						30,000
Sales		12,000	16,000	20,000	24,000	24,000	96,000
Total (A)	30,000	12,000	16,000	20,000	24,000	24,000	126,000
Payments							
Purchases			30,000	24,000	20,000	20,000	94,000
Wages	2,000	2,000	2,000	3,000	3,000	3,000	15,000
Selling/Admin	1,200	1,200	1,200	1,400	1,400	1,400	7,800
Rent	1,800			1,800			3,600
Equipment	16,000			8,000			24,000
Total (B)	21,000	3,200	33,200	38,200	24,400	24,400	144,400
Net cash flow (A − B)	9,000	8,800	(17,200)	(18,200)	(400)	(400)	(18,400)
Balances:							
Start of month	nil	9,000	17,800	600	(17,600)	(18,000)	nil
End of month	9,000	17,800	600	(17,600)	(18,000)	(18,400)	(18,400)

ii)

Sweet Meats
Budgeted trading and profit and loss account for the six months ending 30 September 2003

	£	£
Sales		120,000
Less Cost of sales:		
Purchases	134,000	
Less Closing stock	54,000	80,000
Gross Profit		40,000
Less Expenses:		
Wages	15,000	
Selling and administration expenses	7,800	
Rent	3,600	
Depreciation of equipment	1,000	27,400
Net profit		12,600

iii)

Sweet Meats

Budgeted balance sheet as at 30 September 2003

	£ Cost	£ Acc.Dep'n	£ NBV
Fixed assets			
Equipment	24,000	1,000	23,000
Current assets			
Stock	54,000		
Debtors	24,000	78,000	
Current liabilities			
Creditors	40,000		
Overdraft	18,400	58,400	
Net current assets			19,600
Capital employed			42,600
Represented by:			
Capital		30,000	
Profit for six months		12,600	
			42,600

iv) Report:

- Net profit is £12,600, which is nearly 30 per cent of the capital employed (at 30 September 2003) of £42,600. This would seem to be a reasonable return. It is also 42 per cent of the initial capital of £30,000.

- The cash-flow forecast reveals that the business will experience a cash-flow deficit during July, August and September. It will therefore be necessary to arrange finance, e.g. an overdraft with the bank. This might require security (for example Ramesh's home). Otherwise Ramesh will have to obtain a loan, or raise money by some other means. It may be necessary to prepare a further cash-flow forecast for the six months to 31 March 2004, to see if the money required is likely to increase or decrease. For example, a full year's forecast might show that an overdraft or loan was only necessary until, say, December, in which case the finance needed would only be temporary. Another possibility would be to lease the equipment, rather than buy it. This would obviate the need for the extra finance, at least in the short term.

- Note that although the budgeted profit is £12,600, the cash position deteriorates from £30,000 at the start to an overdraft of £18,400 at the end of the six months. Why is there such a discrepancy?

	£
Starting with cash of	30,000
and making a net profit of	12,600
you might expect to end up with	42,600
instead of an overdraft of	(18,400)
which is a difference of	61,000

The balance sheet (which was a blank to start with) reveals:

Equipment purchased	24,000
Debtors funded	24,000
Stock purchased	54,000
	102,000
but creditors have provided financing of	40,000
	62,000
and the depreciation fund has been built up by	1,000
which explains the difference of	61,000

This explanation is, in fact, a simple cash-flow statement, which is another of the documents to be found in published accounts.

- It is always useful to reconcile the key figures on your three financial statements. For example, you will see that from the trading and profit-and-loss account, your total sales for the period are £120,000. The cash-flow forecast shows that the total cash you expect to receive is £96,000. The difference must be debtors of £24,000 which appear in the balance sheet. These calculations could be shown like this:

	£
Level of sales achieved as per profit-and-loss account	120,000
Less cash received as per cash-flow forecast	96,000
Figure of debtors for the balance sheet	24,000

The same kind of reconciliation could be carried out for purchases/creditors. By doing this you are less likely to make a mistake.

When preparing these statements, do not confuse cash flow with profit. All sales, whether for cash or on credit, are shown on the *profit-and-loss account*. Receipts from sales or debtors are shown on the *cash-flow forecast*. The difference between sales and receipts (debtors) appears on the *balance sheet*. Never include depreciation in the cash-flow forecast. The cash flow occurs when the asset is purchased. However, do remember to include the purchase price of the asset in the cash-flow forecast in the month in which the asset is paid for.

> *You should now be able to attempt Questions 15.1, 15.2 and 15.3 at the end of this chapter.*

4 SUMMARY

Budgeted statements such as *cash-flow forecasts, profit-and-loss accounts* and *balance sheets* enable managers to look into the future and see the possible financial consequences of their plans. They may indicate poor profits, in which case plans should be revised by adjusting selling prices, controlling expenses, etc. Cash-flow problems may be highlighted, in which case timings of cash flows should be examined and extra funding arranged if necessary. Ratios should be examined (see Chapters 25–28) if balance sheets are unsatisfactory and plans revised accordingly.

> You should now be able to attempt Tasks 15.1, 15.2, 15.3 and the objective test at the end of this chapter.

Student activities

Task 15.1

Students on an accounting course are going to hold a 'Brains Quiz'. Devise five questions for the panel to answer, which will demonstrate their understanding of the relationship between financial statements.

Task 15.2

Divide the group into pairs. One member of each pair should prepare a simple question on the relationship between financial statements (Question 15.1 is a good example) that the other member should try to answer.

Task 15.3

Construct a diagram to show the relationship between a cash-flow forecast, a profit-and-loss account and a balance sheet.

Question 15.1

Indra Lingam starts a business on 1 July 2002 with a capital of £50,000, some of which she immediately spends on fixed assets, costing £20,000. Budgeted figures for the first six months are:

	£'000
Sales	420
Cost of materials actually sold	170
Labour	126
Overheads (including depreciation for six months in the sum of £2,000)	98
Materials purchased	190

Payments for labour and overheads can be regarded as evenly spread over the six month period.

	Receipts from debtors £'000	Payments to creditors £'000
July	35	35
August	42	35
September	49	28
October	56	14
November	70	14
December	84	14
	336	140

Required

Tabulate the budgeted figures into:

i) a cash-flow forecast for the first six months;

ii) a budgeted profit-and-loss statement for the period to 31 December 2002;

iii) a budgeted balance sheet as at that date.

Question 15.2

Distant Shores is a privately owned business, which is being planned early in December 2002, with the main purpose of trading in holiday pleasure craft. Initial capital is £100,000, to be banked in the business bank account during December 2002.

The owner proposes to commence trading on 1 January 2003. During December 2002, fixed assets costing £40,000 will be installed and paid for. Sales are estimated to be:

- £12,000 in January 2003;

- £20,000 in February 2003;

- £40,000 per month thereafter.

Gross profit (sales price less the purchase price of the boats) is expected to run at a uniform rate of 25 per cent of the sales price.

Customers will be required to pay for boats by the last day of the second month after that in which the boats were collected by them. For example sales in January should be paid for by 31 March. Purchasing is to be so arranged that initially, and at the end of every month, the stock will be exactly sufficient (and no more) to supply all the expected sales in the following month. Trade creditors are to be paid on the last day of the month after that in which the boats were purchased.

It is expected that wages and salaries will amount to £2,000 in each month and will be paid during the month in which they are incurred. Similarly for general expenses of £3,000 per month. Any temporary excess of payments over receipts is to be financed by a bank overdraft and a bank has agreed to this.

Required

Prepare the following financial statements for Distant Shores:

i) a budgeted cash-flow forecast for the seven months to 30 June 2003, showing the expected bank balances at the end of each of the six months ending 30 June;

ii) a simple budgeted trading and profit-and-loss account for the seven months ending 30 June 2003;

iii) a balance sheet as at that date;

iv) a brief report commenting on the benefits to be gained from preparing such budgeted statements.

Question 15.3

Sid Lapos has owned several businesses that he has built up and then sold. As a result, he has accumulated capital of £125,000 which he plans to invest in a new business, trading in sports equipment to be called *Sid's Sports Equipment and Accessories*. He decides to commence trading on 1 April 2003.

He intends to rent a warehouse at a cost of £30,000 per annum, payable quarterly in advance, starting on 1 April 2003. He will need storage and handling equipment, which will cost £64,000, and this will have to be paid for on 1 April. Life expectancy of this equipment is ten years, with no scrap value. Sid favours the straight-line method of depreciation.

Wages are budgeted for at £8,500 per month, rising to £10,000 per month from 1 July. Selling, administration and distribution costs are expected to be £5,000 per month for the first three months, rising to £6,000 per month thereafter, payable in the month in which they are incurred.

The selling price of goods is expected to average the purchase price plus 60 per cent. Terms of trade are for customers to pay in the month following receipt of goods, and the same terms have been arranged with Sid's suppliers. Planned sales and purchases for the first six months are:

	Sales £	Purchases £
April	50,000	60,000
May	70,000	60,000
June	80,000	60,000
July	90,000	60,000
August	100,000	60,000
September	90,000	60,000
	480,000	360,000

Required

Prepare the following for Sid's Sports Equipment and Accessories:

i)   a monthly cash-flow forecast for the six months ending 30 September 2003;

ii) a budgeted profit-and-loss statement for the same period;

iii) a budgeted balance sheet as at 30 September 2003;

iv) a brief report commenting on the budgeted plans and giving Sid any advice which you consider to be appropriate.

Objective test (tick the appropriate box)

i)   Depreciation of a particular asset for the year ending 31 December 2004 is calculated as being £500. This will have the effect of:

a)   increasing the working capital on the balance sheet by £500 ☐

b)   reducing the cash flow for the year by £500 ☐

c)   decreasing the profit shown by the profit-and-loss account by £500 ☐

d)   increasing the net current assets by £500 ☐

ii) A company borrows £10,000 from its bank on 1 January as a five-year loan. The interest is 15 per cent per annum, payable at the end of each quarter. Select the correct response to the following statements:

a) The loan will be shown on the balance sheet as £8,500 at 31 December. ☐

b) The cash-flow forecast will show £375 under receipts during the month of March. ☐

c) The half-yearly accounts will show £1,500 as bank interest under expenses in the profit-and-loss account. ☐

d) None of these ☐

iii) The following budget information is available for a company in respect of next year:

Cost of sales	£70,000
Purchases	£80,000
Payments for materials	£60,000

Select the correct response to the following statements:

a) Stock at the year end will be worth £20,000. ☐

b) Creditors at the year end will be £20,000. ☐

c) Sales for the year will be £50,000. ☐

d) Gross Loss for the year will be £10,000. ☐

iv) In the example of Sweet Meats in this chapter the minimum amount needed to be introduced (either as a loan or as additional capital) during April to avoid an overdraft at any time during the six months ending 30 September 2003 would be:

a) £18,400 ☐

b) £17,800 ☐

c) £9,000 ☐

d) £17,600 ☐

v) There are other ways of avoiding the overdraft referred to in (iv) above. One possible adequate method might be:

a) to lease the equipment rather than buying it ☐

b) to delay paying creditors for a further two weeks ☐

c) to allow only two weeks rather than one month's credit ☐

d) to pay all wages monthly rather than weekly ☐

CHAPTER 16

Incomplete records

1 OBJECTIVES

At the end of this chapter you should be able to:

- explain what is meant by single entry bookkeeping;
- draw up a statement of affairs;
- make adjustments to cash records for accruals and prepayments;
- apply formal layouts and percentage calculations to deduce missing figures;
- construct a trading and profit-and-loss account and balance sheet from incomplete records.

2 INTRODUCTION

Although large businesses keep sophisticated records, many small businesses do not have the time or expertise to do this. The owners may rely on bank records, odd slips of paper and what they can remember to keep control of the business. This presents a problem at the end of the year when a trading and profit-and-loss account and a balance sheet are required. The information from the business will be incomplete and the accountant will have to make adjustments to the original records to obtain the correct figures.

This process of constructing full accounts from incomplete records is a favourite topic for examiners. Sometimes it is referred to as *single-entry book-keeping*, because the business has not maintained a system of *double-entry bookkeeping* that would have provided all the information required. Usually the main information available is a cash record and bank statement with notes on amounts owed to and owing by the company at the beginning and end of the financial year.

Both in the examination room and in practice, incomplete records problems are not confined to small businesses. A company may maintain a good accounting system, but an event such as a fire, computer breakdown, or theft may mean that some information is missing at the year end. This will entail making many adjustments to arrive at the correct figures for the trading and profit-and-loss account and balance sheet. In this chapter we examine problems concerned with incomplete records. This involves some of the topics that were introduced in Chapter 12 and you may wish to revise that chapter first.

3 | TYPICAL PROBLEMS

At the heart of most incomplete records examination questions is the fact that profit and cash are not the same thing. It is easiest to demonstrate this by looking at the first year of a new business. Later in the chapter we will consider the adjustments made for a continuing business. Let us assume that a trader in his first year of business receives £9,000 cash for *sales* he has made during the year, but is still owed £2,000 by customers at the year end. The sales figure for the profit-and-loss account is £11,000. This is calculated by adding the £2,000 that is owed to the £9,000 already received. In the balance sheet it will be shown that debtors owe the business £2,000.

The adjustments are similar in respect of *purchases* made by the company. If a business has made cash payments to its suppliers totalling £29,000, but still owes £2,500 at the year end for goods it has received, the total figure for purchases in the trading and profit-and-loss account is £31,500. On the balance sheet there will be a figure of £2,500 for trade creditors.

> *You should now be able to attempt Question 16.1 at the end of this chapter.*

4 | PREPAYMENTS

As well as the purchase and sale of goods, a business incurs other expenses. Some of these are not paid completely by the end of the year. Some expenses have been paid in advance and are known as *prepayments*. A good example of an expense paid in advance is rates. The date on which the business has to pay its rate demand may not coincide with the year end of the company so there will be a prepayment. The amount of the prepayment will have to be deducted from the total paid by the business to obtain the correct figure of expense for the profit statement. The prepayment will be shown under current assets on the balance sheet.

Example

Ho Wan in her first year of trading pays a cheque of £30,000 for business rates. This payment covers the twelve months of the current financial year and the first three months of the next year.

Required

What amount should be shown in the profit-and-loss account and balance sheet?

Solution

The correct amount to put in the profit-and-loss account is:

$$\frac{£30,000}{15 \text{ months}} \times 12 \text{ months} = £24,000 \text{ for the year}$$

The figure of £24,000 is put on the profit-and-loss account and a figure of £6,000 is shown under current assets as a prepayment in the balance sheet. This is an asset because it represents something that the business has paid for, but from which it has not yet received the benefit.

5 | ACCRUALS

If a business has not paid for all the expenses it has incurred during the year the amounts still owing at the year end are known as *accruals*. These have to be added to the cash or cheque payments made during the year to obtain the total cost incurred for the profit-and-loss account. The amounts outstanding will be shown on the balance sheet under current liabilities with the heading of Accruals.

Example

The cash record of a business shows that it has paid motor vehicle repairs of £3,600, but there is an invoice outstanding at the year end for £500.

Required

What is the amount of vehicle repairs to be put in the profit-and-loss account for the year and what entry will be made in the balance sheet?

Solution

The total expense incurred to be put in the profit-and-loss account is £4,100. This is the amount of cash paid of £3,600 plus the invoice outstanding of £500. In the balance sheet an amount of £500 will be shown as an accrual under current liabilities as this represents something the business owes at the end of the year.

> *You should now be able to attempt Question 16.2 at the end of this chapter.*

6 | ADJUSTMENTS IN A CONTINUING BUSINESS

In the above examples we saw that where there is an amount owed by the business at the year end and we know the amount of cash paid during the year, the figures must be added to obtain the correct amount to enter on the trading and profit-and-loss account of the business. The amount owed at the year end will appear on the balance sheet.

The position for a business that has been trading for some years previously is very similar, but you may have to make *adjustments* to allow for items in respect of the previous financial year. The rule is to ensure that you always look at the balance sheet at the end of the previous financial year.

7   TRADE CREDITORS AND ACCRUALS

When dealing with *trade creditors* and *accruals* you must remember that any cash payment made during the current financial year will first be used to pay amounts showing as liabilities at the end of the previous financial year. An adjustment must then be made for amounts owing at the end of the current financial year to obtain the correct figure for the profit-and-loss account.

Example

On 31 December 2002 Jane Kingston owed £500 for rent. During 2003 she paid cash of £1,250 in respect of rent, but at the end of that year still owed £600.

Required

What is the figure for rent to be included in the trading and profit-and-loss account for the year ended 31 December 2003?

Solution

The calculation is as follows:

	£
Cash paid in 2003	1,250
Less due on 31 December 2002	500
	750
Add amount due on 31 December 2003	600
Correct figure for year ended 31 December 2003	1,350

The above layout is very suitable for calculating the amount to be entered in the trading and profit-and-loss account.

> *You should now be able to attempt Question 16.3 at the end of this chapter.*

8 | FINDING THE MISSING FIGURE

In some examination questions you may be given the figure for the trading and profit-and-loss account, but some other figure is missing; for example the amount still owing at the year end. This can easily be calculated by using the format above as in the following example.

Example

At 31 December 2003 the trade creditors amounted to £500. The trading and profit-and-loss account for the year ended 31 December 2004 showed a figure for purchases of £900 and our records showed that we paid our creditors £1,000 cash in that year.

Required

What did we owe our creditors at 31 December 2004?

Solution

If we use the above layout, inserting the figures we know, we get:

	£
Cash paid in 2004	1,000
Less due on 31 December 2003	500
	500
Add amount due on 31 December 2004	x
Amount in profit-and-loss account	900

The missing figure must be £400 and this is the amount we owe our trade creditors on 31 December 2004.

> *You should now be able to attempt Question 16.4 at the end of this chapter.*

9 | TRADE DEBTORS AND PREPAYMENTS

Debtors should cause few problems as we are only doing the reverse of the calculations we did above for creditors.

Example

A business is owed £600 at the end of 2003. During 2004 it receives cash of £2,000 from its customers and is owed £500 at the year end.

Required

What is the figure of sales to be shown on the trading and profit-and-loss account?

Solution

Modifying the above layout slightly, the known figures can be inserted:

	£
Cash received in 2004	2,000
Less owed on 31 December 2003	600
	1,400
Add amount owed on 31 December 2004	500
Amount for sales in profit-and-loss account	1,900

Sometimes students experience difficulties when dealing with *prepayments*. If you refer to the previous section on prepayments you will see that we deducted the prepayment at the end of the current financial year from the cash paid in the year. The resulting figure was the correct amount to be shown on the profit-and-loss account. We can simply extend this approach to account for any prepayments made in the previous financial year.

Example

A company had made a prepayment of £600 in respect of insurance as at 31 December 2005. During the year ended 31 December 2006 cash payments for insurance of £4,000 were made. This amount included £1,000 in respect of 2007.

Required

What is the correct figure for insurance to be entered in the profit-and-loss account?

Solution

The main point to remember is that the prepayment at 31 December 2005 of £600 is part of our total liability for the year ended 31 December 2006. The layout is:

	£
Prepayment at 31 December 2005	600
Add cash paid in 2006	4,000
	4,600
Less prepayment at 31 December 2006	1,000
Amount for profit statement for 2007	3,600

10 | USING LAYOUTS

In some problems key figures are missing and a certain degree of ingenuity is required to calculate the missing figure. It may be possible by using the *standard layout* or *format* for a profit-and-loss account or balance sheet to calculate the missing figure by deduction. In some instances relationships between figures can be expressed in *percentage terms* and you need to apply these to calculate the figures. This may require, in addition, the use of a standard layout to arrive at the missing figure.

This is very simple as long as you remember the standard layout for the specific financial statement needed. If you still have difficulty remembering the items you would normally find on a profit-and-loss account and balance sheet, work through the examples in earlier chapters. The following example illustrates the use of layouts.

Example

A business has made a gross profit of £10,000 on sales of £50,000. At the beginning of the year the opening stock was £4,000 and made purchases during the year of £42,000.

Required

What is the figure of closing stock?

Solution

To solve this you must draw up a standard format for the trading and profit-and-loss account, leaving a blank for the missing figure

Trading and profit-and-loss account

	£	£
Sales		50,000
Less Cost of sales		
Opening stock	4,000	
Purchases	42,000	
	46,000	
Less Closing stock	x	
Gross profit		y
		10,000

The missing figures can now be inserted. The cost of sales (y) must be £40,000 to give the gross profit of £10,000. This means that a closing stock figure (x) of £6,000 must be inserted as the figure to be subtracted from the £46,000. The completed layout looks like:

Trading and profit-and-loss account

	£	£
Sales		50,000
Less Cost of sales		
Opening stock	4,000	
Purchases	42,000	
	46,000	
Less Closing stock	6,000	40,000
Gross profit		10,000

A similar approach to the use of layout can be applied if there is a missing figure on the balance sheet. A typical examination problem is for the amount of profits to be omitted and there is insufficient information to construct a profit-and-loss account. The answer is to use a balance-sheet layout to calculate the missing profit figure as in the example below. The same approach can be used to ascertain the amount of drawings.

Example
A sole trader starts his business with £10,000 capital. The closing capital of the business is £15,000 and the owner has made drawings of £8,500.

Required
What was the figure of profit for the year?

Solution
We start by drawing up the part of the balance sheet concerned with showing the capital of a sole trader.

Balance sheet (Extract)

	£	£
Opening capital	10,000	
Add Profit	x	
	y	
Less Drawings	8,500	
Closing capital		15,000

We can now insert the missing figures. To obtain the closing capital of £15,000 after deducting from y the drawings of £8,500, it means that y must be £23,500. To obtain the figure of £23,000 a profit of £13,500 must be added to the opening capital. With the figures inserted the balance sheet is:

Balance sheet (Extract)

	£	£
Opening capital	10,000	
Add Profit	13,500	
	23,500	
Less Drawings	8,500	
Closing capital		15,000

11 │ USING PERCENTAGES

Some figures may be available for the profit-and-loss account, but the cost of sales figure or the sales figure may be missing. However, in such examples the *gross profit percentage* will be given and from this it is possible to calculate the missing figures.

The gross profit can be expressed either as a percentage of cost of sales and is known as the *gross profit mark up*, or as a percentage of sales and is known as the *gross profit margin*.

$$\text{Gross profit mark up} = \frac{\text{Gross profit}}{\text{Cost of sales}} \times 100$$

$$\text{Gross profit margin} = \frac{\text{Gross profit}}{\text{Sales}} \times 100$$

Using the figures: Sales £5,000; Cost of sales £4,000; Gross profit £1,000, the calculations are:

$$\text{Gross profit mark up} = \frac{£1,000}{£4,000} \times 100 = 25\%$$

$$\text{Gross profit margin} = \frac{£1,000}{£5,000} \times 100 = 20\%$$

The procedure for calculating the missing figure where the gross profit percentage is given is as follows:

1. If the gross profit percentage is the margin, then make sales equal 100 per cent.

2. If the gross profit percentage is the mark up, make cost of sales equal 100 per cent.

3. Enter gross profit as a percentage of 100.

4. Calculate the missing figure.

In the following examples various problems are explained. You should work through these very carefully before tackling the relevant questions at the end of the chapter.

Example

L. Aneja makes an average gross profit margin of 25 per cent. For the year the cost of sales figure is £15,000.

Required

What are the figures for sales and gross profit?

Solution

First enter the figures that are known:

	£	
Sales	x	
Cost of sales	15,000	
Gross profit	y	25%

As the gross profit margin is 25 per cent, we make sales 100 per cent. Therefore the cost of sales is 75 per cent:

	£	
Sales	x	100%
Cost of sales	15,000	75%
Gross profit	y	25%

The missing figures can now be added because if cost of sales of £15,000 equals 75 per cent then:

$$\text{Sales} = £15,000 \times \frac{100}{75} = £20,000$$

The completed figures are:

	£	
Sales	20,000	100%
Cost of sales	15,000	75%
Gross profit	£5,000	25%

Example

Sarah Priddy operates a business where the gross profit mark up is 25 per cent on cost of sales. Cost of sales is £4,000.

Required

What is the figure for sales and gross profit?

Solution

First enter the figures which are known:

	£	
Sales	x	
Cost of sales	4,000	
Gross profit	y	25%

As the gross profit mark up is 25 per cent, we make cost of sales 100 per cent and sales are therefore 125 per cent:

	£	
Sales	x	125%
Cost of sales	4,000	100%
Gross profit	y	25%

The missing figures can now be added because if cost of sales of £4,000 equals 100 per cent then:

$$\text{Sales} = £4,000 \times \frac{125}{100} = £5,000$$

The completed figures are:

	£	
Sales	5,000	125%
Cost of sales	4,000	100%
Gross profit	1,000	25%

Example

Nigel Clutton has a business where the gross profit margin is 10 per cent and the figure for sales is £55,000.

Required

What is the figure for cost of sales and gross profit?

Solution

First enter the figures which are known:

	£	
Sales	55,000	
Cost of sales	x	
Gross profit	y	10%

As the gross profit margin is 10 per cent, we make sales 100 per cent and cost of sales is therefore 90 per cent:

	£	
Sales	55,000	100%
Cost of sales	x	90%
Gross profit	y	10%

The missing figures can now be added because if sales of £55,000 equals 100% then:

$$\text{Cost of sales} = £55,000 \times \frac{90}{50} = £49,500$$

The completed figures are:

	£	
Sales	55,000	100%
Cost of sales	49,500	90%
Gross profit	5,500	10%

Example

Fred Paulton has a garden centre where the average gross profit mark up is 50 per cent on cost of sales and the sales value is £60,000.

Required

What is the value for cost of sales and gross profit?

Solution

First enter the figures which are known:

	£	
Sales	60,000	
Cost of sales	x	
Gross profit	y	50%

As the gross profit mark up is 50 per cent, we make cost of sales 100 per cent and sales are therefore 150 per cent:

	£	
Sales	60,000	150%
Cost of sales	x	100%
Gross profit	y	50%

The missing figures can now be added because if sales of £60,000 equals 100% then:

$$\text{Cost of sales} = £60,000 \times \frac{100}{150} = £40,000$$

The completed figures are:

	£	
Sales	60,000	150%
Cost of sales	40,000	100%
Gross profit	20,000	50%

You should now be able to attempt Task 16.1 and Question 16.5 at the end of this chapter.

12 COMBINING LAYOUTS AND PERCENTAGES

In some questions a considerable amount of information may be missing and you will have to use your knowledge of layouts and percentages to calculate the missing figures. You should have no problems if you tackle the question methodically. The following simple procedure will help you:

1. Draw up a standard layout naming all the items you would expect to find in it.

2. Insert any figures which are given in the question.

3. Identify which figures are missing.

4. Calculate the missing figures as a separate working.

5. Complete your layout using the figures you have calculated.

Example

The following figures for a financial year are available:

Sales	£30,000
Opening stock	£4,000
Purchases	£25,000
Gross profit margin	20%

Required

What is the gross profit and cost of sales?

Solution

The first step is to draw up the standard layout for a profit statement, inserting any figures we know:

Profit statement for the year ended . . .

	£	£
Sales		30,000
Less Cost of sales		
Opening stock	4,000	
Add Purchases	25,000	
	29,000	
Less Closing stock	a	b
Gross profit		c

The figures we have missing are:

a) closing stock

b) cost of sales

c) gross profit

We cannot work out the closing stock figure until we have the gross profit and cost of sales and these can be calculated as follows:

	Known figures £	%	Missing figures £
Sales	30,000	100	
Cost of sales	b	80	24,000
Gross profit	c	20	6,000

As we have calculated that the cost of sales figure is £24,000, the closing stock figure must be £5,000 (£29,000 – £24,000). We can now complete the layout.

Profit statement for the year ended . . .

	£	£
Sales		30,000
Less Cost of sales		
Opening stock	4,000	
Add Purchases	25,000	
	29,000	
Less Closing stock	5,000	24,000
Gross profit		6,000

> *You should now be able to attempt Question 16.6 at the end of this chapter.*

13 INCOMPLETE RECORDS AND A NEW BUSINESS

We have examined the various problems that can arise where a business has incomplete records and the various techniques that may be used to calculate any missing figures. We can now put this knowledge together to draw up a trading and profit-and-loss account and a balance sheet for a business.

Question 16.7 at the end of this chapter concerns a *new business* which has not maintained proper records and has now completed the first year of trading. You should make reference to the earlier parts of the chapter if you have difficulties. You will find that when you come to complete the balance sheet at 31 December 2004 there is no figure given for the cash held on that date. You will have to calculate this by drawing up a simple cash statement showing the cash coming in to the business, the cash going out and the balance in hand at the end of the year.

> *You should now be able to attempt Task 16.3 and Question 16.7 at the end of this chapter.*

14 INCOMPLETE RECORDS AND THE ESTABLISHED BUSINESS

If you have been able to draw up the profit statement and balance sheet from the incomplete records of a new business, you should not experience many problems with an *established business*. One new feature is that some questions ask you to draw up a *statement of affairs* at the beginning of the financial year. This statement is nothing more than a simple balance sheet that serves to arrange the information in a convenient order and allows the calculation of the capital.

Example

Magna Company, manufacturers of stone ornaments for the garden, has supplied you with the following financial information of the business as at 1 January 2003:

	£
Premises	30,000
Machinery	15,000
Stock	15,000
Debtors	10,000
Insurance prepaid	500
Creditors	7,000
Cash	2,000
Accrual for maintenance charge	400

Required

Draw up a statement of affairs as at 1 January 2003.

Solution

Magna Company
Statement of affairs as at 1 January 2003

	£	£
Assets		
Premises		30,000
Machinery		15,000
Stock		15,000
Debtors		10,000
Prepayments		500
Cash		2,000
Total assets		72,500
Liabilities		
Creditors	7,000	
Accruals	400	
Total liabilities		7,400
Capital		65,100

Having given a financial structure to the business, it is now possible to deal with any further problems. In Question 16.8 at the end of the chapter the above statement of affairs is the start of the financial year. Use it, with the additional information given, to prepare a profit-and-loss account and balance sheet.

> *You should now be able to attempt Question 16.8 and Task 16.2 at the end of this chapter.*

15   SUMMARY

If a business has not maintained proper accounting records, it will be necessary to make *adjustments* to the information available to construct a *profit-and-loss account* and *balance sheet*. The most common problem is where a record has been kept only of *cash* transactions. Where key figures are missing in an *incomplete records* question, it is normally possible to calculate them by using *layouts* and *percentages*. With an established business it may be necessary to draw up a *statement of affairs*.

> *You should now be able to attempt the objective test at the end of this chapter.*

Student activities

Task 16.1
Collect a number of advertisements of sales bargains from the newspapers. Using the appropriate layouts for margins and mark ups, calculate the relevant figures.

Task 16.2
Take your bank statement for the last three months and draw up a profit-and-loss account for the period. This will mean that you will have to make adjustments to the bank entries for accruals and prepayments at the beginning and end of the period.

Task 16.3
Your cousin has been in business for almost a year, but has not kept proper accounting records. Write her a letter explaining the step-by-step procedure to draw up a trading and profit-and-loss account and balance sheet.

Question 16.1
In the following questions assume it is the first year of trading for the company.

i) Andy Radstock banks £12,000 from his customers during the year and is still owed £2,500 at the year end. What are the correct figures for:

    a) sales on the profit-and-loss account

    b) trade debtors on the balance sheet

ii) Mary Shepton's records showed that she paid £24,600 to her suppliers by cheque during the course of the year and £3,200 by cash. At the end of the year she still owes £5,300. What are the correct figures for:

    a) purchases on the profit-and-loss account

    b) trade creditors on the balance sheet

iii) Extracts from Arthur Mallet's bank and cash records show:

Received	£	Paid	£
Cheques for sales	27,000	Suppliers by cheque	22,000
Cash for sales	4,600	Suppliers by cash	1,900

At the end of the year the business owes £4,600 to its suppliers and the debtors stand at £5,400. What are the correct figures for:

a) sales on the profit-and-loss account

b) trade debtors on the balance sheet

c) purchases on the profit-and-loss account

d) trade creditors on the balance sheet

Question 16.2

In the following questions assume it is the first year of trading for the company.

i) Peter Drew pays a cheque for electricity charges for £8,400 and has an unpaid invoice for £1,200 at the end of the year. What are the correct figures to show for:

    a) electricity expenses in the trading and profit-and-loss account

    b) accruals in the balance sheet

ii) A business in its first year pays cash to its landlord of £6,000 in respect of the rent for the first 18 months. What are the correct figures to show for:

    a) as rent in the trading and profit-and-loss account

    b) under prepayments in the balance sheet

iii) The bank statement of a business shows that the following payments have been made in its first year of trading:

Electricity:	£4,000
Insurance:	£2,400
Repairs:	£3,900
Rates:	£3,000

Investigations reveal that an electricity invoice for £450 has still not been paid and £330 is owed in respect of repairs. Of the amount paid for insurance, £195 represents an advance payment. The payment for rates includes an amount for the first three months of the following year. What are the correct figures to show:

a) for each item on the trading and profit-and-loss account

b) as accruals on the balance sheet

c) as prepayments on the balance sheet

Question 16.3

i) The amount due for electricity for the previous financial year was £200. During the current financial year cash was paid of £800, but there was still £430 owing at the year end. What is the correct figure to be entered in the trading and profit-and-loss account?

ii) During the current financial year an amount of £500 cash was paid for stationery and a further £250 was still outstanding at the year end. An amount of £150 was outstanding from the previous year. What is the correct figure to be entered in the trading and profit-and-loss account?

iii) At the end of 2003 an amount of £3,000 was owing to trade creditors. During the financial year ended 31 December 2004 we paid cash of £12,500 to trade creditors, but still owed £1,600 at the year end. What is the figure for purchases to be entered on the trading and profit-and-loss account for the year ended 31 December 2003?

Question 16.4

In the following questions you have been given certain figures. Calculate the missing figures.

Amount owing to creditors at end of previous financial year £	Cash paid to creditors in current year £	Amount owing to creditors at end of current year £	Amount in profit and loss account in current year £
200	800	300	?
500	750	800	?
500	2,000	?	1,750
400	1,750	?	1,800
700	?	900	1,000
400	?	600	700
?	1,000	200	1,100
?	650	250	850

Question 16.5

i) A business sells its goods at cost plus 20 per cent. The gross profit is £5,000. What are the sales and cost of sales?

ii) A gross profit margin of 25 per cent is made on sales. The cost of sales figure is £60,000. What are the figures for sales and gross profit?

iii) The value of sales for the year is £11,000. The gross profit mark up is 10 per cent. What are the gross profit and cost of sales?

iv) On cost of sales of £108,000 there is a gross profit mark up of 25 per cent. What is the gross profit and sales?

v) A company makes a gross profit margin of 25 per cent on its sales. The cost of sales is £108,000. What is the sales and the gross profit?

Question 16.6

Lewis Harptree has been running a successful business printing calendars for a number of years. At the end of the current financial year it has made sales of £60,000 and started the year with an opening stock of £8,000. During the year it made purchases of £50,000. Unfortunately, a fire at the end of the year means that no figure is available for the stock at the year end. However, the company knows that it makes a gross profit mark up of 25 per cent.

Required

Calculate the following figures:

i)   closing stock at the year end;

ii) the cost of sales for the year;

iii) the gross profit for the year.

Question 16.7

Louise Litton started a mail order business selling dog baskets with £12,000 capital. During the year to 31 December 2004 £10,000 was received from customers and at the year end an amount of £3,000 was still owing. Goods had been purchased to the value of £5,000, but only £4,000 had been paid to suppliers at the end of the year. During the year machinery had been purchased for cash to the value of £6,000. It is estimated that this machinery will last six years and will have no scrap value. Louise has decided to depreciate the machinery using the straight-line method.

A part-time assistant has been employed and paid £2,500 in wages. Rent had been paid of £1,000, but there was still £500 owing at the year end. Insurance had been paid of £1,250 which included an amount of £250 for 2005. Other expenses of the business for the year to 31 December 2004 amounted to £3,500 and these had been paid in full. On 31 December 2002 the closing stock was valued at £2,500.

Required

Draw up a trading and profit-and-loss account for the year ended 31 December 2004 and a balance sheet as at 31 December 2004.

Question 16.8

To answer this question you will need to use the data from the example in Section 16.14. During the course of 1993 Magna Company received £85,000 from customers and at the end of the year was owed £5,000. Suppliers were paid

£62,000, but £10,000 remained owing at 31 December 2003. The following cash payments were also made during the year:

Wages	£6,000
Motor expenses	£1,900
Insurance	£850

You find that of the amount paid for insurance £250 was in respect of the period 1 January 2004 to 30 June 2004. You also discover at the end of 2003 there is still an unpaid bill for maintenance charges of £250. Further investigation reveals that the value of stock at 31 December 2003 is £25,000. The owner of Magna Company informs you that £5,000 had been drawn out in cash during 2003 for his own use. After consideration you decide that the machinery should be depreciated by £2,000 for the year.

Required

Draw up a trading and profit-and-loss account for the year ended 31 December 2003 and a balance sheet as at 31 December 2003.

Objective test *(tick the appropriate box)*

i) Prepayments are shown on the balance sheet as a:

   a) current liability ☐

   b) fixed asset ☐

   c) capital amount ☐

   d) current asset ☐

ii) Accruals are shown on the trading and profit-and-loss account as:

   a) an addition to sales ☐

   b) an addition to the appropriate expenses ☐

   c) a deduction from the appropriate expenses ☐

   d) a deduction from purchases ☐

iii) If a company has debtors at the beginning of the year of £3,000, receives £20,000 from customers during the year and is owed £5,000 at the year end, the sales figure for the profit statement is:

   a) £28,000 ☐

   b) £22,000 ☐

   c) £18,000 ☐

   d) £12,000 ☐

iv) If a gross profit is shown as a mark up, it has been calculated as a percentage of:

   a) cost of sales ☐

   b) purchases ☐

    c)   sales ☐

    d)   closing stock ☐

v) If a gross profit is shown as a margin, it has been calculated as a percentage of:

    a)   purchases ☐

    b)   cost of sales ☐

    c)   opening stock ☐

    d)   sales ☐

vi) If cost of sales are £5,000 and gross profit is £1,000, the gross profit mark up will be:

    a)   20% ☐

    b)   16.7% ☐

    c)   25% ☐

    d)   5% ☐

vii) If sales are £50,000 and gross profit £5,000, the gross profit margin will be:

    a)   9.09% ☐

    b)   20% ☐

    c)   10% ☐

    d)   11.1% ☐

A problem with the bank

Context

You have received the following letters and papers from a friend:

SHIRES AGENCY
Import and Export
35A Alexander Buildings
Nottingham
Tel: 0115 216243

10 November 2004

Dear Emma,

I wonder if you can help me. I have received the enclosed letter from the Bank Manager who is getting a bit shirty. I'm unable to understand why the overdraft is so high as I charge a mark up of 75% on the goods I trade in, which I think is fair enough.

Last year an accountant did some figures for me, but I have lost these. As there was some unpleasantness over non-payment of his fees, I am reluctant to go back to him. However, I have listed at the bottom of this letter the only figures I have been able to find that he did.

Would you please prepare the statements the Bank want? During the year to 30 June 2004 I made sales of £84,700 on credit and I purchased £49,000 of goods from my suppliers. I've lost my bank statements and I don't want to ask for copies from the bank at the moment, but I have drawn up a list of all the money I have received and paid during the year.

Payments
Suppliers	£47,810
Wages	£9,500
Rates	£2,500
Carriage out	£96
Administrative expenses	£9,200
Insurance	£240
Car expenses	£3,500
Postage	£400
Telephone	£600
Electricity	£520

Receipts
Customers	£83,479

I still have to pay my last electricity bill for the year which amounts to £300, and of the amount for insurance, 50% of it refers to the next financial year. On the 30 June 2004 I had stock worth £3,200.

Perhaps I had better explain about the loan. It is from my father, free of interest, and he does not want to be repaid until I have sorted myself out a bit.

I had better explain about the car as well. I think it is important to have a prestige vehicle like the Rolls. It does cost a lot to run and as there has been some misunderstanding over repair bills, the garage now makes me pay before they will let me have the car back and I think their charges are steep. The last accountant said it was best to depreciate the car at 20% on cost and I am happy to go on doing that, although I don't know what it means.

One problem is that I don't know how much money I've taken out of the business during the year for my own needs. Perhaps there is some way you can work this out for me?

By the way, I expect the manager will ask me some pretty shrewd questions and I want to show him I am on the ball when it comes to finance. Could you please tell me briefly what a profit-and-loss account and a balance sheet is and what they show me? If you have any comments or advice on my accounts could you please include them your reply.

I know you will not expect a fee for your help, but I will take you out for a meal next time I see you.

Yours sincerely

Tom

Figures from last accountant

Balances as at 30 June 2003

Owned:	£
Premises at cost	40,000
Car (cost £40,000) net book value	32,000
Stock	2,600
Debtors	2,000
Bank	1,126
	77,726
Liabilities:	
Trade creditors	1,500
Loan from father	10,000
	11,500

The Forest Bank
Baytree Road, Nottingham
Tel: 0115 212788

26 September 2004

T. Shires, Esq.,
35A Alexander Buildings,
Nottingham.

Dear Mr. Shires,

I am surprised to note that despite my previous letters
you have taken no action to reduce your business overdraft
which stood at £4,761 on 30 June 2004. Although I have
asked you to make an appointment to see me on a number of
occasions, you have failed to do so. I must therefore ask
you to attend a meeting at my offices on 7 December 2004. You
must bring your most recent trading and profit-and-loss
account and balance sheet with you.

If you fail to attend the meeting I will have no alternative but to stop all payments from this account and take
legal action for the recovery of the money due to the
bank.

Your faithfully,

G Sherriff
G.Sherriff
Branch Manager

Student activities

i) Construct a balance sheet as at 30 June 2003.

ii) Prepare a trading and profit-and-loss account for the year ended 30 June 2004.

iii) Construct a balance sheet as at 30 June 2004.

iv) Analyse the results of the business in the light of the information given in the two letters.

Format

A letter is required addressed to your friend, which includes:

- A trading and profit-and-loss account for the year ended 30 June 2004.

- A balance sheet as at 30 June 2004.

- Recommendations as to the action your friend should take to resolve his financial problems.

Objectives

In this assignment the student will apply and appreciate the techniques for preparing financial statements where the information is not presented in a straightforward manner and appreciate the implications of the financial statements in a specific business context.

References

Chapter 16 will be of particular use.

Sam Shanklin

Context

You have recently received the following letter from your uncle, Sam Shanklin:

28th November 2004

Dear Jo,

I hear you are on a course in business studies, and I wonder if you can help me.

I am thinking of setting up a business retailing carpets. As you know, I have worked for many years in a carpet store, and understand the market fairly well. Since becoming redundant, I must obviously find some way of making a living. If you think the project is viable, I shall go to an accountant to get his professional advice, but I have no experience of accounts and things like that, and, if you could analyse my proposals, this would help me a lot.

I have found suitable shop premises which I can occupy at a quarterly rental of £1,000 payable in advance on the first day of each quarter, starting on 1st January 2005.

I shall have to buy some shop fittings, for which I have been quoted £13,800. I expect they will last about ten years, before I have to scrap them and buy new.

I shall, of course, be working full-time, but I shall need an assistant. Your cousin, Fred, says he would help, and his wages and so on will cost about £500 per month. I'll pay him monthly.

You could allow for heating and lighting of the shop at, say, £600 per month, starting on 1st January, payable monthly at the end of each month. Telephone charges will be about £200 per quarter, payable at the end of each quarter.

I have arranged with carpet manufacturers to pay for purchases at the end of the month following month of purchase. I expect these to be £1,000 per month, except that, for the first three and last three months of the year (winter being slightly busier than the summer), they will be £100 more per month. I should have one month's purchases in stock at any one time.

Sales, I expect, will be £3,600 per month for the first three months, increasing to £4,000 per month for the following six months, and then dropping back to £3,600 per month for the last three months of the year. Half of these sales will be for cash, the remainder, of necessity, being on credit. Of my credit customers, if past experience is anything to go by, half will pay on time, i.e. in the month following month of sale, and the other half in the month following that. I doubt if any credit customers will go 'bad' during the year, but you could allow a 10% reserve at the year end if you think that would be prudent.

Many customers will require their carpets to be fitted, and I shall sub-contract this work. I estimate this sub-contract work will cost £150 per month, payable one month after completion of the work.

My brother has offered me a loan of £5,000 on 1st January. He suggests 12% (cheaper than the bank) per annum interest, payable half-yearly on 30th June and 31st December. He wants his money back within the next three years. I'll accept his offer, and aim to pay him back in about two years' time.

I'll have to be careful during the first year, but I should make enough money to draw, say, £500 per month out of the business to live on. I've had a preliminary chat with my bank manager about an overdraft. He says 'no go', unless he gets an accountant's report on the project, with a cash-flow forecast, whatever that may be, and also he would want my house as security. So he can get lost! I've decided to finance it myself out of my redundancy lump sum and savings which total £12,500. Do you think this will be enough? I'll aim to keep at least £250 in credit at the bank.

Any figures, advice and so on would be helpful. What do you want for Christmas (within reason!)?

Best wishes,

Uncle Sam

Student activities

Reply to your Uncle Sam, showing him how professional you are. Surprise him. You should include the following in or with your letter:

i)   a cash-flow forecast for the year to 31 December 2005, showing the initial capital he will need to introduce into the business;

ii) a forecast trading and profit-and-loss account for the year ending 31 December 2005;

iii) a forecast balance sheet as at 31 December 2005;

iv) comments on the foregoing three statements, which you consider need explanation, bearing in mind that your uncle, though intelligent, is not experienced in accounting terminology;

v) any other comments and advice which you consider would be helpful to your uncle.

Format

A letter to your uncle with statements and comments suitably appended.

Objectives

In this assignment, the student should show an appreciation and understanding of:

- cash planning and personal cash flow;
- the role of the accountant in giving advice on personal finance;
- simple final accounts;
- planning the financial needs of an organisation or project.

References

Chapters 9 to 16.

PART IV

PARTNERS
IN BUSINESS

CHAPTER 17

Partnerships: the general principles

1 OBJECTIVES

At the end of this chapter you should be able to:

- define a partnership;
- understand some of the legal requirements of partnership accounting;
- describe a partnership agreement;
- appreciate the reasons for the formation of a partnership;
- list the main advantages and disadvantages of partnerships.

2 INTRODUCTION

In Chapter 1 we described the different forms of business organisation, but so far we have only examined the accounts of individuals. You will remember that a *sole trader* is a form of business owned by one person, and this person runs the business exclusively for his or her own benefit. One of the disadvantages suffered by sole traders is that the capital invested in the business is restricted to the amount that the owner can contribute personally, raise through a loan or generate by making a profit. This is the principal reason why sole traders tend to be small businesses. One way of increasing the amount of capital available to the business, and thus increasing its size, is to form a *partnership*. With more than one owner, there is the potential for increasing the amount of capital that can be raised, as well as the range of skills to run the business.

As far as accounting procedures are concerned, a partnership is very similar to a sole trader. The partners have capital accounts in their own names and are able to make drawings during the financial year in anticipation of profits. However, there are also some important differences. In this chapter we shall describe the main features of a partnership before going on to show you how to prepare partnership accounts in Chapters 18 and 19.

3 DEFINITION

A partnership can be defined as a form of business organisation in which two or more people join together to carry on a business with a view to making a profit.

We have already mentioned that, as their names suggest, a partnership differs from a sole trader in terms of the number of owners: a sole trader has only one owner whereas a partnership more than one owner. However, partnerships also have several other important characteristics.

- A partnership is not a separate legal entity from its owners; in other words, the partners do not enjoy a separate legal status from the business. This is important because it means that all the partners are liable for all the partnership activities, including any debts the business incurs. For example, if a *creditor* (an entity or an individual to whom the business owes money) cannot obtain payment from the partnership, any of the partners can be required to pay in full.

- Under the *Limited Partnership Act 1907*, a partnership may have partners whose liability is limited to the amount of capital they have subscribed, but limited partners may not take part in the management of the business.

- Normally a partnership is limited to a maximum of 20 partners. Exceptions to this are professional firms, such as accountants and solicitors, where there is no upper limit.

- Under the *Business Names Act 1985* the names of the partners must appear on the firm's stationery.

> *You should now be able to attempt Task 17.1 at the end of this chapter.*

4 PARTNERSHIP ACCOUNTS

In many ways *partnership accounts* are similar to those of sole traders. The major legislation which governs the operations of partnerships is the *Partnership Act 1890*, which includes the following accounting and reporting requirements:

- proper books of accounts must be kept;
- capital must be distinguished from profit-and-loss;
- a record must be kept of each partner's share of profit/loss and drawings;
- partners may make loans to the business;
- partners must render true accounts and full information on aspects affecting the partnership to any partner or his or her representative.

It is important to remember some features of a partnership that will have a direct effect on the accounting records, the profit-and-loss account and the balance sheet. These are:

- The partners may not contribute equal amounts of capital to the business and may wish this to be recognised in some way.

- Partners can make loans to the business over and above the capital they have invested and may wish to receive interest on their loan.

- Some of the partners may work full-time in the business, whereas others may spend relatively little of their time in the business. The partners who are committing a considerable part of their time to the business may wish to be recompensed for this by receiving a regular salary, for example.

- As with a sole trader, partners can make drawings during the course of the financial year in anticipation of profits. However, they may agree that drawings should be kept to a minimum and in order to encourage this, they may charge interest on drawings.

To comply with the statutory regulations and capture the financial relationships between the partners, the *profit-and-loss account* includes an *appropriation account* in which the transactions between the partners and the partnership that affect profits are shown. Separate *capital accounts* and *current accounts* show each partner's capital and current account balances. The capital accounts are fixed, except where capital is introduced or withdrawn. Each partner's share of the profit/loss and other transactions between the partners and the partnership are shown in his or her current account. We shall be looking at examples of partnership profit-and-loss accounts in Chapter 18 and balance sheets in Chapter 19.

> *You should now be able to attempt Question 17.1 at the end of this chapter.*

5 | PROFIT SHARING

As we stated in our definition, the objective of a partnership is to make a profit. Choosing a method for *sharing* any *profit* amongst the partners is a controversial topic. There is no 'right' way, but there are some standard approaches.

- *A fixed ratio*. Partners may agree to share the profits equally. However, if one partner has contributed more capital or spends more time working for the partnership, they may decide another fixed ratio. For example, if there are three partners, it may be agreed that one partner receives 50 per cent of the profits and the others receive 25 per cent each. There are no set proportions and it is up to the partners to reach agreement.

- *A ratio based on capital balances*. If the partners have contributed unequal amounts of capital, they may agree to share the profits in the same ratio to reflect this. In some instances partners may decide not to have current accounts and other allocations of profit, such as salaries or drawings, are entered directly into their capital accounts. The agreed ratio is usually set on the closing balances on their capital accounts.

- *Making allocations to partners and sharing the balance*. The partners may agree that interest will be paid on the capital contributed by the partners; that partners who spend a certain amount of time working in the business will receive a salary; that interest will be charged on any drawings. All these transactions will be allocations of the net profit earned by the business. Once these allocations have been made, any balance (whether profit or loss) will be shared amongst the partners in an agreed ratio.

6 | THE PARTNERSHIP AGREEMENT

Although not a legal requirement, partners are advised to draw up a *partnership agreement* when they form a partnership so that the relationship between the partners is clearly defined. Some aspects of any partnership agreement affect the *profit-and-loss account* and *balance sheet*. Examples include:

- the amount of capital to be contributed by each partner;
- the proportion in which profits/losses are to be shared/borne;
- the rate of any interest to be paid on capital contributed by the partners;
- the rate of any interest to be paid on loans to the partnership by the partners;
- the rate of any interest to be charged on partners' drawings;
- the amount of any salaries to be paid to the partners.

In the absence of an agreement between the partners about these matters, the *Partnership Act 1890* provides the following rules.

- *Profits and losses.* All partners are entitled to share equally in the capital gains and profits, and must contribute equally towards the losses, whether capital losses or otherwise, incurred by the firm.
- *Interest on capital.* Partners are not entitled to any interest on capital and therefore such interest cannot be deducted in ascertaining the profits of the business.
- *Interest on loans.* Partners are entitled to interest at 5 per cent per annum on any loan capital contributed in excess of the agreed capital subscribed.
- *Salaries.* All partners are entitled to take part in the management of the business, but no partner is entitled to any remuneration for acting in the business of the partnership.

You should now be able to attempt Task 17.2 and Question 17.2 at the end of this chapter.

7 | ADVANTAGES AND DISADVANTAGES OF PARTNERSHIPS

The main *advantages* of a partnership are that:

- there are few legal requirements;

- more capital can be raised to start the business than a sole trader;
- a greater range of skills is available to run the business than a sole trader;
- the burden of managing the business is shared among the partners;
- any losses will be shared among the partners.

The main *disadvantages* of a partnership are that:

- the profits must be shared;
- responsibility for debts incurred by individual partners or the business as a whole must be shared;
- individual partners are responsible for the actions of the others;
- no one has sole control and one partner's wishes may be overruled by the other partners;
- it can be difficult to transfer interest in a partnership.

> *You should now be able to attempt Task 17.3 and Question 17.3 at the end of this chapter.*

8   LIMITED PARTNERSHIP

The *Limited Liability Partnerships Act 2000* creates a new type of business entity, the Limited Liability Partnership (LLP). An LLP is a separate legal entity from its members. Therefore, it may enter into contracts and deeds, sue and be sued and grant floating charges over its assets in its own name. This avoids the problems that exist in relation to partnerships, where technically it is often necessary for every partner to be party to certain documents or litigation, and the creation of floating charges is not possible.

Currently all the partners in a partnership have potentially unlimited liability and are jointly and severally liable for the acts of their fellow partners carried out in the course of business. By contrast, subject to certain exceptions, members of an LLP have limited liability up to the amount of their capital in the LLP. The principle exceptions to limited liability are:

1. Where a member was personally at fault in giving rise to a cause of action (for example, a claim for negligence) he or she may have unlimited personal liability if he/she accepted a personal duty of care or a personal contractual obligation.

2. If an LLP becomes insolvent, members can be required to repay any property withdrawn from the LLP (including profits and interest) in the two years before insolvency. However, this is only the case if at the time of the member withdrawing such property he/she should have or ought to have concluded that there was no reasonable prospect of avoiding insolvent liquidation. The main burden to be borne by a LLP in return for limited liability is public availability of financial statements. An LLP must file audited accounts

(prepared on a 'true and fair view' basis) annually at Companies House which must include the name and profit share of the highest paid member. This test is assessed using the member's actual knowledge and based on some general knowledge, skill and experience of a person carrying on the same functions as that member. It is a defence to show a reasonable belief that the LLP would be able to avoid insolvent liquidation. We will be looking at the accounts of companies in later chapters.

Members' agreement for LLPs are more complex than partnership agreements because the Limited Liability Partnerships Act 2000 expressly excludes the application of existing partnership law to LLPs and their members. Therefore, matters that partnerships agreements can leave unsaid have to be expressly provided for in members' agreements.

If there is no member's agreement, then the Limited Liability Partnerships Act 2000 will apply certain very basic provisions (for example, that profits should be shared by members equally). However, these provisions are very brief and are likely to be insufficient for any LLP. A member's agreement is therefore essential.

Unlike limited partnerships and general partnerships there is no limit on the number of members an LLO may have (with the exception of certain professions, limited partnerships and general partnerships may only have 20 partners).

Limited Liability Partnerships were primarily intended for use by the professional firms, such as accountants. However, LLPs may be used by any type of business operating for profit. They have been available for use since 6 April 2001. A LLP may be suitable for use as a joint venture vehicle or as an alternative to a limited company, particularly for small businesses.

9 | SUMMARY

A *partnership* is a form of business organisation in which two or more people join together to carry on a business with a view to making a profit. The main legislation which governs the operations of partnerships is the *Partnership Act 1890*, the *Limited Partnership Act 1907* and the *Business Names Act 1985*.

Partnership accounts are similar to those of sole traders with the following exceptions:

- The profit-and-loss account includes an *appropriation account* in which the transactions between the partners and the partnership that affect profits are shown.

- Separate accounts are shown for each partner's *capital* and *current account balances*. The former are fixed, except where capital is introduced or withdrawn profit and losses and other transactions between the partners and the partnership adjust current accounts only.

Although not a legal requirement, the *partnership agreement* determines relationships between the partners. In the absence of such an agreement, the rules provided by the *Partnership Act 1890* apply.

As a form of business, a partnerships offers both *advantages* and *disadvantages* compared with a sole trader or limited company.

> *You should now be able to attempt the objective test at the end of this chapter.*

Student activities

Task 17.1
Carry out a small telephone survey to find out the average number of partners that are in the local firms of solicitors in your town.

Task 17.2
Choose a partner or partners from your group with a view to forming a partnership to carry on a business of your choice. Each of you should now draw up your own draft partnership agreement to cover all the aspects of the business relationship between the partners. Then you should all discuss the draft agreements and incorporate all the agreed clauses in a final partnership agreement. How easy was it to reach a final agreement?

Task 17.3
List all the advantages and disadvantages you can recall of partnerships compared with sole traders and private limited companies. You may wish to refer to Chapter 1 when carrying out this task.

Question 17.1
What are the main financial statements produced by a partnership and how do they differ from those of a sole trader?

Question 17.2
In the absence of any agreement between the partners, what are the main provisions of the Partnership Act 1890 relating to the financial relationships of partners?

Question 17.3
Compare the advantages and disadvantages of forming a partnership with those of forming a business as a sole trader. In addition to this chapter, you may wish to refer to Chapter 1 when answering this question.

Objective test *(tick the appropriate box)*

i)   A partnership:

    a)   is limited to a maximum of 50 people   ☐

    b)   enjoys legal status separate from its owners   ☐

    c)   must distinguish capital from share of profit and drawings   ☐

    d)   is governed by the Companies Act 1985   ☐

ii) One of the accounting and reporting requirements of the Partnership Act 1890 is that:

- a) the balance sheet must be in a vertical format ☐
- b) proper books of accounts must be kept ☐
- c) interest on capital must be clearly shown ☐
- d) capital must be increased by profit and reduced by drawings ☐

iii) In the absence of a partnership agreement, the rules of the Partnership Act 1890 apply, which state that:

- a) partners must share profits in proportion to the capital they have contributed ☐
- b) partners are entitled to 5 per cent interest on the capital they have contributed ☐
- c) working partners are entitled to a fair salary ☐
- d) partners share equally in capital gains and profits ☐

iv) A partnership enjoys the following advantages over a sole trader:

- a) it can raise more capital ☐
- b) legal requirements are fewer ☐
- c) the financial liability of the partners is limited ☐
- d) there is no need to keep proper accounting records ☐

v) A partnership enjoys the following advantages over a limited company:

- a) it can raise more capital ☐
- b) legal requirements are fewer ☐
- c) the financial liability of the partners is limited ☐
- d) it has an infinite life ☐

CHAPTER 18

Profit-and-loss account

1 | OBJECTIVES

At the end of this chapter you should be able to:

- explain the purpose of an appropriation account;
- identify the items which appear in an appropriation account;
- prepare a partnership profit-and-loss account;
- apply the provisions of the Partnership Act 1890 in the absence of a partnership agreement.

2 | INTRODUCTION

All the basic rules covered so far with regard to the preparation of the accounts of a *sole trader* also apply to the preparation of the *profit-and-loss account* and *balance sheet* of a partnership, which we will be examining in this chapter and the next. Therefore, you may find it useful to revise Chapters 10 and 11 before proceeding, and also Chapters 6 and 8 which explain the principles of *double-entry bookkeeping*.

There are certain differences between the profit-and-loss account of a sole trader and that of a partnership. The main difference is that the profit-and-loss account of a partnership is expanded into two sections. The additional section is known as the *profit-and-loss appropriation account* or the *appropriation section*. The appropriation account, although not necessarily headed as such, follows on directly from the main profit-and-loss account. It commences with the amount available for appropriation. This is determined by the gross profit less operating expenses, which is a normal feature of a profit-and-loss account of a sole trader, where it is described as the net profit. The other entries in the appropriation account are those which represent the transactions between the partnership and the individual partners. These transactions include salaries, interest on capital, interest on drawings and interest on loans.

The appropriation account is part of the *double-entry bookkeeping system*. If you make an entry to the appropriation account, such as interest paid on capital, a corresponding entry must be made to another account. In partnerships, it is usual for a *current account* to be opened for each partner which will record the corresponding entries to the appropriation account.

> You should now be able to attempt Task 18.1 at the end of this chapter.

3 | SALARIES

Salaries paid to partners are not deductible for tax purposes in ascertaining profits of the partnership as they are rather like drawings, therefore they may not be shown in the main profit-and-loss account as an expense. However, any salaries paid or due to the partners are found to affect the amount remaining to be shared amongst the partners as profit or loss.

Example

James, Curtis and Matlock are in partnership with profits being shared 50 per cent, 25 per cent, and 25 per cent respectively. James is credited with an annual salary of £30,000, and Curtis and Matlock receive £20,000 each. The profit available for appropriation is £190,000.

Required

Write up the entries in the profit-and-loss account appropriation account for the year ended 31 December 2003.

Solution

James, Curtis and Matlock
Profit-and-loss appropriation account for the year ended 31 December 2003

		£	£
Net profit available for appropriation			190,000
Less Salaries:			
	James	30,000	
	Curtis	20,000	
	Matlock	20,000	70,000
Balance of profits to be shared:		120,000	
	James 50%	60,000	
	Curtis 25%	30,000	
	Matlock 25%	30,000	120,000

4 | INTEREST ON CAPITAL

Where partners have contributed different amounts of capital, or their profit sharing ratio is unequal, it is normal to pay an agreed rate of *interest* on the *capital* of each partner. Interest paid on capital is a charge against the profits available for appropriation and therefore, like salaries, it reduces the amount of profit shared among the partners.

Example

James, Curtis and Matlock (see previous example) contribute agreed capitals of £100,000, £150,000 and £170,000 respectively, and their partnership agreement allows for interest at 10 per cent on their capitals to be credited to the partners.

Required

Redraft the appropriation account shown in the previous example to include interest on capital.

Solution

James, Curtis and Matlock
Profit-and-loss appropriation account for the year ended 31 December 2003

		£	£	£
Net profit available for appropriation				190,000
Less Interest on capital:				
	James	10,000		
	Curtis	15,000		
	Matlock	17,000	42,000	
Less Salaries:				
	James	30,000		
	Curtis	20,000		
	Matlock	20,000	70,000	112,000
Balance of profits to be shared:				78,000
	James 50%	39,000		
	Curtis 25%	19,500		
	Matlock 25%	19,500		78,000

> *You should now be able to attempt Question 18.1 at the end of this chapter.*

5   INTEREST ON DRAWINGS

In order to avoid cash-flow problems that might be caused if partners draw substantial amounts in anticipation of profits, there is often an agreement whereby *interest* may be charged by the business on partners' *drawings*. This encourages partners to keep them to a minimum or not to make drawings until profits are calculated. In such cases, interest is charged from the date on which the drawings are made until the date when the account is closed; alternatively, to some mutually agreed date. Where interest is charged, the amounts received by the business are credited to the profit-and-loss appropriation account as income to the business.

Example

James, Curtis and Matlock (see previous examples) regularly make drawings in anticipation of profits. For the current year the interest charged by the business on those drawings was £1,000, £2,000 and £1,000 respectively.

Required

Redraft the appropriation account shown in the previous example to include the interest on drawings.

Solution

James, Curtis and Matlock

Profit-and-loss appropriation account for the year ended 31 December 2003

		£	£	£
Net profit available for appropriation				190,000
Add Interest on drawings:				
	James	1,000		
	Curtis	2,000		
	Matlock	1,000	4,000	
			194,000	
Less Interest on capital:				
	James	10,000		
	Curtis	15,000		
	Matlock	17,000	42,000	
Less Salaries:				
	James	30,000		
	Curtis	20,000		
	Matlock	20,000	70,000	112,000
Balance of profits to be shared:				82,000
	James 50%	41,000		
	Curtis 25%	20,500		
	Matlock 25%	20,500		82,000

> You should now be able to attempt Task 18.2 and Question 18.2 at the end of this chapter.

6 INTEREST ON LOANS

Interest paid on loans provided by the partners in excess of their agreed capitals, unlike interest on partners' capitals, represents a normal business expense. The fact that the loans are provided by the partners is incidental; loans could equally be provided by outsiders to the partnership, in which case the interest paid would be deductible from the normal trading profits. Interest on loans provided by the partners is treated in the same way, thus reducing the net profit available for appropriation. The latter is always the opening line in the appropriation account. Interest paid on partners' loans should be shown as an expense in the profit-and-loss account, and not in the profit-and-loss appropriation account.

7 CAPITAL AND CURRENT ACCOUNTS

With the entries made to the *appropriation account*, it would be possible to make the corresponding entry to the *capital account* of each partner. However, this can be slightly confusing, particularly where interest is paid on capital invested by the partners. The usual system is to maintain a capital account for each partner that shows any capital subscribed and withdrawn, and a *current account* for each partner showing salaries, interest on capital, interest on drawings and share of profit.

Example

Sally and Ann have an interior design business, Sally Ann Partnership. The net profit last year was £80,000. The salaries of the two partners are: Ann £12,000; Sally £18,000. Interest is paid on capital as follows: Ann £7,000; Sally £3,000. The remaining profit is shared equally.

Required

Draw up an appropriation account and a current account for each partner.

Solution

Sally Ann Partnership

Profit-and-loss appropriation account for the year ended . . .

	£	£	£
Net profit available for appropriation			80,000
Less Interest on capital:			
Ann	7,000		
Sally	3,000	10,000	
Less Salaries:			
Ann	12,000		
Sally	18,000	30,000	40,000
Balance of profits to be shared:			40,000
Ann 50%	20,000		
Sally 50%	20,000		40,000

Current account: Ann

	£		£
		Appropriation account:	
		Interest on capital	7,000
		Salary	12,000
		Share of profit	20,000

Current account: Sally

	£		£
		Appropriation account:	
		Interest on capital	3,000
		Salary	18,000
		Share of profit	20,000

Note that the appropriation account has been drawn up in a *vertical format*, whereas the current accounts are traditional double-sided formats. This should not confuse you as far as the principles are concerned. The net profit on the appropriation account is a credit balance. The interest on capital, salaries and share of profits are, therefore, all debit balances, which means that the appropriation account is closed. As the entries to the appropriation account were all debit entries, they are credit entries to the current accounts of the partners. If the partners decide to take all the money owing to them as shown in the current accounts as drawings, the entries would be to credit the cash or bank account and debit the current accounts of the partners, thus closing them.

In the next chapter we will examine current accounts again in the context of the balance sheet.

> *You should now be able to attempt Task 18.3 and Question 18.3 at the end of this chapter.*

8 | SUMMARY

The profit-and-loss account of a partnership is similar to that of a sole trader. However, the net profit is transferred to a following section known as the *appropriation account*. This section shows the financial transactions of the partners, such as salaries, interest on capital and any interest charged on drawings. The balance of net profit, adding interest on drawings and deducting the charges, is allocated to the partners in their agreed profit sharing ratios.

The appropriation account forms part of the *double-entry bookkeeping system*, although it may be drawn up in a vertical format. Salaries, interest on capital and shares of profit represent *debit* balances; the corresponding *credit* balances are shown on the partners' current accounts. Interest on drawings is a credit entry to the appropriation account; the corresponding debit entry is made to the partners' current accounts.

> *You should now be able to attempt the objective test at the end of this chapter.*

Student activities

Task 18.1
Write a letter to the partners of a newly formed business explaining the type of information they can expect to find in an appropriation account.

Task 18.2
You have been talking to a friend who has recently become a partner in a local business. He is aggrieved because he has been charged interest on his drawings. Explain to him the reasons for this and why the same practice is not adopted for a sole trader

Task 18.3
You have been asked by the local Chamber of Commerce to make a presentation on the purpose and content of an appropriation account. Prepare a handout showing the contents of an appropriation account in the form of a diagram, using the appropriation account of James, Curtis and Matlock for your example.

Question 18.1
The following information refers to the Smith & Jones Partnership for the year ended 31 December 2003. Capital invested by the partners is Smith £10,000; Jones £30,000. Interest is allowed on capital at 5 per cent per annum. Profits are shared in the following proportions: Smith 60 per cent; Jones 40 per cent. The net profit available for appropriation for the year amounted to £47,500.

The following information for the year is also available:

	Drawings £	Interest on drawings £	Salaries £
Smith	7,500	750	25,000
Jones	6,000	400	–

Required

Prepare the profit-and-loss appropriation account for the year.

Question 18.2
Stanier, Collett and Hughes are in partnership and share profits equally. The business made a net profit available for appropriation of £99,189 for the year ended 31 December 2003. At the beginning of the year, the balances due to the partners on their current and capital accounts were as follows.

	Capital account £	Current account £
Stanier	54,000	6,660
Collett	54,000	5,130
Hughes	36,000	3,528

The following information for the year is also available:

	Drawings £	Interest on drawings £	Salaries £
Stanier	40,860	1,944	22,500
Collett	34,650	1,449	16,200
Hughes	15,750	1,296	–

The partners have agreed that interest on capital accounts will be allowed at 10 per cent per annum.

Required

i)   Prepare the profit-and-loss appropriation account for the year.

ii) Prepare the current accounts for the partners for the year.

Question 18.3

The following is a summarised list of transactions which was taken from the partnership books of Stirling, Drummond & Webb as at 30 June 2004.

		£	£
Sales			381,690
Purchases		243,222	
Returns in and out		6,450	10,800
Stock at 1 July 2003		54,630	
Discounts allowed and received		4,728	4,131
Wages		48,675	
Bad debts		1,419	
Electricity		1,895	
General expenses		1,263	
Fixtures (cost)		3,563	
Fixtures: Accumulated depreciation		24,000	
Creditors			12,000
Debtors			33,247
Bank overdraft		77,170	
Rates			3,197
Drawings:	Stirling	1,000	
	Drummond	24,030	
	Webb	18,135	
Current accounts as at 1 July 2003:	Stirling	18,375	
	Drummond (overdrawn)	1,857	
	Webb (overdrawn)	1,170	
Capital accounts:	Stirling		37,500
	Drummond		22,500
	Webb		22,500
		531,600	531,600

The following information is also available:

- Closing stock at 30 June 2004 was valued at £44,025.
- A provision of £750 for doubtful debts is to be made.
- At the end of the year, amounts accrued due for electricity and general expenses were £375 and £60 respectively.
- A prepayment of £750 has been paid for rates at the year end.
- Depreciation on fixtures is to be charged at 25 per cent per annum on cost.
- Interest is to be charged on drawings: Stirling £1,125; Drummond £950; Webb £500.
- Interest is to be allowed on capital at 10 per cent per annum.
- Profits are to be shared in the following proportions: Stirling 40 per cent; Drummond 40 per cent; Webb 20 per cent.

Required

i) Prepare the profit-and-loss accounting (including the appropriation section) for the year ended 30 June 2004.

ii) Show the entries in the partners' current accounts for the year.

Objective test (tick the appropriate box)

i) In partnership accounts, interest on drawings is normally shown as:

   a) a debit to the appropriation account and a credit to the current account ☐

   b) a debit to the profit-and-loss account and a credit to the current account ☐

   c) a credit to the profit-and-loss account and a debit to the current account ☐

   d) a credit to the appropriation account and a debit to the current account ☐

ii) Interest on partners loans are shown as:

   a) a credit to the appropriation account ☐

   b) a debit to the appropriation account ☐

   c) credit to the profit-and-loss account ☐

   d) a debit to the profit-and-loss account ☐

iii) Salaries paid to partners are shown as:

   a) credit entries on the partners' current accounts ☐

   b) debit entries on the partners' current accounts ☐

   c) debit entries to the profit-and-loss account ☐

   d) credit entries to the profit-and-loss account ☐

iv) In partnership accounts, the profit-and-loss appropriation account:

    a)   must not show salaries, which are deducted as an expense before arriving at net profit ☐

    b)   must not include interest on capital, which is deducted as an expense before arriving at net profit ☐

    c)   should include interest on loans provided by the partners in excess of their agreed capital ☐

    d)   none of these ☐

v) The current accounts of partners do not include:

    a)   interest on loans ☐

    b)   interest on capital ☐

    c)   salaries of partners when paid as and when due ☐

    d)   drawings ☐

CHAPTER 19

Balance sheet

1 OBJECTIVES

At the end of this chapter you should be able to:

- describe the purpose of a capital and current account for a partner;
- identify the entries which are made in capital and current accounts;
- construct a partnership balance sheet;
- construct the two main financial statements for a partnership.

2 INTRODUCTION

The *balance sheet* for a partnership is drawn up in a similar way to that of a sole trader. It is based on the accounting equation we introduced in Chapter 11:

$$Assets = Capital + Liabilities$$

The balance sheet is a statement of the financial position at one point in time and gives more detailed information than expressed by the accounting equation. It details the fixed assets and current assets of the business, as well as any liabilities. The balance sheet can be drawn up in either a horizontal of a vertical format. If you have forgotten any of the terms we have used so far, you should revise Chapter 11 now.

3 CAPITAL AND CURRENT ACCOUNTS

A *capital account* is shown in the balance sheet for each partner. The balance on each capital account represents the agreed fixed capital invested in the business by the partner. The fixed capital only changes when additional capital is introduced or some capital is withdraw by agreement. Unlike sole trader accounts, where profits or losses for the period adjust the capital accounts of the owner, in partnership accounts the profits or losses for the period adjust each partner's *current account*.

A current account for each partner is shown in the balance sheet. The balance on the account represents the amount due to or from the partner at the date of the balance sheet.

Example

James, Curtis and Matlock are in partnership. The amounts shown on the current accounts as owing to each partner at the beginning of the year were as follows:

James	£7,000
Curtis	£4,000
Matlock	£10,000

The net profit available for appropriation for the year is £190,000. During the year the partners' drawings amounted to:

James	£90,000
Curtis	£40,000
Matlock	£57,000

The following salaries were paid to the partners:

James	£30,000
Curtis	£20,000
Matlock	£20,000

The following interest on capital was paid to the partners:

James	£10,000
Curtis	£15,000
Matlock	£17,000

The following interest on drawings was charged to the partners:

James	£1,000
Curtis	£2,000
Matlock	£1,000

The balance of profits is shared as follows: James 50 per cent, Curtis 25 per cent and Matlock 25 per cent.

Required

Draw up the current accounts for the three partners.

Solution

James

Current account

	£	£
Opening balance due to James	7,000	
Add Salary	30,000	
Interest on capital	10,000	
Share of profit	41,000	88,000
Less Interest on drawings	1,000	
Drawings	90,000	91,000
Closing balance due from James		3,000

Curtis
Current account

	£	£
Opening balance due to Curtis	4,000	
Add Salary	20,000	
Interest on capital	15,000	
Share of profit	20,500	59,500
Less Interest on drawings	2,000	
Drawings	40,000	42,000
Closing balance due from Curtis		17,500

Matlock
Current account

	£	£
Opening balance due to Matlock	7,000	
Add Salary	30,000	
Interest on capital	10,000	
Share of profit	41,000	88,000
Less Interest on drawings	1,000	
Drawings	90,000	91,000
Closing balance due from Matlock		3,000

Of the three closing balances, James owes the partnership £3,000 because he has effectively overdrawn the balance due to him. The other partners are owed money by the business at the year end.

If salaries are paid in cash, it is possible that there are no entries for salaries in the partners' current accounts. However, if salaries are credited to the partners periodically, to be drawn on a different date, entries in respect of salaries will appear in the current accounts. This is because the current account balances represent the amounts due to, or from the partners. If the payment of salaries has been made as and when due, no entry in the current account may be necessary.

> *You should now be able to attempt Task 19.1 and Question 19.1 at the end of this chapter.*

4 APPROPRIATION ACCOUNT AND CURRENT ACCOUNTS

The example in the previous section demonstrates the relationship between the *appropriation account* and the *current accounts* of the partners. What is a *debit* to the appropriation account becomes a *credit* to the current accounts of the partners, and vice versa. You may find it useful to revise your knowledge of double-entry bookkeeping (see Chapter 8) before moving on to the next example which show how the double entry takes place.

Example

Churchward, Dean & Collett are in partnership and agree to share profits in the ratio 3:2:1. Their partnership agreement states that the partners are entitled to receive interest on capitals at 10 per cent per annum; 10 per cent per annum interest is charged on drawings; and Collett is entitled to a salary of £5,000 per annum. In addition, Churchward has guaranteed Dean a minimum total income of £30,000 for the year. The agreed balances at the beginning of the year were as follows:

	Capital account £	Current account £
Churchward	50,000	6,500
Dean	50,000	1,000
Collett	20,000	(3,000)

As you can see, Collett's current account is overdrawn. The net profit for the year available for appropriation was £71,500 and the partners' total drawings for the year were as follows:

Churchward	£25,000
Dean	£15,000
Collett	£15,000

Required

Draw up the profit-and-loss appropriation account for the year, the entries in the current accounts of the three partners and how they would appear on the balance sheet.

Solution

Churchward, Dean & Collett
Profit-and-loss appropriation account for the year ended . . .

		£	£	£
Net profit available for appropriation				71,500
Less Interest on capital	Churchward	5,000		
	Dean	5,000		
	Collett	2,000	12,000	
Less Salary	Collett		5,000	17,000
				54,500
Add Interest on drawings	Churchward	2,500		
	Dean	1,500		
	Collett	1,500		5,500
				60,000
Balance of profits to be shared	3: Churchward	30,000		
	2: Dean	20,000		
	1: Collett	10,000		60,000

Current accounts

	Churchward £	Dean £	Collett £
Opening balance	6,500	1,000	(3,000)
Interest on capital	5,000	5,000	2,000
Share of profits	30,000	20,000	10,000
Salary	–	–	5,000
	41,500	26,000	14,000
Interest on drawings	(2,500)	(1,500)	(1,500)
	39,000	24,500	12,500
Top-up (£30,000 – £25,000*)	(5,000)	5,000	–
Closing balance	34,000	29,500	12,500

*Dean's income is made up of interest on capital and share of profits.

Churchward, Dean & Collett
Balance sheet as at . . . (extract)

		£	£
Capital accounts:	Churchward	50,000	
	Dean	50,000	
	Collett	20,000	120,000
Current accounts:	Churchward	34,000	
	Dean	29,500	
	Collett	12,500	76,000
			196,000

You should now be able to attempt Task 19.2 and Question 19.2 at the end of this chapter.

5 THE FINAL ACCOUNTS

It is now possible to put together all the information from this chapter and the two previous chapters to construct the final accounts of a partnership from a list of data. Remember, the partnership *profit-and-loss account* is the same as for a sole trader, but there is a second section known as the *appropriation account*. The latter shows how the net profit is shared among the partners and the corresponding entries are recorded on the partners' current accounts. The partnership *balance sheet* is also similar to that of a sole trader, but you need to show the closing balances of each partner's current and capital accounts. You can use either the *vertical* or the *horizontal format* for the balance sheet. In the following example, we use the vertical format.

Example

Bond & Riddles are in partnership and have agreed to share profits 60 per cent and 40 per cent respectively. The trial balance drawn up from the partnership books is as follows.

Bond & Riddles
Trial balance as at 31 March 2004

		£	£
Buildings (cost £150,000)		120,000	
Plant and machinery (cost £30,000)		21,000	
Trade debtors		89,772	
Trade creditors			18,375
Stock as at beginning of the year		49,075	
Purchases and sales		119,768	269,580
Carriage inwards		1,688	
Carriage outwards		2,040	
Administration expenses		19,050	
Wages		33,375	
Bad debts		593	
Provision for doubtful debts			630
Capital accounts:	Bond		135,000
	Riddles		60,000
Current accounts:	Bond		3,930
	Riddles		3,060
Drawings:	Bond	18,900	
	Riddles	13,800	
Bank		1,514	
		490,575	490,575

The following information is also available:

- Stock at 31 March 2004 was valued at £72,365.

- Depreciation on buildings is charged at 2 per cent per annum, based on the reducing-balance method; depreciation on plant is charged at 10 per cent per annum using the straight-line method.

- Administration expenses accrued amount to £780 and carriage inwards £70.

- The provision for doubtful debts is to be set at £510.

- Partners are to be credited with salaries of £18,000 each.

- Interest on capital is allowed at 10 per cent per annum.

Required

i) Prepare a partnership trading, profit-and-loss account, including an appropriation section, for the year ended 31 March 2004.

ii) Prepare a partnership balance sheet as at 31 March 2004.

iii) Show the movements on the partners' current accounts for the year and the balances outstanding at the end of the year.

Solution

Bond & Riddles

Trading, profit and loss account for the year ended 31 March 2004

		£	£	£
Sales				269,580
Opening stock			49,075	
Add Purchases		119,768		
Carriage inwards		1,758	121,526	
			170,601	
Less Closing stock			72,365	98,236
Gross profit				171,344
Less Expenses:				
Depreciation:	Buildings		2,400	
	Plant		3,000	
Administration			19,830	
Carriage outwards			2,040	
Wages			33,375	
Bad debts written off		593		
Provision for doubtful debts (£630 – £510)		(120)	473	61,118
Net profit available for appropriation				110,226
Salaries:	Bond	18,000		
	Riddles	18,000	36,000	
Interest on capital:	Bond	13,500		
	Riddles	6,000	19,500	
Share of profits:	Bond	32,836		
	Riddles	21,890	54,726	110,226

Current accounts

	Bond £	Riddles £
Opening balance	3,930	3,060
Interest on capital	13,500	6,000
Salary	18,000	18,000
Share of profits	32,832	21,890
	68,266	48,950
Less Drawings	18,900	13,800
Closing balance due to partners	49,366	35,150

Bond & Riddles

Balance sheet as at 31 March 2004

	£ Cost	£ Accumulated depreciation	£ Net book value
Fixed assets:	150,000	32,400	117,600
Buildings	30,000	12,000	18,000
Plant	180,000	44,400	135,600

continued

	£ Cost	£ Accumulated depreciation	£ Net book value
Current assets:			
Stock	72,365		
Debtors	89,262		
	1,514	163,141	
Less Creditors due within one year:			
Creditors	18,375		
Accruals	850	19,225	143,916
			279,516

	Bond £	Riddles £	Total £
Capital accounts	135,000	60,000	195,000
Current accounts	49,366	35,150	84,516
			279,516

> *You should now be able to attempt Task 19.3 and Question 19.3 at the end of this chapter.*

6 SUMMARY

The entries which are made in the *appropriation section* of a partnership *profit-and-loss account* are reflected in corresponding entries in the *balance sheet* of a partnership. Separate *capital* and *current accounts* are maintained for each partner. The balance sheet of a partnership is similar to that of a sole trader, but in the case of a partnership the closing balances on the partners' capital and current accounts are show separately for each partner.

> *You should now be able to attempt the objective test at the end of this chapter.*

Student activities

Task 19.1
Draw a diagram to show the entries made on the appropriation account and partners' current accounts.

Task 19.2
Devise a checklist of items you would expect to see in the financial statements of a partnership but not in the financial statements of a sole trader.

Task 19.3

Your local Chamber of Commerce has asked you to make a presentation on partnership accounts. Prepare notes for the occasion which focus on the purpose and main features of a partnership balance sheet.

Question 19.1

Tan & Wei are in partnership and share profits equally. The following information for the year is available from the partnership books.

		£
Net profit		11,000
Interest on capital:	Tan	300
	Wei	200
Interest on drawings:	Tan	50
Salaries:	Tan	6,000
	Wei	4,000

Required

Prepare the appropriation account and current accounts for the partners.

Question 19.2

Sikka, Sidhu & Patel are in partnership and share profits equally. The partners receive interest on capital at 5 per cent per annum and Sikka and Sidhu receive a salary of £16,000 and £15,000 per annum respectively. During the year, the three partners each made drawings of £7,500. Their capital balances are Sikka £20,000; Sidhu £25,000; Patel £10,000. The net profit for the year was £41,250.

Required

Draw up the appropriation account and the partners' capital and current accounts as they would appear on the balance sheet.

Question 19.3

The following is a summarised list of transactions which was taken from the partnership books of *Stirling, Drummond & Webb* as at 30 June 2003.

	£	£	£
Sales			381,690
Purchases		243,222	
Returns in and out		6,450	10,800
Stock at 1 July 2002		54,630	
Discounts allowed and received	4,728	4,131	
Wages		48,675	
Bad debts		1,419	
Electricity		1,895	
General expenses		1,263	
Fixtures (cost)		3,563	
Fixtures: Accumulated depreciation	24,000		
Creditors			12,000
Debtors			33,247

		£	£
Bank overdraft		77,170	
Rates			3,197
Drawings:	Stirling	1,000	
	Drummond	24,030	
	Webb	18,135	
Current accounts as at 1 July 2002:	Stirling	18,375	
	Drummond (overdrawn)	1,857	
	Webb (overdrawn)	1,170	
Capital accounts:	Stirling		37,500
	Drummond		22,500
	Webb		22,500
		531,600	531,600

The following information is also available:

- Closing stock at 30 June 2003 was valued at £44,025.

- A provision of £750 for doubtful debts is to be made.

- At the end of the year, amounts accrued due for electricity and general expenses were £375 and £60 respectively.

- A prepayment of £750 has been paid for rates at the year end.

- Depreciation on fixtures is to be charged at 25 per cent per annum on cost.

- Interest is to be charged on drawings: Stirling £1,125; Drummond £950; Webb £500.

- Interest is to be allowed on capital at 10 per cent per annum.

- Profits are to be shared in the following proportions: Stirling 40 per cent; Drummond 40 per cent; Webb 20 per cent.

Required

i) Prepare the profit-and-loss accounting (including the appropriation section) for the year ended 30 June 2003.

ii) Prepare the partnership balance sheet as at 30 June 2003.

iii) Show the entries in the partners' current accounts for the year.

Objective test (tick the appropriate box)

i) Drawings made by a partner are:

    a) credited to the profit-and-loss account ☐

    b) credited to the appropriation account ☐

    c) debited to the profit-and-loss account ☐

    d) debited to the current account ☐

ii) Partners only receive interest on capital if:

   a) they have made a profit ☐

   b) they have agreed to do so ☐

   c) the rules of the Partnership Act 1890 apply ☐

   d) they have contributed unequal amounts ☐

iii) Partners working in a partnership are entitled to a salary if:

   a) they have not invested any capital ☐

   b) it is stated in the partnership agreement ☐

   c) the profit share are unequal ☐

   d) they have made drawings ☐

iv) Normally a partnership balance sheet shows balances for:

   a) the partners' capital accounts only ☐

   b) the partners' capital and current accounts ☐

   c) the partners' capital, current and salary accounts ☐

   d) the partners' capital and salary accounts ☐

v) On a horizontal partnership balance sheet:

   a) the partners' capital accounts go on the left-hand side and current accounts on the right ☐

   b) the partners' current accounts go on the left-hand side and their capital accounts on the right ☐

   c) the partners' capital and current accounts go on the right-hand side ☐

   d) the partners' capital and current accounts go on the left-hand side ☐

CHAPTER 20

Partnership changes

1 OBJECTIVES

At the end of this chapter you should be able to:

- describe the circumstances in which a partnership ceases;
- explain the workings of a realisation account;
- close a partnership where all partners are insolvent;
- explain the rules to apply when a partner is insolvent;
- close a partnership where one of the partners is insolvent;
- account for the introduction of a new partner.

2 INTRODUCTION

One of the disadvantages of a partnership as a form of business is that it has a finite life. There are a number of *partnership changes*, which mean that the business must close, even if it restarts immediately with a new combination of partners. Although the partners may not know in advance when the business will close, at some stage it will for a number of reasons that we will examine in this chapter. When a partnership ends, it is essential to be able to calculate what sum is due to each partner. This will mean following strict procedures so that all partners can be satisfied that they have received their share of the proceeds. This is most conveniently done by opening a *realisation account*.

Another change in the life of a partnership occurs when a new partner joins. It is usual for the new partner to invest capital in the business and the existing partners will want to benefit from this as a reward for building up the business. This is achieved by opening a *goodwill account*.

3 CESSATION OF A PARTNERSHIP

When a partnership ceases to trade we refer to it as the *cessation* or *dissolution* of the partnership. Unlike a limited company, a partnership is affected by changes of ownership and such changes mean that the partnership must be dissolved. We can be assured that at some stage changes in ownership will occur because even if the partners remain the same in the business for a long period of time, they may want to retire and eventually they will die. This does not mean that the business will not carry on, but the books of the existing partnership will have to be closed so that all partners can receive their fair share of the proceeds. Then books need to be opened for the new partnership.

It is possible that one of the partners becomes insolvent. In such a case it is not unusual for the partner concerned to owe money to the partnership, but be unable to pay it. This can arise when the partner has taken excessive drawings that have not been covered by his or her share of any profits. In such instances the remaining partners will have to make good the deficit and this must be accounted for in a fair and reasonable way. The main reasons for a partnership ceasing are:

- the business for which the partnership was formed has come to the end of its natural life;

- for various reasons the partners have agreed not to continue the business; for example, they may wish to change their careers or go off on a cruise;

- the partnership is unable to meet its financial obligations;

- one of the partners becomes insolvent;

- one of the partners dies.

In all these circumstances it will be necessary to close the accounts of the partnership. This is done by opening a realisation account which we examine next.

You should now be able to attempt Task 20.1 and Question 20.1 at the end of this chapter.

4 | REALISATION ACCOUNT

Whenever you are faced with the dissolution of a partnership the first rule is always to open a realisation account. This will act as part of the *double-entry system* (see Chapter 6) and will allow you to close all other existing accounts, calculate any profits or losses due to the partners on the cessation of the business, and pay them the amounts due. In its simplest form the procedure is as follows:

- Open a realisation account.

- Debit the realisation account with the book value of the business's assets.

- Debit the realisation account, thus closing them, and credit the bank account with the expenses of dissolving the partnership.

- Credit the realisation account and debit the bank account with the cash proceeds from the sale of the business's assets.

- Credit the bank account and debit the liability accounts (e.g. creditors) as they are paid.

- Distribute the profit or loss on the realisation account according to the agreed ratios among the partners.

- Pay cash to partners by crediting the bank account and debiting each partner's current and capital account.

If you follow these procedures, all the accounts will be closed with no outstanding balances and the partners will have received their due entitlements. Needless to say, there are some complications that can arise but we will start by considering a simple example.

Example

David and Goliath are in partnership and share profits equally. Their balance sheet as at 31 March 2004 was as follows.

David & Goliath

Balance sheet as at 31 March 2004

	£		£
Fixed assets	16,000	Capital accounts:	
Stock	8,500	David	14,000
Debtors	12,800	Goliath	12,000
Bank	2,100	Creditors	13,400
	39,400		39,400

On 1 April they dissolve the partnership and the following events occurred. The fixed assets were sold for £15,800; the stock was sold for £8,400; the debtors realised £12,700, and the creditors were paid in full.

Required

Close the accounts of the partnership showing all the entries.

Solution

This example can look quite confusing at first, so we will rehearse the stages you need to go through.

1. Open an account for all of the items shown on the balance sheet and enter the balances.

2. Close off the fixed assets, stock and debtor accounts by crediting them and entering the corresponding entries on the debit side of the realisation account.

3. When you have paid off the creditors in full, crediting the bank account and debit the creditors' accounts.

4. At this stage the only accounts that have balances on them are the realisation account, the bank account and the partners' capital accounts.

5. Total both sides of the realisation account. If the balancing figure has to be added on the debit side to make the totals agree there is a profit on realisation. In our example, the balancing figure has to go on the credit side, so there is a loss. This loss must be shared equally between the partners so debit their capital accounts.

6. Calculate the balancing figures on the partners' capital accounts. In both cases you will have debit balances and these are the proceeds they are due. Debit the partners' capital accounts to close them and credit the bank account.

7. Total both sides of the bank account. They should agree. If not you have made a mistake and will have to work through the example again.

Realisation account

	£		£
Fixed assets	16,000	Bank: Sale of assets	15,800
Stock	8,500	Bank: Sale of stock	8,400
Debtors	12,800	Bank: Debtors realised	12,700
		Loss on realisation:	
		David	200
		Goliath	200
	37,300		37,300

Bank account

	£		£
Opening balance	2,100	Creditors	13,400
Realisation: Sale of assets	15,800	Capital accounts:	
Realisation: Stock	8,400	David	13,800
Realisation: Debtors	12,700	Goliath	11,800
	39,000		39,000

Fixed asset account

	£		£
Opening balance	16,000	Realisation account	16,000

Stock account

	£		£
Opening balance	8,500	Realisation account	8,500

Debtors account

	£		£
Opening balance	<u>12,800</u>	Realisation account	<u>12,800</u>

Creditors account

	£		£
Bank	<u>13,400</u>	Opening balance	<u>13,400</u>

Capital account: David

	£		£
Loss on realisation	200	Opening balance	14,000
Bank	13,800		———
	<u>14,000</u>		<u>14,000</u>

Capital account: Goliath

	£		£
Loss on realisation	200	Opening balance	12,000
Bank	11,800		———
	<u>12,000</u>		<u>12,000</u>

In the above example the business's liabilities, the creditors, were paid off in full. If this had not been the case, the entries would have been put through the realisation account. First, the creditors' account would have been closed by debiting with the final balance and crediting the realisation account. When the agreed amount was paid, the bank would have credited and the realisation account debited.

You should now be able to attempt Task 20.2 and Question 20.2 at the end of this chapter.

5 | THE INSOLVENT PARTNER

The above procedure is applied to all cases, with one notable exception and that is when one or more partners becomes *insolvent*. In this case, there will be a debit balance on the relevant partner's account. If the partner had money and paid this into the partnership, you would debit the bank account and close the partner's account by crediting it. But if the partner has no cash, the capital account will show a deficit that must be borne by the remaining partners. This will not be in their profit sharing ratios, however, but in the ratio of their capital accounts.

This procedure for changes incurred when a partner becomes insolvent follows the ruling of a famous legal case *Garner v Murray 1904*. If you have an example where one or more of the partners is insolvent, you must remember this rule and explain you are applying it as set out in the case.

Example

Ursula, Dave & Sandra are in partnership and share profits in the ratio 50 per cent: 25 per cent: 25 per cent respectively. On 31 December their balance sheet was as follows.

Ursula, Dave & Sandra
Balance sheet as at 31 December

	£	£
Fixed assets		23,500
Stock		24,600
Debtors		13,200
		61,300
Less Current liabilities:		
Creditors	38,900	
Overdraft	13,400	52,300
		9,000
Capital accounts:		
Ursula	4,000	
Dave	2,000	
Sandra	2,000	8,000
Add Current accounts:		
Ursula	400	
Dave	200	
Sandra	400	1,000
		9,000

The partnership was dissolved on 1 January when the following events occurred. The fixed assets were sold for £21,000; the stock was sold for £17,600; the debtors realised £12,500; the creditors were paid £38,700. Dave is insolvent and therefore is unable to make any contribution on the dissolution of the partnership.

Required

Draw up the realisation account, bank account and the capital and current accounts.

Solution

Realisation account

	£		£
Fixed assets	23,500	Creditors	38,900
Stock	24,600	Proceeds:	
Debtors	13,200	Fixed assets	21,000
Payment of creditors	38,700	Stock	17,600
		Debtors	12,500
		Loss on realisation:	
		Ursula	5,000
		Dave	2,500
		Sandra	2,500
	100,000		100,000

Bank account

	£		£
Proceeds:		Opening balance	13,400
Fixed assets	21,000	Realisation account:	
Stock	17,600	Payment of creditors	38,700
Debtors	12,500		
Ursula	800		
Sandra	200		
	52,100		52,100

Capital accounts

	Ursula	Dave	Sandra		Ursula	Dave	Sandra
	£	£	£		£	£	£
Loss on realisation	5,000	2,500	2,500	Opening balance	400	200	200
Dave*	200		100	Current accounts:	4,000	2,000	4,000
				Ursula*		200	
				Sandra*		100	
				Bank	800		200
	5,200	2,500	2,600		5,200	2,500	2,600

Garner v Murray

Dave's deficit is £300 and this must be shared between Ursula and Sandra in the ratio of their capital balances which are £4,000 and £2,000 respectively, namely 2:1.

Current accounts

	Ursula	Dave	Sandra		Ursula	Dave	Sandra
	£	£	£		£	£	£
Capital account	400	200	400	Opening balance	400	200	400

> You should now be able to attempt Question 20.3 at the end of this chapter.

6   ADMISSION OF A NEW PARTNER

It is not unusual for a partnership at some stage in its existence to admit a new partner. It could be that business is expanding and new skills or more capital is required, which can be supplied by a new partner. The actual negotiations for admitting a new partner are usually complex. The existing partners will expect the new partner to invest in the partnership and that this capital will reflect a share of the 'worth' of the business. There will also be discussions on what share of the profits/losses will be received/borne by the new partner. In other words, all the issues that are included in the partnership agreement must be renegotiated.

From the accounting point of view, the admission of a new partner is relatively simple. There are a number of different approaches but we will explain one that is frequently used. It will help with the example if you remember the following:

1. The total assets less the total liabilities will give the net worth of the business. The total assets less the total liabilities are referred to as the *net assets*. This is merely an adjustment to the accounting equation we have met in other chapters, which will now read:

$$\text{Assets} - \text{Liabilities} = \text{Capital}$$

or

$$\text{Net assets} = \text{Capital}$$

2. Over the years the business will have developed *goodwill*. This may be difficult to define and measure, but will be made up of such things as the business's name and reputation; the loyalty of its workforce; its customer base; its links with suppliers; the infrastructure of systems and procedures that have been established. The existing partners will consider goodwill as an asset and expect the new partner to recompense them for acquiring a share of the goodwill.

Example

Camden & Lansdown are a partnership and have agreed to share profits equally. Their existing capital accounts each show a balance of £30,000. Camden and Lansdown agree to let Weston join the partnership. He must contribute £50,000 and for this will receive a one-third interest in the partnership. It is agreed that goodwill will be recorded as an asset of the partnership.

Required

Draw up the goodwill account, the bank account and the partners' capital accounts to show the admission of the new partner.

Solution

As Weston has agreed to invest £50,000 for a one-third interest in the capital of the new partnership the new capital will be £50,000 × 3 = £150,000. Using the accounting equation, if the capital is £150,000 the net assets must be the same amount:

	£
Total net assets of the new partnership	150,000
Identifiable net assets of the old partnership (i.e. the existing partners' last capital accounts plus the investment by the new partner of £50,000)	110,000
Difference (goodwill)	40,000

This difference of £40,000 represents goodwill which it has been agreed will be recorded in the books of accounts. Under the *double-entry bookkeeping* system (see Chapter 6), the accounts will look like this.

Goodwill account

	£		£
Lansdown and Camden	40,000		

Bank account

	£		£
Capital: Weston	50,000		

Capital account: Weston

	£		£
		Opening balance	30,000
		Goodwill	20,000

Capital account: Camden

	£		£
		Opening balance	30,000
		Goodwill	20,000

Capital account: Lansdown

	£		£
		Opening balance	30,000
		Goodwill	20,000

You will see that the balances in the old partners' capital accounts after the admission of the new partner stand at £50,000 each and they have each benefited by £20,000. This is recognised by the opening of a goodwill account.

It is usual to leave the goodwill account in the books. It can either be written off immediately in the partners' agreed profit-sharing ratios and their capital accounts debited, or it can be written off over a number of years in the profit-and-loss account.

> *You should now be able to attempt Task 20.3 at the end of this chapter.*

7 | SUMMARY

Partnerships cease during the lifetime of the partners for a number of reasons as well as on the death of one of the partners. When a partnership ceases, it is essential to close the partnership accounts so that the amount due to each partner can be calculated. A *realisation account* is opened and this allows the profit to be calculated on the dissolution of the partnership. The profit is shared among the partners in their agreed profit-sharing ratios.

Sometimes when a partnership ceases, one of the partners is insolvent. In such a case, the insolvent partner is unable to contribute cash to clear any deficit that may exist on the capital account. The rules in *Garner v Murray* apply and these state that the deficit will be borne by the remaining partners in the ratio of their capital accounts.

The admission of a new partner entails an adjustment so that the existing partners can benefit from having built up the business. One method for doing this is to open a *goodwill account*. This is usually written off immediately or over a period of time.

Student activities

Task 20.1
List the reasons for the cessation of a partnership.

Task 20.2
Prepare notes for a presentation to explain the purpose and operation of a realisation account.

Task 20.3
Tom and Andy are considering admitting a new partner. Write them a letter explaining the procedure.

Question 20.1
Mike, Alistair & Helen are in partnership and share profits equally. Their balance sheet at 31 December 1996 is shown below.

Mike, Alastair & Helen
Balance sheet as at 31 December 1996

	£		£
Fixed assets	25,500	Creditors	18,300
Stock	12,600	Overdraft	2,400
Debtors	30,600	Capital accounts:	
		Mike	18,000
		Alistair	15,000
		Helen	15,000
	68,700		68,700

On 1 January 1997 the partnership was dissolved and on that date the fixed assets were sold for £20,800; stock was valued at £10,200; debtors realised £29,900; creditors were paid £17,700; the expenses of realisation were £1,500.

Required

Prepare the accounts to close the partnership.

Question 20.2

Explain the importance of *Garner v Murray* in the dissolution of a partnership.

Question 20.3

Juliet, Pat & Joe are in partnership, sharing profits equally. Their balance sheet at 30 June 1997 is shown below.

Juliet, Pat & Joe
Balance sheet as at 30 June 1997

	£		£	£
Fixed assets	47,500	Creditors		77,400
Stock	49,200	Overdraft		26,900
Debtors	27,100	Capital accounts:		
		Juliet	6,000	
		Pat	8,000	
		Joe	2,000	16,000
		Current accounts:		
		Juliet	200	
		Pat	1,600	
		Joe	2,000	3,500
	123,800			123,800

The partnership is dissolved on 1 July 1997 and on that date the fixed assets were sold for £40,300; the stock was sold for £37,500; debtors realised £26,300; creditors were paid £77,200. Unfortunately, Joe is bankrupt and unable to contribute to the assets of the partnership.

Required

Prepare the accounts to close the partnership.

Objective test *(tick the appropriate box)*

i) Expenses of realisation are:

a) debited to the realisation account and credited to the capital accounts ☐

b) debited to the realisation account and credited to the bank account ☐

c) debited to the bank account and credited to the realisation account ☐

d) debited to the capital accounts and credited to the bank account ☐

ii) Profits on the realisation of a partnership are:

a) debited to the bank account ☐

b) credited to the bank account ☐

c) debited to the partners' capital accounts ☐

d) credited to the partners' capital accounts ☐

iii) When creditors are not paid in full on realisation:

a) the difference is debited to the partners' capital accounts ☐

b) the difference is credited to the bank account ☐

c) the creditor's account is first transferred to the realisation account ☐

d) the creditor's account is first transferred to the capital account in the profit sharing ratio ☐

iv) If a partner is insolvent, any deficit on his or her capital account is shared among the other partners:

a) in the ratio of their capital accounts ☐

b) in the ratio of their current accounts ☐

c) in their profit sharing ratios ☐

d) equally ☐

v) The value of any goodwill is considered to be:

a) the net worth of the business ☐

b) the capital of the business ☐

c) a liability of the business ☐

d) an asset of the business ☐

Jones, Morgan and Thomas

Context

Jones, Morgan and Thomas have been in partnership as garage proprietors for a number of years, but they are seriously considering dissolving the partnership, selling the assets, paying all the bills and going their own separate ways. Although they have employed a bookkeeper who has maintained proper records, their accountant became fed up with the uncertainty of not knowing whether he had a future with the partnership or not, so he left to join Henleys. The partners have approached you for advice, and initially you decide to establish the state of the business at the end of 2003, and the level of profit for that year. The list of balances at the end of 2003 is shown below.

List of balances at 31 December 2003

		£	£
Capital accounts:	Jones		25,000
	Morgan		25,000
	Thomas		20,000
Current accounts:	Jones		9,000
	Morgan		12,000
	Thomas		5,000
Drawings:	Jones	9,000	
	Morgan	9,500	
	Thomas	4,000	
Premises and car showrooms		50,000	
Workshop equipment at cost		10,000	
Depreciation on workshop equipment to 31 December 2003			4,000
Petrol pumps at cost		2,000	
Depreciation on petrol pumps to 31 December 2002			800
Opening stock		23,485	
Debtors and creditors		33,040	19,400
Bank overdraft			1,650
Cash in hand		125	
Purchases and sales		236,890	306,990
Wages		40,660	
Workshop rent received to 30 June 2003			160
Rent, insurance and electricity		5,850	
Telephone		800	
Advertising		1,000	
Sundry office expenses		650	
Sundry materials		1,250	
Repairs and maintenance		750	
		429,000	429,000

After further investigation you ascertain the following additional information:

- Accrued expenses at 31 December 2003 were electricity £150 and sundry office expenses £400.
- Depreciation on fixed assets other than premises and showrooms is charged at 10 per cent per annum using the straight line method.
- The workshop is let at an annual rent of £320.
- Interest at 10 per cent is allowed on the partners' capital accounts.
- The partners' profit sharing ratio is Jones 50 per cent, Morgan 30 per cent and Thomas 20 per cent.
- Closing stock at 31 December 2003 was valued at £30,135.

There is some argument between the partners as to whether they have a well-run business, and whether the business is in a sound state at the end of 2003. They feel that the answers to these questions will influence their decision whether or not to dissolve the business.

You ascertain that the ratios for a comparative firm for the same year are:

Credit period taken by debtors: 75 days

Stock turnover (based on cost of sales): 6 times per annum

Current ratio: 24 : 1

Return on capital employed (based on closing capital): 23%

Gross profit margin: 22%

Net profit margin: 10%

Another consideration that will influence their decision whether to dissolve the partnership or not is the return that could be obtained if each partner invested the amounts due to him in an alternative investment outside the business. Assume that the partners' returns from the business this year are typical of past and future performances.

Student activities

i) Prepare the partnership trading, profit-and-loss account, including an appropriation section, for the year ended 31 December 2003, together with a balance sheet as at that date.

ii) Draw up the detailed current account for each partner for the year.

iii) Assume that on dissolution of the partnership the balance sheet values would be realised. How much would each partner receive? Investigate other alternative investments into which each partner could place the funds released by the partnership dissolution, and provide a list of them, together with their characteristics such as risk level, minimum amounts invested, the period of time the money is tied up, brokerage and investment fees, and any other relevant points. You should restrict your list to investments rather than businesses.

Format

A set of accounts, the calculation of, and a report on, the ratios revealed by the accounts, a list of alternative investment types, a questionnaire, and a report to each partner advising him/her of the action to be taken.

Objectives

The student should show an understanding and appreciation of partnership accounts.

- the construction of partnership accounts;
- their operation;
- the application of capital accounts;
- the application of current accounts;
- the procedures for dissolving a partnership.

References

Chapters 6, and 17 to 20.

PART V

LIMITED COMPANIES

CHAPTER 21

The general principles

1 OBJECTIVES

At the end of this chapter you should be able to:

- define a limited liability company;
- describe the difference between public and private limited companies;
- describe the advantages and disadvantages of limited companies;
- summarise the main differences between sole trader and a limited company accounts;
- explain the meaning of the financial terms associated with limited company accounts.

2 INTRODUCTION

In Chapter 1 we described the different forms of business organisation, and so far we have examined *sole trader* and *partnership accounts*. You will remember that a sole trader is a form of business owned by one person who runs the business for his or her own benefit, whereas a partnership can have more than one owner (usually up to 20). Because a sole trader's business is relatively small, its financial statements are fairly easy to understand. To a large extent, the financial statements of a partnership are similar to those of a sole trader, although by having more than one owner to subscribe capital, partnerships are generally larger businesses. By far the most important financial statements are those of the largest form of business organisation: *limited companies*.

In this chapter we shall be describing the nature of limited companies, and the main differences between public and private limited companies, and limited companies in general and sole traders. We shall be introducing the financial terms that you will need to be familiar with before we examine the internal profit-and-loss account of limited companies. Limited companies are controlled by regulations and we will look at these in the following chapter.

3 PUBLIC AND PRIVATE COMPANIES

You will remember from Chapter 1 that a *limited liability company* (often referred to simply as a limited company) can be defined as a legal entity that is separate from the owners. The owners of the company are known as *shareholders*. Their liability is limited to the amount of money they have invested and/or agreed to invest in the company. This means that, in contrast to sole traders and partnerships, the owners are not responsible for the business's debts.

Because of the owners' benefit from limited liability, there are a number of legal burdens placed on limited companies. On formation of a limited company, certain documents must be registered with the *Registrar of Companies*. Every year the company must send certain financial information to all its shareholders and register certain information with the Registrar of Companies, which then becomes public. In the main, the owners tend not to run the company themselves, but appoint directors to do it for them.

Limited companies are either *public limited companies*, able to offer their shares to the public, or *private limited companies*, which are not permitted to do so. Only a public limited company can use a name which includes the words 'public limited company' or the abbreviation 'plc' (or the Welsh equivalent 'ccc'). A public limited company can have its shares listed for trading on the *London Stock Exchange*. Such a company may be referred to as a *listed* or *quoted company*. In the UK, most public limited companies are quoted on the London Stock Exchange. This means that trading (buying and selling) shares is conducted through the Stock Exchange and is therefore a relatively easy process.

There are approximately 2,000 listed companies and you can probably name many of the major companies. Names of companies that immediately spring to mind are often high street names such as Boots, W. H. Smith, Marks & Spencer, Tesco and Sainsbury, or banks such as Barclays, and National Westminster. Other well-known names are companies in the food and drinks sector such as RHM, Unigate, Bass and Guinness. If you look in any quality newspaper, such as the *Independent*, *The Times* or the *Financial Times*, you will find the names and share prices listed of most of the major public limited companies. Because of their importance in their contribution to the economy in such matters as the numbers they employ and their products and services, information on public limited companies is by far the easiest to obtain. Their activities are reported in the press and they make information about themselves readily available; in particular, their annual report and accounts.

It is an offence for a private limited company to offer its shares to the public, but under the legislation one person alone may form a private company by completing all the formalities. There are many more private companies than public companies – approximately one million in Great Britain. However, some of them are very small with only a handful of employees. As far as reporting requirements are concerned, private companies, and also those public limited companies not listed on the London Stock Exchange, do not have to comply with Stock Exchange requirements. For private companies, there are a number of exceptions and exclusions in respect of the financial information they have to publish.

The most obvious differences between public and private limited companies are their names and the fact that public limited companies can offer their shares to the public, but there are other differences. It is usually easier for public companies to raise large amounts of finance because they can offer their shares to the public. For some business activities considerable sums of capital are required and therefore the company needs to be able to offer its shares to the public. Public limited companies also have a higher public profile and frequently, but not always, are familiar names and have a good reputation. They can often pay high salaries to attract the best staff and can often negotiate favourable terms for many of their transactions because of their size and prestige.

> *You should now be able to attempt Task 21.1 at the end of this chapter.*

4 | ADVANTAGES AND DISADVANTAGES OF LIMITED COMPANIES

Private limited companies have some advantages over public limited companies. As mentioned above, they do not have to disclose so much information publicly and the formalities for setting up a private limited company are somewhat easier. In fact, companies are normally started as private limited companies. If they are successful and grow, the owners may decide to *go public* or *float* the company. This means that they will turn the company into a public company and seek a listing on the London Stock Exchange. Part of the proceeds from the (new) issue of shares to the public goes to the original owners, who inevitably lose some control of the company. However, they are handsomely paid for the interests they are relinquishing and may well end up millionaires.

The main *advantages* limited companies have over sole traders and partnerships are that:

- limited companies can raise more capital;
- they continue even if the owners die;
- the owners' liability is limited to the capital they have agreed to invest in the company.

The main *disadvantages* limited companies have over sole traders and partnerships are that:

- it is more expensive to start a business as a limited company;
- any decisions an individual shareholder may wish to make can be overruled by other shareholders;
- there are considerable legal requirements to be fulfilled;
- some of the financial affairs become public property.

> *You should now be able to attempt Task 21.2 at the end of this chapter.*

<table>
<tr><td>5</td><td>LIMITED COMPANY AND
SOLE-TRADER ACCOUNTS</td></tr>
</table>

The main differences between the accounts of a limited company and those of a sole trader are summarised in the following table. The table introduces some new terms that are associated with limited company accounts and it is useful if these are explained before we begin our examination of the accounts of a limited company.

Limited company and sole-trader accounts compared

Sole-trader accounts	Limited company accounts
Capital is the sum introduced by the owner at the start.	*Share capital* is the amount invested by the shareholders whose liability is limited to their shareholding (or if a share is only partly paid, also to the amount owing on the shares).
Capital is increased by *profit*.	*Profit* is not part of the share capital. It belongs to the shareholders.
Loans are made by banks and other financial institutions or individuals.	*Debentures* represent loans made to the company. They are bonds issued by the company.

The following glossary provides a brief explanation of the terms that are associated with limited company accounts.

- A *shareholder* is an owner of shares in a limited company (or a limited partnership). A shareholder is a member of the company. In other companies the term *stockholder* is frequently used.

- *Share capital* is the part of the finance of a company received from its owners (shareholders) in exchange for shares. Share denominations are 1p, 5p, 10p, 25p, 50p and £1. If you look at the London Share Service page of the *Financial Times*, 25p is the default value.

- *Authorised share capital* is the amount of share capital a company is allowed to issue. The issued share capital may be less than the authorised share capital. The authorised share capital is shown as a note on (or to) the balance sheet and is not part of the figures needed to balance.

- *Called-up capital* is a proportion of the issued shares for which payment has been demanded and paid. It is not unusual for companies to issue shares with part of the amount due paid initially and the balance at some later date.

Example

Sunderland Ltd was formed with a right to issue 500,000 ordinary shares of £1 each, but to date only 400,000 shares have been issued. None of the shares issued has been fully paid, and only 60p per share has been called. No payment has been received for 1,000 of the shares; the full amount of £1 per share has been paid on another 2,000 shares.

Required

Quantify the following:

i)   authorised share capital

ii) issued share capital

iii) called-up share capital

iv) calls in arrears

v)   calls in advance

vi) paid-up capital

Solution

i)   authorised share capital = 500,000 shares × £1 = £500,000

ii) issued share capital = 400,000 shares × £1 = £400,000

iii) called-up share capital = 400,000 shares × 60p = £240,000

iv) calls in arrears = 1,000 shares × 60p = £600

v)   calls in advance = 2,000 shares × 40p = £800

vi) paid-up capital = £240,000 − £600 = £239,400

- *Ordinary shares* are the most common form of share capital and usually carry voting rights. Ordinary shareholders receive dividends (see below) after the preference shareholders (see below) have been paid. The dividends ordinary shareholders receive are proposed at the discretion of the directors. Therefore, ordinary shares are often referred to as *risk capital* or *equity*. In North America, ordinary shares are called *common stock*.

- *Preference shares* entitle the shareholder to a specified rate of dividend and are paid before ordinary shareholders. If there are insufficient profits for any dividend to be paid in one year, the arrears have to be paid to *cumulative preference* shareholders before any other class of share is paid in any subsequent year. *Non-cumulative preference* shareholders are not entitled to any arrears.

- A *dividend* is the distribution of part of the earnings of a company to its shareholders. The directors decide on the amount of the dividend to be recommended for approval at the *annual general meeting (AGM)*. The amount depends on the profits. Dividend policy is too complicated to be discussed here, but usually some profit is retained and perhaps transferred to reserves (kept back for use in the business). Shareholders cannot propose a dividend higher than that recommended by the directors, although they can (unusually) propose a reduction in the dividend if they feel that it would be more advantageous to the company to retain profits, perhaps to improve the liquidity (cash) position.

It is common practice to express the dividend for ordinary and preference shares as pence per share or as a percentage. The table shows examples for ordinary shares.

	Company A	Company B
Number of shares	100,000	1,000,000
Denomination	25p	£1
Share capital	£25,000	£1,000,000
Dividend	10%	5%
Dividend (pence)	2.5p	5p
Total amount of dividend	£2,500	£50,000
Dividend for a shareholding of 1,000 shares gives	£25	£50

- *Debentures* are long-term loans, sometimes held by banks. They are usually secured on specific assets such as property or on all or some of the assets (called a *floating charge*). Interest paid on debentures, like interest charged on bank overdrafts, is charged as an expense in the profit-and-loss account. Debentures are not part of the share capital and debenture holders are not members of the company unless they also hold shares.

- A *minority interest* is the interest of individual shareholders in a company more than 50 per cent of which is owned by a holding company. For example, if 70 per cent of the ordinary shares in a company are owned by a holding company, the remaining 30 per cent represents a minority interest. When the results of all the separate companies in the group are consolidated, it is important to show the amount belonging to minority interests.

- *Exceptional items* are events or transactions of an exceptional nature. For example, a company may have suffered a large loss through fire for which it was uninsured, or perhaps a war led to the loss of its overseas assets. Under FRS 3, *Reporting Financial Performance*, exceptional items are defined as events or transactions that are part of a company's ordinary activities, but because of their size or incidence need to be disclosed. Most exceptional items should be included under the heading to which they relate on the financial statements and be explained in a note to the accounts. If they are sufficiently material, the exceptional item should be disclosed separately on the face of the profit-and-loss account. Some exceptional items must be shown separately on the face of the profit-and-loss account after operating profit and before interest. These are: profits or losses on the sale or termination of an operation; costs of a fundamental reorganisation or restructuring, profits or losses on the disposal of fixed assets.

At one time, companies differentiated between exceptional items and extraordinary items. This practice was open to abuse and profits could be presented to look more favourable than they really were. Under FRS 3, extraordinary items are rare.

- *Corporation tax (CT)* is the tax charged on the total profits of a company resident in the UK arising in each accounting period. The rate depends on the level of profits. At the time that the accounts are being prepared it is unlikely that the amount will have been agreed and therefore an estimate is made and a suitable amount provided for. Because taxation is a large and complicate subject, in the next chapter you will see that we have simplified matters by placing the estimated liability for tax under 'Creditors: Amounts due within one year' on the balance sheet.

- A *transfer to reserves* is where the directors of the company have transferred profits to reserves and indicates that they do no intend to distribute the amount transferred as a dividend in that particular year. Reserves are also shown on the balance sheet in the Financed by or Represented by section.

- A *proposed dividend* is one that has been recommended by the directors of the company but has not yet been paid. Proposed dividends are shown on the balance sheet under *Creditors: Amounts due within one year*. Assuming there are adequate profits remaining after corporation tax and transfers to reserves, a dividend is shown as already described. Many companies issue an interim statement reporting on profits during the financial year, usually during the first six months of the year (see Chapter 21). If interim profits are adequate, they may declare and pay an *interim dividend*. This interim dividend is usually shown in the final accounts for the year as follows:

	£	£
Interim dividend paid	4,000	
Proposed final dividend	8,000	12,000

After all the above appropriations, there is almost always a balance of unappropriated profit. This is transferred to the profit-and-loss account balance on the balance sheet as part of the *shareholders' equity* (also known as *shareholders' funds*). Shareholders' equity comprises the share capital and the reserves of the company.

> *You should now be able to attempt Task 21.3 at the end of this chapter.*

6 | SUMMARY

A *limited liability company* is a legal entity and is separate from its owners. This form of business is more complex and costly to set up than a sole trader or a partnership, but a limited company enables greater sums of capital to be raised, has perpetual existence and the liability of the owners, who are the shareholders, is limited to the amount they have agreed to invest. Although there are many more *private limited companies*, it is the *public limited companies (plcs)* which have a substantial impact on our economy and are much more in the public eye.

The financial statements of limited companies follow the same principles as those of sole traders and partnerships, but contain specialised financial terms. This *financial terminology* not only reflects the company's relationship with its shareholders, but also the *regulatory framework* within which limited companies operate.

> *You should now be able to attempt the objective test at the end of this chapter.*

Student activities

Task 21.1
Obtain the annual report and accounts of a limited liability company and identify the financial terms given in this chapter.

Task 21.2
List the main advantages and disadvantages a limited company business has compared with sole traders and partnerships.

Task 21.3
Your uncle's computer business has recently changed from a sole trader to a limited liability company, but he is confused by some of the terms his accountant is now using. 'For example, my accountant is now talking of dividends instead of drawings', he complains.

Draw up a glossary of terms where those used for a limited liability company differ from those used for a sole trader. Provide simple, brief explanations that your uncle will be able to understand.

Question 21.1
Discuss the difference between private and public limited companies.

Question 21.2
Explain what is meant by the term 'dividend' and use a hypothetical example to illustrate the percentage dividend, dividend in pence per share and the benefit to a shareholder with a holding of 100 shares.

Question 21.3
New Ventures plc has 500,000 issued shares at 25p. The directors have declared a dividend of 10 per cent.

Required
Calculate the following:

i)   the amount of issued share capital;

ii) the dividend in pence;

iii) the total amount of dividend;

iv) the dividend for a shareholding of 150 shares.

Objective test (tick the appropriate box)

i)   The share capital of a limited liability company consists of:

    a)   authorised shares plus profit retained   ☐

    b)   issued share capital plus profit retained   ☐

    c)   issued share capital plus profit brought forward from last year less appropriations   ☐

    d)   none of these   ☐

ii) A limited liability company:

    a)   is a company where the liability of its shareholders is limited to the amount that they have agreed to invest   ☐

    b)   must have at least three shareholders   ☐

    c)   must be quoted on the Stock Exchange   ☐

    d)   must have the letters 'plc' after its name   ☐

iii) A private limited company must have:

    a)   a minimum of 30 shareholders   ☐

    b)   a maximum of 30 shareholders   ☐

    c)   a minimum of two and a maximum of 30 shareholders   ☐

    d)   none of these   ☐

iv) The number of shares in a company is 50,000, the denomination of each share is 25p and the proposed dividend per share is 15 per cent. The total amount of the proposed dividend is:

    a)   £750   ☐

    b)   £7,500   ☐

    c)   £1,875   ☐

    d)   £18,750   ☐

v)   The number of shares in a company is 63,000, the denomination of each share is 50p and the proposed dividend per share is 13p. You own 1,500 shares. If the proposal is approved by the shareholders at the AGM, you will receive:

    a)   £195   ☐

    b)   £97.50   ☐

    c)   £4,095   ☐

    d)   £9.75   ☐

CHAPTER 22

National and international regulations

1 OBJECTIVES

At the end of this chapter you should be able to:

- identify the main documents made publicly available by limited companies;
- explain the main features of limited companies;
- describe the information contained in an annual report and accounts;
- examine critically the information contained in an annual report and accounts.

2 INTRODUCTION

All limited companies must be registered with the Registrar of Companies at Companies House which is under the control of the Department of Trade and Industry. There are a number of legal requirements to be met when a limited liability company is first formed, including filing certain documents with the Registrar. The principal documents required on registration, which we will examine, are the *memorandum of association* and the *articles of association*.

The most useful document published by a limited liability company is the *annual report and accounts*. All limited liability companies have to send every shareholder a copy of their annual report and accounts and file a copy with the Registrar of Companies. As anyone can visit Companies House and obtain a copy for a modest fee; the annual report and accounts is a public document.

Public limited companies that are listed on the Stock Exchange make their annual report and accounts freely available. If you read the financial pages in the press you will find that they carry announcements by public limited companies of their financial results for the year and an address from which to obtain a copy of their annual report and accounts.

Because of the importance of the annual report and accounts to those who are interested in the company, most of this chapter is concerned with the contents of such documents.

3 | THE UK REGULATORY FRAMEWORK

The financial reporting of limited liability companies is controlled by legislation and a number of different regulations. This is known as the regulatory framework. The key elements of the regulatory framework are:

- the *Companies Acts*, the most recent of which is the *Companies Act 1989*, which added to and amended the *Companies Act 1985*;

- the pronouncements of the *Accounting Standards Committee (ASC)* in the form of *Statements of Standard Accounting Practice (SSAPs)* and its successor the *Accounting Standards Board (ASB)* in the form of *Financial Reporting Standards (FRSs)*;

- the requirements of the *London Stock Exchange*, which apply to listed companies only.

The purpose of the regulatory framework is to ensure that those who have an interest in a company can obtain financial information that gives a *true and fair view* of the company's affairs. However, this is not easy. Companies may not wish to disclose certain financial information for number of reasons; for example, if confidential information got into the hands of a company's competitors, it could cause damage to the company, its employees and its shareholders. Occasionally companies do not wish to disclose financial information for the wrong reasons and many company scandals are related to the disclosure, or lack of disclosure, of information.

Smaller companies are exempted from certain provisions in the regulatory framework. For example, the profit-and-loss account and balance sheets they send to the Registrar of Companies do not have to contain the same amount of information as those of larger companies. In this and later chapters we concentrate on larger companies. You will find it easier to obtain information on the large public limited companies that are quoted on the stock exchange and it is these companies that have the greatest impact on our economic life. If you are looking for information on smaller companies, you must be aware that they are likely to have taken advantage of the exemptions permitted to them and therefore you will not be able to obtain all the information to which we refer.

> *You should now be able to attempt Question 22.1 at the end of this chapter.*

4 | COMPANIES ACTS

The first *Companies Act* was passed in 1844. This allowed companies to be incorporated by legislation instead of by special Act of Parliament or Royal Charter. There have been a number of Companies Acts since that date imposing further responsibilities and requirements on companies. The most recent Act is the *Companies Act 1989* which amends the Companies Act 1985. The legislation and other regulations are very lengthy and complex. If you decide to become an accountant, you will have to study them in great detail. However for students of most accounting and business courses it is sufficient to know only the main requirements.

For the purposes of this book, the most important requirements are:

- to keep accounting records sufficient to show and explain the company's transactions;
- to prepare final accounts, which will comprise:

  a profit-and-loss account;

  a balance sheet;

  an auditor's report;

  a directors' report.

The final accounts are laid before the *shareholders* (often referred to as the *members*) at a general meeting. They are circulated before the meeting to all members and debenture holders and delivered to the Registrar of Companies.

The formats, that is, the way the final accounts should be presented, are given in Schedule 4 of the Companies Act 1985. Examples of some of these are given in the following chapters, but the main points are as follows:

- The *balance sheet* has two alternative formats. Format 1 is a vertical layout with the current liabilities deducted from the current assets. Format 2 has the same contents, but in two blocks headed *assets* and *liabilities*, current assets and current liabilities not being netted off. The blocks can be placed in a vertical or a horizontal layout.

- The *profit-and-loss account* has four formats. In format 1 the items are vertically arranged according to function, for example administration costs, distribution expenses. Format 3 arranges the same information in two blocks headed '*charges* and *income*' and these may be presented horizontally. Format 2 classifies costs according to their nature, for example raw materials, wages, depreciation, in a vertical format. Format 4 is a two-block version of format 2.

The Companies Act 1985 states that the profit-and-loss account and balance sheet of a company must give a true and fair view. Unfortunately, the legislation does not define 'true and fair view' and to understand the term we would look for guidance at the ordinary practices of general accountants. These ordinary practices are often referred to as Generally Accepted Accounting Practices (GAAP) and are seen as a combination of company law, accounting standards and Stock Exchange requirements.

There is no legal definition of GAAP and it has no direct legal impact. It is a dynamic concept that constantly changes as circumstances alter through new legislation, standards and practice. This makes it difficult to apply the concept because new practices may not have been fully adopted so it is a problem to decide whether they are 'generally accepted'. The best approach to resolve the issue is to try to determine whether the financial statements meet the needs of users and the objectives of regulatory pronouncements and are not misleading.

The difficulty in defining 'true and fair' does not mean that it is unimportant. Indeed, the Companies Act states that in some circumstances it may be necessary to not comply with the legal provisions to ensure that a true and fair view is given. This is known as the true and fair override. In some instances companies can give a true and fair view by providing more information than is required by the legislation.

If companies depart from the requirements of the legislation to give a true and fair view they must explain the particulars of and reasons for the departure and its effects on the accounts.

> *You should now be able to attempt Question 22.2 at the end of this chapter.*

5 | THE ACCOUNTING STANDARDS BOARD

Although company legislation is complex, it has not been sufficient to control all the accounting activities of companies. At the end of the 1960s some highly publicised events took place that brought accounting into disrepute. In response to this, at the beginning of the 1970s the Institute of Chartered Accountants in England and Wales set up the *Accounting Standards Committee (ASC)*, and the other accounting bodies soon joined. The ASC was formed to define accounting concepts, to narrow difference of financial accounting and reporting treatment, and to codify generally accepted best practice in the public interest by issuing *Statements of Accounting Practice (SSAPs)*.

The ASC issued a total of 25 SSAPs before it was disbanded in 1990.

Although the ASC did much to improve accounting in the UK, the Committee found it increasingly difficult to obtain acceptance by companies of regulations on controversial topics. Some commentators suggested that a tougher enforcement regime was required. In 1987 an independent review of the standard-setting process was carried out and in 1988 proposals for a new structure and system were issued. Figure 22.1 shows the structure of new standard-setting regime which came into being in 1990.

The *Financial Reporting Council (FRC)* is responsible for guiding the *Accounting Standards Board (ASB)* on its work programme and on broad matters of policy. The ASB has a full-time chairman and technical director, as well as part-time members. The *Financial Reporting Review Panel (FRRP)* is responsible for the investigation of any departure from accounting standards by companies. The *Urgent Issues Task Force (UITF)* tackles issues that have not yet been covered by an accounting standard, but which require immediate action. The Accounting Standards Board has a very informative website with a section for students.

The ASB is responsible for issuing new accounting standards and has adopted the SSAPs issued by the ASC. The new standards are known as *Financial Reporting Standards (FRSs)* and so far have had a significant impact on the accounts of companies.

In addition, the UITF has issued a number of pronouncements known as *abstracts* on a range of important topics and the strength of the new standard-setting structure has been increased by legislation. Companies must state whether

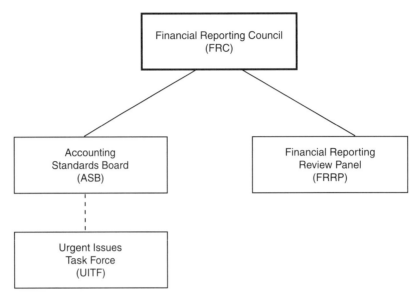

Figure 22.1 *The UK accounting standard-setting structure*

their accounts have been prepared in accordance with accounting standards and give information if they have not done so. If the Secretary of State or the FRRP are dissatisfied with the published accounts of a company, they can apply to the courts and the company concerned may be required to prepare revised accounts that do give a *true and fair view*.

Accounting standards offer a number of benefits to the users and preparers of accounts. The preparers have an authoritative guide to the most appropriate method for accounting for many of the important activities undertaken by companies. The users have additional financial information than that required by legislation alone, as well as information about the basis on which the accounts have been drawn up. This allows comparison of a company's results with other companies and between one year and another.

The main disadvantage of accounting standards is that they impose additional work, and therefore additional costs, on companies. This can be a considerable burden on smaller companies. There is also the difficulty of deciding which accounting method is appropriate to set for all companies, in all industries, and in all circumstances.

At the time of writing this book, the Accounting Standards Board had issued 25 financial reporting standards. Most of these are long and complex documents, some being over 100 pages in length. For large public companies that have many private shareholders and institutional shareholders, such as pension funds, it is appropriate that the regulations are tough so that investors do have protection. Remember that accounting standards help to determine what we mean by Generally Accepted Accounting Practices.

However, we have commented earlier that most UK companies are small. They may be owned and managed by a family or a few friends who have direct knowledge of what the financial transactions of these companies are on a day-to-day basis. These small companies are not listed on the Stock Exchange and their economic transactions will be much simpler than those of the large, public companies. The question arises whether these companies should go through all the expense and difficulties of complying with all accounting standards.

The debate on whether we should have one set of regulations for larger companies and another for smaller companies is known as the 'big GAAP/little GAAP divide'. This dilemma was resolved in 1996 when the Accounting Standards Board issued an exposure draft of the *Financial Reporting Standard for Smaller Entities (FRSSE)*. In 1997 the FRSSE (pronounced 'frizzy') was issued in its final form. It brings together in one document all the accounting guidance that small companies require to prepare their financial statements. This has been achieved by retaining the basic principles of accounting standards and removing the detailed explanatory notes. Some of the more complex standards have been omitted altogether as they only apply to the complex financial transactions undertaken by the large companies.

6 THE LONDON STOCK EXCHANGE

If a company chooses to be listed on the London Stock Exchange, which means that its shares can be traded there, it must comply with additional reporting requirements. However, the requirements of the London Stock Exchange do not have such a big effect on accounting in companies as the legislation and the accounting standards. The aspects of the Stock Exchange requirements that are most relevant to financial accounting are those concerned with the information that listed companies must disclose. As well as requiring some information to be given in the annual report and accounts, the Stock Exchange requires all listed companies to issue *interim reports* and *preliminary profit announcements*. Neither of these documents is covered by legislation although the Accounting Standards Board has issued guidance.

An interim or half-yearly report must be published by listed companies at the end of the first six months of every financial year. These interim statements are very much shorter than the annual report and accounts. Essentially, only profit-related information is required, together with an explanatory statement on the company's performance during the half year. The aim is to give shareholders an overview of the company's progress. The interim report must be sent to the individual shareholders or inserted as a paid advertisement in one national daily newspaper.

Preliminary profit announcements must be made prior to the annual report and accounts being issued; the financial information required is similar to that given in the interim statement. The preliminary profit announcement is intended to ensure that the key financial results for the year are made public as soon as possible to prevent *insider dealing*. This is where individuals who are in possession of information that can affect the share price of a company attempt to take advantage of their knowledge by buying or selling shares.

Stock Exchange regulations require that the annual report and accounts provides significantly more information than that required by the Companies Act 1985. The following short list includes some of the items required:

- A statement by the directors giving the reasons for any significant departures from applicable standard accounting practices.

- A geographic analysis of net turnover and of contribution to trading results of those trading operations carried on outside the UK and Ireland.

- The following particulars regarding each company in which the group interest exceeds 20 per cent of equity capital:

  the principal country of operation;

  particulars of its issued capital and debt securities;

  the percentage of each class of debt securities attributable to the company's interest.

- A statement of the amount of interest capitalised during the year, together with an indication of the amount and treatment of any related tax relief.

> *You should now be able to attempt Task 22.2 at the end of this chapter.*

7 INFORMATION IN THE ANNUAL REPORT AND ACCOUNTS

If you obtain the published annual report and accounts of a major company you will find that it may comprise of anything between 40 and 70 pages. Some documents are even longer. You will most likely find that the financial statements such as the profit-and-loss account and balance sheet contain the word 'Consolidated' in their heading. This is because the accounts are not just for the main company but for all the other companies it owns, namely its subsidiaries. All the profit-and-loss accounts and balance sheets of all the subsidiaries have been brought together and 'consolidated' into one set of accounts. This gives you a much better picture of what is happening in the entire group. If you have the report and accounts of a group of companies you will find a list of the principal subsidiaries usually at the end of the document.

Because most of the published reports and accounts that are readily obtainable refer to groups of companies, we will concentrate on these. The information in the report and accounts can be divided approximately into two main sections. The first half of the document is mainly information that the company chooses to give. The second part of the document is information the company is obliged to give under the regulatory framework. This second part is often printed on a different type or coloured paper. We will concentrate on this section first. In this section we will introduce some new terms that will be covered in detail in later chapters.

The regulatory framework section

Under the Companies Act 1985, accounting standards and, for a listed company, Stock Exchange regulations the following are the main items of information that should be provided:

- *Profit-and-loss account.* This is required by the Companies Act 1985 but will also show certain information on new aquisitions and discontinued activities as required by Financial Reporting Standard 3 – Reporting Financial Performance.

- *Balance sheet.* This is required by the Companies Act 1985 and the vertical format is the most common form of presentation.

- *Cash-flow statement.* This is required by Financial Reporting Standard 1 which was first issued in 1993 and revised in 1996

- *Statement of total recognised gains and losses.* This is a primary financial statement required by Financial Reporting Standard 3.

- *Directors' report.* This is addressed to the members or shareholders and provides a range of information that is usually quite technical. You will also find information on such matters as any political or charitable donations and the employment of disabled persons.

- *Auditors' report.*

- *Notes to the accounts.*

In the subsequent sections we discuss the auditors' report and the notes to the accounts in more detail.

The review section

The first section of the annual report and accounts is a type of review and may even be published as a separate document with that title. Although some of the information in this section will be provided because it is required or 'encouraged as good practice' under the regulatory framework, much of the information will be voluntary. The types of information will vary from company to company, but the following list is an indication of the types of information you may find.

- *Chairman's statement.* It would be highly unusual not to find a statement by the chairman of the company. This will provide an overview of the company's performance and any major events. Not surprisingly the chairman will want to give the most favourable picture to the shareholders.

- *Highlights of the main financial results.* This is often just one page concentrating on the main financial results such as the profit figure and the dividends.

- *Review of the company's activities.* This section will tend to be more factual and detailed than the chairman's statement. Often the main parts of the business and their financial performance and business operations will be discussed. The Accounting Standards Board is encouraging companies to give an operating and financial review, which interprets the financial data, discusses the business, its risks and the structure of its finance.

- *Corporate governance statement.* Following some of the major financial scandals in the 1980s the financial and business community became very concerned over the ethics of business and the way it was governed. A committee was established to consider the problem and a series of recommendations were issued under the title of the Cadbury Report. Companies listed on the Stock Exchange should disclose the extent to which they comply with the Cadbury

Recommendations. A number of companies discuss their approach at some length and you will most likely find a section entitled 'corporate governance'.

- *Historical summaries.* Most companies provide a statement of their main financial results for the last five or ten years. This is a useful source of information when you wish to draw up accounting ratios as discussed in a later chapter.

- *Environmental issues.* As corporate governance became an important topic in annual reports and accounts so has the environment. A number of companies make statements on their environmental policies and in some industries that have a high environmental profile you may find lengthy discussion on their activities and policies.

In this section we have not been able to refer to all items of information you might find. There will certainly be a profusion of photographs and diagrams. You will also find information on topics such as visits to the company by royal personages, charitable and community activities and sporting and scholastic achievements by employees.

You should now be able to attempt Task 22.3 at the end of this chapter.

8 THE AUDITORS' REPORT

All limited companies in the UK are required by law to have their accounts *audited* by a professional accountant qualified under the Companies Act to do so. The auditor must be registered and supervised by the accounting bodies. The annual report and accounts must include a report from the auditors. Although it is brief, it is an essential piece of information in the annual report and accounts and will alert you to any problems that the auditors may believe affect the financial statements.

The auditor's report is addressed to the members of the company, this means the shareholders. There will be an introductory paragraph in which the auditors make clear to which pages of the annual report and accounts they are referring. You will find that these pages will be in the second part of the document, which we called the regulatory framework section. The second paragraph of the auditors' report will state that it is the directors' responsibility to prepare the financial statements and that it is the auditors' responsibility to form an opinion on those financial statements and report upon them. The next section of the auditors' report will be headed 'Basis of Opinion' and the auditor will refer to the manner in which they conducted the audit. The final paragraph is the actual opinion of the auditors and the important phrase is whether the auditors consider that the financial statements give a 'true and fair' view. If this is not the case any reader of the financial statements should take considerable care in drawing any conclusion or making any interpretations.

You should now be able to attempt Task 22.4 at the end of this chapter.

9   NOTES TO THE ACCOUNTS

The financial statements are supported by notes to the accounts, which take up a considerable number of pages. Some of the notes provide explanations or further information on certain figures in the financial statements. Other notes provide new information. The notes are important as they help you to understand better the financial statements and provide more detailed information. It would be impossible to get all the information in the financial statements themselves. The profit-and-loss account, balance sheet and cash-flow-statement are annotated with the appropriate note numbers for the separate items.

The nature, type and detail of the notes varies according to the company and its activities. There are, however, some important notes which are common to most companies and you should be able to find examples of these in your sample annual report and accounts.

- *Accounting policies.* This is a most important note and will either be note number 1 or 2 or may even be on a separate page before the numbered notes. Companies are required to publish their policies in respect of certain accounting treatments. Although these can be very technical they are important as they describe items that are significant in determining the profit and financial position of the company. You should find statements such as depreciation, goodwill, foreign exchange, pensions and research and development.

- *Segmental information.* Large companies will give a breakdown by class of business and geographical area of their turnover and profit. This is most useful in ascertaining the most profitable areas of the company and where it seems to be experiencing risks or problems. This information can be used for constructing accounting ratios as discussed in a later chapter.

- *Directors' emoluments.* In its broadest sense this means the pay of directors and this note usually receives great attention from the press. You will find the pay of the Chairman or the highest paid director if it is not the chairman. You will also find the emoluments of the other directors grouped in bands of £5,000.

- *Employee information.* Companies are obliged to disclose information on the numbers of employees and the staff costs. The number of employees is one way of measuring the relative size of a company and you can work out the turnover and profit per employee and compare these figures to other companies to find out which company has the most 'profitable' employees.

- *Tangible fixed assets.* There are the resources such as buildings, machinery, cars and equipment. Although the assets are grouped under main headings, the note will be very comprehensive and give not only the original cost or value of the items, but additions and disposals as well as the cumulative depreciation and the net book values.

> *You should now be able to attempt Task 22.5 and Question 22.3 at the end of this chapter.*

10 SUMMARY FINANCIAL STATEMENTS

Our review of the regulatory framework demonstrates that companies are being required to disclose increasing amounts of information. This *burden of disclosure* is being questioned for two reasons. First, there is concern that the sheer volume and complexity of the information cannot be handled by the users; in particular, the private shareholders. Secondly, the provision of the information is a cost that has to be borne by companies and some consider that high costs outweigh any benefits that may be gained.

There have been some changes and proposals for further change that seek to address these criticisms. Companies which are listed on the Stock Exchange can publish a *summary financial statement* instead of the full report and accounts if their shareholders agree. A summary financial statement need only contain an abbreviated version of the main financial statements and need not incorporate all the notes to the accounts. This is the minimum information that can be provided, although most companies voluntarily provide more information than this, usually in narrative form.

Summary financial statements are often included in a larger document that may have a title such as 'annual review'. This larger document will contain mostly voluntary information about the activities of the company and there will probably be a number of photographs and diagrams.

The part of the annual review that is the summary financial statement must:

- state that it is only a summary of the information in the company's annual accounts and the directors' report;

- contain a statement by the company's auditors of their opinion on whether the summary financial statement is consistent with those accounts and that report complies with the normal statutory requirements;

- state whether the auditor's report on the annual accounts was unqualified or qualified, and if it was qualified set out the report in full together with any further material needed to understand the qualification.

It is essential that the summary financial statements are derived from, and are consistent with, the company's annual accounts and report. It is also important that the readers are made aware that the summary financial statement does not contain the full information and investment decisions should not be made on the basis of the limited information contained in the summary financial statement.

11   INTERNATIONAL DEVELOPMENTS

Regulatory requirements are not the same in all countries. There are a number of reasons for the differences, the main reasons being:

- *Legal systems in various countries differ.* In the UK we have 'common law' where there is a limited amount of statute law that is interpreted by the courts to build up a large body of case law. In other countries, particularly in other European countries, there is codified law with detailed rules for accounting and financial reporting.

- *Business organisations and ownership.* In some countries there may be many small businesses that obtain significant funding from the state or major banks. In other countries there can be widespread share ownership and the many investors need to receive information about the financial transactions of the company.

- *Stock exchanges* are at different periods in their development and the disclosure requirements and the ability to obtain compliance differs.

- *Taxation systems* differ in many countries depending on the political policies of the country and the trading traditions and objectives.

- *Accounting profession.* The UK has a very strong accounting profession that has been very active in promoting better accounting practices. In some countries the accounting profession does not have so much influence.

- *Cultural factors.* This is a very wide category but you will be aware that different countries have their own characteristics and these will be reflected in the way that they do business and account for it.

The result of these differences is that accounting requirements vary from one country to another and this creates problems for individuals and companies. If you are an investor in the UK with shares in a UK company you may not worry about international accounting differences. If you wish to invest in a company in another country, however, you would want the accounts of that company to be comparable with UK companies so that you could make your investment decision. Similarly, if you are a company in Germany and you wish to attract American investors you will want to list your shares on the New York Stock Exchange. This will mean that you will have to prepare your accounts according to US GAAP. There have been a number of examples where a company prepares its accounts according to the regulations of one country but when it prepares them according to the regulations of another country it has arrived at a different figure, or a profit instead of a loss or vice versa.

As business has become more global so there have been demands for greater international standardization of accounting practices. In 1973 the professional accounting bodies of a number of countries founded the International Accounting Standards Committee (ISAC) to seek a solution. Progress in the early days was slow but there has been an acceleration in developments and in 2001 the IASC was renamed the International Accounting Standards Board and was given a new structure.

The IASB issues International Financial Reporting Standards and the hope is that companies throughout the world will implement these. There has been considerable support for the work of the IASB and some countries, including the UK, are strongly in favour whereas others, such as the US, have expressed reservations. There are a number of huge political and technical difficulties to overcome and it is difficult to predict how successful the attempt to completely internationalise accounting standards will be. International accounting is a fast moving subject and students are recommended to visit the website of the International Accounting Standards Board.

12   SUMMARY

Limited liability companies are either *public limited companies*, able to offer their shares to the public, or *private limited companies*, which are not permitted to do so. All limited companies must register with the Registrar of Companies and file an *annual report and accounts*, which thus become a public document. All companies must also file a *memorandum of association*, which defines the company's constitution and objects, and *articles of association*, which contain the internal regulations of the company.

The activities of limited liability companies are controlled within a *regulatory framework*. This comprises legislation in the form of the *Companies Acts*, pronouncements of the *Accounting Standards Board* and, for *listed companies*, the requirements of the *London Stock Exchange*.

The annual report and accounts is the most useful document issued by limited companies. The annual report and accounts of a public limited company is readily available and discloses information required by the regulatory framework and also information on other issues.

Student activities *(questions with answers at the end of the book)*

Task 22.1
Visit the website of the Accounting Standards Board and draft a brief report on the main features of the FRSSe.

Task 22.2
Search the financial press for the announcement of the interim results of a well known company. Read a number of financial newspapers and collect the comments made on the interim results. Do different newspapers make similar statements or do they vary?

Task 22.3
On which pages of your sample annual report and accounts is the following information:

- Notice of the annual general meeting
- Auditors' report
- Chairman's statement

- Directors' report
- Profit-and-loss account
- Balance sheet
- Five or ten year summary of results

Task 22.4

Answer the following questions using the information in your sample annual report and accounts:

i)   Who are the auditors?

ii) Which accounting standards (if any) are noted in the auditors' report?

iii) On what date did the auditors sign their report?

iv) What fee was charged by the auditors for their services?

Task 22.5

Examine the notes in your sample annual report and accounts and answer the following questions:

i)   What was the issued share capital of the company at the year end?

ii) How many authorised shares are there?

iii) What was the emolument (salary) of the chairman?

iv) What was the total value of stocks at the year end?

v)   What was the total of wages and salaries?

Question 22.1

Select the correct response to the following statements:

	True	False
i) Only public limited companies are quoted on the Stock Exchange.	☐	☐
ii) There are no limits to the number of shareholders there can be in a limited company.	☐	☐
iii) All limited companies must put the letters 'plc' after their names.	☐	☐
iv) The share prices of private limited companies are published each day in the *Financial Times*.	☐	☐
v) If a private limited company is unable to pay all its debts, the shareholders are responsible for them.	☐	☐

Question 22.2

List the main types of information you would expect to find in the annual report and accounts of a public limited company.

Question 22.3

Insert the missing word or phrase in the following statements:

i) An auditors' report should normally state that the accounts give a . . . view.

ii) The Companies Act 1989 mainly introduced requirements on the regulation of auditors and . . .

iii) A company which can offer its shares to the public is known as a . . .

iv) The . . . is responsible for issuing accounting standards.

v) The regulatory framework consists of three elements: company legislation, . . . and . . .

Objective test (tick the appropriate box)

i) A limited liability company:

   a) does not need to comply with accounting standards ☐

   b) is always quoted on the Stock Exchange ☐

   c) must have the letters 'plc' written after its name ☐

   d) is a company where the liability of its shareholders is limited to the amount that they have agreed to invest ☐

ii) A summary financial statement includes:

   a) exactly the same information as the statutary account ☐

   b) the same information as the interim report ☐

   c) all the notes to the accounts ☐

   d) a statement by the company's auditors ☐

iii) A limited liability company is required to circulate shareholders with copies of its final accounts by:

   a) a Statement of Standard Accounting Practice (SSAP) ☐

   b) the Companies Act 1985 ☐

   c) a Statement of Recommended Practice (SORP) ☐

   d) a Financial Reporting Standard (FRS) ☐

iv) The Companies Act 1985 gives the format for the appropriate presentation of the balance sheet. The format must be:

   a) in vertical format ☐

   b) in horizontal format ☐

   c) in blocks of assets and liabilities either in vertical format or horizontal format ☐

   d) any of these ☐

v) In addition to the requirements of the Companies Acts, the Stock Exchange requires a listed company to produce:

a) a statement by the directors giving reasons for significant departures from accounting standards ☐

b) an auditors' report ☐

c) a directors' report ☐

d) all of these ☐

CHAPTER 23

Financial statements of a limited company

1 OBJECTIVES

At the end of this chapter you should be able to:

- describe the financial statements of a limited company;
- explain the main elements of a profit-and-loss account;
- explain the main elements of a balance sheet;
- understand a cash-flow statement for a limited company.

2 INTRODUCTION

In the previous chapter we looked at the main features of the financial statements of limited companies and introduced some new financial terms you will come across in limited company accounts. In this chapter we will look at three important financial statements published by limited companies: the statutory *profit-and-loss account*, *balance sheet* and *cash-flow statement*.

First we will examine the internal profit-and-loss account and balance sheet produced by limited companies, before going on to look at the structure and content of the statutory accounts. The internal financial statements are simply the working documents produced by the company's accountants from which the published statutory accounts are drawn. When we examine the statutory accounts, we will concentrate on the published accounts of a group of companies, which are known as *consolidated accounts*, as these are the type of accounts you are most likely to encounter. In this chapter we give only a brief introduction to the profit-and-loss account and balance sheet as they are dealt with in more depth in later chapters.

3 THE INTERNAL FINANCIAL STATEMENTS

We are now ready to start using some of the financial terms associated with limited company financial statements by looking at a simple example of the *internal financial statements*. In this example we are not attempting to demonstrate how the accounts might appear in their published form, or the precise terms used, but to illustrate how the accounts are constructed. The information contained in internal accounts such as these is then used to prepare the statutory, published accounts. We will be examining the published accounts individually later in this chapter.

You will see that a limited company profit-and-loss account adopts the same principles as we used for a sole trader profit-and-loss account, but a limited company profit-and-loss account also shows what happens to the net profit. For example, some will be used to pay corporation tax; some will be used to pay dividends to the shareholders and the balance may be left in the company in order to allow it to grow. A limited company *balance sheet* is also similar to that of a sole trader, the main difference is that the balance sheet of a limited company also contains information concerning the interests of the shareholders.

Example

The books of Hartlepool plc showed the following figures at 31 December 2003:

	£'000	£'000
Sales		1,250
Opening stock at 1 January 2003	50	
Purchases	610	
Wages and salaries	250	
Rates	20	
Insurance	15	
Light and heat	10	
Office expenses	30	
Miscellaneous expenses	50	
Buildings	280	
Plant and equipment	200	
Cumulative provision for depreciation on plant and equipment		80
Motor vehicles	120	
Cumulative provision for depreciation on motor vehicles		30
Debtors	130	
Bank (in credit)	116	
Creditors		50
Share capital:		
8% Preference shares (100,000 authorised)		
Issued 50,000 of £1 each		50
Ordinary shares (500,000 authorised)		
Issued 400,000 of £1 each		400
Reserves brought forward at 1 January 2003		15
Profit and loss account balance		
brought forward at 1 January 2003		6
	1,881	1,881

The following additional information is provided as at 31 December 2003:

Stocks are valued at	£60,000
Accruals:	
Wages and salaries	£10,000
Light and heat	£3,000
Prepayments:	
Rates	£5,000
Insurance	£3,000
Depreciation for the year:	
Buildings	Nil
Plant and equipment	20% of cost
Motor vehicles	25% of cost
Proposed dividends:	
Preference shares	pay full dividend
Ordinary shares	15p per share
Provide for corporation tax	£70,000
Transfer reserve is	£60,000

Required

Prepare a trading and profit-and-loss account for Hartlepool plc for the year ending 31 December 2003 and a balance sheet as at the same date presented in vertical format.

Solution

Hartlepool plc

Trading and profit-and-loss account for the year ending 31 December 2003

	£'000	£'000
Sales		1,250
Less Cost of sales:		
Opening stock	50	
Add Purchases	610	
	660	
Less Closing stock	60	600
		650
Gross profit		
Less Expenses:		
Wages and salaries (£250 + £10)	260	
Rates (£20 − £5)	15	
Insurance (£15 − £3)	12	
Light and heat (£10 + £3)	13	
Office expenses	30	
Depreciation of plant and machinery	40	
Depreciation of motor vehicles	30	
Miscellaneous expenses	50	450
Net profit		200
Corporation tax charge		70
Profit for the year available for appropriation		130

continued

Proposed dividends		
Preference dividend of 8%	4	
Ordinary dividend of 15p per share	60	64
		66
Profit-and-loss account balance		
brought forward from previous year		6
		72
Transfer to reserves		60
Profit and loss account balance		
carried forward to next year		12

Hartlepool plc

Balance sheet as at 31 December 2003

	Cost	Accumulated depreciation	Net book value
	£'000	£'000	£'000
Fixed assets			
Buildings	280	–	280
Plant and equipment	200	120	80
Motor vehicles	120	60	60
	600	180	420
Current assets			
Stock	60		
Debtors	130		
Prepayments	8		
Bank	116	314	
Creditors: amounts due within one year			
Creditors	50		
Accruals	13		
Proposed dividends	64		
Current taxation	70	197	
Net current assets (Working capital)			117
Capital employed			537
Financed by:			
Share capital			
Authorised:			
8% Preference shares			
100,000 of £1 each (£100,000)			
Ordinary shares			
500,000 of £1 each (£500,000)			
Issued and fully paid:			
8% Preference shares 50,000 of £1 each	50		
Ordinary shares 400,000 of £1 each	400	450	
Reserves brought forward	15		
Add Transferred from profit-and-			
loss account	60	75	
Profit-and-loss account balance		12	
at 31 December 2003		537	

> *You should now be able to attempt Questions 23.1, 23.2 and 23.3 at the end of this chapter.*

4　PUBLISHED ACCOUNTS

In some annual accounts you may find that the profit-and-loss account and balance sheet are headed *consolidated*. This is because the financial statements are for a group of companies, normally a *holding company* and a number of *subsidiary companies*. To allow shareholders to appreciate the activities of the entire group, the individual companies' financial statements are added together to form the consolidated accounts.

As explained earlier in this chapter, limited liability companies are not obliged to publish all the details in their profit-and-loss accounts and balance sheets. What they do have to publish, and therefore make publicly available, is determined by the regulatory framework, although certain companies are exempt from these requirements. These are mainly small and medium-sized companies and in this section we will only be looking at the *consolidated published accounts* of large companies. You will find it useful to have a copy of the published accounts of a large company as you work through this chapter.

The key financial statements published are the *profit-and-loss account* and the *balance sheet*. Under the Companies Act 1985 a company must use one of four different formats for the former and one of two for the latter. Each company can choose which formats to adopt. As well as giving the financial results for the current financial year, the figures for the previous financial year must also be shown.

If you look at the published profit-and-loss account and balance sheet in a company's accounts, you will see that normally they occupy one page each. However, at the side of these two statements are many items referring to note numbers. The *notes* are also included in the document and take up many pages.

The reason why companies use notes is because the regulatory framework requires certain information to be given and it is impossible to include it all in the financial statement itself. The notes are therefore used to explain and expand on items in the profit-and-loss account and balance sheet. For simplicity we have not given the notes or the previous year's figures in the examples that follow in the next section.

5　THE PUBLISHED PROFIT-AND-LOSS ACCOUNT

When you first look at the *profit-and-loss account* of a limited company you will see that it differs in many ways from that of the sole trader, which we looked at earlier. One major difference is that you do not find the detailed information on costs. The reason for this is that limited companies are not obliged to disclose this information. Because of the different types and sizes of limited companies, and the diverse nature of their business transactions, their profit-and-loss accounts will look different. However, there will always be a considerable number of similarities.

The Companies Act 1985 gives no less than four alternative formats for the presentation of the published *profit-and-loss account*. Two are *vertical* and two are *horizontal*. You will find that most UK companies use one of the two vertical formats. Of these, one analyses expenses by their purpose or function and the other by type. The requirements of the Companies Act have been greatly expanded by FRS 3 Reporting Financial Performance which we will consider in Chapter 24.

The profit-and-loss account using format 2 shows the costs analysed by the item of expense. The ordering of the items for format 2 is shown below, using the same terminology as in the legislation.

1. Turnover

2. Change in stocks of finished goods and work-in-progress

3. Own work capitalised

4. Other operating income

5. (a) raw materials and consumables

    (b) other external charges

6. Staff costs

    (a) wages and salaries

    (b) social security costs

    (c) other pension costs

7. (a) depreciation and other amounts written off tangible and intangible fixed assets

    (b) exceptional amounts written off current assets

8. Other operating charges

9. Income from shares in group undertakings

10. Income from participating interests†

11. Income from other fixed asset investments

12. Other interest receivable and similar income

13. Amounts written off investments

14. Interest payable and similar charges

15. Tax on profit or loss on ordinary activities

16. Profit or loss on ordinary activities after taxation

    *Minority interests

17. Extraordinary income

18. Extraordinary charges

19. Extraordinary profit or loss

20. Tax on extraordinary profit or loss

    *Minority interests

21. Other taxes not shown under the above items

22. Profit or loss for the financial year

† In relation to group accounts, 'Interest from participating interest' is to be replaced by two items: 'Income from interest in associated undertakings', and 'Income from other participating interests'.
* 'Minority interests' was introduced by Schedule 4A:17 and should be treated in the same way as those to which an Arabic number is assigned.

Once a format has been adopted, it should be used in subsequent years, unless in the directors' opinion there are special reasons to change.

> *You should now be able to attempt Tasks 23.1 and 23.2 at the end of this chapter.*

6   THE PUBLISHED BALANCE SHEET

The *balance sheet* of a limited company looks very similar to the vertical-format balance sheet of a sole trader. The balance sheet of a limited company is made up of three main sections.

* *Assets. Fixed assets* are assets that are held in the business on a continuing basis. They include *tangible assets*, such as land, factories and machines, and *intangible assets*, such as spending on research and development, and goodwill. *Current assets* are assets that are not held in the business on a continuing basis; in other words, they are part of the trading cycle. Many current assets are converted into cash within twelve months, but you should not assume that this is necessarily the case; for example, a company may have long-term debtors. Current assets include, in order of liquidity stocks, debtors and cash.

* *Creditors. Current liabilities* are debts where repayment is due within one year, such as overdrafts or goods bought on credit. Current liabilities are subtracted from current assets to give *net current assets* or *working capital*. The value of fixed assets can then be added to give *total assets less current liabilities*. *Long-term liabilities* are debts on which repayment is due after one year, such as long-term bank loans. This figure can be subtracted from total assets less current liabilities to give *net assets*. The legal term for current liabilities, which

is shown on a published balance sheet, is *Creditors: amounts falling due within one year*. Long-term liabilities are referred to as *Creditors: amounts falling due after more than one year*.

- *Capital and reserves*. The company's issued share capital, which is the value of shares (based on their nominal value rather than on their current market price) is added to the company's reserves or retained profit to give *capital employed*. This must balance with the figure for net assets.

The Companies Act 1985 gives two alternative formats for the balance sheet. Format 1 is essentially a *vertical format*, deducting liabilities from assets. Format 2 is a *horizontal format* with all the assets on one side and all the liabilities on the other.

There are some problems with limited company balance sheets. First, the balance sheet does not show what the company is 'worth'. This is mainly due to the fact that some of the *fixed assets*, including land and buildings, are likely to have been purchased many years ago. They may be stated at *historic cost* (original cost) less *depreciation*, or they may have been revalued at some time. In either case, it is doubtful whether the amount on the balance sheets represents the current market value of these assets.

Another problem is that the balance sheet has been drawn up on a *going concern* basis, a concept we discussed in an earlier chapter. If the business were to go into liquidation, some of the fixed assets would not be sold for the amount they are shown at in the balance sheet. This is particularly true of specialised machinery and equipment, for which there may be no demand and therefore no potential purchaser.

In addition to these problems, there is uncertainty over the value of any *intangible assets* shown in the balance sheet. These are resources of the company to which a monetary value has been attributed, but which do not have any physical substance. For example, the business may have paid a research company a considerable sum for a licence to manufacture a product for the next 15 years and this licence will be shown as a valuable intangible asset on the balance sheet. Other intangible assets, such as *patents* and *trademarks* cause relatively few problems, but one which causes considerable controversy is goodwill. We will study these problems in a subsequent chapter.

You should now be able to attempt Question 23.3 at the end of this chapter.

7   THE PUBLISHED CASH-FLOW STATEMENT

In 1996 the Accounting Standards Board issued a revised FRS 1 cash-flow statement. The Companies Act does not require this financial statement so FRS 1 is very important. It does not apply to small entities but apart from special companies, which are exempt, you should find a cash-flow statement in the annual report and accounts of all major companies.

The purpose of a cash-flow statement is to report the cash generation and absorption of a company and provide information that assists investors and other users in their assessment of the liquidity, solvency and financial adaptability. FRS 1 defines cash as cash in hand and deposits less overdrafts repayable on demand. Repayable on demand means without notice or within one working day. Liquid resources are defined as current asset investments held as readily disposable stores of value. This means that the company can dispose of them without affecting its business and the amount of cash that will result from the disposal is reasonably certain.

The accounting standard lays down eight different headings and is very specific on how the cash flows should be categorised under these headings. Without going into the fine details, the following are the standard headings and the types of cash flows.

Operating activities

These are the cash effects of transactions and other events relating to operating or trading activities.

Returns on investments and servicing of finance

These are cash inflows from interest and dividends received and cash outflows such as interest paid, finance costs, the interest element of finance lease rental payments and dividends paid on non-equity shares of the entity.

Taxation

These are cash flows to or from taxation authorities in respect of the company's revenue and capital profits.

Capital expenditure and financial investment

These are related to the purchase or disposal of a fixed asset and any current asset investment.

Acquisitions and disposals

These are the cash flows from sales and acquisitions of trades and businesses.

Equity dividends paid

These are the dividends paid on the company's equity shares, excluding any advance corporation tax.

Management of liquid resources

The cash inflows include withdrawals from short-term deposits not qualifying as cash and disposal or redemption of any other investment held as liquid resources. The cash outflows include payments into short-term deposits not qualifying as cash and acquisition of any other investments held as liquid resources.

Financing

This is cash inflow from the issue of shares, debentures and loans. The cash outflow is the repayment of amounts borrowed, the capital element of finance lease rental payments, payments to reacquire or redeem the company's shares and payment of expenses and commission on any issue of equity shares.

It has been argued that the preparation of a cash-flow statement can be a burden on a company because it will have to maintain additional records. This is doubtful because companies of the size to which the standard applies will be keeping such records as the survival of the business depends on the ability to generate cash.

Another advantage of cash is that it is definite and relatively easy to audit. We saw in earlier chapters that profit is derived from a series of concepts and conventions and is therefore less certain. This may mean that the cash-flow statement is more easily understood and more useful to a number of users, although no research has substantiated this argument. It is true to say that many users may find the knowledge of cash flows of a company of interest. If you are a creditor, for example, you are more interested in whether the company will be able to pay you than its profitability.

> *You should now be able to attempt Task 23.3 at the end of this chapter.*

8	**SUMMARY**

There are a number of differences between the financial statements of a sole trader or partnership and those of a limited company. These give rise to new financial terms. As well as preparing financial statements for its own purposes, a limited company is required to publish a *profit-and-loss account*, *balance sheet* and a *cash-flow statement*. However, the published financial statements do not include as much information as those prepared for internal purposes.

The published balance sheet is similar in principle to that of a sole trader, but uses some special financial terms. It should be treated with care as it does not necessarily represent what the business is 'worth'. There are problems concerning the valuation of *tangible fixed assets* and the account treatment of *intangible assets*.

A third financial statement for limited companies is the *cash-flow statement* which was introduced by FRS 1. Although there have been some criticisms of the statement, it is now firmly established as a major means of disclosure of information.

> *You should now be able to attempt the objective test at the end of this chapter.*

Student activities *(questions with answers at the end of the book)*

Task 23.1

The Institute of Directors intends to publish a simple guide to published accounts. Write a suitable preface and contents page for the proposed publication.

Task 23.2

Obtain the published accounts of three different companies and compare their balance sheets. Attempt to explain any differences in their form and contents.

Task 23.3

Examine the published accounts of a company and identify the notes that make reference to the cash-flow-statement.

Question 23.1

The balance sheet of Aldeburgh plc revealed the following balances as at 31 December 2004:

	£'000
Fixed assets at cost:	
Land and buildings	6,791
Plant and equipment	13,887
Motor vehicles	1,953
Accumulated depreciation of fixed assets:	
Land and buildings	1,939
Plant and equipment	7,308
Motor vehicles	1,036
Stocks	11,278
Creditors	9,387
Debtors	9,099
Investments	2,261
Cash at bank and deposits	3,801
Bank overdraft	2,888
Debentures	9,509
Profit and loss account	544
Current taxation	1,022
Reserves	13,876
Proposed dividends	469
Ordinary share capital	793
Preference share capital	299

Required

Complete the following form, grouping the above balances as single figures under suitable headings.

Aldeburgh plc
Balance sheet as at 31 December 2004

	£'000	£'000	£'000
Fixed assets			
Tangible assets		....	
Investments		....	....
Current assets			
Stocks	....		
Debtors	....		
Cash and deposits	....	....	
Creditors: Amounts due within one year			
Bank overdraft	....		
Trade creditors	....		
Taxation	....		
Dividends proposed	....	....	
Net current assets			....
Total assets less current liabilities			....
Creditors: Amounts due after more than one year			
Loans			....
Financed by:			
Capital and reserves			
Called up share capital			....
Reserves		....	
Profit-and-loss account		....	....

Question 23.2

You have received the following memorandum from your managing director.

Memorandum

It is planned to form a new company called *Lowestoft Transport Limited*. We intend to start operations on 1st October 2005 and therefore the first financial year will end on 30th September 2006. Plans are well advanced for a start in 2005.

We have bought a garage and office premises for £50,000, four lorries at £50,000 each, and plant and equipment for £40,000. I suggest depreciation rates of 4% per annum for the premises and 12.5% per annum for the lorries and plant and equipment, all starting from 1st October 2005.

Operating expenses are estimated as follows for the first year:

Drivers' wages	£29,000
Manager and office staff	£21,000
Fuel oil	£8,000
Maintenance and repairs	£7,000
Rates	£4,000
Insurances	£6,000
Miscellaneous expenses	£3,000
Administration expenses	£9,000

We propose that the capital of Lowestoft Transport Ltd will be 200,000 ordinary shares of £1 each. There will be a five-year bank loan of £60,000 with interest at 10% per annum. Sales turnover is estimated at £150,000 for the first year.

As a matter of policy, we will allow for debtors at two months of sales turnover, and for the fuel oil, maintenance and repairs and miscellaneous expenses, we will allow for one month's credit.

Insurance and rates will be for a full year, so there will be no need to allow for prepayments at the year-end. We can also ignore stocks, taxation and dividends. You may assume that both costs and sales occur evenly throughout the year.

The cash-flow-forecast shows that the above proposals result in a balance at bank of £3,500 at 30th September 2006. Please prepare a budgeted profit-and-loss account for this first year together with a budgeted balance sheet at the year end.

John Lever

Managing Director

Required

Prepare the budgeted accounts for the year to 30 September 2006 as requested by your managing director. These should be in vertical format.

Question 23.3

The books of Colchester plc reveal the following figures as at 31 December 2004:

	£'000	£'000
Sales		87,100
Sales returns	85	
Opening stock at 1 January 2004	2,375	
Purchases	63,450	

continued

	£'000	£'000
Purchases returns		120
Rent received		1,050
Office expenses	1,685	
Insurances	175	
Wages	3,820	
Rents		2,000
Rates		1,650
Bad debts written off	2,150	
Provision for bad debts at 1 January 2004		1,000
Profit-and-loss account balance at 1 January 2004		85
Reserves		101,500
Premises	131,000	
Equipment	6,000	
Provision for depreciation of equipment		1,600
Debtors	23,500	
Bank and deposits	11,125	
Creditors		26,560
Share capital, authorised and issued:		
5,000,000 7% preference shares of £1 each		5,000
100,000,000 ordinary shares of 25 pence each		25,000
	249,015	249,015

The following additional information is provided as at 31 December 2004.

	£'000
Wages accrued	130
Prepayments	
Insurance	25
Rent payable	550
Rent receivable for 2004, but unpaid as at 31 December 2004	180
Stock at 31 December 2004	2,625
The provision for bad debts is to be increased by	250
Transfer to reserves	3,500
Provision for Corporation Tax	4,750

Proposed dividends:

  Pay the preference dividend

  Pay a dividend on the ordinary shares of 18% (4.5p per share)

Depreciation should be provided on the equipment using the straight line basis. Expected life is five years, with scrap value at the end of that time of £2,000,000.

Required

Prepare a trading and profit-and-loss account (with appropriation account) for the year ending 31 December 2004 and a balance sheet as at that date for Colchester plc, presented in vertical format.

Objective test (tick the appropriate box)

i)   The requirement for a company to publish its profit-and-loss account in a particular format is contained in:

    a)   legislation   ☐

    b)   accounting standards   ☐

    c)   Stock Exchange regulation   ☐

    d)   none of these   ☐

ii) A balance sheet can show only:

    a)   fixed tangible assets   ☐

    b)   intangible assets   ☐

    c)   current assets   ☐

    d)   all of these   ☐

iii) A cash-flow statement is required under:

    a)   FRS 1   ☐

    b)   FRS 3   ☐

    c)   SSAP 3   ☐

    d)   SSAP 10   ☐

iv) The net profit of a company this year is £9,876, the net profit brought forward from last year is £1,234, the transfer to reserves is £3,654, the provision for corporation tax is £3,456, and the proposed dividend is £1,432. Therefore, the net balance on the profit-and-loss account carried forward to next year is:

    a)   £100   ☐

    b)   £2,568   ☐

    c)   £5,432   ☐

    d)   £19,652   ☐

v)   A company purchases another business for £335,000. The acquired business's premises are worth £290,000, its plant and machinery is worth £24,000, and its furniture and fittings are worth £12,000. The business's creditors amount to £8,000. Therefore, the figure for goodwill is:

    a)   £1,000   ☐

    b)   £1,700   ☐

    c)   £17,000   ☐

    d)   £318,000   ☐

CHAPTER 24

Statements of financial performance

1 | OBJECTIVES

At the end of this chapter you should be able to:

- explain the main requirements of FRS 3;
- describe the structure of the profit-and-loss account;
- understand the key terms;
- describe the other statements related to the profit-and-loss account.

2 | INTRODUCTION

The profit-and-loss account we have described in earlier chapters served for many years but increasingly showed a number of weaknesses. In particular, the statement tended to emphasise the importance of profit but not how that profit was achieved. It also allowed companies some degree of creativity in how they presented the profit figures and this could be misleading. The Accounting Standards Board wished to improve the information provided to users and therefore issued FRS 3, Reporting Financial Performance.

In bringing about these changes the ASB wished to give a more comprehensive picture of the total financial performance of a company to users. Thus, companies have to provide more details of their activities. Increasingly, the accounting profession is moving away from a relatively simple approach to measuring profit and trying to identify the elements of the overall performance of a company. FRS 3 is by no means the last word and we can expect further changes and revisions in the future.

In this chapter we will examine the main requirements of FRS 3. In particular we will look at the new structure for the profit-and-loss account and the types of information to be provided. We will also look at other statements, related to the profit-and-loss account, which companies are now required to provide. It will be extremely helpful if you have obtained a set of published accounts so that you can work through this chapter and refer to the accounts.

3   KEY REQUIREMENTS

One of the key abuses that FRS 3 tackles is that known as 'extraordinary items'. When we look at a profit-and-loss account we are interested in the profit or loss arriving from the ordinary activities of the business, that is the day-to-day operations. During the course of the year there will be a number of events, such as closure of factories, thefts, fires where there is no insurance, redundancies and so forth. The question arises as to how such events should be treated in the profit-and-loss account.

Prior to the introduction of FRS 3 events that were not part of ordinary activities could be treated as either exceptional or extraordinary. With extraordinary items companies found that they could calculate a figure of profit before taking these into account. When items that were not ordinary and involved large costs arose there was an obvious temptation for companies to call these extraordinary items and thus flatter their profit figures. Under FRS 3 that is no longer possible.

The Accounting Standards Board has defined extraordinary items as abnormal events that arise from transactions outside of the ordinary activities of the company. Such events are not expected to recur. The ASB has gone so far as to state that it does not expect extraordinary items to appear on the profit-and-loss account now that FRS 3 is in force.

Nevertheless, companies will also have transactions or events that are unusual and FRS 3 has defined these as exceptional items. These are events or transactions that are within the ordinary activities of the company and that need to be disclosed because of their size or incidence. Without the separate disclosure of exceptional items the profit-and-loss account would not give a true and fair view. The standard goes on to carefully specify how exceptional items are treated on the profit-and-loss account so that users are not misled.

In addition to stopping the abuse of extraordinary items, the accounting standard requires companies to give a better analysis of their operations. Two issues are dealt with, that of *discontinued operations* and that of *newly acquired business*.

Firstly, during the course of a year a company may discontinue some of its operations. In other words it will sell or terminate a part of the business permanently. For example, a hotel company may choose to sell all of its hotels in a particular country or a manufacturing company may decide to cease making one of its products. Before FRS 3 the investor did not know from the profit-and-loss account what the financial impact was from the cessation of part of the operations. FRS 3 requires companies to separately provide information on the profit-and-loss account on continuing and discontinued items.

The second issue is where a company makes an acquisition during the course of the financial period. Where a company has a newly acquired acquisition it must analyse turnover and operating profit between that from existing operations and that from newly acquired business.

You should now be able to attempt Task 24.1 and Question 24.1 at the end of this chapter.

4 | STRUCTURE OF THE PROFIT-AND-LOSS ACCOUNT

As you can imagine, all this additional information would make for a very long and detailed profit-and-loss account. Some information can be shown as a note. We show below the types of headings that one would expect to see on a profit-and-loss account drawn up according to FRS 3. We have left out the figures for clarity and also the previous year, which is required to be shown. We have also only shown the profit-and-loss account as far as operating profit. There is still considerable information to be shown following that figure.

Profit-and-loss account: simplified example

Turnover		
Continuing operations	X	
Acquisitions	X	
	X̲	
Discontinued operations	X̲	X
Cost of sales		(X̲)
Gross profit		X̲
Net operating expenses		X̲
Operating profit		
Continuing operations	X	
Acquisitions	X	
	X̲	
Discontinued operations	(X̲)	X

Although the standard requires all the headings from turnover to operating profit to be subdivided between those arising from continuing operations and those from discontinued, only the analysis for turnover and operating profit need be shown on the face of the profit-and-loss account, as we have shown above. All the additional information regarding costs can be allocated to a note.

As we stated earlier, the above profit-and-loss account is only a simplified example. The main information that would be shown on the face of the profit-and-loss account after the figure of operation profit is:

Interest payable

Taxation

Minority interests

Dividends

Retained profit for the financial year

Earnings per share

Two items that you may not have encountered before are minority interests and earnings per share. We will discuss earnings per share in a later chapter. Minority interests arise where the holding company does not own 100 per cent of a subsidiary. It may hold 90 per cent and other investors will hold the remaining

10 per cent. When the results of all the separate companies in a group are consolidated, it is important to show the amount belonging to these minority interests.

> *You should now be able to attempt Task 24.2 and Question 24.2 at the end of the chapter.*

5 STATEMENT OF TOTAL RECOGNISED GAINS AND LOSSES

As well as the profit for the year as shown on the profit-and-loss account, a company may have other gains and losses that are not shown on the profit-and-loss account but are likely to appear on the balance sheet. For example, if a company decides that some of its assets have increased in value it may decide to revalue them. This means that the figure for the asset will be increased in the balance sheet and the figure in reserves must also be increased by the same amount. This is good news for shareholders but the problem is that the transaction may not be easily noticed on the balance sheet.

The *statement of total recognised gains and losses* is designed to capture this type of information and bring it to the attention of the users of financial statements. The statement is therefore a primary statement. In other words it must have the same prominence as the profit-and-loss account, balance sheet and cash-flow statement. The statement will usually have the following types of information

Statement of total recognised gains and losses

Profit for the year from the profit-and-loss account

Surplus on revaluation of fixed assets

Surplus/deficit on revaluation of investment properties

If a company has no gains and losses other than the profit for the year a statement to that effect must be given immediately following the profit-and-loss account.

Before we finish this section, it is worth emphasising that we are considering *recognised* gains and losses. In the example used above of the company revaluing the asset, there has been a gain but the company still owns the asset. It is not until the company sells the asset will this gain be *realised*.

> *You should now be able to attempt Question 24.3 at the end of this chapter.*

6 OTHER DISCLOSURES

The other two main disclosures to be made by companies under FRS 3 are a *reconciliation of movements in shareholders funds* and a *note of historical cost profits and losses*. You will most probably find this information somewhere in the notes of the published accounts you are using. They are not primary statements but the information should be disclosed if it is available.

The reconciliation of movements in shareholders' funds is intended to pull together several separate pieces of information that shareholders find of importance – in other words, those aspects of financial performance that reflect their interest in the company. The statement is fairly brief and would include the following information:

Profit for the financial year	X
Dividends	(X)
	X
Other recognised gains and losses (taken from the statement of total recognised gains and losses)	X
New share capital	(X)
Net addition to shareholders funds	X
Opening shareholders' funds	X
Closing shareholders funds	X

You may not be able to find the note of historical cost profits and losses in the set of published accounts you have obtained. It will only be present where the profit reported by the company deviates materially from that if the pure historical cost convention had been used. This will occur where the company has used the legislative exemption to revalue its assets.

> You should now be able to attempt Task 24.3 at the end of this chapter.

7 SUMMARY

The profit-and-loss account required by the Companies Act has been found to contain a number of deficiencies. Over the years a number of companies have abused the ambiguity allowed in the regulations. In addition, investors became too fixed on a single profit figure.

The Accounting Standards Board has sought to bring about improvements by issuing FRS 3, *Reporting Financial Performance*. This standard has stopped the practice of companies labelling some items as extraordinary and thus manipulating the profit figure used by investors for decision making. The standard has also improved the quality of the information disclosed by requiring a distinction between continuing and discontinued items. Information is also required regarding financial performance due to acquisitions.

The standard has also introduced another primary statement – the *statement of total recognised gains and losses*. This is designed to capture those transactions that do not go through the profit-and-loss account but are put directly to reserves on the balance sheet. The standard has also introduced other disclosures in the form of a *reconciliation of movements in shareholders' funds* and a *note of historical costs profits and losses*.

The standard has substantially increased the amount and the quality of information disclosed to users. For the untrained person, the information is complex and profit is likely to fluctuate more than before the issue of the standard. The ASB, however, believes that investors should not be fixed on a final figure of profit but should consider the separate elements of financial performance that make up that profit.

Student activities

Task 24.1
Select the published accounts of three companies and compare the way in which information on continuing and discontinued operations is presented. Do these differences affect your understanding of the accounts?

Task 24.2
From a set of published accounts, extract the data relating to continuing and discontinued operations and construct separate profit-and-loss accounts. What conclusions do you draw from these accounts?

Task 24.3
Search for a set of published accounts that contains a note of historical cost profits and losses. Discuss why this is important in understanding the figure of profit shown on the main profit-and-loss account.

Question 24.1
Write a letter to an investor explaining why the distinction between continuing and discontinued operations is useful.

Question 24.2
List the main types of information you would expect to find in a profit-and-loss account after operating profits.

Question 24.3
As far as the ordinary shareholder is concerned, why is the distinction between recognised and realised gains and losses important?

Objective test *(tick the appropriate box)*

i)   The Accounting Standards Board:

    a)   requires all companies to show extraordinary items on the balance
       sheet   ☐

b) requires all companies to show extraordinary items on the profit-and-loss account ☐

c) states that extraordinary items must never appear on the profit-and-loss account ☐

d) believes that extraordinary items will rarely appear on the profit-and-loss account ☐

ii) The statement of total recognised gains and losses:

a) must be shown in the notes to the accounts ☐

b) is a section of the main profit-and-loss account ☐

c) is a primary statement following the profit-and-loss account ☐

d) is part of the reconciliation of movements in shareholder funds ☐

iii) A surplus on revaluation of fixed assets appears as:

a) part of the operating profit ☐

b) an item on the statement of total recognised gains and losses ☐

c) as a separate note to the accounts ☐

d) as a discontinued item ☐

iv) An issue of new share capital would be shown in the:

a) statement of total recognised gains and losses ☐

b) reconciliation of movements in shareholder funds ☐

c) note of historical cost profits and losses ☐

d) the main profit-and-loss account ☐

v) Information about the financial impact relating to costs of sales on continuing and discontinued operations should be shown:

a) on the profit-and-loss account ☐

b) as a note ☐

c) both on the profit-and-loss account and as a note ☐

d) either on the profit-and-loss account or as a note ☐

CHAPTER 25

Statements of financial position

1 OBJECTIVES

At the end of this chapter you should be able to:

- describe the main feature of a balance sheet;
- explain the accounting treatment of fixed assets;
- explain the treatment of liabilities and provisions;
- explain the complexities of share capital and reserves.

2 INTRODUCTION

Although the a balance sheet was the first financial statement required by legislation in the middle of the nineteenth century, it fell out of favour. As new legislation required a profit-and-loss account and early accounting standards required more disclosures, so the balance sheet seemed less important. Investors, understandably, wanted to know about profit and how much dividend they were going to receive.

In recent years the balance sheet has been attracting more attention. One reason is that a few companies found that they could carry out creative accounting by using the balance sheet and it was difficult to detect. Another reason was the realisation that the profit-and-loss account gave only one part of the picture and the balance sheet is required to complete it.

The Accounting Standards Board has issued a number of standards that have a direct effect on the balance sheet. The aim of these has been to stop the abuses that were taking place and to improve the quality and quantity of the information on the balance sheet. In this chapter we will look at the present structure of the balance sheet. We will then consider separate aspects of the balance sheet and the requirements of the relevant accounting standards.

As with the previous chapter, you will find it useful to have a set of published accounts to refer to as you work through this chapter.

You should now be able to attempt Question 25.1 at the end of this chapter.

3 | MAIN FEATURES

The Companies Act 1985 sets out two formats for the balance sheet. We have considered these formats in earlier chapters with one being vertical and the other horizontal. The vertical format is the one most used by limited companies but it is important to remember that they both provide the same information.

The balance sheet has a number of items and in the Companies Act 1985, each heading is referenced by letters, roman and arabic numbers. These do not have to be disclosed in the published accounts and are only a method by which the legislation can make clear to different types of companies the information that has to be shown.

In the following example we give the letters, roman and arabic numbers. The main rules are:

1. If an item is preceded by a letter or roman number, it must be shown on the face of the balance sheet.

2. Where an arabic number precedes a number of items they may be amalgamated if their individual amounts are not material and it conveys the information more effectively.

3. Where an arabic number precedes a number of items the title may be altered and they can be shown in a different position.

Do not be surprised if the balance sheet you have does not show all this information. There are a number of reasons why it may be missing:

- companies may have a nil figure so the item is not shown;
- some headings are more relevant to other European Union companies than those in the UK;
- the information may be contained in the notes to the accounts.

Do not forget that the company should also show the figures for the preceding year.

> *You should now be able to attempt Task 25.1 at the end of the chapter.*

4 | FIXED ASSETS

Fixed assets can be divided into two main types. *Tangible* assets are those that have physical substance – you can touch them. Examples are buildings, machinery and fixtures. The other kind of fixed assets are known as *intangibles*. Examples are patents, trademarks and goodwill. There are issues concerning both of these main types and some of the solutions are common to both. We will consider tangible fixed assets first as, in many ways, they are the least controversial. We will then tackle some of the major issues of intangible assets.

The two main questions concerning tangible fixed assets are how they are to be valued and also how they are to be depreciated. The valuation aspect is fairly straightforward and also applies to intangible assets. The rules are to be found in the Companies Act 1985 and can be summarised as follows:

1. Where an asset is purchased the valuation is the purchase price plus any incidental expenses incurred.

2. Where an asset is made by a company for its own use the valuation is the cost of raw materials, consumables and other direct costs e.g. labour. A company may also include a reasonable proportion of indirect costs and interest on any capital borrowed to finance production of the asset.

3. If there is a permanent diminution in the value of a fixed asset – if it decreases in value, a provision must be made in the profit-and-loss account and the asset should be disclosed at the reduced amount in the balance sheet.

Proforma balance sheet (vertical format)

			£	£	£
A	CALLED UP SHARE CAPITAL NOT PAID*				X
B	FIXED ASSETS				
	I	Intangible assets			
		1 Development costs	X		
		2 Concessions, patents, licences, trade marks and similar rights and assets	X		
		3 Goodwill	X		
		4 Payments on account	X		
				X	
	II	Tangible assets			
		1 Land and buildings	X		
		2 Plant and machinery	X		
		3 Fixtures, fittings, tools and equipment	X		
		4 Payments on account and assets in course of construction	X		
				X	
	III	Investments			
		1 Shares in group undertakings †	X		
		2 Loans to group undertakings †	X		
		3 Participating interest †	X		
		4 Loans to undertakings in which the company has a participating interest †	X		
		5 Other investments other than loans	X		
		6 Other loans	X		
		7 Own shares	X		
				X	
					X
C	CURRENT ASSETS				
	I	Stocks			
		1 Raw materials	X		
		2 Work in progress	X		

continued

			£	£	£
	3	Finished goods and goods for resale	X		
	4	Payments on account	X		
				X	
II	Debtors				
	1	Trade debtors	X		
	2	Amounts owed by group undertakings †	X		
	3	Amounts owed by undertakings in which the company has a participating interest †	X		
	4	Other debtors	X		
	5	Called up share capital not paid*	X		
	6	Prepayments and accrued income **	X		
				X	
III	Investments				
	1	Shares in group undertakings †	X		
	2	Own shares	X		
	3	Other investments	X		
IV	Cash at bank and in hand			X	
				X	

D PREPAYMENTS AND ACCRUED INCOME **   X

E CREDITORS: AMOUNTS FALLING DUE WITHIN ONE YEAR

1	Debenture loans	X	
2	Bank loans and overdrafts	X	
3	Payments received on account	X	
4	Trade creditors	X	
5	Bills of exchange payable	X	
6	Amounts owed to group undertakings †	X	
7	Amounts owed to undertakings in which the company has a participating interest †	X	
8	Other creditors including taxation and social security	X	
9	Accruals and deferred income **	X	
			(X)

F NET CURRENT ASSETS (LIABILITIES)   X

G TOTAL ASSETS LESS CURRENT LIABILITIES   X

H CREDITORS: AMOUNTS FALLING DUE AFTER MORE THAN ONE YEAR

1	Debenture loans	X
2	Bank loans and overdrafts	X
3	Payments received on account	X
4	Trade creditors	X
5	Bills of exchange payable	X
6	Amounts owed to group undertakings †	X
7	Amounts owed to undertakings in which the company has a participating interest †	X
8	Other creditors including taxation and social security	X
9	Accruals and deferred income ***	X

(X)

continued

		£	£	£
I	PROVISIONS FOR LIABILITIES AND CHARGES			
	1 Pensions and similar obligations †	X		
	2 Taxation, including deferred taxation	X		
	3 Other provisions	X		
			(X)	
J	ACCRUALS AND DEFERRED INCOME ***		(X)	
				X
				X
K	CAPITAL AND RESERVES			
	I Called up share capital			X
	II Share premium account			X
	III Revaluation reserve			X
	IV Other reserves			
	1 Capital redemption reserve		X	
	2 Reserve for own shares		X	
	3 Reserves provided for by the articles of association		X	
	4 Other reserves		X	
				X
	V Profit-and-loss			X
				X

(*), (**), (***). These items may be shown in either of the positions indicated.

These rules appear simple but there are problems in practice and there are some that are controversial. The rule that a company may capitalise, that is charge as part of the fixed asset, the interest costs on money it has borrowed, is viewed with suspicion by some as it presents an area where creative accounting may take place. The rule on permanent diminution also raises some problems and we will return to these when we consider intangible assets.

In addition to the above provisions a company may choose to use the 'alternative accounting rules'. Where it is appropriate a company can abandon the normal historic-cost convention and use either the current cost or market value instead of the production cost or purchase price.

Although this rule may seem odd at first glance it was introduced to improve the information on balance sheets. The main example is property where a company may have purchased one building in 1925 another in 1937 and a third in 1999. If these are all shown at their purchase price there is little information content. The buildings purchased in 1925 and 1937 should be worth much more today if they have been well maintained. To show the original cost on the balance sheet could mislead the reader. Note, however, that a company is not forced to revalue its assets and this can make the comparison of two companies a problem.

Fixed assets have to be depreciated under the Companies Act 1985 and FRS 15 *Tangible Fixed Assets* provides detailed guidance. In essence, depreciation is the allocation of cost (or revalued amount) less the residual value over the economic life of the asset. Depreciation is not a way of valuing assets.

Prior to FRS 15 there was considerable flexibility in the way that companies could value and depreciate fixed assets. The standard now sets strict rules. It states that depreciation should be on a systematic basis and performed throughout the asset's useful economic life. It does not state the method of depreciation that should be used.

The question of the correct accounting treatment for intangible assets has caused serious debate over many years. It would seem that we have a solution in the UK with the issue of FRS 10 *Goodwill and Intangible Assets* and FRS 11 *Impairment of Fixed Assets and Goodwill*. Intangible assets includes patents, trademarks, licences and goodwill.

It would need a separate book to explain all the provisions of these two accounting standards so we will just look at one issue – that of goodwill. Goodwill arises when one business buys another for more than the value of its net assets. It is argued that the purchaser must expect to pay more for the entire business, which can include such items as buildings, machinery and stock, because intangible assets are also being acquired. Examples of such intangible assets are the reputation of the business, the established network of suppliers and customers, the loyalty of key employees and the infrastructure of efficient systems and procedures. All of these intangible assets can be grouped together in the general category of goodwill.

Example

A company purchases another successful business for $1,000,000. The acquired business's premises are worth $750,000 and its furniture and fittings are worth $100,000. The business's creditors amount to $50,000.

The figure for goodwill can be calculated as follows:

	$	$
Purchase price		1,000,000
Less fair value of net assets		
Premises	750,000	
Furniture	100,000	
	850,000	
Creditors	(50,000)	800,000
Goodwill		200,000

We suspect that you can see some problems with the above calculation. The mathematics is correct but what if the premises were, in fact, worth $850,000. What if the purchaser was having a bad negotiating day and paid $1,200,000 for the business? Does this mean that goodwill is worth $200,000?

Even if we can answer the above questions there remains the problem of how we treat goodwill in the accounts. If you remember your double entry, then there will be a credit to cash of $1,000,000 and we therefore need to debit some asset accounts. If we do regard goodwill as an asset because we have purchased it, do we put it on the balance sheet? If so, for how long and how do we determine the annual depreciation?

There are no easy answers to the above questions and it took the accounting profession many years of debate before FRS 10 *Goodwill and Intangible Assets* was issued. It is a long standard with many rules and in this chapter we will only consider the main points.

- Goodwill can only be shown in the balance sheet when one business acquires another as a going concern.

- Where goodwill and other intangible assets have limited lives they will be amortised to the profit-and-loss account over those lives.

- It is assumed that the lives of goodwill and intangible assets will be no more than 20 years.

- Where it can be argued that an asset has a life of over 20 years, or even an indefinite life, an impairment review must be conducted to ensure that the value is not lower than that shown in the balance sheet.

In the last point we mentioned an impairment review. The rules for this are given in FRS 11 *Impairment of Fixed Assets and Goodwill*. At this stage in your studies, it is sufficient to know that there is a standard without studying its contents.

> *You should now attempt Tasks 25.2 and 25.3 and Question 25.2 at the end of this chapter.*

5   EQUITY AND DEBT

On the face of it share capital would not seem to be as complicated as goodwill and other intangible assets. At its simplest share capital or equity is the amount that the owners have invested in the business. Unfortunately the financial world is far more complex than that and accountants and lawyers have created a whole array of techniques for raising finance for a company. These techniques are known as capital instruments and include bank loans, convertible debt, ordinary shares, preference shares and options and warrants to subscribe for these shares. Ordinary shares are only one way out of many that a company can use to raise finance.

It may seem that as long as the company has been able to raise the money it does not matter how we classify the technique used. However, as we will see in a later chapter, users of accounts make great use of a ratio known as the gearing ratio in order to interpret a company's financial performance. This is a measure of the proportion of debt to equity. If the ratio is to be of use we need to be very clear as to what is debt and what is equity.

The Accounting Standards Board has issued FRS 4 *Capital Instruments*, to help us sort out the distinction. Essentially, a company's shares should remain in shareholders' funds on the balance sheet. Capital instruments should be reported as liabilities if the company has to transfer 'economic benefits' – in other words pay out cash or transfer other property. Unfortunately some capital instruments, known as convertibles, can look like shares and liabilities. The main example of these hybrid capital instruments is convertible debt. This is like conventional debt but also allows the holder to acquire shares in the future – to convert the debt to equity.

As you can imagine, financiers invent more and more complex capital instruments so that it can become very difficult to determine what is debt and what is equity. The approach of the Accounting Standards Board to resolve this issue is to require issuers to make substantial disclosures in the annual report and accounts. If you examine the set of published accounts that you have obtained, you may find some examples of these disclosures.

6 | SUMMARY

This is a complex chapter and may seem far removed from the introduction of the balance sheet that you met in the first chapters. You must remember that the principles are the same. The accounting ratio is:

$$Assets = Liabilities + Capital$$

As the business world becomes more complex it becomes harder to identify and measure economic transactions.

Tangible fixed assets such as buildings, machinery and fixtures raise their own problems. Decisions must be made on values and amortisation and company legislation and accounting standards have produced some strong guidelines. The issues surrounding intangible assets and goodwill are more complex. Although we now have accounting standards that set out certain provisions, it is still too early to be confident that all eventualities have been covered.

As far as equity and debt are concerned, the Accounting Standards Board has addressed the main problems. But the financing of business activities is complex and competitive. There is no way to predict what wonderful schemes some accountants and lawyers will dream up in the future to confuse the distinction between debt and equity.

Student activities (questions with answers at the end of the book)

Task 25.1
Select the published accounts of three companies and compare the way in which the balance sheets are presented. Do the differences affect your understanding of the balance sheets?

Task 25.2
List the main roles for valuing fixed assets.

Task 25.3
Select a number of published accounts and list any intangible assets you find. What industrial or company differences might explain the types of intangible assets?

Question 25.1
In your opinion, why does the balance sheet attract more attention in recent years?

Question 25.2

In your opinion, what other methods are possible in the accounting treatment of goodwill apart from the approach required by the accounting standard?

Question 25.3

What is meant by the term capital instruments? Describe two different types.

Objective tests (*tick the appropriate box*)

i) The Companies Act sets out:

    a) two formats for the balance sheet ☐

    b) four formats for the balance sheet ☐

    c) one format for the balance sheet ☐

    d) no format for the balance sheet ☐

ii) Depreciation on tangible fixed assets is a method of:

    a) allocating costs over the life of the asset ☐

    b) ensuring that any permanent diminution is recorded ☐

    c) giving the up-to-date value of the asset ☐

    d) misleading shareholders ☐

iii) Under FRS 10, goodwill is assumed to:

    a) last indefinitely ☐

    b) have a life of no more that 20 years ☐

    c) be worthless as soon as it is purchased ☐

    d) have a life of no more than five years ☐

iv) The gearing ratio is the proportion of:

    a) debt to equity ☐

    b) bank loans to preference shares ☐

    c) equity to tangible fixed assets ☐

    d) equity to intangible assets ☐

v) The accounting standard dealing with capital instruments is:

    a) FRS 3 ☐

    b) FRS 4 ☐

    c) FRS 10 ☐

    d) FRS 11 ☐

PART VI

THE ANALYSIS OF FINANCIAL STATEMENTS

CHAPTER 26

Ratio analysis

1 OBJECTIVES

At the end of this chapter you should be able to:

- identify the purposes of ratios;
- calculate the main performance ratios;
- calculate the main liquidity ratios;
- interpret the meaning of these ratios and recognise their limitations.

2 INTRODUCTION

Ratio analysis is a technique used to describe and interpret the relationships of certain financial data in the financial statements that would otherwise be devoid of meaning. It allows the comparisons to be made between:

- companies of different sizes;
- a particular company and the industry average;
- the same company over a period of time.

It is important to note that there are different definitions of some of the ratios and different ways of calculating them. In this chapter we will adopt the definitions and methods of calculation most frequently used.

3 PURPOSE OF RATIO ANALYSIS

Ratio analysis can be used for the following purposes:

- to assess a company's financial performance;
- to evaluate the financial stability of a company;
- to predict the future performance and stability of a company.

To demonstrate the ratios we are going to use the profit-and-loss account and balance sheet of Ivy Stores, a business that has been trading in health foods for a number of years. The profit-and-loss account for the year ending December 2003 and the balance sheet at that date are shown below. To make the exercise easier, we have ignored taxation.

Ivy Stores

Profit-and-loss account for the year
ending 31 December 2003

	£'000	£'000
Sales		500
Less cost of sales		375
Gross profit		125
Less expenses:		
Salaries	30	
Rent	10	
Administration	9	
Depreciation	20	
Interest	5	74
Profit before tax		51

Ivy Stores

Balance sheet as at 31 December 2003

	£'000	£'000		£'000	£'000
Fixed assets at cost:			Capital	70	
Fixtures	80		*Add* Profit	51	
Vehicles	60			121	
Less cumulative depreciation			*Less* Drawings	50	
		86			71
Net book value		54	Loan		50
Current assets:					
			Creditors: amounts due within one year		
Stock	78		Trade creditors		63
Debtors	46				
Cash	6	130			
		184			184

4 PERFORMANCE OR PROFITABILITY RATIOS

There are a number of ratios that can be used to assess the financial *performance* or *profitability* of an organisation. Because the terms used in the ratios may be defined in several different ways, it is important to state the precise meaning of the terms you are using. We will use the following:

- *return* is defined as profit before interest and tax;
- *capital employed* is defined as fixed assets plus current assets less current liabilities (Creditors: amounts due within one year).

There are no standard definitions of the above terms, so it is important to find out what definitions have been used in any ratios quoted in order to understand fully what is being referred to and the implications of the ratio calculated. We have defined the term *return* as profit before interest and tax. You should be able to find this figure on the profit-and-loss account of a business. In the accounts of a limited company it may be labelled *operating profit*.

There are five main *financial performance* or *profitability ratios* and we will calculate them one at a time using the above profit-and-loss account and balance sheet.

1. The *prime ratio or return on capital employed (ROCE)* measures the percentage total return on the investment of funds (i.e. capital plus loans). The formula is:

$$\frac{\text{Profit before interest and tax}}{\text{Capital employed}} \times 100$$

Example
Using the data given in the financial statements of Ivy Stores, calculate the prime ratio.

Solution
The first step is to find the figure for profit before interest and tax. On the profit-and-loss account no figure for tax is shown. The figure of £51,000 profit is therefore before tax. However, if you look at the costs, you will see that the organisation had to pay interest of £5,000 on a loan. As we want the figure of profit before interest, we must add the figure of £5,000 to the profit of £51,000 (£56,000). Next, find the figure for capital employed, which we defined as fixed assets (£54,000) plus current assets (£130,000) less creditors: amounts due within one year (£63,000). This results in a figure of £121,000. Then, substituting the figures in the formula, the correct answer is:

$$\frac{£56,000}{£121,000} \times 100 = 46.3\%$$

The resulting percentage should reflect the element of risk in the investment and can be compared with interest rates for other investments where there is barely any risk, such as building society interest rates. It is also useful to compare the prime ratio over time. However, if we want to know how this profitability has been achieved or how it can be improved, we need to look at two subsidiary ratios.

2. The *profit margin* or *return on sales (ROS)* measures the percentage return on sales (net profit per £1 of sales). The formula is:

$$\frac{\text{Profit before interest and tax}}{\text{Sales}} \times 100$$

Example
Using the data given in the financial statements of Ivy Stores, calculate the profit margin.

Solution

You have already found the figure for profit before interest and tax, so now you need to look up the figure for sales, which you will also find on the profit-and-loss account. When you substitute the figures in the formula the correct answer is:

$$\frac{£56,000}{£500,000} \times 100 = 11.2\%$$

Profit margin can be improved by increasing the selling prices and/or reducing costs.

3. *Capital turnover* measures the level of activity in the business as reflected by sales in relation to the capital employed. In other words, it measures the number of times the net assets (the capital employed) are utilised or turned over to achieve those sales. It is usually expressed as the number of times rather than a percentage. The formula is:

$$\frac{\text{Sales}}{\text{Capital employed}}$$

Example

Using the data given in the financial statements of Ivy Stores, calculate the capital turnover.

Solution

You used both these figures when calculating the two previous ratios, so you simply have to substitute them in the formula to arrive at the correct answer:

$$\frac{£500,000}{£121,000} = 4.13 \text{ times}$$

The level of activity should be as high as possible for the lowest level of investment. Capital turnover can be improved by increasing sales activity or decreasing capital employed (perhaps by reducing loans), or by selling off fixed assets which are no longer used.

These three ratios are interrelated. The *profit margin* multiplied by the *capital turnover* gives the *prime ratio*.

Example
Multiply the profit margin for Ivy Stores for 1994 by the capital turnover.

Solution

Your answer should be the same figure as the prime ratio:

$$11.2\% \times 4.13 = 46.3\%$$

A business can improve its *prime ratio* by reducing costs and/or raising prices, which will improve its *profit margin*. Alternatively, it can increase its sales volume and/or reduce its capital employed, which will improve its *capital turnover*.

4. In some profit-and-loss accounts you may also be given the figure for gross profit, as in the above example. In some industries, retailing in particular, the

gross profit figure is considered an essential feature of management control and a guide to pricing and purchasing policies. The *gross profit mark up* measures gross profit as a percentage of cost of sales. The formula is:

$$\frac{\text{Gross profit}}{\text{Cost of sales}} \times 100$$

Example

Using the data given in the financial statements of Ivy Stores, calculate the gross profit mark up.

Solution

You will need to look at the profit-and-loss account to find the figures for gross profit and cost of sales. Substituting the figures in the formula, the correct answer is:

$$\frac{£125}{£375} \times 100 = 33.3\%$$

5. The *gross profit margin* or the *gross profit percentage* measures gross profit as a percentage of sales. The formula is:

$$\frac{\text{Gross profit}}{\text{Sales}} \times 100$$

Example

Using the data given in the financial statements of Ivy Stores, calculate the gross profit margin.

Solution

You used the figure for gross profit in the last ratio, so you need only look up the sales figure in the profit-and-loss account. Substituting the figures in the formula, the correct answer is:

$$\frac{£125}{£500} \times 100 = 25\%$$

As with the other profitability ratios, trends and inter-company comparisons are useful when interpreting *gross profit mark up* and *gross profit margin*. We will discuss these topics in the next chapter.

5   LIQUIDITY OR WORKING CAPITAL RATIOS

Liquidity or working capital ratios reflect the financial stability of a business and shows how effectively the business is managing its working capital. There are five main ratios.

1. The *current test ratio* or *working capital ratio* gives an overall view of the financial stability of a company. *Working capital* or *net current assets* is the term used for current assets less creditors: amounts due within one year. The current test ratio is usually expressed as a ratio of $x:1$ rather than a percentage. The formula is:

$$\frac{\text{Current assets}}{\text{Creditors: amounts due within one year}}$$

Example

Using the data given in the financial statements of Ivy Stores, calculate the current test ratio.

Solution

You will need to look at the balance sheet to obtain the figures you need for this ratio. Substituting the figures in the formula, the correct answer is:

$$\frac{£130,000}{£63,000} = 2.1:1$$

It is useful to consider what the ratio $2.1:1$ means. In simple terms we are saying is that the business has £2.10 of current assets for every £1 of current liabilities. Therefore, if the creditors had to be paid, the business should have enough current resources to do so without having to obtain a loan or sell off its fixed assets.

In many industries there are benchmarks of what is considered to be a good current test ratio. Generally, if the ratio drops below $1.5:1$ it may indicate a lack of liquidity; a ratio of above $2:1$ could indicate poor management of working capital. A ratio of $0.9:1$ would indicate that the business may be unable to pay its creditors. However, it is essential to relate the ratio to the type of business and its trend over a period of time.

2. The *acid test, quick* or *liquid capital ratio* is a more stringent test of liquidity than the current test ratio. It is similar to the current ratio except that it excludes stock. It shows the relationship between the business's liquid assets and its current liabilities. The acid test ratio is usually expressed as a ratio of $x:1$ rather than a percentage. The formula is:

$$\frac{\text{Current assets} - \text{Stock}}{\text{Creditors: amounts due within one year}}$$

which, in our example, is the same as:

$$\frac{\text{Debtors} + \text{Cash}}{\text{Creditors: amounts due within one year}}$$

Example

Using the data given in the financial statements of Ivy Stores, calculate the acid test ratio.

Solution

Your calculations should be either:

$$\frac{\text{Current assets} - \text{Stock}}{\text{Creditors: amounts due within one year}}$$

$$\frac{£130,000 - £78,000}{£63,000} = 0.8:1$$

or

$$\frac{\text{Debtors} + \text{Cash}}{\text{Creditors: amounts due within one year}}$$

$$\frac{£46,000 - £6,000}{£63,000} = 0.8:1$$

Generally the ratio should not fall below 1:1. However, this would not be true of all businesses. For example, some businesses collect from debtors weekly, but pay their creditors monthly. This results in a low level of debtors and higher level of creditors, varying according to the time of the month. It is hard to generalise about ideal levels of liquidity, but trends and inter-firm comparisons make this an important ratio to use as a measure of liquidity.

3. The *debt collection period* or *credit ratio*, measures the average time in days (or months) that debtors take to settle their accounts. It attempts to give an indication of the effectiveness of working capital management. The formula is:

$$\frac{\text{Debtors at the end of the year}}{\text{Sales}} \times 365 \text{ days (or 12 months)}$$

Example

Using the data given in the financial statements of Ivy Stores, calculate the debt collection period.

Solution

You will need to look at the balance sheet to obtain the figures you need for this ratio. Substituting the figures in the formula, the correct answer is:

$$\frac{£46,000}{£500,000} \times 365 = 33 \text{ days}$$

or

$$\frac{£46,000}{£500,000} \times 12 = 1.1 \text{ months}$$

This means that on average Ivy Stores' customers take 33 days or 1.1 months to pay. If company policy or the industry average is one month's credit, then 45 days (the average length of the credit period) is what we would expect, so 33 days indicates good management; 76 days would indicate bad management. It appears that the management of Ivy Stores is very efficient in collecting the money that is owed to the business, although we would want to make comparisons to ensure that we are drawing the correct conclusions.

4. The *credit period ratio* measures the average time in days (or months) that the business takes to settle accounts with their creditors. The formula is:

$$\frac{\text{Creditors}}{\text{Purchases}} \times 365 \text{ days (or 12 months)}$$

Sometimes we do not know the figure for purchases and therefore have to use the cost of sales figure. This is not quite such a good measure, because it is affected by changes in stock levels. However, as long as we are consistent, it is possible to draw conclusions from it.

Example
Using the data given in the financial statements of Ivy Stores, calculate the credit collection period.

Solution
You will need to look at the balance sheet to obtain the figures for this ratio.
Substituting the figures in the formula, the correct answer is:

$$\frac{£63,000}{£375,000} \times 365 = 61 \text{ days}$$

or

$$\frac{£63,000}{£375,000} \times 12 = 2.016 \text{ months}$$

5. The *stock turnover ratio* measures the level of activity in regard to stock held by the organisation. Holding stock is expensive and an organisation should attempt to sell its stock and replace it as often as it can in a financial period. This is known as *turning over stock* and the formula is:

$$\frac{\text{Cost of sales}}{\text{Stock}}$$

In some instances the profit-and-loss account does not disclose the cost of sales figure and you may have to use the sales figure.

Example
Using the data given in the financial statements of Ivy Stores, calculate the stock turnover ratio.

Solution
You will need to look at the profit-and-loss account to obtain the cost-of-sales figure and the balance sheet for the stock figure. Substituting the figures in the formula, the correct answer is:

$$\frac{£375,000}{£78,000} = 4.8 \text{ times}$$

This ratio shows that Ivy Stores has turned over its stock 4.8 times in the financial period. To assess whether this is good, you would need to compare this result with the ratio of other retailers, the industry average or for Ivy Stores for a number of financial periods.

6   LIMITATIONS OF RATIOS

The main *limitations* of ratio analysis are as follows.

- There are no agreed definitions of the terms used.
- Data drawn from different sources may not be comparable.
- The figures you need to construct the ratios may not be available and you may have to use less precise alternatives.
- If there is high inflation, the figures in the financial statements may be misleading.
- The business may have used an unusual accounting treatment, the effect of which is not apparent.
- Not all aspects of a business that should be taken into account are shown in the figures in the financial statements. For example, a company's products may have a good reputation or it may suffer from poor industrial relations.

Despite these limitations, ratio analysis is an invaluable method for interpreting the financial statements of an organisation. You should not treat them as absolute answers, but as an indication of where your investigations should be directed to find out the underlying reasons for the financial performance. In the next chapter we consider other ratios and how they may be interpreted.

> *You should now be able to attempt Tasks 26.1, 26.2 and 26.3 and Questions 26.1, 26.2 and 26.3 at the end of this chapter.*

7   SUMMARY

Ratio analysis is a key technique for interpreting the financial statements of organisations. We have used five ratios to assess *financial performance* or *profitability*. By considering these ratios, and the relationship between them, it is possible to draw conclusions concerning the financial performance of an organisation. It is also possible to assess the liquidity of an organisation and the effectiveness of the management in controlling working capital. The calculation of the ratios can highlight where there are weaknesses and where management can take action.

Although accounting ratios are powerful tools for interpreting financial statements they have their limitations. One difficulty if you are conducting comparisons is the lack of precision in terminology. It is important to ensure that the definitions you use are applied consistently.

> *You should now be able to attempt the objective test at the end of this chapter.*

Student activities

Task 26.1

Obtain an annual report and accounts of a company in an industry that interests you. Turn to the financial statements and find:

- the profit-and-loss account or the consolidated profit-and-loss account;
- the consolidated balance sheet or the balance sheet of the company.

The latter is probably that of the holding company, showing mainly (as assets) the investment in the subsidiary companies of the group. Ignore this balance sheet. Choose the consolidated or group balance sheet, which means that it is the combined balance sheet of all the companies in the group. Try to find the items you need to calculate all the ratios described in this chapter. You may need to look up the notes to the accounts to find some of them.

Calculate the ratios for the current year and last year. Comparative figures for last year are usually provided. Look for the changes between this year and last year. Which are good and which are bad? Is there anything in the reports, notes and so forth that indicates reasons for any of these changes? Is there any ratio that you cannot work out because the figures are not provided?

Task 26.2

Invent an imaginary company, and compose its accounts for the last two years. The accounts need only be in sufficient detail for the seven ratios described in this chapter to be calculated from them. Try to arrive at figures such that three or four of the ratios show favourable changes and the other ratios show unfavourable changes. Pencils and rubbers are recommended for your rough workings! Present your final accounts and ratios in an acceptable format, and append your comments on the causes of the favourable/unfavourable changes.

Task 26.3

Read the financial pages of the newspaper and extract any items that refer to ratios.

i) Compare them with the ratios examined in this chapter.

ii) Construct a frequency table to illustrate the most quoted ratios.

Question 26.1

The following information is available in respect of Norwich Ltd for the year ending 31 December 2004:

Debtors amount to £33,600, and the debt collection period is one month.

Gross profit is 25% of sales.

Net profit is 5% of sales.

Sales: WDV (written down value) of fixed assets is a ratio of 2:1.

Purchases totalled £336,000.

Creditors are equal to one month's purchases.

Opening stock at 1 January 2004 was £28,000.

Expenses are the difference between gross and net profits.

Share capital is 239,120 shares of £1 each.

Dividends proposed are half of the net profit.

The current test ratio is 2:1 at 31 December 2004.

Bank overdraft is £9,520 at 31 December 2004.

Required

Prepare a trading and profit-and-loss account for Norwich Ltd for the year ending 31 December 2004, and a balance sheet as at that date, in as much detail as possible, taking into account all the above information.

Hint: Prepare a blank set of accounts, fill in any given figures, calculate other figures from them using the ratios provided and then any missing figures can be calculated from them.

Question 26.2

Using the data given in the financial statements for Ivy Stores in this chapter, calculate the profitability ratios using profit after interest instead of profit before interest and comment on the differences.

Question 26.3

The relative sizes of assets and liabilities of businesses in different industries vary. Given below are the assets and liabilities of five different industries. The figures given are the *percentages of capital employed*. This should help you compare and contrast the relative sizes of the various components of the balance sheets.

Company	A %	B %	C %	D %	E %
Fixed assets					
Buildings	18	25	76	21	51
Plant & Machinery	9	60	1	47	8
Office equipment	5	4	4	5	15
Vehicles	72	3	2	5	10
Current assets					
Stocks	4	8	8	37	45
Debtors	1	25	17	26	1
Current liabilities	(9)	(25)	(8)	(41)	(30)
Capital employed	100	100	100	100	100

The industries represented are:

- commercial vehicle manufacturer;
- public transport (buses);
- general engineering;
- food retailing;
- hotel and leisure.

Required

Match the numbers of the industries against the companies.

Company	Industry
A	____
B	____
C	____
D	____
E	____

Hint: a cash business will have relatively low debtors; an engineering company will have a relatively high investment in plant and machinery.

Objective test (*tick the appropriate box*)

i) Capital employed is calculated by:

    a) adding fixed and current assets   ☐

    b) adding back interest on loans   ☐

    c) adding fixed assets and net current assets   ☐

    d) adding fixed assets and net current assets and deducting long-term loans   ☐

ii) The prime ratio results from multiplying:

    a) profit before interest and tax by capital employed   ☐

    b) the gross profit ratio by the capital turnover ratio   ☐

    c) the profit margin ratio by the capital turnover ratio   ☐

    d) the capital turnover ratio by the current test ratio   ☐

iii) If debtors are £20,000, creditors £7,000, cash £6,000 and overdraft £6,000, then:

    a) the current test ratio is 1.54:1   ☐

    b) the current test ratio is 2.25:1   ☐

    c) the acid test ratio is 1.54:1   ☐

    d) the acid test ratio is 2:1   ☐

iv) If sales are £80,000, purchases £60,000 and gross profit £20,000, then gross profit mark up is:

a) 25% ☐

b) 50% ☐

c) 33.3% ☐

d) 20% ☐

v) The debt collection period in days is calculated by:

a) dividing debtors by purchases and multiplying by 365 ☐

b) adding debtors to sales and multiplying by 365 ☐

c) dividing debtors by sales and multiplying by 365 ☐

d) dividing creditors by sales and multiplying by 365 ☐

Use the following data to answer (vi) to (vii) below

	£'000
Gross profit	243
Profit before interest and tax	77
Capital employed	804
Sales	1,320
Current assets	642
Creditors: amounts due within one year	285
Stock	208
Debtors	131

vi) The current test ratio is:

a) 2.25:1 ☐

b) 1.52:1 ☐

c) 3.09:1 ☐

d) none of these ☐

vii) The acid test ratio is:

a) 2.25:1 ☐

b) 1.52:1 ☐

c) 3.09:1 ☐

d) none of these ☐

viii) The debt collection period is:

a) 36 months ☐

b) 36 days ☐

c) 36 weeks ☐

d) none of these ☐

ix) The capital turnover ratio is:

    a) 1.64 times ☐

    b) 1.52 times ☐

    c) 2.25 times ☐

    d) 3.09 times ☐

x) The profit margin ratio is:

    a) 58.3% ☐

    b) 18.4% ☐

    c) 1.84% ☐

    d) 5.83% ☐

CHAPTER 27

Investment ratios

1 OBJECTIVES

At the end of this chapter you should be able to:

- explain and calculate gearing ratios;
- demonstrate the importance of earnings per share;
- explain and calculate ratios used by investors.

2 INTRODUCTION

In Chapter 26 we considered the main accounting ratios relating to *financial performance* or *profitability* and *liquidity* or *working capital management*. These ratios are very useful to those responsible for managing the company and to others outside the company, such as lenders, creditors and investors, as a means of assessing the company. In the previous chapter we showed how ratios are related and how the interpretation of one ratio is assisted by considering the significance of another ratio.

This chapter continues the theme by considering the importance of *gearing ratios*, which relate to the financial structure of the business. Most businesses are funded not only by their owners (in the case of a limited company, the shareholders), but also by long-term loans. The balance between these two sources of funds can have a dramatic impact on the profit of a company and the decisions we may make about it.

Finally, we will look at a number of *investment ratios* most commonly used by investors. These are given in the financial pages of broadsheet newspapers such as the *Financial Times* and it is helpful in your assessment of a company to understand what information these ratios convey. A fundamental ratio for investors is earnings per share and we will consider this in some detail.

3 GEARING RATIOS

Gearing ratios are concerned with the financial structure of the business. Businesses fund their operations through investment by their owners and by borrowing from banks and other organisations. In a limited company the investment by the owners (the shareholders) is known as *equity* and consists not only of the share capital but also of any profits that have been retained in the company to help it grow. The borrowings are known as *debt*. As with all ratios the precise definitions of equity and debt can cause problems, but in the example in this section we will use these straightforward definitions. We further define debt as being long-term debt (over twelve months).

If you consider the above definitions you can see that equity plus long-term debt must be equal to fixed assets plus current assets less current liabilities otherwise the balance sheet would not balance. Equity plus long-term debt is therefore equal to capital employed. *Gearing* refers to the proportion of debt and equity in a company's financial structure. A company that is highly geared is a company that has a high proportion of debt in relation to its equity. A low-geared company has a low proportion of debt in relation to its equity. The importance of this is that the higher the gearing a company has, the greater the risk to shareholders in poor economic conditions, but the greater their return if business is going well.

We can demonstrate the importance of gearing by calculating two ratios: *return on capital employed (ROCE)* and *return on equity*. The first ratio we explained in the previous chapter. Return on equity is the return that shareholders receive after interest has been paid and the formula is:

$$\frac{\text{Profit after interest}}{\text{Equity}} \times 100$$

Example

Two similar companies both make the same profit before interest and tax in the financial year. They both have the same capital employed. However, Bonito plc is a low-geared company and Loftus plc is a high-geared company. The figures for the two companies are as follows.

	Bonito plc	Loftus plc
Equity	£450,000	£250,000
Long-term debt	£50,000	£250,000
Profit before interest	£150,000	£150,000
Interest charge on debt	10%	10%

Required

Calculate the return on capital employed and return on equity and comment on your results.

Solution

	Bonito plc £	Loftus plc £
Profit before interest	150,000	150,000
Interest charge on debt (10%)	5,000	25,000
Profit after interest	145,000	125,000
Return on capital employed	30%	30%
Return on equity	32%	50%

Both companies have the same return on capital employed because they both have the same figure for profit before interest, but they have different capital structures. Bonito plc has a low level of debt and pays low interest charges. The profit after interest of £145,000, however, has got to be expressed as a percentage of equity of £450,000 to give a return of 32 per cent. The highly geared company, Loftus plc, has a higher interest charge, but the lower figure of profit after interest of £125,000 is the return on equity investment of £250,000. It would be safe to assume that the shareholders in Loftus plc are much happier with their return of 50 per cent, than those in Bonito plc with a return of 32 per cent.

Now we will use gearing ratios to analyse these same companies in a different situation.

Example

Let us assume that there is a severe economic recession and the profits of Bonito plc and Loftus plc both slump to £25,000.

Required

Calculate the return on capital employed and return on equity and comment on your results.

Solution

	Bonito plc £	Loftus plc £
Profit before interest	25,000	25,000
Interest charge on debt (10%)	5,000	25,000
Profit after interest	20,000	0
Return on capital employed	5.0%	5.0%
Return on equity	4.4%	0%

The results are very dramatic. The shareholders in Bonito plc receive a return of 4.4 per cent, whereas those in Loftus plc receive none. In the following year, if profits were to sink lower or interest charges were to increase, the shareholders of Loftus plc would be very dissatisfied.

In the above examples we used gearing ratios, but these suffer from the problem that the terms they used can be defined in a number of different ways. Another ratio related to gearing, known as *interest cover*, is very popular because it avoids these problems and yet provides a similar interpretation. It is calculated by using the formula:

$$\frac{\text{Profit before interest and tax}}{\text{Interest charge}}$$

Quite simply, interest cover is number of times the interest could be paid out of the profits available for the purpose; in other words, the number of times the interest is covered by the available profits.

Example

Using the same two companies, the results for the first year are as follows.

	Bonito plc	*Loftus plc*
Equity	£450,000	£250,000
Long-term debt	£50,000	£250,000
Profit before interest	£150,000	£150,000
Interest charge on debt	10%	10%

Required

Calculate the interest cover.

Solution

	Bonito plc	*Loftus plc*
Profit before interest	£150,000	£150,000
Interest charge on debt (10%)	£5,000	£25,000
Interest cover	30 times	6 times

It is easy to see from this that Bonito plc could pay the interest charge 30 times and therefore there is considerable cover, whereas the cover in Loftus plc is much lower.

---

4 | EARNINGS PER SHARE

As an investor in a company you will be interested in the dividends you receive. But you must remember that, although a company may pay out some of the profit in dividends, the remainder is retained in the company. This amount also belongs to the shareholders.

To be certain that we are dealing with the right figure of profit (refer to your set of accounts) the term *earnings* is used. The total earnings figure is of some interest but the critical figure for investors is how much earnings they are getting on each share: the earnings per share. The basic calculations is:

$$\frac{\text{Earnings}}{\text{Issued ordinary shares}}$$

As so often with accounting at the higher levels, the calculations are easy once we have agreed on what we are trying to calculate. FRS 14 *Earnings Per Share* sets out definitions of the terms used.

- earnings per share are the profit in pence attributable to each equity share;

- earnings are the net profits after tax, interest, minority interests and dividends on other classes of shares;

- Issued ordinary shares are all ordinary shares in circulation during the years. The weighted average approach is taken to calculate this amount.

The last point needs some explanation. If a company were to keep the same number of shares for the year there would be no problems but companies may issue more shares during the year. Some will be at market price but a company can also issue bonus shares and also make a rights issue.

Bonus shares are issued when a company decides to issue more shares to their current shareholders without expecting the shareholders to pay. The company may do this because it feels that the market share price is too high and it would therefore be better to have more shares in circulation. The bonus shares are usually issued in proportion to the existing holdings of shareholders. For example, for every two shares you hold at a specific date you will receive one bonus share.

A rights issue occurs when the company wishes to raise more money but also wishes to give some benefits to existing shareholders. If you wish to raise money it is better to go to existing shareholders (assuming they are happy) rather than to strangers! The rights issue usually involves an exercise price that is less than the value of the currently issued shares. For example, the current market price may be $1.80 but an existing shareholder can purchase one share for $1 for every five shares held.

If you look at the set of accounts that you have, you may experience difficulty in calculating the EPS just from the face of the accounts. This is because many companies have to make various adjustments in the calculation.

You should now be able to attempt Tasks 27.1 and 27.2 and Questions 27.1 and 27.2 at the end of the chapter.

5 | DIVIDEND PERFORMANCE

As the term suggests, *investment ratios* are used by those who are interested in making investment decisions. Anyone concerned with making a decision to buy, sell or hold shares in a particular company will base their decision on a number of factors. Knowledgeable investors will obtain the annual report and accounts of the company concerned and calculate the ratios that we have already described. They will also refer to the financial press where they will find other ratios that should help them to assess the performance of the company. The ratios in the financial press are designed specifically for investors and we describe the main ones below.

Dividend net tells us the dividend that has been paid in the latest year. It is calculated net of income tax and the answer is given in pence. The formula is:

$$\frac{\text{Total dividend}}{\text{Number of ordinary shares}}$$

Dividend cover is very similar to the interest cover ratio we described when we were looking at gearing ratios. It is the number of times that the dividend will go into the profit after tax. The higher the number of times, the more profit the company is retaining and the safer the dividend is likely to be in future years. A company with a very low dividend cover will have difficulty in paying out the same amount of dividend if its profits decline in the future. The formula is:

$$\frac{\text{Profit after tax}}{\text{Total dividends}}$$

Yield gross shows the actual return in the form of dividend on the price which has been paid for the share. Dividends are normally quoted on the *par* (face value) of the share (the original authorised value). This value may be very different from the price which has to be paid in the market place. Therefore an investor will want to know what return is being received in the form of a dividend on the present market price of the share. The formula is:

$$\frac{\text{Gross dividend per share}}{\text{Current share price}}$$

In the previous section we showed the calculations for earnings per share. Once this figure has been calculated, you will want to know how much you would be willing to pay to obtain these earnings. To help in this decision the following formula is used:

$$\frac{\text{Current share price}}{\text{Earnings per share}}$$

The answer will show you the number of years it will take you to cover your investment if the earnings remain at the present level. However, you must take care in interpreting this because the figure will show the investment market's expectations. If you have one company with a price earnings ratio of 10 and another with a ratio of 20, it is tempting to think that the former is better because you will cover your investment in ten years. However, the ratio of 20 indicates that the market believes that the latter company has a bright future and is therefore willing to pay more for its shares than the current level of earnings would justify.

6 MARKET CAPITALISATION

This is concerned with ascertaining the market value of a company. When we discussed the balance sheet of limited companies in previous chapters, we took great care to emphasise that the balance sheet does not show what the company is worth. One way of ascertaining the market value of a company is to use the following formula:

$$\text{Current share price} \times \text{Number of ordinary shares in issue}$$

All these investment ratios are helpful for making investment decisions, but it is important to remember that share prices can go down as well as up. No matter how sophisticated your analysis is, it is impossible to predict the future. There have been a number of spectacular company failures where investors have lost their money and employees their jobs; very few of these failures had been predicted.

 You should now be able to attempt Task 27.3 and Question 27.3 at the end of this chapter.

7 | SUMMARY

There is almost no limit to the number of ratios that can be calculated. However, to interpret ratios effectively, some basis of *comparison* is required.

One major impact on the financial performance of companies is their financial structure. This can be considered as the balance between equity and long-term debt and is known as *gearing*. A highly geared company offers a good return to shareholders in strong economic conditions, but can be very risky if there is a recession. Gearing ratios present problems because of differences in definition of the terms used to calculate them. As a result, many people prefer to use *interest cover*, as this avoids such problems.

Task 27.1
Select several sets of published accounts and calculate the gearing ratios. Consider why these may differ.

Task 27.2
Examine the set of accounts that you are using and the notes relating to the calculation of earnings per share. How does this compare to the explanation in the chapter?

Task 27.3
Imagine that you have £50,000 to invest. Select three companies using the techniques in the chapter. Keep a record of the movement in their share prices over a three-month period.

Question 27.1
Explain why the gearing ratio is important to investors and the financial risks they are willing to take.

Question 27.2
What is meant by bonus shares and rights issues. How do these affect the calculation of the EPS?

Question 27.3
Select ten large listed companies and calculate their market capitalisation. Rank the companies both by their market capitalisation and their last figure of annual revenue. Discuss the differences in the ranking.

A simple guide to the balance sheet

Context

Your local Chamber of Commerce has become increasingly concerned about the standard of financial knowledge particularly among its junior managers in the locality. It has decided to launch a series of conferences, seminars and publications to improve basic financial knowledge.

As part of this programme, it has asked you to prepare a draft of a small booklet to be entitled. *A Simple Guide to the Balance Sheet.*

The aim of the guide is to provide managers with a simple, clear and concise:

- description of what a balance sheet is;

- explanation of the basic concepts underlying a balance sheet;

- description of what the principle components of a balance sheet signify;

- exposition of how a balance sheet can be analysed and interpreted.

To this end, it has suggested that you obtain an actual example of a balance sheet, taken from a published report and accounts of a public limited company, and include a copy of it in your booklet, suitably annotated and explained.

Student activities

i)   Obtain from a friend, relation, library or company, a number of published reports and accounts. Find the balance sheets in them. There may be several. Choose the one that is headed 'group' or 'consolidated'. Select the balance sheet that is well presented, in vertical format, and with clear, simple headings. More important, choose one from an industry that interests you. Obviously, you will have to take a photocopy of the balance sheet page if you have to return or not deface the original.

ii) Decide on the plan of your booklet, in order to cover the points that the local Chamber of Commerce requires.

iii) Decide what you are going to do with the balance sheet, for example:

- leave it unmarked, and include it as one of the pages;

- put reference numbers or symbols on it to which you can refer in your text;

- write your actual annotations on it; in which case, it could be in the form of a large pull-out or fold-out chart, with the copy of your balance sheet in the middle, perhaps;

- choose another way of presenting it which is an improvement on the three previous suggestions.

iv) Write the draft guide, bearing in mind that it should be in a format which is suitable for printing by professional printers.

Format

A booklet, any suitable size, with a title page, introduction, simple, clear and concise text, containing the balance sheet in a form as suggested in activity (iii) above, and with diagrams, graphs, and so forth, which you consider to be appropriate. It should not be more than the equivalent of twelve A4-size pages, including title page, and diagrams, and the balance sheet itself.

Hints

The guide should be interesting to someone who probably will not want to devote more than, say, half an hour to reading it. Avoid too much detail: keep to the major items that have been explained in this book. There will inevitably be a number of items in the published accounts that you will not understand unless you read a more advanced text than this present book. Ignore these items.

Read through all the notes to the accounts, and the chairman's report in the published report and accounts; you are bound to come across something of interest that will help you explain, interpret or comment upon the items on the balance sheet.

Objectives

In this assignment, the student should show an appreciation and understanding of:

- the uses and limitations of accounting concepts as they affect the recording of financial data;

- simple final accounts;

- interpretation of financial information in order to measure performance against the perceived objectives of the organisation.

CHAPTER 28

Interpretation of financial statements

1 OBJECTIVES

At the end of the chapter you should be able to:

- prepare a trend analysis;
- make conclusions from a comparative analysis;
- describe different data presentations;
- interpret cash-flow statements.

2 INTRODUCTION

In previous chapters we have tended to look at ratios in isolation. We have explained the calculation of the individual ratios for such issues as profitability and liquidity and explained what these mean. We have not yet, however, brought them together so that you can get a full picture of the company. A considerable part of interpretation relies on experience but there are a number of techniques you can use. These will help your interpretations to become more sophisticated and we consider the main ones in this chapter.

A crucial point to bear in mind is that an individual ratio has very little meaning by itself – you need to compare your ratio with something else. In this chapter we will look at trend analysis where you compare ratios over a period of time and comparative analysis where you use other companies or industry performance as benchmarks. We complete the chapter by taking a broader view of the interpretation of financial performance and position as well as cash-flow statements.

3 TREND ANALYSIS

Trend analysis is concerned with the trend of ratios over a period of time. The calculation of ratios for a single financial period can be very helpful. However, you need to be able to compare the ratios for one organisation with other ratios, in order to enhance your analysis. One basis of comparison is with another company in the same industry, or possibly with a number of other companies. It is also possible to obtain average ratios for a particular industry against which you can make comparisons. Another approach is to calculate ratios for the same company for a number of consecutive financial periods. Not only does this reveal movements in individual ratios over time, but it also allows an interpretation of the significance in changes in the balance of ratios. The method of calculating ratios is exactly the same as in Chapter 24 and we will concentrate on the *gross profit percentage* and the *profit margin*.

Example

Arbutus plc is a large retailer and has divided its costs into two main categories. One is the cost of sales and this is deducted from the sales figure to give the gross profit. The other costs are all associated with running the store and tend not to change. In the first quarter of 1997, the company experienced very high sales and decided to expand its store. This led to a significant increase in the costs of running the store commencing in April. Unfortunately sales declined in May. The figures for the period January to May are as follows.

	Jan £	Feb £	Mar £	Apr £	May £
Sales	120,000	135,000	172,000	200,000	172,000
Gross profit	72,600	81,600	100,800	117,200	100,800
Store costs	39,000	39,000	39,000	50,000	50,000
Net profit	33,600	42,600	61,800	67,200	50,800

Required

Calculate the gross profit percentage and the profit margin and comment on your results.

Solution

An initial investigation of these figures may give no cause for alarm. The gross profit and net profit both increased each month until May when the decline in sales had an understandable effect. Even the increase in store costs in April did not prevent an increase in profits. However, if the ratios are calculated, the picture looks very different.

	Jan £	Feb £	Mar £	Apr £	May £
Sales	120,000	135,000	172,000	200,000	172,000
Gross profit	72,600	81,600	100,800	115,200	94,600
Gross profit percentage	60.5%	60.5%	58.6%	57.6%	55.0%
Store costs	39,000	39,000	39,000	50,000	50,000
Net profit	33,600	42,600	61,800	65,200	44,600
Profit margin	28.0%	31.6%	35.9%	33.6%	25.9%

Looking first at the gross profit percentage, matters started to go wrong as early as the month of March. The ratio had dropped to 58.6 per cent which suggests that the store had either reduced its selling prices or that costs had risen but were not passed on to the customer. This decline continued throughout the remainder of the period. Although the profit margin increased from January to March, as the increase in turnover was achieved without increasing store running costs, the position changed in April. The increase in running costs to £50,000 did not affect the absolute profit figure because sales were still increasing, but the profit margin illustrates that the sales had not increased sufficiently to cover all the increase in the costs. Consequently, in May, when sales declined, the company suffered.

The above example shows the importance of trend analysis as a technique for giving early warning of problems. Absolute figures can be very misleading, particularly when sales are increasing; ratios permit a more rigorous interpretation of the results.

> *You should now be able to attempt Questions 28.1, 28.2 and 28.3 at the end of this chapter.*

4 | COMPARATIVE ANALYSIS

In previous chapters we have stressed the value of comparing the ratios for one company with those of other companies. It is important to ensure that the companies you are comparing have common characteristics and this is usually done by taking companies from the same industry. You would not expect, for example, a transport company, a publishing company and a nursing home to have the same financial and operating structures.

For the first part of the analysis we will consider the profitability ratios for three companies. At the year end the ratios are as follows:

Profitability ratios

Three-company comparison

Company	A	B	C
Return on capital employed	20%	20%	25%
Profit margin	10%	8%	10%
Capital turnover	2 times	2.5 times	2.5 times

Looking at the return on capital employed, company C is the best performer with 25% and the other two lagging someway behind at 20 per cent. You will remember from an earlier chapter that the return on capital employed can be explained by

- profit margin, which measures the percentage return on sales;
- capital turnover, which measures the level of activity in the business as reflected by sales in relation to the capital employed.

If the profit margin is multiplied by the capital turnover ratio the result will be the return on capital employed (ROCE).

Moving on to the separate elements of the ROCE, B has a lower profit margin than the others. This is because the selling price of its products is lower than the other two companies or its costs are higher. It may even be a combination of the two. You can investigate product prices either through the Internet, sales material from the company or even a telephone call to the sales and marketing department. You can examine the costs by calculating further ratios but, for a thorough investigation, you will need more information than you would normally find in a company's published accounts.

When conducting these investigations you should also collect information on the environment in which the companies are operating. For example, company B's prices may be lower for a number of reasons including

1. it is a new entrant to the business and is holding prices low as a strategy to gain greater market share;

2. its products, although similar to the other two companies, are not so well designed;

3. it is operating in parts of the market where the customer base is not so affluent – for example, prices can be set higher in London than in some other cities; or

4. the other two companies have 'brand' recognition and can therefore charge premium prices

Looking at capital turnover, company A is the worst. In other words it does not use its facilities as efficiently as the other companies in generating sales. You can see that if company A improved its capital turnover to 2.5 times it would also have a return on capital employed of 25 per cent. There can be a host of reasons for inefficiencies, including bad management. Company A could be a good takeover prospect if it could be acquired at the right price. The new management could resolve the inefficiencies and obtain a return on capital employed of 25 per cent.

As regards working capital ratios, we will take another three hypothetical companies and see what conclusions we can draw:

Working capital ratios
Three-company comparison

Company	X	Y	Z
Current ratio	2:0	1.3:1	2.5:1
Debtors' ratio	45 days	15 days	90 days
Stock turnover	4.5 times	6.0 times	2.5 times

The above three ratios, examined in Chapter 26, measure the following:

• the current ratio shows how effectively a company is managing its working capital;

- the debtors' ratio measures the average time in days that debtors take to settle their accounts;
- the stock turnover ratio measures the level of activity in relation to stock held by the organisation.

There is no ideal ratio for the current test but generally we expect companies to fall within the range 1.5 : 1 to 2.0 : 1. Company Y's current ratio is on the very low side and we might have some concerns about whether it could pay its debts if it were called on to do so.

Company Z's current ratio looks high and suggests that there may be inefficiencies within the company. Remember that a high current ratio means that the company has to finance it in some way and this could entail interest charges on money borrowed.

Further analysis shows that company X takes 45 days to collect money that it is owed by its customers. This is the equivalent to allowing one month's credit. Company Z, however, takes 90 days and this suggests that it is not so efficient in collecting the money it is owed. Company Z should therefore look at its policy on allowing credit to customers and the procedures it has in place for collecting debts. Where the collection period is very long, we would be concerned that some of the debtors may turn out to be bad debts.

A final note on the debtors' period is one of caution. Company Y has a very short period and this suggests that a part of the business is on a cash basis. The comparison therefore may not be valid.

As far as stock turnover is concerned, we like to see a fairly rapid turnover as holding items in stock costs money. That is why many large manufacturers have introduced such systems as just in time. On the other hand, companies such as retailers do need to ensure that they have a sufficient stock to meet customer demand. In some segments of retailing, for example cars and furniture, it is common for a customer to wait some time for delivery. In other segments, such as food and clothing, the customer expects immediately delivery.

Assuming that the three companies are comparable, then Z has a very low stock turnover and this should be investigated. The stock turnover for company Y is very high compared to the others and this could be a worrying sign. If the company is meeting the demand of its customers then it suggests great efficiency but we would wish to ensure that this is so.

You should now be able to attempt Tasks 28.1 and 28.2 at the end of this chapter.

5   DATA PRESENTATION

It is essential that you prepare your data in such a way that they help your interpretation and allow for an informative presentation to anyone else. In the previous section we presented the data in the form of simple tables. This is an excellent technique for examination rooms. It is also a good way for you to be able to contrast and compare the data and to make an interpretation.

Data can also be presented diagrammatically and you will be familiar with such techniques as bar charts and graphs. If you look at a set of published accounts you will most likely see some of these formats being used. The financial press also uses diagrammatic formats for conveying data. There are some rules, however, on how these should be constructed and in this section we cover the basic principles.

Rules for data presentation

The main lessons to remember are:

- the graphs must represent the facts clearly and accurately;
- the graphs must be easily understood;
- they must hold the reader's attention.

The exact type of graph will depend to some extent on your own preferences but the following advice will be helpful:

- use a pie chart where the amounts are expressed as a part or a percentage of a total;
- a bar chart is effective where a comparison is to be made, for example where there are two amounts one larger than the other;
- if there are changes over time, for example profit over ten years, a line graph may be used.

You can find good examples, and poor, of graphs in textbooks and the financial press. Do remember to give your chart a title and a number if you have more than one chart.

6   INTERPRETING CASH-FLOW STATEMENTS

It is generally agreed that the cash-flow statement provides useful information. It is possible to calculate a type of gearing ratio for cash by comparing the operating cash flows to financing flows. This demonstrates a company's reliance on external funding. As far as further analysis is concerned it is essential to do comparisons over a period of time and with other companies. You are trying to find unexpected changes in trends or unusual comparators. The following guidelines will assist in your analysis:

- Cash is not the same as profit. You must expect the cash flows to move significantly from year to year. What you are seeking is to identify the underlying trend in cash flows.
- Profits and cash flows will not keep the same relationship from year to year. You would expect that earned profits are being converted into positive cash flows at some stage.
- Management of liquid resources is highlighted and it can be useful to refer to this when considering working capital ratios.

7 | SUMMARY

This chapter is concerned with improving your ability to conduct an analysis of financial statements. The techniques of trend analysis and comparative analysis are examined. In addition the use of diagrams both to assist in the analysis and presentation of the results is discussed. Finally, we offer some guidance on the interpretation of cash-flow statements.

The main point to remember in your analysis is that you must compare your ratio with another ratio. With trend analysis you compare ratios for the same company over a period of time. Comparative analysis involves comparing the ratios of the selected company with similar companies. It is also possible to compare with the industry averages and these statistics are available in many libraries.

The use of bar charts and line graphs is common in the analysis of financial statements. It is important to remember that there are rules for the preparation of such diagrams. If these are not followed the user may be misled and you can find examples of misleading diagrams in published accounts.

Of all the financial statements the cash-flow statement, possibly because of its recent introduction, has the least number of ratios associated directly with it. We have offered some general guidance and would re-emphasise our earlier advice. Always compare with other ratios!

Student activities

Task 28.1
Obtain the published accounts of 3 companies. Calculate and compare their profitability ratios.

Task 28.2
Obtain the published accounts of a company and the average ratios for the industry which the company belongs to. Explain why your selected company differs from the industry average.

Task 28.3
Take the ratios for the companies which you have calculated using both trend analysis and comparative analysis and present these in diagrammatic form.

Question 28.1
The following three-year figures have been extracted from the accounts of Goldrush Ltd.

	2001 £	2002 £	2003 £
Profit before interest and tax	15,000	16,000	17,000
Sales	125,000	123,000	122,000
Capital employed	75,000	88,000	113,000

Required

Calculate the prime ratio, profit margin and capital turnover, and comment on your results.

Question 28.2

Your managing director has asked you to analyse the accounts of Tobias Woolfe plc, a competitor, for the last three years. There is a rumour that this company is experiencing serious financial difficulties. The company's figures are as follows.

	2001	2002	2003
	£'000	£'000	£'000
Sales turnover	92,727	99,161	133,911
Gross profit	28,745	29,579	35,464
Profit before interest and tax	9,467	9,635	11,112
Profit after tax	7,458	8,771	8,211
Capital employed	52,303	55,854	70,890
Current assets	36,742	36,939	51,236
Creditors: amounts due within one year	24,333	26,125	39,061
Stocks	10,298	8,953	9,426
Debtors	13,420	14,158	20,258
Balances at bank and cash	13,024	13,828	21,552

Required

Prepare a brief report for your managing director, which should include the following:

i) calculation of the prime ratio, profit margin, capital turnover, gross profit percentage, current test, acid test and the debt collection period;

ii) an explanation of what each ratio indicates;

iii) interpretation of the resulting ratios, paying particular attention to trends, with comment on whether they confirm the rumour of serious financial difficulties at Tobias Woolfe plc.

Question 28.3

Orchardlea plc is a wholesale fruit company. Abbreviated results for the last two years are shown below.

Orchardlea plc

Profit-and-loss accounts for the years ending 31 December

	2002		2003	
	£'000	£'000	£'000	£'000
Sales		350		560
Cost of sales		280		462
Gross profit		70		98
Administration costs	30		37	
Interest charge	5		5	
Selling and distribution costs	14	49	14	56

continued

	£'000	2002 £'000	£'000	2003 £'000
Net profit		21		42
Retained profits brought forward		84		91
		105		133
Proposed dividends		14		35
Retained profits carried forward		91		98

Orchardlea plc
Balance sheets as at 31 December

	£'000	2002 £'000	£'000	£'000	2003 £'000	£'000
Fixed assets						
Land			50			50
Buildings			35			105
Equipment			70			161
			155			316
Current assets						
Stock	56			98		
Debtors	35			84		
Bank	84	175		63	245	
Creditors: amounts due within one year						
Creditors	35			28		
Dividends	14	49		35	63	
		126			182	
		281			498	
Creditors: amounts due after one year		50			50	
Represented by:						
£1 ordinary shares		140			350	
Retained profits		91			98	
		281			498	

Required

Calculate any seven performance, liquidity and gearing ratios you consider appropriate for each of the years 2002 and 2003 and comment briefly on your results.

Objective test *(tick the appropriate box)*

i) If the profit margin is multiplied by the capital turnover ratio, the result will be:

   a) the debtors' collection period   □

   b) the sales turnover   □

   c) the current ratio   □

   d) the return on capital employed   □

ii) If the current ratio is 3:1, you might conclude a company is:

    a) run very inefficiently ☐

    b) run very efficiently ☐

    c) will have difficulty in paying creditors ☐

    d) has a just-in-time system ☐

iii) If a company has a debtors' collection period of 20 days, you might conclude:

    a) it has a low sales figure ☐

    b) a proportion of sales are on a cash basis ☐

    c) its credit control system is very weak ☐

    d) the profit margin will be high ☐

iv) The return on capital employed ratio is also known as the:

    a) sales margin ratio ☐

    b) prime ratio ☐

    c) acid test ratio ☐

    d) liquidity ratio ☐

v) By using ratio analysis, it is justified to compare with companies:

    a) of a different size ☐

    b) in a different industry ☐

    c) in a different country ☐

    d) none of these ☐

PART VII

OTHER TYPES OF ORGANISATION

CHAPTER 29

Clubs and societies

1 OBJECTIVES

At the end of this chapter you should be able to:

- draw up accounts appropriate to clubs or societies;
- understand differences between the accounts of trading-for-profit and not-for-profit organisations;
- convert receipts-and-payments accounts into income-and-expenditure accounts;
- construct and interpret balance sheets of clubs and societies.

2 INTRODUCTION

The principles of preparing accounts of clubs and societies are similar to those used for the preparation of sole traders, with some adjustments to make the accounts appropriate to this kind of non profit-making organisation.

You will see that many club accounts are produced as receipts-and-payments accounts, simply being a summary of the cash and bank entries for the period. Other accounts take into consideration the principles of capital and revenue and accruals and prepayments. It would be helpful, therefore, if you would revise these topics, particularly in Chapter 16 where we considered the effects of accruals and prepayments at the beginning and end of accounting periods.

3 DEFINITION

A club is an organisation formed by a number of persons joining together in order to pursue a purpose that is mainly non profit-making and usually of a recreational nature. Examples of such clubs are small local sports clubs for rugby, cricket, football and judo, or other recreational pursuits such as winemaking, theatregoing, and societies for the appreciation of music or art.

Some clubs and societies are formed for purposes which are not entirely recreational and have more far-reaching objects. For example, Tottenham Hotspur Football Club is listed on the London Stock Exchange, and most of the clubs in the Football League are professional organisations. Similarly, building societies are subject to special legislation and nowadays operate in a similar way to many banks. Such clubs and societies are organisations that are outside the scope of this chapter.

4 CLUB ORGANISATION

The organisation of clubs or societies may range from the very formal where there are clear rules agreed by the members about the club's objects, election of officers and operations, to the very informal where such questions are resolved as and when they arise. It is usual for club members to elect annually at the annual general meeting (AGM) the *club officers* and the *club committee*. The officers are usually the chairman, sometimes called the chairperson or chair, the secretary, who is responsible for the administrative aspects of running the club, and the treasurer, who is responsible for the financial affairs of the club or society.

The treasurer is responsible for collecting club subscriptions from the members, paying the expenses that the club incurs, and maintaining the accounting records of the club. The treasurer usually presents an accounting statement to the club members at the AGM, which shows them a financial summary of the the club's financial transactions over the period being considered by the AGM, normally a year. A statement showing the club's financial position at the end of the year is also presented. The precise form of the annual financial statement presented to the membership will depend upon the type of financial records kept, and the skill of the treasurer in accounting for the club's transactions.

5 FINANCIAL RECORDS

The elected treasurer is often a person who may have very limited accounting knowledge. Consequently, in these circumstances the treasurer will keep the books of the club in the simplest way possible. This will probably mean simply recording in a *cash book* the cash receipts and the cash payments of the club for the period. Payments and receipts by cheque that have to be passed through the club's bank account are also regarded as cash transactions for this purpose. Indeed, the statements received by the treasurer from the bank from time to time can be of great assistance in keeping the cash book.

Example

Cash book

Receipts			Payments			Balance
Date	Details	£	Date	Details	£	£

6   RECEIPTS-AND-PAYMENTS ACCOUNT

Where a receipts-and-payment account is the statement that is presented to the membership at the AGM, it represents a summary of the entries that will have been recorded in the cash book for the year.

The receipts-and-payments account will show:

- the balance of cash in hand and/or at the bank at the beginning of the period;
- an analysis of the cash receipts that have been received by the club during the period;
- an analysis of the cash payments that have been made by the club during the period;
- the balance of cash in hand and/or at the bank at the end of the period.

Example

The Grace Cricket Club

Receipts-and-payments account for the year ended 31 December

	£	£
+ *Receipts*		
Subscriptions received	X	
Match fees	X	
Net receipts from bar	X	
Net receipts from raffles	X	
Net receipts from socials	X	
Other receipts	<u>X</u>	X
− *Payments*		
Purchase of equipment	X	
Repairs to pavilion	X	
Catering costs	X	
League fees	X	
Groundsman's wages	X	
Umpires' expenses	X	X
Other expenses	<u>X</u>	<u>X</u>
= *Excess of receipts over payments*		X
+ Opening balance of cash/bank		<u>X</u>
= *Closing balance of cash/bank*		<u><u>X</u></u>

Notes

All the items are recorded on a cash basis, therefore no adjustment is made for either outstanding expenses for the period due to be paid after the period end, or for income due for the period but not received by the period end. You will recall from Chapter 10 that where such adjustments are made the accounts are said to be prepared on an accruals basis. Therefore a receipts and payments account is not prepared on an accruals basis.

There is no attempt to differentiate between expenditure on items that have an extended life, such as equipment, and expenditure on items where the benefits arise almost immediately, such as league fees. We have seen in Chapter 15 that the former are regarded as capital expenditure items and the latter as revenue expenditure. A receipts and payments account treats these items in an identical manner as simply payments.

Where a receipts-and-payments account is produced, then it is not possible also to produce a balance sheet of the society or club at the period end without substantial adjustments to the figures to convert them to an accruals basis. The financial position of the club is shown simply by the balance of cash and/or bank at the period end.

Because of such drawbacks in using a receipts-and-payments account, some club or society treasurers prepare statements for the members that give a more comprehensive and informative picture of the club's surplus or deficit for the period, together with its state of affairs at the end of the period. These are known as *income-and-expenditure accounts* and *balance sheets*, and are prepared along similar lines to those of sole traders.

7 | THE ACCUMULATED OR GENERAL FUND

Unlike sole traders or partnerships, clubs and societies do not have capital as such, as they do not trade for profit. Instead they have what is known as an *accumulated fund* or *general fund*, and instead of revealing a profit or loss for a period they record a *surplus* or *deficit*. A surplus is where income for the period exceeds expenditure, and a deficit is where expenditure exceeds income. Any surplus or deficit for a period made by a club is treated in a way similar to a profit or loss made by a sole trader; a surplus is credited or added to the accumulated fund and a deficit is debited to or charged against the accumulated fund.

The value of the accumulated fund can be calculated at any time by valuing the net assets of the club. This will be equal to the accumulated fund. The net assets are made up of the assets less the liabilities, and you may remember that a similar technique was used to calculate the value of the owner's capital when dealing with the accounts of sole traders in Chapter 16.

Example

The Coarse Rugby Club wishes to value its accumulated fund at the beginning of the season on 1 September 20X1. It owns a clubhouse which is valued at £25,000 in which the fixtures and fittings are worth £2,000 and the bar stock is valued at £900. £10,500 remains outstanding on a loan that was obtained from the brewery four years ago to finance the construction of the clubhouse.

The stock of shirts, shorts, and so forth is worth £200, and the rugby equipment is valued at £100. The club owes six month's rent to 31 August 20X1 for the pitch, which is rented at a rate of £500 per annum. Club members owe ten annual subscriptions at £10 each, and a delivery of beer valued at £300 on 31 August 20X1 has not been paid for and remains outstanding. The bank balance stands at £1,250.

Required

Calculate the club's accumulated fund as at 1 September 20X1.

Solution

The recommended approach to this problem is to draw up a statement of assets and liabilities of the club at the date of the valuation of the accumulated fund. This statement is known as a *statement of affairs*.

The Coarse Rugby Club

Statement of affairs as at 1 September 20X1

	£	£
Assets		
Clubhouse	25,000	
Fixtures and fittings	2,000	
Rugby equipment	100	
Rugby kit	200	
Bar stock	900	
Bank Balance	1,250	
Subscriptions $(10 \times £10)$	100	29,550
Less liabilities		
Loan	10,500	
Creditors:		
Beer	300	
Rent payable	250	11,050
Valuation of accumulated fund		18,500

Note that the calculation of the accumulated fund enables a balance sheet to be constructed that can provide the basis for recording the club transactions on double entry lines, thus enabling accruals and prepayments to be taken into consideration when preparing club income and expenditure accounts. The balance sheet in vertical form may appear as follows:

The Coarse Rugby Club

Balance sheet as at 1 September 20X1

	£	£
Capital employed		
Fixed assets		
Clubhouse	25,000	
Fixtures & fittings	2,000	
Rugby equipment	100	
Rugby kit	200	27,300
Current assets		
Bar stock	900	
Subscriptions $(10 \times £10)$	100	
Bank	1,250	
	2,250	

continued

	£	£
Less current liabilities		
Creditors:		
Beer	300	
Rent payable	250	
	550	
Net current assets		1,700
Net assets		29,000
Financed by		
Accumulated fund		18,500
Loan from Brewery		10,500
		29,000

> You should now be able to attempt Question 29.1 at the end of this chapter.

8 CONVERSION OF A RECEIPTS-AND-PAYMENT ACCOUNT TO AN INCOME-AND-EXPENDITURE ACCOUNT

An income-and-expenditure account is really the profit-and-loss account of a *non-trading organisation*, and like a profit-and-loss account it contains only the revenue items of income and expenditure for the period to which it refers. You will remember from Chapter 16 that whether or not those revenue items are actually received or paid within that period, they are included as income and expenditure for the period.

In comparing the characteristics of an income-and-expenditure account with those of a receipts-and-payments account, the main differences are as follows.

Income-and-expenditure account:

- includes items outstanding and unpaid for the period (accruals), items due but not received, and items paid in advance (prepayments);
- excludes capital receipts and capital payments;
- includes depreciation charges;
- the balance represents the surplus or deficit for the period.

Receipts-and-payments account:

- includes cash transactions only made in the period;
- may include payments and receipts of items of a capital and revenue nature;
- the balance represents the cash and/or bank balance at the end of the period.

In order to convert a receipts-and-payments account to an income-and-expenditure account, the following steps should be made.

1. Identify the revenue items in the receipts-and-payments account and treat the revenue receipts as income and the revenue payments as expenditure.

2. Draw up a statement of affairs of assets and liabilities at the commencement of the period, but clearly showing the accruals, prepayments and stocks in respect of the revenue items that appear in the income and expenditure account.

3. Identify the accruals, prepayments and stocks at the end of the period in respect of the revenue items that appear in the income-and-expenditure account.

4. Adjust the items in (1) above so that the accruals, prepayments and stocks in (2) and (3) create the income and expenditure appropriate to the period for which the accounts are prepared.

5. Any capital items of expenditure that appear in the receipts-and-payments account must be added to the capital items taken from the statement of affairs at the commencement. Suitable adjustments for any sales of assets should be made, to take into consideration the profits and losses on their disposal which are credited to the income and expenditure account.

6. Any other capital payments, such as the repayment of a loan, should be deducted from the liability in the balance sheet.

7. The balance of the income-and-expenditure account for the year is then transferred to the opening accumulated fund balance which was calculated from the statement of affairs. A surplus is added to the accumulated fund (assuming that the fund is in credit), and any deficit for the year is deducted from the accumulated fund.

8. The balance sheet may then be constructed in the normal way, bringing into the balance sheet the assets and liabilities and accruals and prepayments from the statement of affairs adjusted by the transactions in (3) and (5) above.

Example

Refer to the example in the previous section. Having prepared the opening balance sheet, the Coarse Rugby Club treasurer wishes to produce the income and expenditure account for the year to 31 August 20X2. He has already produced a receipts and payments account, as follows:

	£	£
Receipts		
Subscriptions received	600	
Match fees	250	
Net receipts from bar	3,100	
Net receipts from raffles	920	
Net receipts from socials	540	
Other receipts	30	5,440

continued

	£	£
Payments		
Purchase of tables for clubhouse	510	
Repairs to clubhouse	1,220	
Loan repayment	1,000	
Interest on loan	1,050	
Rugby equipment	100	
Rugby kit	100	
Rent of pitch	250	
Bank charges	100	4,330
Excess of receipts over payments		1,110
Opening balance of cash/bank		1,250
Closing balance of cash/bank		2,360

At the end of the year, amounts due amounted to:

Rent	£500
Beer for bar	£700
Subscriptions	4 members
Band for social	£140
Bar stock was valued at £500	

It is club policy to depreciate fixed assets using the diminishing balance method as follows:

Rugby equipment	25% per annum
Rugby kit	50% per annum
Fixtures and fittings	20% per annum
Clubhouse	10% per annum

Required

Draw up the club's income and expenditure account for the year, and the balance sheet as at 31 August 20X2.

Solution

The Coarse Rugby Club

Income and expenditure account for the year ended 31 August 20X2

	£	£	£
Income			
Subscriptions (£600 − £100 + £40)		540	
Match fees		250	
Bar profits (£3,100 Stock − £900 + £500 Creditors +£300 − £700)		2,300	
Raffle profits		920	
Social profits (£540 − £140)		400	
Other income		30	4,440

continued

	£	£	£
Expenditure			
Repairs to clubhouse		1,220	
Interest on loan		1,050	
Rent of pitch (£250 − £250 + £500)		500	
Bank charges		100	
Depreciation			
Rugby equipment 25% (£100 + £100)	50		
Rugby kit 50% (£200 + £100)	150		
Fixtures & fittings 20% (£2,000 + £510)	502		
Clubhouse 10% (£25,000)	2,500	3,202	6,072
Deficit of expenditure over income			1,632

The Coarse Rugby Club

Balance sheet as at 31 August 20X2

	£	£
Capital employed		
Fixed assets		
Clubhouse (£25,000 − £2,500)	22,500	
Fixtures & fittings (£2,000 + £510 − £502)	2,008	
Rugby equipment (£100 + £100 − £50)	150	
Rugby kit (£200 + £100 − £150)	150	24,808
Current assets		
Bar stock	500	
Subscriptions (4 × £10)	40	
Bank	2,360	
	2,900	
Less current liabilities		
Creditors:		
Beer	700	
Band for social	140	
Rent payable	500	
	1,340	
Net current assets		1,560
Net assets		26,368
Financed by		
Accumulated fund	18,500	
Less Deficit for the year	1,632	16,868
Loan from Brewery (£10,500 − £1,000)		9,500
		26,368

> *You should now be able to attempt Task 30.3 and Questions 30.2 and 30.3 at the end of this chapter.*

9 | SUMMARY

The accounts of clubs and societies are often in the form of *receipts-and-payments accounts*, which are nothing more than summaries of the cash and/or bank transactions that have taken place over the period. An alternative presentation, the *income-and-expenditure account*, takes into consideration both the accruals and prepayments and the different natures of capital and revenue expenditure in determining the club's income and expenditure for the period.

Clubs or societies do not trade for profit, therefore the excess of income over expenditure for the period is known as a *surplus*. Any excess of expenditure over income is known as a *deficit*. The surplus or deficit adjusts the club's *accumulated fund* in the balance sheet. The accumulated fund replaces the capital account normally found in the accounts of businesses which trade for profit such as sole traders.

> You should now be able to attempt the objective test at the end of this chapter.

Student activities

Task 29.1
There are many people who act as honourary (unpaid) treasurers of such clubs or societies considered in this chapter. Discuss with a club treasurer the way in which he keeps the financial records, the books, of the club. Consider the following questions.

i)   Is a complete set of books maintained or simply a cash book?

ii) Does the treasurer produce a receipts and payments account or an income and expenditure account at the year end?

iii) If a receipts and payments account only is produced, can you help the treasurer produce an income and expenditure account for the period?

iv) Is an annual balance sheet produced? If not, can you help the treasurer produce an opening statement of affairs and a closing balance sheet?

Task 29.2
Now you know how to keep the financial records of a club or society, the next time the club of which you are a member requires a treasurer, volunteer to put yourself up for election to that position. If you are elected, maintain the records in such a way as to enable a club income and expenditure account and a club balance sheet to be prepared when you present the financial report to the members at the AGM.

Task 29.3
Imagine you are the treasurer of the Coarse Rugby Club (see Section 29.8). You are expected to present the income and expenditure account and balance sheet at

the AGM which is held in the club bar. Prepare a speech which you consider will be appropriate for the members of the club attending.

Question 29.1

The Mozart Music Club has the following assets and liabilities at 30 September 20X2:

Subscriptions overdue from members: £45

Affiliation fee overdue to Music Club Associates: £25

CD player (at cost): £1,080

Record and disc library (at valuation): £560

Rent of premises prepaid: £60

Printing costs of September magazine not yet paid: £100

Fixtures and fittings (at cost): £800

Electricity for September quarter not yet paid: £40

Cash at bank: £222

Cash in hand: £48

The CD player was purchased two years ago and has an anticipated life of five years, with an estimated sale value of £80 at the end of that time. The fixtures and fittings were installed four years ago and are being depreciated over ten years with no residual value. The straight line method of depreciation is used.

Required

Draw up a statement of affairs and determine the value of the accumulated fund on 30 September 20X2.

Question 29.2

Adelaide Vintage Car Club is preparing its accounts for the year to 31 December 20X2 for the annual general meeting. The treasurer cannot decide whether to produce a receipts and payments account or an income and expenditure account, so he decides to produce both. The information available is as follows.

The balance at bank on 1 January 20X2 was £900. During the year subscriptions were received of £1,600, of which £50 represented amounts overdue at the beginning of the year, and £100 paid in advance. £75 of subscriptions were outstanding at 31 December 20X2. A summary of the other cash/bank entries is shown below.

Receipts	£	Payments	£
Interest received	70	Bank charges	62
Sales of parts	1,250	Rent of premises	400
Raffles (net)	261	Purchase of parts	642
		Socials (net)	124
		Electricity	105
		Printing & Stationery	206
		Furniture	420
		Books	160

Other information:
  Parts for resale:
    Stocks at 1 January 20X2: £50; 31 December 20X2: £80
    Amounts due to suppliers on 1 January 20X2: £144; 31 December 20X2: £300

  Printing costs for raffle tickets outstanding on 31 December 20X2: £56

  Electricity outstanding for December quarter 20X2: £25

  Stationery:
    Stock at 1 January 20X2: £24; 31 December 20X2: £46
    Amount due to supplier at 31 December 20X2: £25

  Other assets at the beginning of the year were:
    Vintage Rolls Royce (at cost): £4,000
    Furniture (at valuation): £1,280
    Library (at valuation): £340

Library and furniture should be depreciated at 20 per cent on the value in the accounts at the year end. The Rolls Royce is not depreciated.

Required

i)   Prepare a statement of affairs at 1 January 20X2.

ii) Prepare a receipts and payments account for the year ended 31 December 20X2.

iii) Prepare an income and expenditure account for the year ended 31 December 20X2.

iv) Prepare a balance sheet as at 31 December 20X2.

Question 29.3

The following opening balances were taken from the books of Viney Green Golf Club on 1 January 20X1:

  Golf course at cost: £100,000

  Clubhouse at cost: £50,000

  Investment in building society: £12,000

  Subscriptions in advance: £800
                 in arrears: £1,200

  Bar stock: £9,700

  Equipment at cost: £7,000

  Cash in hand and at bank: £2,500

Analysis of the bank statements and cash book for the year revealed the following transactions:

Receipts:	£	Payments:	£
Subscriptions	52,000	Course maintenance	34,100
Green fees	1,000	Bar wages	6,000
Sale of equipment	100	General expenses	14,100
Bar takings	46,200	Cost of professional	4,000
Interest received	980	Purchase of equipment	2,400
		Bar purchases	25,180

Outstanding balances at 31 December 20X1 were as follows:

Creditors for bar supplies: £2,000

Subscriptions in advance (20X2): £1,800

Subscriptions in arrears (20X1): £700

Bar stocks at 31 December 20X1 were £8,650. Insurance paid in advance (included in general expenses) £1,200. Depreciation on equipment and the club-house (a temporary one) is to be provided at 20 per cent per annum on cost at the year end. The equipment sold originally cost £500.

Required

Prepare an income and expenditure account for the club for the year ended 31 December 20X1 and a balance sheet as at that date.

Objective test (tick the appropriate box)

i) The receipts and payment account represents a summary of:

   a) the bank account □

   b) the cash account □

   c) both □

   d) neither □

ii) The receipts and payments account fails to differentiate between:

   a) capital and revenue expenditure □

   b) accruals and prepayments □

   c) income and expenditure □

   d) cash and non-cash items □

iii) The statement of affairs is drawn up primarily to establish, at the beginning of the period:

   a) total fixed assets □

   b) value of the accumulated fund □

   c) total current liabilities □

   d) total assets □

iv) Subscriptions received in cash are £1,125. This includes £25 outstanding at the beginning of the year when £40 was prepaid, and at the end of the year £60 was prepaid and £50 was overdue. The subscription income for the year to be included in the income and expenditure account was:

a) £1,250 ☐

b) £1,130 ☐

c) £1,135 ☐

d) £1,265 ☐

v) Net cash received from bar sales less payments amounted to £2,161 for the year. The opening stock was £440, and the closing stock was £280. The final delivery last year of £920 was unpaid at the end of that year, and this year £640 of deliveries remains unpaid. A private social had been supplied with drinks amounting to £600, and this amount remains unpaid at the end of this year. The bar net income for the year was:

a) £2,881 ☐

b) £4,781 ☐

c) £1,711 ☐

d) £3,471 ☐

CHAPTER 30

Manufacturing organisations

1 OBJECTIVES

At the end of this chapter you should be able to:

- appreciate the link between manufacturing accounts and trading, profit-and-loss accounts;
- understand the classification of costs necessary for the drawing up of a manufacturing account;
- explain what is meant by work-in-progress;
- explain what is meant by finished goods;
- understand their accounting treatment;
- produce final accounts for a manufacturing organisation.

2 INTRODUCTION

In earlier chapters you saw how the final accounts of sole traders, partnerships and limited companies include a statement called the *trading, profit-and-loss account*, which is often abbreviated to the *profit-and-loss account*. You should revise these chapters now to ensure that you are completely familiar with their contents. The profit-and-loss account may be made up of three sections:

- the *trading section*, which compares the sales and the cost of sales in order to obtain the *gross profit* for the period;
- the *profit-and-loss section*, which compares the gross profit with the expenses or overheads of the business in order to obtain the *net profit* for the period;
- the *appropriation section*, which is used in limited companies and partnerships in order to record what happens to the net profit. In a partnership it is shared between the partners, whereas in a limited company the appropriation section records what proportion of the profit is distributed as a dividend and what proportion is retained.

As the trading section compares the sales and cost of sales to obtain the gross profit, it assumes that the organisation is one that simply buys and sells goods or services. However, many organisations are involved in a manufacturing process where raw materials are worked on and converted into something else, which is then sold. In this kind of organisation the trading, profit-and-loss account is inadequate, and for this reason the *manufacturing account* has been developed as an additional statement to those discussed above. In building up a manufacturing account the costs are listed in the account according to the costs which are incurred when a product is manufactured. These product costs are *classified* according to costing principles.

3 | PRODUCT DIRECT COSTS

Product direct costs are costs that can be traced directly to the product or products that are being manufactured by the enterprise and comprise:

- direct materials;
- direct wages;
- direct expenses.

Direct materials are those materials or parts and subassemblies that are used in the production of and feature in the final form of the products which are produced by the enterprise.

Example

Direct material	Product
Wood, screws, handles	Desk
Printed circuit boards, disk drives, cases	Computer
Steel, wheels, power train	Motor vehicle

Direct wages (direct labour) are those wages paid to the personnel who are directly involved in the production of each of the items produced. They include wages paid to operators of the machinery used to manufacture the products, wages paid to the workers who assemble the products and wages paid to those who finish them, such as painting, polishing and testing.

Direct expenses are those costs that can also be directly traced to the products that are being produced, but cannot be classified under direct materials or direct wages. For example, if in the manufacture of a machine the supply and installation of electronic controls is subcontracted to an outside expert, the resultant cost is neither direct material nor direct wages. Nevertheless, this cost is clearly a product direct cost and would therefore be charged as a direct expense of manufacturing the product on which the technician worked.

The total of direct materials consumed, direct wages and direct expenses incurred is known as the *prime cost* of a product, and is often shown as such in the manufacturing account.

4 | OVERHEADS

If a cost is not a product direct cost as described above, it is classified as a *product indirect cost* or *overhead*. Overheads are those items of revenue expenditure that, although incurred to enable business operations to take place, nevertheless cannot be traced directly to individual products where a range of products is manufactured. Overhead costs are often shared by the entire output. Overheads can be classified as:

- production overheads;
- administration overheads;
- selling overheads;
- distribution overheads.

Only the production overheads are charged in the manufacturing account as part of the cost of production. Costs under the other overhead classifications are charged against the profit-and-loss account.

Production (manufacturing or *factory) overheads* are incurred as part of the cost of manufacture, but cannot be traced as direct costs to the products produced.

Example

Production overhead

Factory rent and business rates

Factory cleaning costs (cleaners' wages and materials)

Depreciation of factory machinery

Power

Factory light and heat

Supervisors' salaries

Maintenance wages and expenses

The addition of prime cost and production overheads is known as *total production cost* or *total manufacturing cost* or *total factory cost of finished goods.*

5 THE MANUFACTURING ACCOUNT

The following example shows the basic *manufacturing account* layout, which incorporates direct costs and production overheads.

Example

Manufacturing account for the year ended (date)

	£	£
Direct costs		
Direct materials consumed	X	
Direct wages	X	
Direct expenses	X	
Prime cost		X
Production overheads		X
Total production cost of finished goods		X

The following costs have been incurred by Manchester Manufacturers Ltd for the year ended 31 December 20X1.

	£'000
Office salaries	300
Depreciation of machinery	60
Machinery maintenance	82
Factory maintenance	105
Operators' wages	662
Factory rent	100
Factory insurance	30
Direct materials consumed	317
Office stationery	32
Factory canteen	204
Factory manager's salary	29
Accountancy and legal fees	49
Depreciation of delivery vans	37
Telephone	18
Electricity	43
Power for factory machinery	102
Production sub-contract work	95
Business rates – office	32
– factory	65

Required

i) Identify from the list of costs those that should be included in a manufacturing account.

ii) Classify the costs you have identified as either direct costs or overheads.

iii) Arrange the production costs in the form of a manufacturing account showing prime cost and total production cost of finished goods.

Solution

Manchester Manufacturers Ltd.
Manufacturing account for the year ended 31 December 20X1

	£'000	£'000
Direct costs		
Direct materials	317	
Direct wages (operators' wages)	662	
Direct expenses (subcontract)	95	
Prime cost		1,074

continued

Production overheads

Depreciation of machinery	60
Machinery maintenance	82
Factory maintenance	105
Factory rent	100
Factory insurance	30
Factory canteen	24
Factory manager's salary	29
Power for factory machinery	102
Business rates – factory	65

Total production overheads	597
Total production cost of finished goods	1,671

You should now be able to attempt Question 30.1 at the end of this chapter.

---

6   CHANGES TO THE TRADING ACCOUNT

The introduction of the manufacturing account into the final accounts of an organisation requires some minor changes to the *trading* section of the traditional profit-and-loss account. You will recall that the trading account establishes the *gross profit* of the enterprise by comparing the sales income with the *cost of goods sold* or *cost of sales*. The following example shows a typical layout.

Example

Trading, profit and loss account for the year ended (date)
(Trading section only)

	£	£
Sales		X
Cost of goods sold:		
Opening stock	X	
Add purchases	X	
	X	
Less closing stock	X	
Cost of goods sold		X
Gross profit		X

The above trading section assumes that the items sold are obtained by purchasing them. If manufacturing takes place, the manufactured items are sold. Therefore the *purchases* in the trading section are replaced by a transfer of the *production cost of finished goods* from the manufacturing account. The trading section of the profit-and-loss account accompanying the introduction of a manufacturing account is as follows.

Trading, profit and loss account for the year ended (date)
(Trading section only)

	£	£
Sales		X
Cost of goods sold:		
Opening stock	X	
Add production cost of finished goods	X	
	X	
Less closing stock	X	
Cost of goods sold		X
Gross profit		X

The opening and closing stocks included in this trading section refer to stocks of *finished goods*. These are goods that have completed the manufacturing process and have been transferred to a part of the business where completed products are held in a condition where they may be sent to the customer.

7	DIRECT MATERIAL STOCKS

So far we have drawn up the basic manufacturing account on the basis of direct materials consumed forming part of the prime cost, making the assumption that the quantity of direct material *purchased* is the same as the quantity of direct material *consumed*. However, in practice this is rarely the case, as for a number of reasons it is considered to be beneficial for an organisation to maintain stocks of direct materials. As a result the difference in direct material stock levels at the beginning and the end of an accounting period must be taken into consideration in order to obtain a value of *direct material stock consumed* in the period. This figure is obtained by including adjustments to the direct materials purchased figure in the manufacturing account. This is achieved by bringing in the values of opening and closing stock levels in the following manner.

	£
Direct materials:	
Opening stock at the beginning of the period	X
Add purchases during the period	X
Less closing stock at the end of the period	X
Cost of direct materials consumed during the period	X

Example
The revised *manufacturing account* layout that incorporates the calculation of *direct materials consumed* is as follows.

Manufacturing account for the year ended (date)

	£	£	£
Direct costs			
Direct materials:			
Opening stock	X		
Add Purchases	X		
	X		
Less closing stock	X		
Direct materials consumed		X	
Direct wages		X	
Direct expenses		X	
Prime cost			X
Production overheads			X
Total production cost of finished goods			X

Occasionally the cost of *carriage inwards on direct materials purchased* is incurred. In this case, the carriage inwards cost is simply added to the cost of direct materials purchased, as carriage inwards is simply part of the cost of obtaining direct materials.

> *You should now be able to attempt Question 30.2 at the end of this chapter.*

8   WORK IN PROGRESS

In practice it is not possible for the end of an accounting period to correspond to a circumstance where all the production is made up of completed or finished goods. It is inevitable that there will be some production which is only partially complete. This incomplete production is known as *work in progress (WIP)*. At the beginning of an accounting period there will be opening WIP and at the end of the period, closing work-in-progress.

In assessing the production cost of finished goods for the accounting period, the impact of *differences* in opening and closing levels of work in progress must be considered when the manufacturing account is drawn up. The way this is done depends on how WIP is valued. The alternative ways in which it can be valued are outside the scope of this chapter, but it is quite normal to value WIP at total production cost up to the stage of production reached.

We have already seen that total production cost is made up of *prime cost* plus *production overhead*, and the point at which the adjustment for the difference between opening and closing WIP is incorporated into the manufacturing account is based on this valuation principle. The adjustment for opening and closing stocks of *direct materials* is incorporated by adding the opening stocks and deducting the closing stocks from the costs that feature in the manufacturing account. Similarly, the adjustment for the opening and closing stocks of *finished goods* is incorporated by adding the opening stocks and deducting the closing stocks from the costs that feature in the trading section of the profit-and-loss account. The adjustment for WIP is similarly treated in the manufacturing account by adding the value of the opening stocks of work in progress and deducting the value of closing stocks of work in progress. Because work in progress is normally valued at total production cost up to the stage of production reached, the work in progress adjustment is recorded in the manufacturing account by adjusting the total production cost for the period.

The revised *manufacturing account* layout, which incorporates the valuation of WIP, is as follows.

Example

Manufacturing account for the year ended (date)

	£	£	£
Direct costs			
Direct materials			
Opening stock	X		
Add Purchases	X		
Add Carriage inwards	X		
	X		
Less Closing stock	X		
Direct materials consumed		X	
Direct wages		X	
Direct expenses		X	
Prime cost			X
Production overheads			X
Total production costs			X
Work-in-progress adjustment			
Add Opening work in progress		X	
Less Closing work in progress		(X)	
			X
Total production cost of finished goods			X

The total production cost of finished goods is then transferred to the trading section of the trading, profit-and-loss account as described in Section 30.6.

> *You should now be able to attempt Question 30.3 at the end of this chapter.*

9   MANUFACTURING PROFIT

We have seen that the sales income of an organisation is usually shown in the trading section of the trading, profit-and-loss account. This figure refers to the sales to third parties that have been made during the accounting period to which the final accounts relate.

In some circumstances an organisation sets up an accounting system which records *internal sales* from one part of the business to another. For example, an internal price may be set at which the finished goods are transferred or sold by the manufacturing part of the business to the selling part of the business. This price is recorded in the accounts to show the *sales* by the manufacturing account which become the *purchases* by the trading account. There are a number of reasons why firms adopt this practice:

- Where a fixed price per unit is set for the transfer of finished goods from the manufacturing facility into the finished goods warehouse, a profit or loss on manufacturing can be established.
- The manufacturing facility is motivated to control costs so that the production of the finished goods is achieved within a fixed price, otherwise a loss on manufacturing would result.
- The selling function receives the goods from manufacturing already including a profit element. This is similar to them purchasing the goods for resale from an outside source.
- Different managers may be responsible for each part of the business. This can provide a measure of profits or losses for each part of the business, which may be used to measure managers' individual performances.

The effect of creating an internal selling price for goods transferred from manufacturing is to bring a sales figure into the manufacturing account. This figure is normally described as *sales value of finished goods produced*. The result of bringing this additional element into the manufacturing account is to create an internal profit on manufacture known as *profit on finished goods produced*. The following example shows the layout of the revised manufacturing account which incorporates these changes.

Example

Manufacturing account for the year ended (date)

	£	£	£
Sales value of finished goods produced			X
Direct costs			
Direct materials:			
Opening stock	X		
Add Purchases	X		
Add Carriage inwards	X		
	X		
Less Closing stock	X		
Direct materials consumed		X	
Direct wages		X	
Direct expenses		X	
Prime cost		X	
Production overheads		X	
Total production costs		X	

continued

	£	£	£
Work-in-progress adjustment:			
Add Opening work-in-progress		X	
Less Closing work-in-progress		(X)	
Total production cost of finished goods			X
Profit or loss on finished goods produced			X

10 OTHER CHANGES TO THE FINAL ACCOUNTS

When a *profit or loss on finished goods produced* is recorded in the manufacturing account, other changes to the trading, profit-and-loss account are necessary. In this case the *sales value of finished goods* figure is transferred to the trading section of the trading, profit-and-loss account as referred to earlier. The *profit or loss on finished goods produced* in the manufacturing account is transferred to the profit-and-loss section of the trading, profit-and-loss account and is added to (or subtracted from, if a loss) the *gross profit* from trading. From the total of these two profits the non-manufacturing expenses or overheads of the business are deducted to give the net profit for the period.

Example

Using the example in section 30.5 of *Manchester Manufacturing Ltd*, the following list of balances on the accounts for the year ended 31 December 20X1 have been expanded to include those which are entered in the trading, profit-and-loss accounts as well as those for the manufacturing account. Opening and closing work in progress have also been introduced. The company has decided to transfer finished goods from the factory to the finished goods warehouse at £15 per unit and during the year 120,000 units were transferred.

	£'000
Office salaries	300
Depreciation of machinery	60
Machinery maintenance	82
Factory maintenance	105
Operators' wages	662
Factory rent	100
Factory insurance	30
Direct materials purchased	336
Factory canteen	204
Office stationery	32
Factory manager's salary	29
Accountancy and legal fees	49
Depreciation of delivery vans	37

continued

	£'000
Telephone	18
Electricity	43
Power for factory machinery	102
Production sub-contract work	95
Business rates – office	32
– factory	65
Sales	2,466
Stocks as at 1 January 20X1:	
Direct materials	127
Finished goods	61
Work in progress	43
Stocks as at 31 December 20X1	
Direct materials	146
Finished goods	76
Work in progress	59

Required

i) Draw up a manufacturing account and trading, profit-and-loss account for the year ended 31 December 20X1.

ii) Clearly show the following in the respective accounts:

the sales value of finished goods produced;

the profit or loss on finished goods produced;

the gross or trading profit;

the total gross profit;

the net profit.

Solution

Manchester Manufacturing Ltd
Manufacturing account for the year ended 31 December 20X1

	£'000	£'000	£'000
Sales value of finished goods produced			
120,000 units at £15 per unit			
(to trading section of trading, profit-and-loss account)			1,800
Direct costs			
Direct materials			
Opening stock	127		
Add Purchases	336		
	463		
Less Closing stock	146		
Direct materials consumed	317		
Direct wages (operators' wages)	662		
Direct expenses (sub-contract)	95		
Prime cost		1,074	

continued

	£'000	£'000	£'000
Production overheads			
Depreciation of machinery	60		
Machinery maintenance	82		
Factory maintenance	105		
Factory rent	100		
Factory insurance	30		
Factory canteen	24		
Factory manager's salary	29		
Power for factory machinery	102		
Business rates – factory	65		
Total production overheads		597	
Total cost of production		1,671	
Work in progress adjustment			
Opening work in progress	43		
Less Closing work in progress	(59)		
Increase in work in progress		(16)	
Production cost of finished goods			1,655
Profit or loss on finished goods produced or *manufacturing profit* (to profit-and-loss section of trading, profit-and-loss account)			145

Trading, profit-and-loss account for the year ended 31 December 20X1

	£'000	£'000
Sales		2,466
Cost of sales		
Opening stock	61	
Sales value of finished goods produced	1,800	
	1,861	
Less Closing stock	76	
Cost of goods sold		1,785
Gross or trading profit		681
Profit on finished goods produced or manufacturing profit (from manufacturing account)		145
Total gross profit		826
Expenses or overheads		
Office salaries	300	
Office stationery	32	
Accountancy and legal fees	49	
Depreciation of delivery vans	37	
Telephone	18	
Electricity	43	
Business rates – office	32	511
Net profit		315

11 ACCRUALS AND PREPAYMENTS

Like profit-and-loss accounts, manufacturing accounts are prepared on an *accruals* basis. This means that the expenses charged in the manufacturing account for the accounting period are not restricted to those that have actually been paid for. Adjustments must be made for those expenses that have been *incurred* by adding to the amounts paid any amounts *accrued*, that is amounts due at the end of the period. For example, wages that are paid a week in arrears would involve the final week's pay being paid in the first week of the new year. The amount of that payment would be added to the old year's wages as an *accrual* to ensure that the wages figure *incurred*, rather than the wages figure *paid*, is included in the accounts for the old year.

Similarly, if an amount has been paid in the period that includes an element that refers to the succeeding period, an adjustment to account for the *prepayment* element is made. For example, a proportion of rent paid in the old year may refer to the new year. In this case the amount of rent which refers to the new year must be deducted from the charge for the old year as a *prepayment* so that the charge for the old year is restricted to the amount properly chargeable to that period. See Chapter 16 which goes into this aspect in more detail.

12 APPORTIONMENT OF OVERHEAD COSTS

Manufacturing organisations often incur some *overhead costs* that are shared between the factory and the office. Business rates are an example of this. They can be paid as a single invoice, but require apportioning between the manufacturing account and the profit-and-loss account on an equitable basis. The share of the business rates chargeable to production appears in the manufacturing account as an overhead; the proportion chargeable to the office premises is charged in the profit-and-loss account.

It is normal for students to be given the basis of apportionment of such shared overheads in examination questions, often as percentages or fractions. If such information is not available, then an equitable basis must be chosen. The following are examples of the ways in which some overhead costs can be apportioned between the manufacturing account and the profit-and-loss account.

Example

Cost	Basis of apportionment
Business rates	Floor areas of office and factory
Rents	Floor areas of office and factory
National insurance	Number of personnel in office and factory
Insurance – buildings	Floor areas of office and factory
– plant	Capital values of plant in office and factory

403

> *You should now be able to attempt Tasks 30.1, 30.2 and 30.3 and Questions 30.4 and 30.5 at the end of this chapter.*

13 SUMMARY

The use of the trading, profit-and-loss account to record the financial results of an organisation becomes inadequate when the organisation is one which manufactures the products. The *trading section* of the trading, profit-and-loss account is based on the assumption that the cost of sales or cost of goods sold are *purchased*. In a manufacturing organisation this is clearly not the case. The *manufacturing* account is drawn up before the trading, profit-and-loss account, and records the cost of converting the raw materials into the finished goods which are ultimately sold. It *classifies* the costs of production into the direct costs of direct materials consumed, direct wages and direct expenses, and indirect costs, which are otherwise known as production overheads. The figure for direct or raw materials consumed is obtained by adjusting the direct materials purchased by the opening and closing stocks of raw materials. Unfinished production at any time is known as *work-in-progress*. In order to obtain the production cost of finished goods, the total cost of production must be adjusted by the opening and closing work in progress of the period.

In some circumstances a *manufacturing profit* is calculated by arranging for an internal price to be set for the transfer of finished goods transferred from the factory to the warehouse or sales function. In these circumstances the manufacturing account records a profit or loss on finished goods produced by bringing in a *sales value of finished goods manufactured*. This profit or loss is transferred to the profit-and-loss account to be added to (or subtracted from, if a loss) the normal gross or trading profit.

As there is no legal requirement under partnership or company legislation for a manufacturing account to be included in the published accounts of an organisation, it is generally used for internal purposes only. Consequently, the manufacturing account is never seen as part of the published report and final accounts, even though the organisation may be one involved in the manufacture of products.

> *You should now be able to attempt the objective test at the end of this chapter.*

Student activities

Task 30.1

You have been asked by a local manufacturing company to advise them of the advantages and disadvantages of sharing the profits between manufacturing and trading activities. Write a report to the managing director of the company setting out how this might be achieved, the alternative transfer pricing methods which might be considered, the merits of such a system, and any other points which they should bear in mind before making such a change.

Task 30.2

Construct a diagram to illustrate the relationships between the figures in the manufacturing account, the trading, profit-and-loss account, and the balance sheet.

Task 30.3

A local businessman has been operating a successful manufacturing company for a number of years, but has only prepared a trading and profit-and-loss account at the year end. Make a list of the benefits he could gain by preparing a manufacturing account.

Question 30.1

Barnstaple Bolts Ltd manufactures nuts, bolts and other fasteners. The following financial information was taken from the books for the year ended 31 March 20X1.

	£
Raw materials consumed	100,235
Factory indirect wages	60,277
Factory manager's salary	25,616
Factory business rates	6,211
Factory rent	14,118
Depreciation of machinery	5,200
Direct wages	126,306
Insurance of machinery	2,198
Maintenance of machinery	14,205
Maintenance of factory	7,236
Factory power	2,876
Consumable materials	274
Factory heating	3,206

Required

Prepare a manufacturing account for Barnstaple Bolts Ltd for the year ended 31 March 20X1 showing clearly:

i)   the prime cost;

ii) the production cost of finished goods.

Question 30.2

Kidderminster Kitchens Ltd produces flat-pack kitchen units from the basic raw materials. The following information was extracted from the books of the company for the year ended 30 June 20X5.

	£
Purchases of raw materials	105,200
Manufacturing wages:	
Direct	177,211
Indirect	116,300
Factory rent	40,000
Business rates	35,290
Insurance	7,302
Building maintenance	14,603
Depreciation of machinery	4,800
Stocks of raw materials:	
1 July 20X4	8,457
30 June 20X5	9,666
Maintenance of machinery	16,934
Consumable materials	3,298
Factory manager's salary	27,300
Factory power	45,874
Heat and light	12,875
General expenses	7,216
Depreciation of factory fixtures and fittings	5,400

Required

Prepare a manufacturing account for Kidderminster Kitchens Ltd showing clearly:

i)   the cost of raw materials consumed;

ii) the prime cost;

iii) the production cost of finished goods.

Question 30.3
The following financial information was taken from the books of Wolverhampton Wagonwheels Ltd at the 31 December in respect of the year ended on that date.

	£
Stock of raw materials on 1 January 20X1	82,000
Stock of raw materials on 31 December 20X1	62,000
Work in progress on 1 January 20X1	25,000
Work in progress on 31 December 20X1	55,000
Purchases of raw materials	258,000
Fuel and power	37,800
Heat and light	4,800
Wages: Direct	202,000
Indirect	24,500
Direct expenses (sub-contractors' charges)	7,200
Carriage inwards on raw materials	3,900
Depreciation: Plant and machinery	61,000
Tools	4,700

continued

	£
Machine lubricants	6,300
Factory insurance	2,100
Factory general expenses	32,100

Required

Prepare a manufacturing account for Wolverhampton Wagonwheels Ltd for the year ended 31 December in good form.

Question 30.4

J. Colwyn owns a small manufacturing business. The following financial information was extracted from his books for the year ended 31 December 20X6.

	£
Sales	625,500
Sales returns	1,250
Purchases of raw materials	132,200
Purchase returns	2,350
Plant and machinery (cost £350,000)	230,000
Office furniture (cost £15,000)	10,000
Factory power	30,000
Heat and light (factory 80%, office 20%)	10,000
Creditors	165,000
Debtors	110,000
Cash at bank	108,000
Stock of raw materials: 1 January	42,500
Stock of finished goods: 1 January	53,200
Manufacturing wages	160,000
General expenses (factory $\frac{2}{3}$, office $\frac{1}{3}$)	30,000
Insurance (factory $\frac{6}{7}$, office $\frac{1}{7}$)	9,800
Freehold factory at cost	200,000
Business rates (factory $\frac{6}{7}$, office $\frac{1}{7}$)	63,000
Motor vehicles (cost £220,000)	82,000
Office salaries	62,000
Work in progress: 1 January	25,000
Drawings	55,000
Carriage inwards	2,650

The following information is also available:

Stocks at 31 December 20X6

	£
Raw materials	31,000
Finished goods	56,350
Work in progress	23,450

Depreciation is to be provided on the following fixed assets using the reducing balance method:

Plant and machinery	10%
Office furniture	15%
Motor vehicles	20%

Required

i) Prepare a manufacturing account and trading, profit-and-loss account for the year ended 31 December 206 and a balance sheet as at that date.

ii) Calculate J. Colwyn's capital as at 1 January 20X6.

Question 30.5

Portsmouth Printers Ltd prints repair manuals for the car trade, and the details extracted from the financial books of the company for the year ended 31 August 20X4 are as follows.

	£
Stocks as at 1 September 20X3.	
Direct materials	13,550
Work in progress	6,720
Finished books	12,490
Purchases and expenses incurred for the year:	
Direct materials	290,720
Indirect materials	3,700
Direct wages	106,500
Factory power	9,200
Light and heat (office 40%, factory 60%)	6,120
Direct expenses	1,120
Postage	1,210
Carriage inwards	3,120
Telephone	2,100
Factory salaries	22,720
Office salaries	21,210
Factory insurances	2,410
Other insurances	920
Depreciation – factory plant and machinery	10,000
– office equipment	1,300
Office expenses	3,200
Advertising	1,960
Business rates (office 20%, factory 80%)	10,200
Rent (office 30%, factory 70%)	9,000
Sales of finished goods for the year	752,390

The following additional information is relevant to the above accounting period:

Finished books printed during the accounting period are transferred from the factory at a manufacturing price of £5 per book. 113,000 books were completed during the year.

	£
Stocks at 31 August 20X4	
Direct materials	18,211
Work in progress	9,300
Finished goods	16,100
Expenses prepaid at 31 August 20X4	
Factory insurances	110
Other insurances	140
Rent	1,000
Expenses accrued due at 31 August 20X4	
Direct wages	4,200
Factory power	700
Light and heat	880

Required

Prepare the manufacturing account and trading, profit-and-loss account for the year ended 31 August 20X4.

Objective test (tick the appropriate box)

i) The total of the direct material consumed, direct labour and direct expenses is known as:

   a) total production cost ☐

   b) prime cost ☐

   c) total factory cost ☐

   d) overheads ☐

ii) The materials cost that is ultimately charged against profits is made up of:

   a) opening stock plus purchases plus closing stock ☐

   b) purchases less closing stock ☐

   c) purchases plus carriage inwards ☐

   d) opening stock plus purchases plus carriage inwards minus closing stock ☐

iii) Stocks of finished goods appear as adjustments in:

   a) the manufacturing account ☐

   b) the trading section of the profit-and-loss account ☐

   c) the profit-and-loss section of the profit-and-loss account ☐

   d) the balance sheet ☐

iv) The work-in-progress adjustment appears in:

   a) the manufacturing account ☐

b)   the trading section of the profit-and-loss account ☐

c)   the profit-and-loss section of the profit-and-loss account ☐

d)   the balance sheet ☐

v)   When a manufacturing profit is shown in the manufacturing account, the value of finished goods transferred to the trading account section of the profit-and-loss account is made up of:

a)   total cost of goods produced ☐

b)   total production cost of finished goods ☐

c)   profit on finished goods produced ☐

d)   prime cost ☐

Lansdown Bowls and Tennis Club

Context

You are the treasurer of Lansdown Bowls and Tennis Club, which was founded in June 20X5. The following receipts and payments account for the period ended 30 June 20X6 June is taken from the club's books.

Receipts	£	Payments	£
Bank balance 1 July 20X5	3,100	Sports equipment	1,400
Subscriptions	1,800	Ground maintenance	2,200
Refreshment sales	16,600	Light and heat	380
Tournament fees	640	Refreshment purchases	6,000
Donations	50	Bar salaries	5,000
		Club house rent	1,500
		Bank balance 30 June 20X6	5,710
	22,190		22,190

The following information is also available:

	£
Stock of bar refreshments at 30 June 20X6	1,250
Subscriptions owing for the current year	460
Ground maintenance fee owing	140

A number of residents living close to the clubhouse are petitioning for the bar to be closed because of a problem of noise in the evenings. The club members are not only concerned by the threat to their social facilities, but also by the financial impact it might have on the club. The bar occupies some 80 per cent of the clubhouse and the changing rooms and other facilities approximately 20 per cent. In the event of the bar closing, the clubhouse rent would remain the same.

Student activities

i) Draw up a bar account and an income and expenditure account for Lansdown Bowls and Tennis Club for the year ending 30 June 20X6.

ii) Write a brief report to the club members outlining the consequences if the bar had to close.

Format

A report is required, addressed to club members, which should show a bar account and an income-and-expenditure account for the club. It should also provide an explanation of the financial implications for the club if the bar has to close.

Objectives

In this assignment the student will gain an understanding of the advantage of an income-and-expenditure account over a receipts and payments account for a club, and appreciate how the information it provides may be interpreted.

References

Chapter 29.

Nacho Surfboards

Context

Nacho Surfboards makes and sells surfboards. Robbie Nach started up his business three years ago in a garage, but it has grown rapidly. Although Mr Nach has always kept somewhat rudimentary accounts, the following information is available.

Nacho Surfboards

Trading and profit-and-loss account for the year ending 31 December 20X6

	£	£
Sales		159,400
Opening stock	17,200	
Purchases of raw materials	47,600	
	64,800	
Less Closing stock	30,700	34,100
Gross profit		125,300
Less Expenses		
Rent and rates	6,600	
Wages and salaries	75,000	
Power	1,600	
Heat and light	4,880	
Expenses	3,200	
Depreciation on plant and machinery	2,500	93,780
Net profit		31,520

The breakdown of the opening and closing stock figures is as follows:

Stock	at 1 January 20X6	at 31 December 20X6
	£	£
Raw materials	6,400	9,000
Work-in-progress	2,200	2,200
Finished goods	8,600	19,400

Costs are allocated as follows:

Rent and rates	50% to manufacturing
Wages and salaries	20% to manufacturing as indirect wages
	60% to manufacturing as direct wages
Heat and light	£500 to manufacturing
Expenses	50% to manufacturing as direct expenses

Student activities

Mr Nacho has asked you to try and improve his management information by showing the cost to the business of the goods manufactured and the profit made on trading.

i)   Draw up a manufacturing account for the year ending 31 December 20X6.

ii) Draw up a trading and profit-and-loss account for the year ending 31 December 20X6.

iii) Write a brief report to Robbie Nacho explaining the figures.

Format

A report is required which provides a manufacturing account and a profit-and-loss account for the year ending 31 December 20X6, as well as an explanation of the financial statements and the information they convey.

Objectives

In this assignment the student will appreciated the value of constructing a separate manufacturing account and trading and profit-and-loss account and the information these two financial statements convey.

References

Chapter 30.

ANSWERS

CHAPTER 1

Question 1.5

All limited companies are regulated by the Companies Act 1985. This requires companies to prepare final accounts at the end of each financial year. Both private limited companies and public limited companies must deposit certain information with the Registrar of Companies and it thus becomes public.

OBJECTIVE TEST 1

i) c   ii) c   iii) d   iv) a   v) c

CHAPTER 2

Question 2.3

i) c   ii) e   iii) a   iv) f   v) b   vi) d

OBJECTIVE TEST 2

i) c   ii) b   iii) a   iv) d   v) b

CHAPTER 3

Question 3.3

A partnership is not legally required to have a qualified accountant to conduct an audit. Indeed, there is no need for an audit. If the business is sufficiently large to warrant the cost of employing a qualified accountant, the following advantages should be enjoyed:

- better financial information for assessing the performance of business;
- improved information for controlling and monitoring the business and making decisions;
- an improved financial strategy leading to better access to and lower cost of capital;
- tax planning.

The different accounting qualifications are explained in the chapter.

OBJECTIVE TEST 3

i) a   ii) b   iii) c   iv) d   v) c

CHAPTER 4

Question 4.3

Keith Wilson: Stock valuation

	£	£
20 tables at £24 each		480
Less Repolishing	30	
Advertising	60	90
		390

OBJECTIVE TEST 4

i) b   ii) c   iii) d   iv) b   v) d

CHAPTER 5

Question 5.5

Natalie must ensure that she has a system to record the number of garments purchased and the number sold. A purchase order should be sent to the supplier and a goods received note should be issued on receipt of the garments. The number of garments received should be entered on a stock record card when they arrive in the Stores Department. Goods should only be released on receipt of an order and the transaction should be entered on the stock record card. Periodically, the actual number of garments in stock should be checked against the balance shown on the stock record card and any discrepancies investigated.

OBJECTIVE TEST 5

i) b   ii) c   iii) b   iv) c   v) b

CHAPTER 6

Question 6.1

Capital Account

				£
		1 March	Bank	10,000

Loan Account

				£
		1 March	Bank	3,000

Bank Account

		£			£
1 March	Capital Account	10,000	1 March	Van Account	7,500
1 March	Loan Account	3,000	1 March	Office Services	50
			2 March	Advertising Account	35
			2 March	Petrol Account	20

Van Account

		£	
1 March	Bank Account	7,500	

Office Services Account

		£	
1 March	Bank Account	50	

Advertising Account

2 March	Bank Account	£ 35	

Petrol Account

2 March	Bank Account	£ 20	

OBJECTIVE TEST 6

i) b   ii) d   iii) c   iv) d   v) d

CHAPTER 7

Question 7.5

Bob Chipping: Bank reconciliation statement

	£
Balance on the bank statement	607
Add deposits not yet cleared	264
	871
Less cheques not yet presented	539
Balance as per cash book	332

OBJECTIVE TEST 7

i) c   ii) a   iii) c   iv) a   v) b

CHAPTER 8

OBJECTIVE TEST 8

i) c   ii) b   iii) d   iv) b   v) b

CHAPTER 9

Question 9.6

i) See opposite

T. Cherry
Cash flow forecast January to December

	Jan £	Feb £	Mar £	Apr £	May £	Jun £	Jul £	Aug £	Sep £	Oct £	Nov £	Dec £	Total £
Cash inflows													
Cash sales	625	1,250	1,875	3,750	5,000	5,000	3,750	3,125	3,125	2,500	2,500	1,875	34,375
Credit sales	–	625	1,250	1,875	3,750	5,000	5,000	3,750	3,125	3,125	2,500	2,500	32,500
Total inflows	625	1,875	3,125	5,625	8,750	10,000	8,750	6,875	6,250	5,625	5,000	4,375	66,875
Cash inflows													
Equipment	16,000	–	–	–	–	–	–	–	–	–	–	–	16,000
Fittings	–	–	3,500	–	–	–	–	–	–	–	–	–	3,500
Cutters's wage	250	250	250	250	250	250	250	250	250	250	250	250	3,000
Materials	–	–	3,250	3,250	3,250	3,250	3,250	3,250	3,250	3,250	3,250	3,250	32,500
Packaging (no. sold)	–	30	60	90	180	240	240	180	150	150	120	120	1,560
Rent	2,500	–	–	2,500	–	–	2,500	–	–	2,500	–	–	10,000
Overheads	–	400	400	400	400	400	400	400	400	400	400	400	4,400
Telephone	–	–	–	250	–	–	250	–	–	250	–	–	750
Printing	–	50	50	50	50	50	50	50	50	50	50	50	550
Insurance	300	–	–	300	–	–	300	–	–	300	–	–	1,200
Advertising	60	60	310	60	60	60	310	60	60	60	60	60	1,220
Total outflows	19,110	790	7,820	7,150	4,190	4,250	7,550	4,190	4,160	7,210	4,130	4,130	74,680
Bal b/f	–	(18,485)	(17,400)	(22,095)	(23,620)	(19,060)	(13,310)	(12,110)	(9,425)	(7,335)	(8,920)	(8,050)	
Net cash flow	(18,485)	1,085	(4,695)	(1,525)	4,560	5,750	1,200	2,685	2,090	(1,585)	870	245	
Bal c/f	(18,485)	(17,400)	(22,095)	(23,620)	(19,060)	(13,310)	(12,110)	(9,425)	(7,335)	(8,920)	(8,050)	(7,805)	(7,805)

ii)   Capital required £23,620

OBJECTIVE TEST 9

i) a   ii) d   iii) b   iv) d   v) c

CHAPTER 10

Question 10.3

Llanelli Language Courses

Trading and profit & loss account for the year ending 31st December 2002

			£	£
Sales	2,900	@ £89		258,100
Less Cost of sales:				
Opening stock	350	@ £55	19,250	
Add Purchases	3,150	@ £59	185,850	
	3,500		205,100	
Less Closing stock	600	@ £59	35,400	
	2,900			169,700
Gross profit				88,400
Less Expenses:				
Salaries and wages			14,500	
Postages			5,800	
Packing			1,450	
Rent of warehouse			12,000	
Advertising			15,500	
Insurances			2,850	
Power, light and heat			3,400	
Depreciation of equipment			800	
Stationery			1,350	
Telephone			3,450	
Research and development			5,100	66,200
Net profit				22,200

OBJECTIVE TEST 10

i) b   ii) d   iii) c   iv) a   v) c

CHAPTER 11

Question 11.6

Brennan Nantais
Balance sheet as at 30th September 2002

	£'000 £'000		£'000 £'000
Fixed assets		Capital (£100+£31−£11)	120
Warehouse & office	94	Long-term loan (£20−£5)	15
Fixtures & fittings			
(£8+£4)	12		
Delivery van			
(£12−£12+£15)	15		
	121		
Current assets		Current liabilities	
Stocks (£9+£63−£55)	17	Creditors (£18+£63−£59)	22
Debtors (£17+£86−£83)	20 37	Overdraft (£2−£83+£5+	
		£59+£4+£3+£11)	1 23
	158		158

OBJECTIVE TEST 11

i) d   ii) b   iii) d   iv) c   v) b   vi) b   vii) b   viii) b   ix) b   x) c

CHAPTER 12

Question 12.3

Dolgellau Camping Equipment Company
Trading and profit & loss account for the year ending 31st March 2004

	£	£	£
Sales			378,500
Less Returns inwards		4,100	374,400
Less Cost of sales:			
Opening stock		120,600	
Add Purchases	261,700		
Less Returns outwards	7,700	254,000	
		374,600	
Less Closing stock		102,500	272,100
Gross profit			102,300
Add Rent receivable		7,500	
Add Discounts received		2,400	9,900
			112,200
Less Expenses:			
Salaries and wages		45,700	
Office expenses		8,400	*continued*

Insurances	3,100		
Less Prepaid	900	2,200	
Electricity	1,600		
Add accrued	700	2,300	
Stationery		6,200	
Advertising	8,400		
Add Accrued	500	8,900	
Telephone		2,100	
Business rates	7,500		
Less Prepaid	1,500	6,000	
Discounts allowed		600	82,400
Net profit			29,800

Dolgellau Camping Equipment Company
Balance sheet as at 31st March 1995

	£	£	£	£
Fixed assets				
Warehouse, shop & office			210,000	
Fixtures and fittings			12,800	222,800
Current assets				
Stocks		102,500		
Debtors	13,000			
Add prepayments				
(£900 + £1,500)	2,400	15,400		
Cash in hand		500	118,400	
Current liabilities				
Creditors	18,700			
Add accruals (£700 + £500)	1,200	19,900		
Overdraft		30,000	49,900	
Net current assets (Working capital)				68,500
Capital employed				291,300
Represented by:				
Capital at start of year			287,500	
Add Profit for the year			29,800	
			317,300	
Less Drawings			26,000	
Owner's worth				291,300

OBJECTIVE TEST 12

i) b   ii) d   iii) c   iv) a   v) d   vi) c   vii) a   viii) c   ix) d   x) c

CHAPTER 13

Question 13.5

i)   Table comparing original and suggested depreciation calculations

	Fixtures and Fittings			Estate Car			Total
Method of depreciation	Straight line	Reduced balance	RB > SL	Straight line	Reduced balance	RB > SL	RB > SL
Percentage rate per annum	10%	20%		20%	20%		
	£	£	£	£	£	£	£
Original cost 1.1.×4	40,000	40,000		18,000	18,000		
Depreciation y/e 31.3.95	4,000	8,000	4,000	3,600	3,600	nil	4,000
Reduced balance 31.3.95	36,000	32,000		14,400	14,400		
Depreciation y/e 31.3.96	4,000	6,400	2,400	3,600	2,880	(720)	1,680
Reduced balance 31.3.96	32,000	25,600		10,800	11,520		
Depreciation y/e 31.3.97	4,000	5,120	1,120	3,600	2,304	(1,296)	(176)
Reduced balance 31.3.97	28,000	20,480		7,200	9,216		
Cumulative depreciation:							
Year ending 31.3.×5	4,000	8,000	4,000	3,600	3,600	nil	4,000
Year ending 31.3.×6	8,000	14,400	6,400	7,200	6,480	(720)	5,680
Year ending 31.3.×7	12,000	19,520	7,520	10,800	8,784	(2,016)	5,504

ii)   £5,680 more (total cumulative depreciation in above table)

	£
iii) Original capital figure from Question 13.4	201,790
Less additional depreciation charged against profits, see ii) above	5,680
Revised capital figure at 1st April 2004	196,110

	£
iv) Original net profit figure from Question 13.4	20,240
Add reduction in depreciation charge	176
Revised net profit figure	20,416

	£
v) Owner's worth at 31st March 2007, as from Question 13.4	208,830
Less increase in depreciation charge for all 3 years	5,504
Owner's worth at 31st March 2007 (revised)	203,326

	£
or	
Capital at 1.4.2006, revised as iii) above	196,110
Add revised profit year ending 31st March 2007 as iv) above	20,416
	216,526
Less drawings, year ending 31st March 2007	13,200
Owner's worth at 31st March 1997 (revised)	203,326

OBJECTIVE TEST 13

i) c   ii) b   iii) a   iv) d   v) c

CHAPTER 14

Question 14.3

Golf Links: Calculations

	Trainers £	Trampolines £	Track-suits £
Purchases	9,000	4,000	900
Less Closing stock (£500 @ £3)	1,500	100	900
Cost of sales	7,500	3,900	nil
Sales	10,000	5,400	nil
Profit	2,500	1,500	nil
Purchases	9,000	4,000	900
Less Cash paid	6,000	4,000	nil
Creditors	3,000	nil	900
Sales	10,000	5,400	nil
Less Cash received	9,500	5,400	nil
Debtors	500	nil	nil
Less provision for bad debts	100	nil	nil
	400	nil	nil

Bank account

Receipts		Payments	
Capital	5,000	Car	1,200
Loan	2,000	Rent	500
Cash a/c	9,500	Trainers	6,000
		Tramp's	4,000
		Drawings	700
		Bal c/d	4,100
	16,500		16,500
Bal b/d	4,100		

Cash account

Receipts		Payments	
Trainers	9,500	Bank	9,500
Trampolines	5,400	Petrol	500
		Electricity	200
		Drawings	4,500
		Bal c/d	200
	14,900		14,900
Bal b/d	200		

Golf Links
Trading and profit & loss account for the year ending 31st December 2005

	£	£
Sales		15,400
Less Cost of sales:		
Purchases	13,900	
Less Closing stock	2,500	11,400
Gross profit		4,000

Less Expenses:

Petrol	500	
Electricity	200	
Rent [£500 *Less* prepaid £100]	400	
Depreciation of estate car	300	
Provision for bad debts	100	
Interest on loan	200	1,700
Net profit		2,300

Golf Links

Balance sheet as at 31st December 2005

	£	£ Cost	£ Accum. Dep'n	£ NBV
Fixed assets				
Estate car		1,200	300	900
Current assets				
Stocks		2,500		
Debtors	500			
Less Provision for bad debts	100			
		400		
Prepayment		100		
Cash at Bank		4,100		
Cash in hand		200		
			7,300	
Current liabilities				
Creditors		3,900		
Accrual [loan interest]		200		
			4,100	
Net current assets (or working capital)				3,200
Net total assets (or capital employed)				4,100
Less Long-term loan				2,000
				2,100
Represented by:				
Capital		5,000		
Add Net profit		2,300		
		7,300		
Less Drawings: Bank	700			
Cash	4,500	5,200		
			2,100	

OBJECTIVE TEST 14

i) c   ii) d   iii) c   iv) d   v) c

CHAPTER 15

Question 15.3

i)

Sid's Sports Equipment and Accessories

Cash-flow forecast for the six months ending 30th September 2003

	Apr £	May £	Jun £	Jul £	Aug £	Sep £	Total £
Receipts							
Capital	125,000						125,000
Sales	0	50,000	70,000	80,000	90,000	100,000	390,000
Total inflows	**125,000**	**50,000**	**70,000**	**80,000**	**90,000**	**100,000**	**515,000**
Payments							
Purchases		60,000	60,000	60,000	60,000	60,000	300,000
Wages	8,500	8,500	8,500	10,000	10,000	10,000	55,500
Selling & administration	5,000	5,000	5,000	6,000	6,000	6,000	33,000
Rent	7,500	0	0	7,500	0	0	15,000
Equipment	64,000	0	0	0	0	0	64,000
Total outflows	**85,000**	**73,500**	**73,500**	**83,500**	**76,000**	**76,000**	**467,500**
Net cash flow	**40,000**	**(23,500)**	**(3,500)**	**(3,500)**	**14,000**	**24,000**	**47,500**
Balances:							
Start of month	0	40,000	16,500	13,000	9,500	23,500	0
End of month	40,000	16,500	13,000	9,500	23,500	47,500	47,500

ii)

Sid's Sports Equipment and Accessories

Budgeted trading and profit-and-loss account for the six months ending 30th September 2003

	£	£
Sales		480,000
Less Cost of sales		
Purchases	360,000	
Less Closing stock	60,000	300,000
Gross profit		180,000
Less Expenses:		
Wages	55,500	
Selling & administration	33,000	
Rent	15,000	
Depreciation of equipment	3,200	106,700
Net profit		73,300

iii)

Sid's Sport Equipment and Accessories
Budgeted balance sheet as at 30th September 2003

	£ Cost	£ Accumulated depreciation	£ NBV
Fixed assets			
Equipment	64,000	3,200	60,800
Current assets			
Stock	60,000		
Debtors	90,000		
Cash at bank	47,500	197,500	
Current liabilities			
Creditors	60,000		
Overdraft	0		
		60,000	
Net current assets			137,500
Capital employed			198,300
Represented by			
Capital		125,000	
Profit for 6 months		73,300	198,300

OBJECTIVE TEST 15

i) c   ii) d   iii) b   iv) a   v) a

CHAPTER 16

Question 16.8

Magna Company
Cash statement

	£		£
Opening balance	2,000	Purchases	62,000
Sales	85,000	Wages	6,000
		Mtce expenses	1,900
		Insurance	850
		Drawings	5,000
		Closing balance	11,250
	87,000		87,000

Magna Company
Profit statement for the year ended 31st December 2003

	£	£
Sales		80,000
Less cost of sales		
Opening stock	15,000	
Purchases	65,000	
	80,000	
Less Closing stock	25,000	55,000
Gross profit		25,000
Less Operating expenses		
Wages	6,000	
Insurance	1,100	
Mtce expenses	1,750	
Depreciation	2,000	10,850
Net profit		14,150

Magna Company
Balance sheet as at 31st December 2003

	£	£	£
	Cost	Accum. depn	NBV
Premises	30,000		30,000
Machinery	15,000	2,000	13,000
	45,000	2,000	43,000
Current assets			
Stock	25,000		
Debtors	5,000		
Prepayments	250		
Cash	11,250	41,500	
Less Current liabilities			
Creditors	10,000		
Accruals	250	10,250	31,250
			74,250
Capital as at 1st January	65,100		
Add Profit for year	14,150		
	79,250		
Less Drawings	5,000		74,250

OBJECTIVE TEST 16

i) d   ii) b   iii) b   iv) a   v) d   vi) a   vii) c

CHAPTER 17

Question 17.3

See Chapter 1 and Chapter 17.

OBJECTIVE TEST 17

i) c   ii) b   iii) d   iv) a   v) b

CHAPTER 18

Question 18.3

Stirling, Drummond & Webb
Profit-and-loss account for the year ended 30th June 2004

	£	£	£
Sales			381,690
Less Returns inwards			6,450
			375,240
Opening stock		54,630	
Purchases	243,222		
Less Returns outwards	10,800	232,422	
		287,052	
Less Closing stock		44,025	
Cost of sales			243,027
Gross profit			132,213
Discounts received			4,131
			136,344
Discounts allowed		4,728	
Bad debts written off		1,419	
Provision for bad debts		750	
Wages		48,675	
Rates (£1,000 − £750)		250	
Electricity (£1,895 + £375)		2,270	
General expenses (£1,263 + £60)		1,323	
Depreciation – Fixtures (25% × £24,000)		6,000	
Printing and stationery		3,563	68,978
Profit available for appropriation			67,366

	Stirling £	Drummond £	Webb £	
Interest on Drawings	1,125	950	500	
Interest on Capital	(3,750)	(2,250)	(2,250)	
	(2,625)	(1,300)	(1,750)	(5,675)
Profit to be shared	40%	40%	20%	61,691
Share of profits	24,676	24,676	12,339	61,691

Current Accounts

	£	£	£
Opening balances	4,035	(1,875)	(1,170)
Interest on capital	3,750	2,250	2,250
Interest on drawings	(1,125)	(950)	(500)
Drawings	(24,030)	(18,135)	(18,375)
Share of profits	24,676	24,676	12,339
Closing balances	7,306	5,966	(5,456)

OBJECTIVE TEST 18

i) d   ii) d   iii) a   iv) d   v) c

CHAPTER 19

Question 19.3

Stirling, Drummond & Webb
Profit and loss account for the year ended 30th June 2003

	£	£	£
Sales			381,690
Less Returns inwards			6,450
			375,240
Opening stock		54,630	
Purchases	243,222		
Less Returns outwards	10,800	232,422	
		287,052	
Less Closing stock		44,025	
Cost of sales			243,027
Gross profit			132,213
Discounts received			4,131
			136,344
Discounts allowed		4,728	
Bad debts written off		1,419	
Provision for bad debts		750	
Wages		48,675	
Rates (£1,000 – £750)		250	
Electricity (£1,895 + £375)		2,270	

General expenses (£1,263 + £60)			1,323	
Depreciation – Fixtures (25% × £24,000)			6,000	
Printing and stationery			3,563	
				68,978
Profit available for appropriation				67,366

	Stirling £	Drummond £	Webb £	
Interest on Drawings	1,125	950	500	
Interest on Capital	(3,750)	(2,250)	(2,250)	
	(2,625)	(1,300)	(1,750)	(5,675)
Profit to be shared	40%	40%	20%	61,691
Share of profits	24,676	24,676	12,339	61,691

Current accounts

	£	£	£
Opening balances	4,035	(1,875)	(1,170)
Interest on capital	3,750	2,250	2,250
Interest on drawings	(1,125)	(950)	(500)
Drawings	(24,030)	(18,135)	(18,375)
Share of profits	24,676	24,676	12,339
Closing balances	7,306	5,966	(5,456)

Balance sheet as at 30th June 2003

	Stirling £	Drummond £	Webb £	Total £
Capital accounts	37,500	22,500	22,500	82,500
Current accounts	7,306	5,966	(5,456)	7,816
				90,316

	Cost	Accum. depn	NBV
Fixed assets			
Fixtures	24,000	18,000	6,000
Current assets			
Stock	44,025		
Debtors (£77,170 – £750)	76,420		
Prepayment	750		
			121,195
Current liabilities			
Creditors	33,247		
Accruals	435		
Bank overdraft	3,197	36,879	
			84,316
			90,316

OBJECTIVE TEST 19

i) d   ii) b   iii) b   iv) c   v) c

CHAPTER 20

Question 20.3

Realisation account

	£		£
Fixed assets	47,500	Creditors	77,400
Stock	49,200	Proceeds:	
Debtors	27,100	Fixed assets	40,300
Payment of creditors	77,200	Stock	37,500
		Debtors	26,300
		Loss on realisation:	
		Juliet	6,500
		Pat	6,500
		Joe	6,500
	201,000		201,000

Bank account

	£		£
Proceeds on realisation:		Opening balance	26,900
Fixed assets	40,300	Realisation account:	
Stock	37,500	Payment of creditors	77,200
Debtors	26,300	Pat	1,500
Juliet	1,500		
	105,600		105,600

Capital accounts

	Juliet	Pat	Joe		Juliet	Pat	Joe
	£	£	£		£	£	£
Loss on realisation	6,500	6,500	6,500	Opening balance	6,000	8,000	2,000
Joe*		1,200	1,600	Current accounts:	200	1,600	1,700
Bank		1,500		Juliet and Pat		200	2,800
				Bank	1,500		2,800
	7,700	9,600	6,500		7,700	9,600	6,500

$$* \quad \frac{£2,800}{£14,000} \times £6,000$$

OBJECTIVE TEST 20

i) b   ii) d   iii) c   iv) a   v) d

CHAPTER 21

Question 21.3

i)   Amount of issued share capital = £125,000

ii) Dividend = $2\frac{1}{2}$p

iii) Total amount of dividend = £12,500

iv) Dividend for a shareholding of 150 shares = £3.75

OBJECTIVE TEST 21

i) d   ii) a   iii) d   iv) c   v) a

CHAPTER 22

Question 22.3

i)   An auditor's report should normally state that the accounts give a true and fair view.

ii) The Companies Act 1989 mainly introduced requirements on the regulation of auditors and group accounts.

iii) A company which can offer its shares to the public is known as a public limited company.

iv) The Accounting Standards Board is responsible for issuing accounting standards.

v)   The regulatory framework consists of three elements: company legislation, accounting standards and Stock Exchange regulations.

OBJECTIVE TEST 22

i) d   ii) d   iii) b   iv) d   v) b

CHAPTER 23

Question 23.3

Colchester plc
Trading and profit & loss account for the year ending
31st December 2004

	£'000	£'000	£'000
Sales (*Less* returns)			87,015
Less Cost of sales			
Opening stock		2,375	
Add Purchases (*Less* returns)		63,330	
		65,705	
Less Closing stock		2,625	63,080
Gross profit			23,935
Add Rents receivable			1,230
			25,165
Less Operating expenses			
Office expenses		1,685	
Insurances (£175 – £25)		150	
Wages (£3,820 + £130)		3,950	
Rent (2,000 – £550)		1,450	
Rates		1,650	
Bad debts		2,150	
Increase in provision for bad debts		250	
Depreciation of equipment		800	12,085
Net profit this year			13,080
Add Balance of profit & loss account b/f from last year			85
Net profit available for appropriation			13,165
Appropriations			
Corporation tax charge			4,750
			8,415
Transfer to general reserve		3,500	
Proposed dividends			
7% preference shares	350		
Ordinary shares	4,500	4,850	8,350
Unappropriated profit c/f to next year			65

Colchester plc
Balance sheet as as 31st December 2004

	£'000	£'000 Cost	£'000 Acc.Dep'n	£'000 NBV
Fixed assets				
Premises		131,000	–	131,000
Equipment		6,000	2,400	3,600
		137,000	2,400	134,600

Current assets			
Stock		2,625	
Debtors	23,500		
Less Provision for bad debts	1,250		
		22,250	
Prepayments [25+550+180]		755	
Cash at bank and deposits		11,125	36,755
Creditors: amounts due within			
one year			
Creditors		26,560	
Accruals		130	
Taxation		4,750	
Proposed dividends		4,850	36,290
Net current assets			465
			135,065
Financed by			
Share capital, authorised and issued			
5,000,000 7% preference shares of £1 each		5,000	
100,000,000 ordinary shares of 25p each		25,000	30,000
General reserve: B/f from last year		101,500	
Add Transferred from profits this year		3,500	105,000
Profit and loss account balance			65
			135,065

OBJECTIVE TEST 23

i) b   ii) d   iii) a   iv) a   v) b

CHAPTER 24

OBJECTIVE TEST 24

i) d   ii) c   iii) b   iv) b   v) d

CHAPTER 25

OBJECTIVE TEST 25

i) a   ii) a   iii) b   iv) a   v) b

CHAPTER 26

Question 26.3

Company	Industry
A	Public transport (buses)
B	General engineering
C	Hotel and leisure
D	Commercial vehicle manufacturing
E	Food retailing

OBJECTIVE TEST 26

i) c   ii) c   iii) d   iv) c   v) c   vi) a   vii) b   viii) b   ix) a   x) d

CHAPTER 27

Question 27.3

Your answer will depend on the ratios you have decided to calculate. The following provides the main points of a possible answer.

Orchardlea plc

		1996	1997
Prime ratio $= \dfrac{\text{Profit before interest and cash}}{\text{Capital employed}}$		$\dfrac{26}{281} = 9.3\%$	$\dfrac{47}{498} = 9.4\%$
Profit margin $= \dfrac{\text{Profit before interest and cash}}{\text{Sales}}$		$\dfrac{26}{350} = 7.4\%$	$\dfrac{47}{560} = 8.4\%$
Capital turnover $= \dfrac{\text{Sales}}{\text{Capital employed}}$		$\dfrac{350}{281} = 1.24$ times	$\dfrac{560}{498} = 1.12$ times
Gross profit percentage $= \dfrac{\text{Gross profit}}{\text{Turnover}}$		$\dfrac{70}{350} = 20.0\%$	$\dfrac{98}{560} = 17.5\%$
Current test $= \dfrac{\text{Current assets}}{\text{Current liabilities}}$		$\dfrac{175}{49} = 3.6:1$	$\dfrac{245}{63} = 3.9:1$
Acid test $= \dfrac{\text{Current assets} - \text{stock}}{\text{Current liabilities}}$		$\dfrac{119}{49} = 2.4:1$	$\dfrac{147}{63} = 2.3:1$
Debt collection period $= \dfrac{\text{Debtors}}{\text{Turnover}} \times 365$		$\dfrac{35}{350} \times 365 = 36.5$ days	$\dfrac{84}{560} \times 36 = 54.8$ days
Gearing $= \dfrac{\text{Debt}}{\text{Equity}}$		$\dfrac{50}{231} = 21.6\%$	$\dfrac{50}{448} = 11.2\%$
Interest cover $= \dfrac{\text{Profit before interest and cash}}{\text{Interest charge}}$		$\dfrac{26}{5} = 9.3\%$	$\dfrac{47}{5} = 9.4\%$

The prime ratio has increased very slightly, despite the fact that capital employed has nearly doubled (from £281,000 to £498,000) due to the increase in share capital. Capital turnover has dropped, but the increase in profit margin has made up for this.

The current test has increased slightly, but the acid test has dropped a little, indicating an increase in stock levels. Both ratios are rather high, which should prompt an investigation into the composition of the current assets. For example, the balance at the bank could indicate an idle asset, although the amount held at the bank dropped in 1997. Debtors have increased and the reason for the increase in the debt collection period should be investigated.

The gearing ratios have improved significantly due to the increased profit and the additional investment by the shareholders, whilst debt was held at the same level.

OBJECTIVE TEST 27

i) c   ii) a   iii) c   iv) b   v) a

CHAPTER 28

OBJECTIVE TEST 28

i) d   ii) a   iii) b   iv) b   v) a

CHAPTER 29

Question 29.3

Viney Green Golf Club
Statement of affairs as at 1st January 2001

	£	£
Assets		
Golf course	100,000	
Clubhouse	50,000	
Investment	12,000	
Subscriptions in arrear	1,200	
Bar stocks	9,700	
Equipment	7,000	
Cash	2,500	182,400
Liabilities		
Subscriptions in advance		800
Capital or Accumulated fund		181,600

Viney Green Golf Club

Income and expenditure account for the year ended 31st December 2001

	£	£	£
Income			
Subscriptions			
(£52,000 − £1,200 + £700 − £1,800 + £800)		50,500	
Green fees		1,000	
Bar takings	46,200		
Bar cost of sales			
Opening stock	9,700		
Purchases	27,180		
	36,880		
Less Closing stock	8,650		
Cost of sales	28,230		
Bar gross profit	17,970		
Bar wages	6,000		
Bar net profit		11,970	
Interest received		980	64,450
Expenditure			
Course maintenance		34,100	
General expenses (£14,100 − £1,200)		12,900	
Professional		4,000	
Depreciation			
Clubhouse (£20% × £50,000)		10,000	
Equipment (£7,000 − £500 + £2,400) × 20%		1,780	
Loss on sale of equipment (£500 − £100)		400	63,180
Surplus for the year			1,270

Viney Green Golf Club

Balance sheet as at 31st December 2001

	£
Accumulated fund	
Opening balance	181,600
Add Surplus for the year	1,270
	182,870

	Cost	Accum. Dep'n	NBV
	£	£	£
Fixed assets			
Golf course	100,000	–	100,000
Clubhouse	50,000	10,000	40,000
Equipment	8,900	1,780	7,120
	158,900	11,780	147,120

Current assets

Stock	8,650	
Subscriptions in arrears	700	
Insurance prepaid	1,200	
Investment	12,000	
Cash/Bank	17,000	39,550

Current liabilities

Subscriptions in advance	1,800		
Bar supplies	2,000	3,800	35,750
			182,870

OBJECTIVE TEST 29

i) c   ii) a   iii) b   iv) b   v) a

CHAPTER 30

Question 30.5

Portsmouth Printers Ltd
Manufacturing account for the year ended 31st August 2003

	£	£
Sales value of finished goods produced:		
113,000 books @ £5 per book		565,000
(to trading section of trading and profit and loss account)		
Direct costs:		
Direct materials		
Opening stock	13,550	
Purchases	290,720	
Carriage inwards	3,120	
	307,390	
Less Closing stock	18,211	
Cost of direct material consumed		289,179
Direct wages (£106,500 + £4,200)		110,700
Direct expenses		1,121
Prime cost		401,000
Production overheads:		
Indirect materials	3,700	
Factory power (£9,200 + £700)	9,900	
Light and heat (60% of £6,120 + £880)	4,200	
Factory salaries	22,720	
Insurances (£2,410 − £110)	2,300	

continued

Depreciation:

Plant and machinery	10,000	
Business rates (80% of £10,200)	8,160	
Rates (70% of £9,000 – £1,000)	5,600	
Total production overheads		66,580
Total cost of production		467,580
Work in progress adjustment:		
Opening work in progress	6,720	
Less Closing work in progress	(9,300)	
Work in progress adjustment		(2,580)
Total production cost of finished goods		465,000
Profit on finished goods produced or		
Manufacturing profit		100,000
(to profit and loss section of trading, profit and loss account)		

Portsmouth Printers Ltd

Trading and profit and loss account for the year ended 31st August 2003

	£	£
Sales		752,390
Finished goods:		
Opening stock	12,490	
Production cost of finished goods		
(from manufacturing account)	565,000	
	577,490	
Less Closing stocks	16,100	
Cost of goods sold		561,390
Gross profit or trading profit		191,000
Manufacturing profit (from manufacturing account)		100,000
Total gross profit		291,000
Other overheads:		
Light and heat (40% of £6,120 + £880)	2,800	
Postage		1,210
Telephone	2,100	
Office salaries	21,210	
Other insurances (£920 – £140)	780	
Depreciation:		
Office equipment	1,300	
Office expenses	3,200	
Advertising	1,960	
Business rates (20% of £10,200)	2,040	
Rent (30% of £9,000 – £1,000)	2,400	
Total other overheads		39,000
Net profit		252,000

OBJECTIVE TEST 30

i) b   ii) d   iii) b   iv) a   v) b

INDEX